OECD/G20 Base Erosion and Profit Shifting Project

Measuring and Monitoring BEPS, Action 11 - 2015 Final Report

OECD
BETTER POLICIES FOR BETTER LIVES

Please cite this publication as:
OECD (2015), *Measuring and Monitoring BEPS, Action 11 - 2015 Final Report*, OECD/G20 Base Erosion and Profit Shifting Project, OECD Publishing, Paris.
http://dx.doi.org/10.1787/9789264241343-en

ISBN 978-92-64-24133-6 (print)
ISBN 978-92-64-24134-3 (PDF)

Series: OECD/G20 Base Erosion and Profit Shifting Project
ISSN 2313-2604 (print)
ISSN 2313-2612 (online)

Photo credits: Cover © ninog – Fotolia.com

Corrigenda to OECD publications may be found on line at: *www.oecd.org/about/publishing/corrigenda.htm*.

Foreword

International tax issues have never been as high on the political agenda as they are today. The integration of national economies and markets has increased substantially in recent years, putting a strain on the international tax rules, which were designed more than a century ago. Weaknesses in the current rules create opportunities for base erosion and profit shifting (BEPS), requiring bold moves by policy makers to restore confidence in the system and ensure that profits are taxed where economic activities take place and value is created.

Following the release of the report *Addressing Base Erosion and Profit Shifting* in February 2013, OECD and G20 countries adopted a 15-point Action Plan to address BEPS in September 2013. The Action Plan identified 15 actions along three key pillars: introducing coherence in the domestic rules that affect cross-border activities, reinforcing substance requirements in the existing international standards, and improving transparency as well as certainty.

Since then, all G20 and OECD countries have worked on an equal footing and the European Commission also provided its views throughout the BEPS project. Developing countries have been engaged extensively via a number of different mechanisms, including direct participation in the Committee on Fiscal Affairs. In addition, regional tax organisations such as the African Tax Administration Forum, the *Centre de rencontre des administrations fiscales* and the *Centro Interamericano de Administraciones Tributarias*, joined international organisations such as the International Monetary Fund, the World Bank and the United Nations, in contributing to the work. Stakeholders have been consulted at length: in total, the BEPS project received more than 1 400 submissions from industry, advisers, NGOs and academics. Fourteen public consultations were held, streamed live on line, as were webcasts where the OECD Secretariat periodically updated the public and answered questions.

After two years of work, the 15 actions have now been completed. All the different outputs, including those delivered in an interim form in 2014, have been consolidated into a comprehensive package. The BEPS package of measures represents the first substantial renovation of the international tax rules in almost a century. Once the new measures become applicable, it is expected that profits will be reported where the economic activities that generate them are carried out and where value is created. BEPS planning strategies that rely on outdated rules or on poorly co-ordinated domestic measures will be rendered ineffective.

Implementation therefore becomes key at this stage. The BEPS package is designed to be implemented via changes in domestic law and practices, and via treaty provisions, with negotiations for a multilateral instrument under way and expected to be finalised in 2016. OECD and G20 countries have also agreed to continue to work together to ensure a consistent and co-ordinated implementation of the BEPS recommendations. Globalisation requires that global solutions and a global dialogue be established which go beyond OECD and G20 countries. To further this objective, in 2016 OECD and G20 countries will conceive an inclusive framework for monitoring, with all interested countries participating on an equal footing.

A better understanding of how the BEPS recommendations are implemented in practice could reduce misunderstandings and disputes between governments. Greater focus on implementation and tax administration should therefore be mutually beneficial to governments and business. Proposed improvements to data and analysis will help support ongoing evaluation of the quantitative impact of BEPS, as well as evaluating the impact of the countermeasures developed under the BEPS Project.

Table of contents

Tables

Figures

Boxes

Abbreviations and acronyms

ACE	Allowance for corporate equity
AETR	Average effective tax rate
AMNE	Activities of multinational enterprises database
AMTR	Applicable marginal tax rate
ATAF	African Tax Administration Forum
B2C	Business-to-consumer
BEA	Bureau of Economic Analysis
BEPS	Base erosion and profit shifting
BMD3	Benchmark Definition of Foreign Direct Investment, Third Edition
BMD4	Benchmark Definition of Foreign Direct Investment, Fourth Edition
BOP	Balance of payments
BvD	Bureau van Dijk
CbCR	Country-by-Country Reporting
CDIS	Co-ordinated Direct Investment Survey
CFA	Committee on Fiscal Affairs
CFC	Controlled foreign corporations
CIAT	Inter-American Centre of Tax Administrations
CIT	Corporate income tax
CTJ	Citizens for Tax Justice
EBIT	Earnings before interest and taxes
EBITDA	Earnings before interest, taxes, depreciation and amortization
ECJ	European Court of Justice
EITI	Extractive Industries Transparency Initiative
ETR	Effective tax rate
EPO	European Patent Office
EU	European Union
FDI	Foreign direct investment
FISIM	Financial services indirectly measured

FL-ATR	Forward-looking average effective tax rates
FL-METR	Forward-looking marginal effective tax rate
G20	Group of Twenty
GAAP	Generally Accepted Accounting Principles
GAAR	General anti-avoidance rules
GIE	Gross interest expense
GDP	Gross domestic product
GOS	Gross operating surplus
HMRC	Her Majesty's Revenue and Customs
ICTD	Sussex University International Centre for Tax and Development
IFRS	International Financial Reporting Standards
IMF	International Monetary Fund
IP	Intellectual property
IRS	Internal Revenue Service
JCT	United States Congressional Joint Committee on Taxation
KBC	Knowledge based capital
LOB	Limitation-on-benefits
MAP	Mutual agreement procedure
MiDi	Micro database on direct investment
MNE	Multinational enterprise
MTR	Marginal tax rate
NA	National Accounts
NGO	Non-government organisation
NIE	Net interest expense
NOS	Net operating surplus
NSO	National statistical office
OECD	Organisation for Economic Co-operation and Development
PCT	Patent Co-Operation Treaty
PE	Permanent establishment
PPT	Principal purposes test
R&D	Research and development
SAAR	Specific anti-avoidance rules
SOI	Statistic of Income Division
SPE	Special purpose entity

STAN	Structural Analysis Database
STR	Statutory tax rate
TFDE	Task Force on the Digital Economy
UNCTAD	United Nations Conference on Trade and Development
USTPO	United States Patent and Trademark Office
VAT	Value-added tax
WHT	Withholding tax
WIOD	World Input-Output Database
WP	Working Party
WTO	World Trade Organization

Executive summary

The adverse fiscal and economic impacts of base erosion and profit shifting (BEPS) have been the focus of the OECD/G20 BEPS Project since its inception. While anecdotal evidence has shown that tax planning activities of some multinational enterprises (MNEs) take advantage of the mismatches and gaps in the international tax rules, separating taxable profits from the underlying value-creating activity, the *Addressing Base Erosion and Profit Shifting* report (OECD, 2013) recognised that the scale of the negative global impacts on economic activity and government revenues have been uncertain.

Although measuring the scale of BEPS proves challenging given the complexity of BEPS and the serious data limitations, today we know that the fiscal effects of BEPS are significant. The findings of the work performed since 2013 highlight the magnitude of the issue, with global corporate income tax (CIT) revenue losses estimated between 4% and 10% of global CIT revenues, i.e. USD 100 to 240 billion annually. Given developing countries' greater reliance on CIT revenues, estimates of the impact on developing countries, as a percentage of GDP, are higher than for developed countries.

In addition to significant tax revenue losses, BEPS causes other adverse economic effects, including tilting the playing field in favour of tax-aggressive MNEs, exacerbating the corporate debt bias, misdirecting foreign direct investment, and reducing the financing of needed public infrastructure.

Six indicators of BEPS activity highlight BEPS behaviours using different sources of data, employing different metrics, and examining different BEPS channels. When combined and presented as a dashboard of indicators, they confirm the existence of BEPS, and its continued increase in scale in recent years.

- ***The profit rates of MNE affiliates located in lower-tax countries are higher than their group's average worldwide profit rate.*** For example, the profit rates reported by MNE affiliates located in lower-tax countries are twice as high as their group's worldwide profit rate on average.

- ***The effective tax rates paid by large MNE entities are estimated to be 4 to 8½ percentage points lower than similar enterprises with domestic-only operations***, tilting the playing-field against local businesses and non-tax aggressive MNEs, although some of this may be due to MNEs' greater utilisation of available country tax preferences.

- ***Foreign direct investment (FDI) is increasingly concentrated.*** FDI in countries with net FDI to GDP ratios of more than 200% increased from 38 times higher than all other countries in 2005 to 99 times higher in 2012.

- ***The separation of taxable profits from the location of the value creating activity is particularly clear with respect to intangible assets, and the phenomenon has***

grown rapidly. For example, the ratio of the value of royalties received to spending on research and development in a group of low-tax countries was six times higher than the average ratio for all other countries, and has increased three-fold between 2009 and 2012. Royalties received by entities located in these low-tax countries accounted for 3% of total royalties, providing evidence of the existence of BEPS, though not a direct measurement of the scale of BEPS.

- ***Debt from both related and third-parties is more concentrated in MNE affiliates in higher statutory tax-rate countries.*** The interest-to-income ratio for affiliates of the largest global MNEs in higher-tax rate countries is almost three times higher than their MNE's worldwide third-party interest-to-income ratio.

Along with new empirical analysis of the fiscal and economic effects of BEPS and hundreds of existing empirical studies that find the existence of profit shifting through transfer mispricing, strategic location of intangibles and debt, as well as treaty abuse, these BEPS indicators confirm that profit shifting is occurring, is significant in scale and likely to be increasing, and creates adverse economic distortions. Furthermore, empirical analysis indicates that BEPS adversely affects competition between businesses, levels and location of debt, the location of intangible investments, and causes fiscal spillovers between countries and wasteful and inefficient expenditure of resources on tax engineering. The empirical analysis in this report, along with several academic studies, confirms that strong anti-avoidance rules reduce profit shifting in countries that have implemented them.

However, these indicators and all analyses of BEPS are severely constrained by the limitations of the currently available data. The available data is not comprehensive across countries or companies, and often does not include actual taxes paid. In addition to this, the analyses of profit shifting to date have found it difficult to separate the effects of BEPS from real economic factors and the effects of deliberate government tax policy choices. Improving the tools and data available to measure BEPS will be critical for measuring and monitoring BEPS in the future, as well as evaluating the impact of the countermeasures developed under the BEPS Action Plan.

While recognising the need to maintain appropriate safeguards to protect the confidentiality of taxpayer information, this report makes a number of recommendations that will improve the analysis of available data. Some of the information needed to improve the measurement and monitoring of BEPS is already collected by tax administrations, but not analysed or made available for analysis. The focus of the report's recommendations in this area is on improved access to and enhanced analysis of existing data, and new data proposed to be collected under Actions 5, 13 and, where implemented, Action 12 of the BEPS Project.

The report recommends that the OECD work with governments to report and analyse more corporate tax statistics and to present them in an internationally consistent way. For example, statistical analyses based upon Country-by-Country Reporting data have the potential to significantly enhance the economic analysis of BEPS. These improvements in the availability of data will ensure that governments and researchers will, in the future, be better able to measure and monitor BEPS and the actions taken to address BEPS.

Chapter 1

Assessment of existing data sources relevant for BEPS analysis

Key points:

- This chapter assesses a range of existing data sources with specific reference to the availability and usefulness of existing data for the purposes of developing indicators and undertaking an economic analysis of the scale and impact of BEPS and BEPS countermeasures.
- This chapter concludes that the significant limitations of existing data sources mean that, at present, attempts to construct indicators or undertake an economic analysis of the scale and impact of BEPS are severely constrained and, as such, should be heavily qualified.
- While there are several different private data sources and aggregated official sources currently available to researchers, they are all affected by various limitations that affect their usefulness for the purposes of analysing the scale and impact of BEPS and BEPS countermeasures.
- One of the key challenges with currently available data sources is that it is difficult for researchers to disentangle real economic effects from the effects of BEPS-related behaviours.
- Private firm-level financial account databases are useful, but are not comprehensive in their coverage, have significant limitations in their representativeness in some countries, do not include all MNE entities and/or all of their associated financial information, and do not have information about taxes actually paid.
- Some of the limitations of the currently available data also affect the ability of individual governments to analyse how BEPS impacts their economies and tax revenues.
- While tax return data covering all subsidiaries of MNEs are potentially the most useful form of data, most countries do not have or make such data available for the purposes of economic and statistical analysis, even on an anonymised or confidential basis. For example, it is difficult to determine the share of total corporate income tax paid by MNEs, relative to purely domestic companies, as currently very few countries make such data available.
- Recent parliamentary and government enquiries have shed new light on the tax affairs of some high profile MNEs. While this information represents a rich and emerging source of evidence of the existence of BEPS, such information relates to the activities of a small number of MNEs and is of limited use in undertaking a broader analysis. In some cases, this information is not included in the available firm-level financial account databases, which highlights the inadequacy of relying exclusively upon them.
- Separating real economic effects from tax effects requires both data and estimation methodologies, since even with good data, BEPS is not observable and must be estimated. Nevertheless, more comprehensive and more detailed data regarding MNEs is needed to provide more accurate assessments of the scale and impact of BEPS.

1.1 Introduction

1. Assessing currently available data is an important part of BEPS Action 11. Having a proper understanding of the available data and its limitations is a fundamental issue for the development of indicators showing the scale and economic impact of BEPS, as well as for the development of economic analyses of the scale and impact of BEPS and BEPS countermeasures.

2. It cannot be overemphasised that the results obtained from any analysis are only as robust as the data and methodology underpinning them. This is particularly true in the case of analysing BEPS, since BEPS involves multinational enterprises (MNEs) that can establish intra-group arrangements that achieve no or low taxation by shifting profits away from jurisdictions where the activities creating the profits are taking place. These intra-group cross-border arrangements are often very complex, involving multiple related entities, and related party transactions are typically not separately identifiable (and available) in tax or financial account databases.

3. Hence, it is crucial to establish an understanding of the currently available data – what is available; the coverage and representativeness of that data; whether it is tax return or financial account data; whether it is macro or micro-level data; its reliability and robustness (what quality control measures are in place for the data collection); whether it is comparable across jurisdictions; and who has access to it.

4. This chapter provides an initial assessment of the data currently available for analysing BEPS and BEPS countermeasures, which is relevant to both the development of potential indicators and the undertaking of refined economic and statistical analyses. It is important to note that most analyses, including government policy analyses and decisions, are made with partial information. For policymakers, using available data to conduct some analysis is better than working without empirical-based evidence at all, but such analyses must also recognise the limitations of currently available data and how those limitations may affect the reported results.

5. The purpose of the assessment undertaken in this chapter is to describe what is available, as well as outline the benefits and limitations of the different types of data. Based on this assessment, Action 11 also involves the identification of new types of tools and data that should be collected in the future. New data could include capitalising on existing data that is currently unavailable, either due to confidentiality reasons or because it is not currently processed or analysed, as well as additional information needed for monitoring BEPS in the future, taking into account ways to reduce administrative costs for tax administrations and businesses. A detailed discussion of potential new tools and data is set out in Chapter 4.

1.2 Potential criteria for evaluating available data for BEPS research

6. An assessment requires establishing a set of criteria to be used for evaluating the different types of data with respect to their usefulness for analysing BEPS. Having a thorough understanding of the available data will provide a solid base for working towards 'best practices' in future data collection to 'fill the gaps' and strive for more comprehensive data and comparability across countries, recognising the trade-offs between the objectives of improved tax policy analysis and the need to minimise administrative costs for tax administrations and businesses.

7. Box 1.1 briefly outlines a set of criteria that could be considered.

Box 1.1. Criteria for assessing data

Coverage/Representativeness – BEPS is a global issue and significant profit shifting may occur through "small" entities with large profits but with little economic activity. Determining the coverage and representativeness of the underlying data is critical to assessing the results of any analysis. Most databases are limited to individual countries or a region, and there is no truly comprehensive global database of MNE activity.

Usefulness for separating real economic effects from tax effects – Separating BEPS-related activity from real economic activity is important, but must be estimated. National Accounts and macroeconomic statistics, such as foreign direct investment data, combine both real and BEPS-related activity. Firm-level data provides researchers with more information to attempt to more accurately separate BEPS-related activities from a firm's real economic activities.

Ability to focus on specific BEPS activity – BEPS is driven by practices that artificially segregate taxable income from the real economic activities that generate it. A MNE's financial profile can be very different between financial and tax accounts. Differences in financial and taxable income can be large, and the country of taxation can differ from the firm's country of incorporation. In some cases, specific tax information may be available for a limited number of MNEs from specific parliamentary enquiries.

Level of detail – As BEPS behaviours involve cross-border transactions, typically between related parties, information on related and unrelated party transactions should be used when available. Affiliate-level information should supplement worldwide consolidated group information when available. Different types of foreign direct investment data should be used when available.

Timeliness – Access to timely information enables policymakers to monitor and evaluate the changes in the BEPS environment and the effects of legislation. If the time lag is too long, empirical analysis may be more of an historical assessment, rather than an analysis of recent developments.

Access – Many BEPS behaviours cannot be identified as specific entries on tax returns or financial accounts. Analysis of the data is required to separate BEPS behaviours from real economic activity. Thus, policymakers need economic analyses of BEPS and BEPS countermeasures, rather than just compilations of descriptive statistics. The extent to which access to data is provided to statisticians and economists within government, and potentially outside of government, with strict confidentiality rules, represents an important policy issue.

8. ***Coverage/Representativeness***: BEPS is a global issue so comprehensive coverage across all countries would be ideal. Many macro-level aggregate data are available for most countries. Coverage of the entities that form part of MNEs is an important issue. A number of firm-level databases are available for individual countries, and the few private "global" databases are increasing coverage across multiple countries.

9. Even where data for a particular country exists, coverage issues may continue to complicate a rigorous assessment of BEPS. One aspect concerns the coverage of financial information for the entities included in the firm-level databases. Missing financial information may have an equally detrimental effect on an analysis as if the entity were not included in the database. Aggregation of financial information in respect of entities within MNE groups can also distort and limit the analysis.

10. Incomplete coverage of firms for any number of reasons means that the data collected may be from a non-random sample and so, potentially, a non-representative sample of firms. Extrapolating results beyond a non-random sample has limitations which

may be partially addressed by weighting or sensitivity analysis. This is likely to be a significant issue in the analysis of BEPS because of the potential concentration of BEPS in certain types of entities (e.g. located in low or no-tax countries). This is particularly problematic if those entities engaging in more BEPS-related behaviours are more likely to avoid or minimise the disclosure of relevant financial information.

11. Tax return information is generally filed only for entities that have a taxable presence in a country. Some countries may require foreign-owned companies that have a physical presence in the country, but not a tax presence, to register with a designated body. Many countries' tax administrations do not have information about the other affiliates of a MNE group, other than those with a permanent establishment in the country. For example, in South Africa, a foreign company that is physically present in South Africa must register as an external company with the Companies and Intellectual Property Commission. External companies do not have to file annual financial reports with the Commission, but the South African Revenue Service could obtain a list of these companies from the Commission. Many countries have entered into bilateral or multilateral Double Taxation Agreements and Exchange of Information Agreements that enable them to exchange information as well as conduct simultaneous or joint audits on a taxpayer.

12. ***Usefulness for separating real economic effects from tax effects***: BEPS is a tax issue with financial and economic ramifications. As noted below, BEPS affects the reported taxes, but also affects many non-tax variables, including macroeconomic aggregates, such as gross domestic product (GDP) or foreign direct investment (FDI), and firm-level/group financial information, such as reported financial profits or tax return information.

13. Estimating the effects of BEPS requires disentangling real economic activity across countries from tax-related (and specifically BEPS-related) behaviours across countries. In fact, there are three different categories of effects that ideally would be separately estimated: (i) real economic activity across countries independent of tax; (ii) real economic activity across countries influenced by differences in non-BEPS-affected tax rates (e.g. responsiveness of capital investment to a change in a country's effective tax rate); and (iii) BEPS-related activities across countries that include financial flows, legal contracts and structuring to shift profits away from where value is generated. In some cases, the structuring involves placing just enough economic activity (staff and functions for example) in a jurisdiction to attempt to justify the tax minimisation strategy. Only category (iii) effects should be attributed to BEPS.

14. Macroeconomic aggregates, such as FDI include both real and BEPS-related investment and returns, which are difficult or impossible to separate. In their current reporting of FDI, most countries have not been able to separate FDI related to real investment (greenfield and expansion investment) from financial transactions (mergers and acquisitions and the accumulation of reinvested earnings). While BEPS behaviours are more likely to be concentrated in the latter, there could be instances where, for example, a small operational facility (greenfield investment) is set up in a foreign jurisdiction with the main purpose of justifying a BEPS arrangement under current national rules. In addition, financial transactions may take place for legitimate business reasons and should not be automatically associated with BEPS.

15. The International Monetary Fund (IMF)[1] recently conducted a project on bilateral asymmetries in FDI reporting for the Co-ordinated Direct Investment Survey (CDIS). The project confirmed that methodological differences and insufficient data coverage are the

main reasons for bilateral asymmetries. Bilateral data on transactions other than FDI are also important for analysing BEPS, for example trade in goods and services, royalty payments and payments/receipts for services (e.g. legal, management and accounting services). Coverage of bilateral flows between non-OECD/G20 countries and countries with low corporate tax rates is often missing.[2] Bilateral information does not provide analysts with a view of the full chain of a transaction including the origin, transit points and the final destination.[3] Being able to see more than the first destination is important given that many flows are routed via special purpose entities (SPEs) for tax-motivated reasons.

16. The 4th edition of the OECD *Benchmark Definition of Foreign Direct Investment* (BMD4) recommends that countries explicitly separate FDI statistics on SPEs and non-SPEs for reporting purposes, which will result in more meaningful measures of real FDI. Separate reporting of flows through SPEs also identifies particular financial flows, which in some cases have facilitated BEPS behaviours. With the implementation of the latest standards, nine countries (in addition to the four that have done so for several years) have now reported data separating resident SPEs. More data will become available as more countries are included in the new OECD database of FDI statistics later in 2015.[4]

17. Micro-level data makes separating real and BEPS-related effects more likely, since individual firm data allows adjustment for industry, size of company, situation in the MNE group, and other non-BEPS tainted variables. In other words, analysis with micro-level data makes it possible to identify and control for more, but not necessarily all, non-tax characteristics of both affiliated firms and MNE groups that could affect BEPS.

18. ***Ability to focus on specific BEPS activity***: Differences between tax return and financial account data represent an important limitation affecting the use of non-tax financial account information for analysis of tax policy issues generally and BEPS specifically. This is likely to be amplified in instances where an entity's financial profile reported for accounting purposes does not correlate with its economic value-add in the jurisdiction in which it resides (particularly for subsidiaries of foreign headquartered MNEs and unlisted domestically headquartered MNEs). There are three main examples of such book/tax differences. Firstly, book/tax income differences can include permanent exemption of intragroup dividends and timing differences such as accelerated tax depreciation. Companies in a MNE group report financial profits that include exempt intragroup dividends. Differences between the tax consolidation rules and the statutory accounting consolidation rules can affect consolidated accounts.

19. A second book/tax difference relevant to BEPS analysis is the tax residence of the company compared to the country of incorporation, where financial reporting is required.[5] Due to differences in international tax rules, some companies have tax residence in a country other than the country of incorporation, or in some cases companies have been able to exploit mismatches between the tax laws of different countries with the result being that they are not tax residents of any country. Also, financial accounts generally do not show the sales or income of an entity across different countries, so analyses generally assign all of the sales and income to the country of incorporation. For example, a branch of a company could be earning income in a low-tax rate country, yet it is reported as income of the company incorporated in a high-tax country, thus distorting both the location of profits and the measure of the tax rate.

20. A third book/tax difference is the actual tax variable. Financial statement accounts under International Financial Reporting Standards (IFRS) or Generally Accepted Accounting Principles (GAAP) include tax expense, which is an accrual measure of tax

associated with current year income, and which includes both current and deferred income tax expense.[6] For a constantly growing company, deferred income tax expense may also accumulate over long periods, resulting in a near zero effective tax rate. For example, if three subsidiaries of a MNE are operating in different countries, all of which have accelerated tax depreciation allowances for capital spending, an expansion in capital investment over a ten year period could result in a build-up of significant deferred tax liabilities (for accounting purposes). Also, deferred tax expense can accumulate into deferred tax assets (e.g. tax credit carry forwards) or deferred tax liabilities (e.g. accelerated depreciation), which are affected by changes in future statutory tax rates. The total tax expense will be affected by a one-off change in the year that statutory tax rates are changed, due to a re-evaluation of the deferred tax asset or liability. Cash income tax payments are sometimes reported, but cash tax payments may reflect tax from current and prior years and potentially interest and penalties. A further discrepancy could arise if the amount of tax reflected in financial statements includes amounts that would not ordinarily be regarded as tax on profits. For example, where resource royalties are treated as a tax expense rather than (or as well as) a deductible cost of inputs.

21. In addition, many BEPS strategies cannot be observed directly in financial (accounting) statements, as they rely on heterogeneous classification of legal forms, financing contracts and companies' residence by tax authorities.[7]

22. Current tax return information is not a panacea for all the problems facing an analysis of BEPS. Individual country tax administrators or their tax policy analysis agencies with access to tax return information will only have information included in the tax returns filed in their country. In many cases, this will not include returns for other entities of the worldwide group that do not have to file returns in the country. Detailed information about intra-group related party transactions may not be included since it may not have been requested or may not be required for the computation of tax liability (the latter limitation being legally binding for tax authorities in some countries with respect to the information that can be requested). An additional issue is that all of the information reported on corporate income tax returns may not be included in a database processed from the tax returns (e.g. often only information specific to the calculation of tax liability is included, so information from the balance sheet, which could be helpful in the analysis of BEPS, may not be processed).

23. ***Level of detail***: The use of firm-level financial account and tax return data is more likely to allow for the separation of real economic activity from BEPS and focusing on specific BEPS behaviours. With respect to financial account data, the use of unconsolidated financial account data in combination with consolidated financial account data provides further insights. Where available, information on related party transactions should be used in analysing BEPS. For example, group worldwide leverage and interest expense ratios only include external third-party borrowing. Related party borrowing, which is a significant BEPS channel, does not show up in the consolidated group worldwide financial accounts. Related party borrowing is reflected in unconsolidated affiliates' financial accounts, but is generally not separately reported in financial accounts. Concerning tax return data, using micro-level data to understand the heterogeneity of individual firms and BEPS behaviours is preferable to aggregated tax statistics where deviations from the average are masked.

24. ***Timeliness of the information***: Access to timely information will enable policymakers to respond faster in countering new BEPS channels that may arise over time. If the time lag is too long, the analysis undertaken will be of more historical interest

than for policy action purposes. Financial statement information is publicly available annually, often 2-4 months after the firms' fiscal year has closed. Tax return information is often not filed until late the following year, and the processing of the tax return information for analysis purposes is often two years after the calendar year.

25. ***Access to the information***: MNEs file tax and regulatory reports with governments, and those tax reports are available to the tax administration agency. In many countries, the confidentiality of the tax return data prevents any sharing of the information beyond the tax administration agency. Thus government tax policy analysis outside of the tax administration may be limited to specific requests for anonymised records or aggregate statistics. Non-government access to corporate tax return records is typically not permitted, except for a few countries and only for strictly controlled research projects with strict confidentiality rules. Aggregate corporate tax return data is published by a number of countries, including information by industry and for certain taxpayer attributes such as total assets or total revenue. Based on information collected in a recent OECD Committee on Fiscal Affairs (CFA) WP2 on Tax Policy Analysis and Tax Statistics (WP2) survey, only eight of the 37 respondent countries were able to provide data on MNEs' share of corporate income tax revenues.

26. ***Other data issues***: There are many other data issues that reduce the signal-to-noise ratio (real information content) of any empirical tax policy analysis. Analysis must be undertaken with available data, but the analysts and users of the analysis should be aware of the data limitations. A few of the additional data issues related to BEPS analysis include:

- Balance sheets typically reflect purchased intangibles only, since for both tax and financial accounting most expenditures for intangible investments are deducted immediately (expensed) rather than capitalised;
- Intangibles are not limited to intellectual property, such as patents, trademarks and copyrights, but may also include other important items, such as trade names, brands, assembled workforce, and managerial systems, that are important to take into account when considering the sources of real economic activity and value creation;
- Headline statutory tax rates are often not the tax rate applicable at the margin of BEPS behaviour, due to specific country tax rules or administrative practices;
- Effective tax rates, both tax paid and financial tax expense, can also reflect specific non-BEPS related incentives, such as R&D tax credits;
- Available data may be collected through a sampling process to reduce the burden on respondents and the processing costs, but this raises issues of appropriate weighting;
- Existing data collection and processing may capture previous profit shifting structures and transactions, but may not capture recent and new structures and transactions to shift profits; and
- Recent data may be impacted by the financial crisis and changing macroeconomic conditions and may not be directly comparable to previous conditions.

1.3 Currently available data for BEPS analysis

27. Table 1.1 below provides an overview of 11 different types of data sources that have been used to analyse BEPS. It is based on responses to the Action 11 Request for Input, as well as discussions with academics and CFA WP2 delegates. The data sources range from macro aggregate statistics to micro firm/group level statistics; tax return data; financial account statistics; and detailed reports of individual MNEs.

Table 1.1. Overview of the current data sources

MACRO	National Accounts (NA)	This information measures the economic activity in a country and includes variables such as operating surplus, which may be used in BEPS analysis. It is easily accessible from international organisations, such as the OECD and the IMF. However, the underlying information used to construct the data is itself tainted by BEPS behaviours - meaning that even widely used measures such as GDP will be distorted by a BEPS component that is difficult to disentangle. There are significant definitional differences between National Accounts and tax data.
	Balance of Payments (BOP)	BOP statistics include all monetary transactions between a country and the rest of the world, including payments for exports and imports of goods, services, financial capital and financial transfers. This encompasses information on flows widely used to shift profits, such as purchases and sales of trading stock and services, royalties and interest. It is accessible (from the IMF and the World Bank, for example), but does not distinguish between transactions respecting the arm's length principle and manipulated transactions.
	Foreign Direct Investment (FDI)	FDI statistics cover all cross-border stocks and flows between enterprises forming part of the same group, including (i) direct investment (equity or debt) positions; (ii) direct investment financial flows (equity, reinvestment of earnings, debt); and (iii) direct investment income flows (dividends, distributed branch profits, interest). The IMF only reports on FDI positions, not flows, and the amount of information available from individual countries differs. The OECD has statistics on FDI positions, income and flows, but there are currently gaps and inconsistencies. While not directly related to the scale / revenue loss attributed to BEPS, FDI data depicts intra-group cross-border transactions that can provide at least indirect evidence of profit shifting by analysing the disconnect between the amount of FDI and the size of the economy, or the concentration of FDI in countries with a low effective tax burden on corporations. There are several issues with FDI data, including bilateral asymmetries in the capturing of the same FDI transaction and different types of transactions (e.g. greenfield investment, mergers & acquisitions, intra-group financing). There is also no distinction between real and purely financial investment, which would allow for a comparison that is highly relevant for an analysis of BEPS. Changes in data coverage over time can affect trends in macroeconomic variables, e.g. FDI.
	Trade	Aggregate data on bilateral trade by product can be used to analyse profit shifting through mispricing. This is accessible from the United Nations Comtrade database and the OECD database on intermediate trade in goods and services. There can be large discrepancies between figures reported for the same bilateral trade flow by the importing and exporting country (and non-trivial measurement issues concerning quantity and current price trade data). In addition, any re-invoicing arrangements using low-tax jurisdictions as conduits in the supply chain to extract a margin will distort the pricing between suppliers and related party purchasers.

		The CEPALSTAT database covers some Latin American countries, but there is no differentiation between related and non-related parties. The raw underlying customs data (expanded on in the micro data section) used for merchandise trade statistics may also show, in some countries, separate figures for trade between affiliated parties. There is no database equivalent to Comtrade for trade in services, an important element for BEPS analysis. Trade in services by country is usually available with data segregated by royalty payments and entrepreneurial services, among others, but the availability of data and the level of detail differ between countries. In addition, the service component of trade flows (which includes royalties and other payments for the use of IP) is likely to be underestimated due to the underreporting and mispricing of IP. There often appears to be some difficulty in practice in how National Statistics Offices differentiate between payments recorded as trade in services and payments recorded as primary income flows in the BOP, which can result in significant differences in bilateral trade statistics.
	Corporate income tax (CIT) revenue	Aggregate tax revenue data is accessible from international organisations (OECD Revenue Statistics, IMF Government Finance Statistics and World Bank Global Development Indicators) and often from National Accounts and tax authorities. It is typically used to estimate CIT-to-GDP ratios, for example, as well as implicit tax rates (ratios of CIT revenues to a proxy CIT base taken from the National Accounts). However, the biggest drawback is comparability across countries, particularly between developed and developing countries. Often, there is no clear distinction between national and subnational revenue, the relative size of the corporate taxed sector, or between resource and non-resource revenue. The lack of detail and consistency is an important issue for developing countries and, because BEPS involves cross-border transactions with all countries, comparable data for both developed and developing countries, is critical. Recently available data from the International Centre for Tax and Development (ICTD) improves comparability of data for developing countries.[8] The OECD Revenue Statistics presents a unique set of detailed and internationally comparable tax data in a common format for all OECD countries from 1965 onwards. The Revenue Statistics has been expanded to include non-OECD countries in other regions which enhances comparability across a wider range of countries.
MICRO	Customs (trade) data	Customs data is a useful source for understanding the mispricing of traded goods and services. This is an important component for understanding transfer pricing behaviour by related parties. As noted in the macro-section, the service component of trade flows (which includes royalties and other payments for the use of IP) is likely to be underestimated due to the underreporting and mispricing of IP. Availability of such data is country specific and not available in many countries. Studies in France and the United States have measured pricing differences between related and non-related parties, by country of destination and product characteristics.
	Company financial information from public / proprietary databases	This information can be sourced from published financial statements of MNEs, open-access sources such as OpenCorporates, and commercial databases (e.g. Bureau van Dijk (Bvd) ORBIS and Amadeus, S&P Compustat Global Vantage, Bloomberg, Oriana, Osiris, OneSource, Mergent, Alibaba.com SPARK, DataGuru.in, Ruslana). Companies (at least public companies) are typically obliged to publish financial statements (consolidated and/or unconsolidated). Problems with the suitability of this data for BEPS analysis include: different reporting requirements for accounting and

MICRO (continued)		tax purposes, no distinction between related party and independent party transactions, coverage that is far from comprehensive, and the heterogeneity of reporting across countries and companies. Databases that consolidate companies' balance sheet and income account data are improving their coverage over time, but still have weak coverage of developing countries in particular[9], but also of some OECD countries[10], such as Germany. This is because data availability in larger datasets depends on underlying national sources. A further drawback is the level of consolidation available for some countries. Company financial statements are used in research on profit shifting through debt financing, for example[11]. An important limitation in these studies is the limited country coverage and comparability across countries.
	Company financial information from government databases	Detailed financial information is available (although with limitations applying to access) from publicly administered databases such as the United States Bureau of Economic Analysis and German Bundesbank MiDi database. In some other countries, access to data via research centres or via controlled remote-access/execution is also being considered.
	Tax return CIT information	A range of financial and tax information is available to tax authorities as companies are required to file a tax return. The extent of information reported to the tax administration varies across countries. In some countries, there are strict rules limiting the reported information to that required for the calculation of tax liability only; in other countries, companies are required to file broader information used for risk analysis such as data on foreign subsidiaries. Many governments do not report corporate tax revenues separately for MNEs and purely domestic companies from tax returns, and have no systematic data regarding intra-group transactions. Some countries publish tax statistics that show the data in aggregate or by sector. Full access to the detailed micro-level company tax data is generally restricted to tax authorities, made available often on specific request for tax policy analysis, and in a few countries to outside researchers under strict confidentiality conditions.
	Tax audit information	Information from audits of tax return filings, both assessments and settlements, has been cited as a potential source of information about BEPS. This source of information is generally not available for tax policy analysis, even on an aggregated basis,
	Detailed specific company tax information	The specifics of individual MNEs' tax situations are becoming public through legislative enquiries, such as in the United Kingdom, the United States and more recently Australia. More granular tax information than what is available from the MNEs' financial statements or from global databases (for these companies) has become available. The European Commission has also launched a series of in-depth investigations into specific tax rulings and regimes that could be considered as EU State Aid to MNEs.

1.4 Initial assessment of currently available data for analysing BEPS

28. Analysis of BEPS requires identifying where MNE behaviours or arrangements "achieve no or low taxation by shifting profits away from jurisdictions where the activities creating those profits take place. No or low taxation is not *per se* a cause of concern, but it becomes so when it is associated with practices that artificially segregate taxable income from the activities that generate it." This description of BEPS is important in assessing the currently available data.

29. ***Firm-level data is needed for the best analysis of BEPS***. Among the economic community, there is general agreement that the increased availability and use of firm-

level data is an important improvement in analysing BEPS. Earlier studies of macro aggregate-level statistics found very large reported effects of profit shifting due to tax rate differentials, but aggregate-level statistics are less able to separate real economic activity from BEPS behaviours. Dharmapala (2014) presents a good summary of the existing economic empirical literature and how micro-level analysis better refines the analysis of profit shifting. Academic estimates of the responsiveness of profit shifting to tax rate differentials are generally lower from firm-level financial data than from macro level data or tax return data.

30. As mentioned earlier, publicly-available, private-source micro data has limitations in analysing BEPS. The proprietary databases integrate publicly-available financial information reported to various governmental agencies. The coverage and completeness of the data varies significantly across countries. In addition, the available financial information reflects accounting concepts, not tax return concepts. As a result, these databases still provide only indirect information about the presence of BEPS (tax return data would provide a more direct source of information and could be used in conjunction with relevant financial accounts databases). In addition, the ability of researchers using this firm-level data to isolate BEPS depends critically upon the empirical methods used to control for any differences in profitability explained by real economic factors.

31. National Accounts statistics, such as FDI and royalty payments, can provide some insights into transactions that can be part of arrangements to shift profits, so can thus be potential indicators of the scale of BEPS, but better estimates of the scale and economic effects of BEPS require micro-level data (importantly, the same micro data used to create the National Accounts). Improving the data and analysis of BEPS is also important for sound, evidence-based fiscal and monetary policies – government policymakers (fiscal) and central banks (monetary) rely heavily on macroeconomic statistics that are currently tainted by BEPS behaviours (Lipsey, 2010).

32. Figure 1.1 illustrates how BEPS behaviours affect corporate tax payments and company financial accounts, and also countries' National Accounts. Company A is located in Country A that has a statutory tax rate of 30%, while Company B, its affiliate, is located in Country B with a statutory tax rate of 10%. Company B sells goods to Company A for 150 that would have been sold for 100 to an independent party. As a result, the sales in Company B are overstated by 50 while the purchases in Company A are overstated by 50. This has ramifications for the value added measures in the National Accounts by overstating value added in Country B and understating valued added in Country A. This example shows how BEPS behaviours can distort GDP figures across countries. Only very few National Statistical Offices are able to adjust even partly for this distortion, especially in cases concerning payments for (if recorded) and transfers of intellectual property. The extent to which currently available data is tainted by BEPS is likely to be reduced over time, ultimately leading to more accurate statistics.

Figure 1.1. Example of non-arm's length transfer pricing affecting National Accounts and firm-level reports

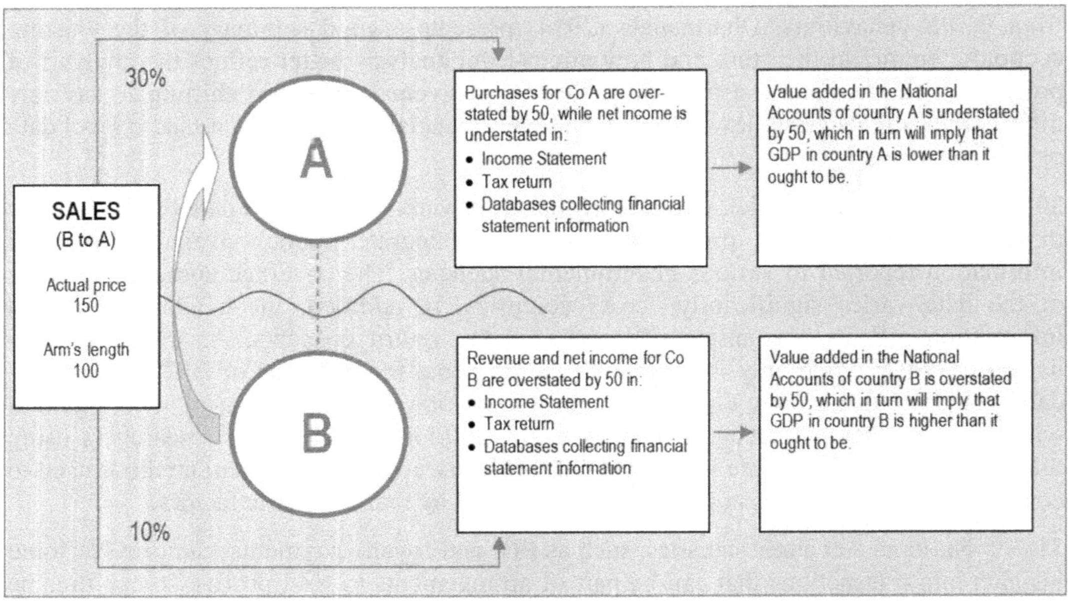

33. ***More complete information about global MNE activity is needed to analyse BEPS***. The analysis of BEPS would benefit from seeing the complete picture of the activities of the MNE and its related entities. In particular, the ability to identify the financial and taxation impacts of the activities of related entities relative to the economic contributions made to the global value chain by the entities in each jurisdiction. Many tax administrations currently only receive tax returns for the MNE entities required to file taxes in their country. They might not have access to information about related party affiliates undertaking transactions with the taxpayer in their country. The incomplete picture can often result in BEPS behaviours not being transparent for identification and quantification. Similarly, an incomplete picture of a MNE's financial arrangements can obscure BEPS behaviours from researchers using financial accounts.

34. Incomplete coverage of a MNE's economic activity across countries is particularly problematic for analysis of BEPS if the coverage is non-random. In that case, the sample of business entities may not be representative of the overall population. The potential for non-representativeness in analysing BEPS is likely to occur in two particular situations.

35. First, if the missing businesses or activities are in either high-tax rate or low-tax rate countries. Since BEPS typically involves profit shifting from high-tax to low-tax or no-tax rate countries, arrangements to segregate profits from real economic activity would be most likely to show up in those entities. For example, large reported profits in no-tax countries, where there is little if any real economic activity or value creation would be a result of BEPS.

36. Second, entities engaged in BEPS behaviours may be less likely to report any corporate holdings, offshore structures or activity that could highlight their BEPS actions to tax authorities or publicly available sources, where their activities may become subject to media and public attention. This may be because there is often discretion in some of the public reporting (e.g. materiality exceptions), or the penalties for non-reporting may

be small relative to the benefits of avoiding disclosure of tax and financial information that may include evidence of BEPS behaviours. Hoopes (2015) summarises academic research on issues of disclosure and transparency, including several studies[12] with regard to geographic/segment reporting, which have found selective disclosure particularly by tax aggressive MNEs.

37. It should also be noted that some MNEs are voluntarily becoming more transparent in their tax reporting. The driving forces behind this include the Extractive Industries Transparency Initiative (EITI), requirements by the European Commission, increasing public and government scrutiny that may affect reputation, and good governance motives.

38. An additional concern about incomplete coverage and lack of representation arises if BEPS behaviours differ across countries (e.g. R&D intensive countries may be more susceptible to BEPS behaviours involving intangibles while other countries may be more affected by financial restructuring[13]), but the available data is not sufficiently representative of the population such that it can capture the differences. Lack of representation has been noted by Cobham and Loretz (2014)[14] with respect to tax policy analysis of developing countries. A recent IMF analysis concluded that developing countries are likely to have significantly higher BEPS concerns than developed countries due to lower tax administrative capacity to stop BEPS behaviours. Also, many studies of profit shifting are based on the Amadeus database, which includes only European countries, so the results may not be applicable to non-European countries.

39. The most comprehensive (and widely-used by researchers) global database is the proprietary BvD ORBIS database. It is an extensive database of almost 100 million financial accounts from many countries, and is being continually updated, expanded and improved. Although a useful global database, it has limitations,[15] and is based upon financial account rather than tax return data. With respect to its representativeness for the purposes of BEPS empirical analysis, Cobham and Loretz (2014) note the Eurocentric nature of the sample and its weakness in coverage of low-income countries. Table 1.2 is a summary of the Cobham and Loretz data analysis, plus a comparison to the geographic distribution of both the Fortune Global 500 MNE groups and GDP.

Table 1.2. Regional distribution of MNE subsidiaries in ORBIS by location of subsidiary and group headquarters, compared with regional distribution of top 500 MNE groups and GDP, 2011

	Location of Subsidiary						%
Location of the group headquarters	Europe	North America	Australasia	Latin & Central America & Caribbean	Middle East & Africa	Total	Representation by location of group headquarter
Europe	208,048	9,933	3,451	1,465	835	223,732	69%
North America	28,901	23,095	2,363	803	125	55,287	17%
Australasia	9,303	4,624	20,318	276	84	34,605	11%
Latin & Central America & Caribbean	3,910	556	432	672	11	5,581	2%
Middle East & Africa	2,349	297	75	32	567	3,320	1%
Total	252,511	38,505	26,639	3,248	1,622	322,525	100%
% Representation by location of subsidiary	78%	12%	8%	1%	1%	100%	
Fortune Global 500[1]	29%	28%	41%	3%	0%	100%	
GDP[2]	27%	24%	34%	8%	7%	100%	

Notes:

1. Regional distribution of top 500 companies in 2014 (Fortune Magazine)

2. GDP from IMF (current 2011 prices: 2011 used to compare with latest year used by Cobham and Loretz from Orbis)

Source: Cobham, A. & Loretz, S. 2014. International distribution of the corporate tax base: Implications of different apportionment factors under unitary taxation

40. For example, Table 1.2 shows that MNEs headquartered in Europe accounted for 69% of the affiliates in the ORBIS database; in comparison, MNEs from the rest of the world accounted for only 31%. Of the total affiliates with key financial information included, 78% were in Europe, while 22% were located in the rest of the world. This is only a summary of the number of firms, and does not indicate how representative the database is in terms of economic activity or taxes. The lack of representative data is likely to be worse for developing countries. Furthermore, it does not indicate whether actual data is available for all the firms included.

41. Many academic studies have observed and estimated the existence of profit shifting (including profit shifting from specific BEPS channels) with limited financial account data, and in a few cases using tax return data, as described in Chapter 3. Importantly, these studies find that BEPS is occurring and the extent of BEPS is large and statistically significant. The limitations of the currently available data are problematic in estimating the global scale and economic impact of BEPS. There is concern that sample selection may result in underestimation of findings on aggregate profit shifting.[16] Other studies include both BEPS and individual tax evasion in their analyses of BEPS and are thus likely to overstate the scale of BEPS.

42. Recent public enquiries by legislative and/or parliamentary committees, such as in the United Kingdom, the United States, and more recently Australia, into the tax strategies of some high profile MNEs, have shed significant light on the tax affairs of the affected parent companies and their affiliates.[17] In addition, The European Commission has launched a series of in-depth investigations into specific tax regimes that could be considered as EU State Aid to MNEs.[18] Investigative journalism has also brought much useful information into the public domain.

43. What is striking is that when one looks into the micro data available, much of this newly revealed information does not appear to be visible – either because certain affiliates are not included or, where they are included, the financial information is missing. This reveals a clear disconnect between the information revealed through

targeted public enquiries of some MNEs and the limited available tax information for those same MNEs from consolidated financial statements. Box 1.2 explains this further.

Box 1.2. Public enquiries reveal data missing from many academic studies

Evidence emerging from several recent public enquiries into the tax affairs of a number of high profile MNEs reveals clear deficiencies in the available data sources used by researchers in analysing BEPS. The public enquiries revealed new information on the earnings, structure and tax affairs of parent companies and their affiliates. The table below shows an example of one of the MNE's reported pre-tax income.

The parent company, X, located in a high-tax jurisdiction, reported between 29 and 43 percent of pre-tax earnings for the years 2009 to 2011. X's affiliate, Y, located in a low-tax jurisdiction, earned nearly two-thirds of the group's total pre-tax income in 2010 and 2011, and half of the total in 2009.

Global Distribution of Specific MNE reported Earnings:

Entity	Location	Pre-tax income		
		2011	2010	2009
		%	%	%
X (Parent)	High tax country	31	29	43
Y (Affiliate)	Low tax country	64	65	50
Other		5	6	7
Total		100	100	100

While Affiliate Y earned the majority of the pre-tax income, it paid virtually no taxes to any government for these three years. Due to different rules for determining tax residence, a key entity incorporated in the low-tax country was not taxable in any country. Thus, several tens of billions of the parent's local currency were only taxed at a 0.06% tax rate over three years.

In a micro database used by many researchers to analyse BEPS, the financial information for the key affiliate (Y) in the low tax country was missing. This reveals a clear disconnect between the information revealed through targeted public enquiries of some MNEs and the incomplete available financial information for those same MNEs from financial accounts. Much of the important information for tax analysis is simply absent. The fact that such observed instances of BEPS are not visible in firm-level financial account databases highlights concerns regarding the reliability and representativeness of one of the most frequently used existing data sources.

44. ***Additional analysis of tax return information is needed.*** As noted above, significant differences exist between tax return information and financial accounts, which make financial account information problematic as a sole source for analysing BEPS, even if it was comprehensive.

45. Tax return information submitted to individual countries is also not comprehensive in terms of the full picture of the MNE group, but it is less likely to be subject to underreporting due to the significant financial penalties for tax non-compliance. Tax return data will have accurate information about the country of tax residence, taxable income, tax paid, tax credits, and tax consolidation, which reduces significant noise present in financial accounts. Information obtained from tax audits can identify new types of BEPS behaviours, and could potentially be used if compiled and analysed systematically to monitor BEPS behaviours in the future.[19]

46. Although significant data from tax returns is provided to tax administrations by companies, much of the data is not processed and incorporated in databases for tax policy analysis purposes. In a survey by the OECD CFA WP2, a majority of countries cited lack of data as the key constraint in analysing BEPS. Most of the 37 respondent countries reported that corporate tax returns are in a database, although corporate tax data for tax policy analysis is often available in aggregate form or upon request for individual companies. Only eight countries were able to report the aggregate corporate income tax collections from MNEs. Thus, although corporate tax return data has been provided by companies to government tax administrations, it is not currently available in easily accessible form for tax policy analysis.

47. ***Making the most of available information and identifying gaps***. Companies and governments are being required to do more with less under tight budgetary constraints. Compliance burdens and tax administrative costs are significant, and additional information should only be requested and processed if the benefits exceed the costs. Information collection where possible should be aligned to current recordkeeping and reporting of MNE business to assure better data integrity and minimise compliance costs.

48. Much of the academic work that has been done and the interest shown in doing more is constrained by lack of access to micro data that is representative of entities in an individual country or across countries, and that is not missing critical information. This is equally true in some instances for government analysts, who could do more tax policy analysis with access to better data, but in many countries the degree of granularity (for example, separating MNEs from purely domestic corporations) is not sufficient, and availability of disaggregated data is quite different across countries.

49. In many cases, information has been provided by businesses to tax administrations, but the data are not processed and are not presently available for tax policy analysis. The amount and detail of data currently made available for tax policy analysis of BEPS behaviours differs across countries. Policy making could be better informed with knowledge of, for example, corporate taxable income, income subject to lower statutory tax rate or exemptions, corporate tax credits, and withholding tax bases and revenues. The lack of distinction in the data between (i) MNEs (inbound / outbound) and domestic-only corporations, and (ii) related and third party transactions, is also a significant limitation in some countries. With increasing use of electronically filed tax returns, the cost of processing the filed information will be reduced, but will still be significant for many countries. Nonetheless, maximising the information and insight from currently provided data, based on best practices in several countries would be beneficial. The Action 11 Request for Input and the CFA WP2 survey identified what could be considered as some best practices to improve data collection, processing, and economic analysis in several countries, which are briefly described in Box 1.3.

Box 1.3. Some current best practices in using available data for BEPS analysis

Germany – The Deutsche Bundesbank houses the Micro database on Direct Investment (MiDi), which is a full census of foreign firms' affiliates in Germany. It covers directly or indirectly owned foreign affiliates of German parent companies above a certain size and ownership threshold, including affiliates in developing countries. It contains unconsolidated (sometimes consolidated) balance sheet data at the firm level, ownership variables (links between affiliates and parent company), as well as other useful information such as liabilities to shareholders and (or) affiliates; total balance sheet of affiliates and parent company; and shares in the assets and liability positions of non-residents. The data includes profit after tax, but does not include other income statement information, such as taxes or income/expense information for analysing specific BEPS channels. The MiDi data is confidential and available only on site at the Research Centre at the Central Office of the Deutsche Bundesbank in Frankfurt for approved research projects and under strict confidentiality rules.

Sweden – Government analysts in Sweden have access to detailed, anonymised taxpayer information from filed tax returns. The firm-level information also includes balance sheet information, the number of domestic employees, employee compensation, and the value of tangible and intangible assets. The data distinguishes between MNEs and purely domestic firms, with a further breakdown available by sectors. Information on foreign source income and related party transactions (e.g. controlled foreign corporations), and the amount of R&D expenditures undertaken in the country is not captured in tax returns. A useful practice that could be replicated in other countries is using information available from other sources, such as commercial sources to supplement the government's database. However, the Swedish data lacks detailed income information on foreign subsidiaries.

Latin America – Some tax authorities, such as in Argentina, request companies to present special forms with information relating to transactions with related parties as well as with entities located in non-cooperative jurisdictions, and non-related parties. The information covers trade in goods and specifies prices, volumes and trading partners. Some Latin American countries share data extracted from these forms (e.g. effective tax rates, intragroup transactions, and transactions with parties located in tax havens) with international organisations, such as the Inter-American Centre of Tax Administrations (CIAT), upon request, even if they are not shared with the public. This suggests that there are opportunities for international organisations to construct comparable data for developing countries[20].

United States – The United States Bureau of Economic Analysis (BEA) surveys both UNITED STATES headquartered firms (and their affiliates abroad) and subsidiaries in the United States of foreign headquartered firms. Both surveys are done on an annual basis with more detailed benchmark surveys done every five years. MNE firms operating in the United States are required by law to respond to these surveys, but the survey information is not shared with tax or financial reporting authorities to enable verification, and confidentiality is assured. The aggregated data are publicly available, and the micro data can be accessed by non-government researchers under strict confidentiality rules. The current data does not enable full consolidation, can include some double counting of affiliated entities, and does not identify hybrid securities that can be used for shifting income. The data for each affiliate includes the country of location of its physical assets as well as its country of incorporation, though neither of these are necessarily its country of tax residence.

Box 1.3. Some current best practices in using available data for BEPS analysis ***(continued)***

The United States Internal Revenue Service (IRS) collects tax return information on controlled foreign corporations (CFCs) of United States parents, plus tax return information on United States subsidiaries of foreign parents. Some of the tax return data is compiled and tabulated for published aggregate tables and compiled micro data is available for certain government analysts as well as certain approved non-government researchers. While most corporate micro data for analysis are stratified random samples, in the international area micro data is more likely to be for the population of multinational corporations. This enables a relatively complete picture of all the CFCs of United States parents though some information on lower tiers may be missing. Data are reported by country of incorporation and therefore the country of reporting for some entities, particularly hybrid or stateless entities, does not necessarily reflect the country of tax residence. For United States subsidiaries with foreign parents, data are generally limited to United States activity. The CFC data is important in tax policy analysis particularly because it includes linkages with affiliated entities.

50. In 2011, the OECD Expert Group for International Collaboration on Microdata Access was formed to examine the challenges for cross-border collaboration with micro data. The resulting 2014 report[21] notes: "*The challenge in the 21st Century is to change practices in access to micro data so that the access services can cross borders and support trans-national analysis and policy making. This is necessary to reflect the increasingly international (global) reach and impact of comparative analysis and shared policy making.*"

51. Instead of suggesting new legislation, substantial new infrastructure, or new technology for doing so, the report seeks smarter deployment of what already exists in most OECD countries. Of course, in the micro-level tax return data context for BEPS, data collection, dissemination and access is still not ideal. The report highlights the importance of comparability and thus working towards homogeneity in data collection across countries. It states that regional and international shared policy making needs the support of evidence drawn from comparative analysis and/or the combined data of the national parties to the collaboration. Working with available firm/group-level financial statements, for example, reveals the heterogeneity across reporting standards for accounting purposes worldwide. The level of detail (and whether this is provided geographically or by segment) in which groups choose to report certain items like sales, assets, profits and employees differs widely. There are also vast differences in the mandatory information required by different tax authorities.

52. It is important to emphasise that in most cases BEPS must be estimated rather than directly observed from tax returns, financial accounts or customs records. For example, identifying deviations from arm's length pricing is a highly fact-intensive analysis. Analysis of customs data for individual product pricing must distinguish between sales to related parties and third-parties, and analysis of relatively unique transfers of intangible assets requires analysis of "comparable" transactions. Comparisons of profits and effective tax rates across thousands of companies require sophisticated statistical analysis to truly separate tax aspects from real economic activity. Simple descriptive statistics can only provide indications, rather than correlation or causation, of potential BEPS behaviours, and statistical analysis of large databases may also only be able to provide rough measures or indications of BEPS due to current data limitations.

Nonetheless, analysis of available data by statistical and economic analysis will provide additional insights beyond descriptive statistics.

53. Processed corporate tax return information for MNEs and their foreign affiliates have been analysed by governments and, in some countries, academic researchers. Linkage of tax return information with other business administrative records within governments could increase the insights from existing data. However, access to existing tax return information for tax analysis purposes is not always possible. In addition, many government tax policy agencies and tax administrations have limited resources to conduct empirical statistical and economic analysis. Some countries provide good examples of what can be achieved as there are co-operative research programmes between government and academics for analysis of data under strictly controlled and confidential circumstances by academics with specific research programmes. This promotes robust economic and statistical analysis based on access to firm-level data.

54. Although having a large database with many observations is helpful for statistical analysis, such a database may exclude important available information. Sometimes the quality and depth of an analysis is more insightful than the quantity of observations providing a non-random and/or less in-depth analysis. Thus, although examples of BEPS behaviours by some major MNEs should not be extrapolated to all MNEs, detailed information from public enquiries should be considered. Existing databases used for economic analysis of BEPS should be checked to see if identified cases of BEPS are included in the data. Finally, this assessment of the currently available data for economic analysis of BEPS and potential countermeasures has identified significant data limitations, data issues, and in some cases data gaps in the various data sources currently available for analysing BEPS and BEPS countermeasures.

Bibliography

Akamah, H.T., O.-K. Hope and W.B. Thomas (2014), *Tax havens and disclosure aggregation*, Rotman School of Management Working Paper, No. 2419573.

Australia (2014), *Parliament of Australia: Inquiry into tax disputes*, www.aph.gov.au/Parliamentary_Business/Committees/House/Tax_and_Revenue/Inquiry_into_Tax_Disputes (accessed 19 December 2014).

Beer, S. and J. Loeprick (2013), *Profit shifting: Drivers and potential countermeasures*, WU International Taxation Research Paper Series, No. 2013-03, http://dx.doi.org/10.2139/ssrn.2271539.

Buettner, T and G. Wamser, G. (2007), *Intercompany loans and profit shifting: Evidence from company-level data*, CEsifo Working Paper Series, No. 1959.

Bureau Van Dijk, *ORBIS Database*, Bureau Van Dijk Electronic Publishing.

Cederwall, E. (2015), *Making sense of profit shifting: Jack Mintz*, Tax Foundation interview, http://taxfoundation.org/blog/making-sense-profit-shifting-jack-mintz.

Cobham, A. and S. Loretz (2014), *International distribution of the corporate tax base: Impact of different apportionment factors under unitary taxation*, ICTD Working Paper, No. 32.

Dharmapala, D. (2014), *What do we know about base erosion and profit shifting? A review of the empirical literature*, Fiscal Studies, Vol. 35, pp. 421–448.

European Commission (2014), *State aid: Commission extends information enquiry on tax rulings practice to all member states*, http://europa.eu/rapid/press-release_IP-14-2742_en.htm (accessed 8 January 2014).

Hanlon, M. (2003), *What can we infer about a firm's taxable income from its financial statement?*, National Tax Journal, Vol. 56, Issue 4, pp. 831-863.

Hoopes, J. 2015, *Taxes and disclosure: A brief summary of the research*, (mimeo).

Hope, O.K., M. Ma and W.B. Thomas (2013), *Tax avoidance and geographic earnings disclosure*, Journal of Accounting & Economics, Vol. 56(2-3), pp. 170-189.

House of Lords Select Committee on Economic Affairs (2013), *Tackling corporate tax avoidance in a global economy: is a new approach needed?*, First Report of Session 2013–14, www.publications.parliament.uk/pa/ld201314/ldselect/ldeconaf/48/48.pdf (accessed 14 October 2014).

Huizinga, H., L. Laeven and G. Nicodeme (2008), *Capital structure and international debt shifting*, Journal of Financial Economics, Vol. 88, pp. 80-118.

IMF (2014), *Co-ordinated Direct Investment Survey: Project on bilateral asymmetries*, IMF Policy paper, http://data.imf.org/?sk=D732FC6E-D8C3-44D1-BFEB-F70BA9E13211.

Koch, R. and A. Oestreicher (2014), *Comments on Categories A and B: Indicators of the scale and economic impact*, Comments in response to the OECD BEPS Action 11 request for input, www.oecd.org/ctp/tax-policy/comments-action-11-establishing-methodologies.pdf.

Lipsey, R. E. (2010), *Measuring the location of production in a world of intangible productive assets, FDI and intrafirm trade*, Review of Income and Wealth, Series 56, Special Issue No. 1.

Lisowsky, P. (2010), *Seeking shelter: Empirically modelling tax shelters using financial statement information*, Accounting Review, Vol. 85, No. 5.

OECD (2015), *Implementing the latest international standards for compiling foreign direct investment statistics: How multinational enterprises channel investments through multiple counties*, OECD, Paris, www.oecd.org/daf/inv/How-MNEs-channel-investments.pdf.

OECD (2014), *OECD expert group for international collaboration on microdata access: Final report*, OECD Publishing, Paris, www.oecd.org/std/microdata-access-executive-summary-OECD-2014.pdf.

OECD (2013), *Addressing Base Erosion and Profit Shifting*, OECD Publishing, Paris, http://dx.doi.org/10.1787/9789264192744-en.

Prichard, W., A. Cobham and A. Goodall (2014), *The ICTD Government Revenue Dataset*, ICTD Working Paper, No. 19, http://dx.doi.org/10.2139/ssrn.2496442.

United Kingdom (2015), *Parliament: Commons Select Committee on Tax avoidance and evasion*, www.parliament.uk/business/committees/committees-a-z/commons-select/public-accounts-committee/inquiries/parliament-2010/tax-avoidance-evasion-hsbc/ (accessed 19 December 2014).

United States Homeland Security & Governmental Affairs (2013), *US Senate Subcommittee on permanent investigations*, www.hsgac.senate.gov/subcommittees/investigations/hearings/offshore-profit-shifting-and-the-us-tax-code_-part-2 (accessed 2 February 2015).

Weyzig, F. (2014), *The capital structure of large firms and the use of Dutch financing entities*, Fiscal Studies, Vol. 35(2), pp. 139-164.

Notes

1. IMF (2014), Coordinated Direct Investment Survey: Project on bilateral asymmetries.
2. BEPS Monitoring Group, submission to Action 11 Public Consultation, May 2015.
3. Cederwall, E. (2015), Making Sense of Profit Shifting: Jack Mintz. Tax Foundation.
4. OECD 2015. Implementing the latest international standards for compiling foreign direct investment statistics: How multinational enterprises channel investments through multiple countries.
5. Koch, R. & Oestreicher, A. (2014), in response to the OECD BEPS Action 11 Request for Input.
6. For financial accounting purposes, the objective is to record both current-year and future-year tax liabilities (tax expense) associated with the current-year economic activities of a firm. This differs from actual, current-year tax payments that may have been generated by prior-year economic activities and do not include the future tax payments from current-year economic activities. See Hanlon (2003) and Lisowsky (2010).
7. Koch & Oestreicher (2014).
8. Prichard, Cobham and Goodall (2014).
9. See e.g. Cobham & Loretz, (2014).
10. See Weyzig (2014).
11. E.g. Weyzig (2014), Buettner and Wamser (2007), Huizinga et al. (2008).
12. Hope et al. (2013) examined firms' responses to a United States accounting rule change in 1998, which allowed firms to stop providing segment reporting at the geographic level. The analysis found that firms that discontinued geographic segment reporting were those that had lower effective tax rates, consistent with firms' interest in not reporting information that would potentially reveal tax avoidance behaviour. In a similar paper, Akamah et al. (2014) find that firms with operations in tax havens are more likely to aggregate their geographic segment disclosures.
13. Cederwall, E. (2015), Making Sense of Profit Shifting: Jack Mintz. Tax Foundation.
14. Cobham and Loretz (2014) use the largest commercially available database of company balance sheets, ORBIS. Using a dataset of over 200,000 individual companies in over 25,000 corporate, they state coverage is severely limited among developing countries, and increasingly so for lower-income countries, and "where there are non-random reasons for information to be missing (e.g. accounts in low-tax jurisdictions are less likely to be included in the dataset), this will result in systematic biases to the results."
15. In response to the OECD (2014) BEPS Action 11 Request for Input, Reinald Koch and Andreas Oestreicher list some of the limitations: there is no distinction between interest and dividend income, or between intra-group and third party transactions; the

publishers of the data rely on extent to which companies publish reports; there are missing companies in the data as well as missing financial information from companies that are included; it is not a random sample as it depends on information released by business sector; and it can be assumed that information is lacking in particular for entities that are used for tax planning purposes.

16. Beer and Loeprick (2013) estimate profit shifting, and find significant effects, but note the selection criterion reduced their sample by more than 60%, "possibly resulting in a bias as incomplete accounting information may be correlated to less transparent corporate governance and more aggressive tax optimization." "Such a bias would likely result in an underestimation of findings on aggregate profit shifting."

17. Commons Select Committee on Tax avoidance and evasion in the United Kingdom (2015); House of Lords Select Committee on Economic Affairs (2013); The Permanent Subcommittee on Investigations in the United States (2013); Inquiry into Tax Disputes in Australia (2014).

18. European Commission (2014).

19. Michael Durst, submission to Action 11 Public Consultation, May 2015.

20. BEPS Monitoring Group, submission to Action 11 Request for Input, September 2014

21. (OECD 2014), *OECD Expert Group for International Collaboration on Microdata Access: Final Report*.

Chapter 2

Indicators of base erosion and profit shifting

Key points:

- While there is a large and growing body of evidence of the existence of BEPS, through empirical analysis and specific information relating to the affairs of certain MNEs that has emerged from numerous legislative and parliamentary enquiries, the scale of BEPS and changes in BEPS over time are difficult to measure.
- This chapter presents six indicators to assist in tracking the scale and economic impact of BEPS over time, while noting the strengths and limitations of each indicator. The six indicators point to a disconnect between financial and real economic activities, profit rate differentials within top global MNEs, tax rate differentials between MNEs and comparable non-MNEs and profit shifting through intangibles and interest.
- The use of any indicators to identify the scale and economic impact of BEPS can only provide "general indications" and the interpretation of any such indicators must be heavily qualified by numerous caveats.
- While no single indicator is capable of providing a complete picture of the existence and scale of BEPS, a collection of indicators or a "dashboard of indicators" can provide broad insights into the scale and economic impact of BEPS and provide assistance to policymakers in monitoring changes in BEPS over time.
- This chapter also provides calculations for the indicators, using samples of existing available data. The data used to produce these calculations are affected by the considerable limitations of existing available data sources described in detail in Chapter 1. As a result, the indicators are illustrative rather than definitive, as the insights that can be discerned from these indicators are greatly affected by the limitations of the existing available data.
- Future access to more comprehensive and improved data would allow much greater insight to be obtained from the use of these indicators as well as two potential indicators that could be constructed with improved future data.
- The six BEPS indicators show strong indications of BEPS behaviours using different sources of data, employing different metrics, and examining different BEPS channels. When combined and presented as a dashboard of indicators, they provide evidence of the existence of BEPS, and its continued increase in scale. Improved data availability can provide better insights in the future.

2.1 Introduction

55. One of the key components of Action 11 is the development of "indicators" that can be used to identify the scale and economic impact of BEPS, to track changes in BEPS over time and to monitor the effectiveness of measures implemented to reduce BEPS.

56. The first step in developing useful indicators of BEPS is defining the concept. BEPS relates to arrangements that achieve no or low taxation by shifting profits away from the jurisdictions where the activities creating those profits take place or by exploiting gaps in the interaction of domestic tax rules where corporate income is not taxed at all. No or low taxation is not *per se* a cause of BEPS, but becomes so when it is associated with practices that artificially segregate taxable income from the activities that generate it. The important distinguishing characteristic of BEPS is tax planning strategies that result in a disconnect between the geographic assignment of taxable profits and the location of the underlying real economic activities that generate these profits. As a result of this disconnect, MNEs may be able to shift profits from higher-taxed countries to lower-taxed countries without a corresponding material change in the way the taxpayer operates, including where products and services are produced, sales and distribution occur, research and development is undertaken, and how the taxpayer's capital and labour are used. In some cases, BEPS involves placing just enough economic activity in a jurisdiction to attempt to justify the tax planning strategy.

57. An overriding objective in the construction and analysis of BEPS indicators in Action 11 is to develop metrics that help portray the extent of practices that artificially segregate taxable income from the activities that generate it.

2.2 Indicator concept

58. Dictionary definitions of indicators include:

- An index that provides an indication, especially of trends
- A meter or gauge measuring and recording variation
- A device to attract attention, such as a warning light
- An instrument that displays certain operating conditions such as temperature
- A pointer on a dial showing pressure or speed

59. As with any gauge, the degree of precision depends on the available information and the accuracy of the measurement tools. Given currently available data and distortions caused in that data by BEPS which is being measured, at this stage BEPS indicators can only provide some general insights into the scale and economic impact of BEPS, but will necessarily lack the precision that may become possible if more comprehensive and improved data sources were to be used in the future (see Chapter 1 for a detailed assessment of the limitations of currently available data). More refined analysis and estimates of BEPS, based on multi-variate statistical estimation, are possible with currently available data, but also involve significant uncertainties and limitations (see Chapter 3 for a detailed examination of the approaches to undertaking such estimation). Over time, the proposed indicators will provide a general sense of the trend in a number of key metrics associated with BEPS behaviours.

60. The concept followed in developing the BEPS indicators has been to create a "dashboard of indicators" that provides an indication of the scale of BEPS and help policymakers monitor changes in the scale of BEPS over time. The indicators are crude proxies for a more refined and sophisticated estimate of the dimensions of BEPS. Given currently available data, indicators are probably the appropriate approach to showing consistent trends on the general scale of BEPS. Multiple indicators can help identify trends regarding the scale of BEPS and changes in BEPS and specific BEPS behaviours. An important requirement of an indicator is that it provides more signal than noise in measuring the scale of BEPS. To the extent that various potential indicators provide the same signal (i.e. a high correlation) on the same dimension, then only the clearest indicator should be used.

61. While no single indicator can be used to provide a complete picture of the scale or economic impact of BEPS, if a number of separate indicators referring to different dimensions are pointing in the same direction, they may provide more solid information on the presence of and trends in BEPS.

2.3 Indicators as a component of Action 11

62. The following chart provides an overview of the different analyses carried out under Action 11. This chapter presents six BEPS indicators that can be developed from current data, which is identified as the "current state" category in the chart. Also included here is the analysis of the scale and economic impact of BEPS that is addressed in Chapter 3 on the economic analysis of BEPS. The current data limitations are a significant challenge to the development of both indicators and economic analyses. Even within tax administrations there is limited information on the operations of MNEs. In a recent country survey conducted by the Committee on Fiscal Affairs' WP2 on BEPS-related research, only eight countries, out of 37 respondents, could report the total amount of tax revenue collected from MNEs operating in their country.

63. Over time, to the extent that new data sources become available, it is expected that more accurate estimates of the scale and economic impact of BEPS and the impact of countermeasures will be possible. Many of the indicators in this chapter have been developed not only with existing available data in mind, but with a view towards how such indicators could be enhanced if more comprehensive and improved data were to become available in the future. The "future state" in the chart represents what would be considered the next step in the development of more effective BEPS indicators and estimation methodologies. In this "future state", many of the indicators would provide even more insight and more targeted indicators and deeper economic analyses could be developed from the emergence of new data sources. In the "ideal state", the indirect indicators of BEPS would evolve into more accurate, direct estimates of BEPS and the effectiveness of the BEPS counter-measures. In the "ideal state", additional and more comprehensive information derived from actual tax return data would be necessary to achieve the most precise estimations of BEPS and its economic impact.[1]

64. One important outcome of developing BEPS indicators with currently available data is a clearer understanding of the usefulness and limitations of the current data. These insights are discussed in more detail in Chapter 1's assessment of current data. Such an understanding is helpful in informing any consideration of what future new data might be needed.

Figure 2.1. Future path of BEPS measurement

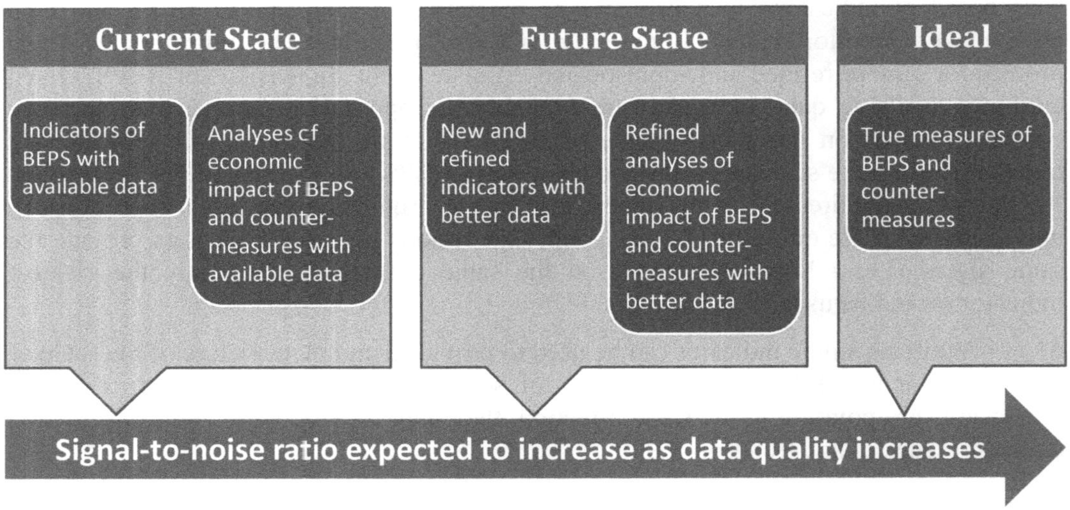

2.4 Guidelines for indicators

65. The following are specific guidelines that were used in developing BEPS indicators:

66. ***A number of different indicators should be included to form a "dashboard of BEPS indicators".*** Multiple indicators showing the general scale of BEPS and particular BEPS channels are needed given limitations in currently available data. The six indicators include indicators based on both macro (aggregate) and micro (firm-level) data. Certain indicators will be more useful than others for understanding the effectiveness of different BEPS countermeasures.

67. ***Alternatives should be considered for summarising indicators.*** A single indicator may provide information on both the level of BEPS and changes in BEPS over time. A ratio may be the most effective way to indicate the level, while trends or changes in time may be more effectively presented as an index with reference to an initial year value of the indicator.

68. ***Financial and tax flows should be related to economic activity.*** The most useful indicators of the general scale of BEPS should link BEPS-related financial and tax flows to measures of real economic activity, such as GDP, sales, employment or the amount of capital used by firms. In other words, in constructing indicators to be used in evaluating BEPS, it is important to distinguish between shifts in profits among countries that reflect changes in real economic activity and BEPS-related transfers of profits that are not in response to changes in the location of real economic factors, labour and capital, that produce the income. It should be understood, however, that any indicator of BEPS, such as income relative to assets, sales, operating expenses or employment or any other economic measure will vary across countries for a number of reasons unrelated to BEPS. The economic sources of variation in profits relative to assets, for example, include differences in the ratio of capital to labour used in different businesses and locations, differences in market conditions, differences in profitability over the economic cycle, and differences in factor productivity.

69. ***Indicators should distinguish between BEPS and real economic effects of current-law corporate income tax features.*** Indicators should focus on tax shifting due to

BEPS, not real economic responses to tax rate differences that reflect the impact of current-law provisions adopted by legislators, including incentives to expand business operations in their country. Legislated or discretionary tax incentives can have an important impact on reported corporate income tax payments that reflect the location of real economic activity. The challenge in developing indicators is distinguishing between the economic effects and BEPS. However, artificial cross-border arrangements to exploit legislated differences in tax structures, including statutory tax rate differences, are considered BEPS.

70. ***The BEPS indicators should be able to be refined with potential new data sources***. The initial indicators are based on currently available data for a large number of countries. New methodologies and data sources will be identified going forward to analyse the scale of BEPS and the effectiveness of countermeasures to reduce BEPS. In some cases the initial indicators could be calculated from new data sources which could provide more targeted and accurate information for estimating BEPS.

71. ***Bad indicators should be avoided; caveats should be highlighted***. Almost as important as developing effective indicators of BEPS is the need to avoid using poor, imprecise and misleading indicators. Indicators should have a high signal-to-noise ratio. In other words, indicators should provide a high ratio of information about BEPS behaviours relative to real economic effects and other non-BEPS factors. Any indicator will have limitations which should be highlighted. All indicators will require careful interpretation in analysing BEPS.

72. ***Indicators should be simple, clear and timely***. Indicators will be used by policymakers, so they should be simple, clear and well-described. However, their caveats and limitations should also be clearly noted. Where possible, indicators should not have significant time lags.

73. ***Indicators should be adaptable to extended uses***. The initial indicators focus on the global perspective, but some indicators should have the potential to be extended to be used by individual countries or for specific industries. The development of disaggregated indicators should be considered for future analysis.

2.5 A significant caution

74. One of the biggest challenges to developing and interpreting indicators is that BEPS "taints" available measures of real economic activity such as corporate income tax bases, financial accounting statements, and even national aggregate measures of economic activity in the corporate sector. This is a serious limitation that is difficult to overcome with current data and methodologies available for measuring BEPS.

75. The data used to measure most of the indicators unavoidably mix the influence of real economic activities, corporate income tax policies adopted to encourage business development, and BEPS.

76. It is important to note that each indicator provides a single perspective of the scale or composition of BEPS based on currently available data. The indicators are not equivalent to coefficients in regression equations used to measure the responsiveness of BEPS to corporate income tax rate differentials. A regression equation is designed to take into consideration or "control for" the simultaneous impacts of other economic variables on BEPS. However, in most cases, the indicators do provide high-level "controls" for some of the major non-BEPS factors through the use of ratios of tax variables to

economic measures and differentials in tax measures between affiliates and their MNE worldwide group measures.

77. These limitations must be kept in mind in interpreting the information that each indicator or combination of indicators provides in helping portray the magnitude of BEPS and evaluating progress over time in reducing BEPS. It may be the case that, in the future, new and better data sources may help overcome some of these data limitations.

2.6 Six indicators of BEPS

78. Six BEPS Action 11 indicators are described in this section. The discussion for each indicator includes a description, the rationale for the indicator and the data source that can be used to estimate the indicator. Calculations of the indicators use existing available data. The data used to produce these calculations are affected by the considerable limitations of existing available data sources outlined in detail in Chapter 1. As a result, the indicators are designed to be illustrative rather than definitive, as the insights that can be discerned from these examples are greatly affected by the limitations of the existing available data. Each indicator also contains a statement of some of the important issues in estimating and interpreting the indicator, including limitations which might be considered a type of "user-warning".

79. This chapter presents six specific indicators in the following five categories:

A. Disconnect between financial and real economic activities

1. Concentration of high levels of foreign direct investment (FDI) relative to GDP

B. Profit rate differentials within top (e.g. top 250) global MNEs

2. Differential profit rates compared to effective tax rates
3. Differential profit rates between low-tax locations and worldwide MNE operations

C. MNE vs. "comparable" non-MNE effective tax rate differentials

4. Effective tax rates of large MNE affiliates relative to non-MNE entities with similar characteristics

D. Profit shifting through intangibles

5. Concentration of high levels of royalty receipts relative to research and development (R&D) spending

E. Profit shifting through interest

6. Interest expense to income ratios of MNE affiliates in high-tax locations

80. In addition, two possible additional indicators are discussed that could be estimated from improved future data when it becomes available.

81. Indicators 1 and 5 are based on macro-level data on a country-by-country basis. Indicators 2-4 and 6 are calculated from MNE, firm-level financial information from the ORBIS database[2] for unconsolidated affiliates and/or worldwide consolidated groups.

82. In order to partly distinguish between BEPS and real economic impacts, most of the indicators are constructed using various comparison groups, such as different groups of countries, different groups of MNE affiliates or worldwide MNE measures vs. affiliate measures. The objective is to compare measures where BEPS is likely to be relatively

important to measures that are more likely to reflect real economic activities. The use of these comparison groups is designed to increase the signal-to-noise ratio of the indicators.

2.7 General structure of the indicators

83. This section discusses general advantages, limitations, issues and possible extensions that apply generally to the indicators. In addition, there are more specific comments about these dimensions in the introduction to the indicator categories. Finally, there are additional considerations that are discussed for specific indicators.

2.7.1 General advantages

84. Some of the advantages of using indicators include the following:

- Indicators can be calculated historically and on an annual basis to track the direction of changes in BEPS over time.
- Some indicators can be updated relatively quickly from data available on a timely basis.
- Indicators can be calculated in the future with more accurate, comprehensive data, while still tracking indicators using existing data.
- Indicators can be calculated, refined and extended by academic and other researchers to improve the indicators' ability to measure BEPS. This will contribute to the transparency of the process.
- Use of multiple indicators recognises that there is no single metric currently available to precisely measure the scale of BEPS and changes in BEPS over time. When multiple indicators provide similar results, there may be more substantial evidence of the presence of profit shifting.

2.7.2 General limitations

85. While there may be additional limitations that apply to a particular indicator, there are several important limitations that apply more broadly to all of the indicators. These limitations need to be included in any discussion of the indicator results.

- Non-tax economic factors are likely to explain a portion of the observed cross-country and over-time variations in the indicators of BEPS. For example, both firm-level and aggregate data will be influenced by the economic cycle, which may contribute to the variation of the indicators over time, independent of BEPS. Factors such as the size of a country, the level of its GDP per capita or its GDP growth could explain a part of the observed variation across countries. *The indicators must be evaluated with this key limitation in mind.* For example, Indicator 1 based on FDI data needs to be interpreted with more caution than the other indicators because attracting high levels of real FDI may be a result of an attractive investment climate in the recipient country.
- There are important limitations related to the availability and quality of the reported data: missing affiliates in financial data, incomplete data, variation in how data is reported by country, changes in the way aggregate variables are measured over time (FDI, for example).

2.7.3 General extensions

86. There are common options for extending the indicator analysis that apply to all indicators:

- Indicators are designed so that they can be calculated with currently available data or with new data sources that become available in the future. As more accurate and disaggregated data becomes available, the ratio of signal-to-noise for individual indicators is likely to improve.
- One possibility for extension could be a combination of tax return information available to tax administrations with the publicly available financial information used in estimating the firm-level indicators. Tax administrations could use the combined information to estimate specific indicators and track the impact of BEPS countermeasures over time.

87. In developing specific indicators, single global indicators could be extended to specific countries or industries (e.g. firm-level data could be analysed by major industry). This disaggregation, if permitted by the data, could help control for some of the variation in real economic factors.

88. The following sections describe each of the six specific indicators, as well as the two possible future indicators using future data. Annex 2.A1 shows formulas for calculating the indicators.

2.8 Disconnect between financial and real economic activities

89. The indicator in this category uses macro (aggregate) data to develop an indirect indicator of BEPS using foreign direct investment (FDI) data.

90. FDI measures cross-border investments by a resident of one country (direct investor) in an enterprise (direct investment enterprise) in another country. Importantly, the investments being measured are those representing a "lasting interest" in the investment enterprise. The included investments are between affiliates with at least a 10% ownership link. In other words, FDI measures investments by related parties.

91. The indicator uses FDI stocks (positions) that represent the cumulative annual net investments of foreign direct investors in a country. In theory, the stock reflects all prior annual investments and disinvestments in a country. FDI stocks can be broken down to debt and equity direct investments.

2.8.1 Specific considerations for indicators of financial and economic disconnects

2.8.1.1 Strengths

- Indicator based on important global economic variables which include BEPS financial flows.
- Measures previously cited by many BEPS researchers.
- Can be easily explained.

2.8.1.2 Limitations

- FDI information includes financial stocks, as well as stocks related to real economic activities. The indicator has to be carefully evaluated in reaching conclusions about the presence of BEPS. In addition, not all BEPS behaviours are captured by FDI statistics.
- Countries report transactions related to BEPS, such as transactions with special purpose entities, in different ways. This introduces cross-country variations in FDI based on reporting differences.

2.8.1.3 Issues

- FDI is measured relative to GDP. However, other measures of real economic activity, such as trade flows (both imports and exports), and annual capital formation could be used in constructing the indicator.

Indicator 1: Concentration of foreign direct investment relative to GDP

Description: This macro-economic indicator is the ratio of the stock of FDI to a country's GDP, a measure of real economic activity. The indicator compares the FDI ratio in countries with relatively high values of FDI to GDP ratios to the same ratio in the rest of the included countries. Two versions of the FDI measure are presented.

The first is *net* FDI equal to the FDI stock in a country owned by foreign investors from OECD countries minus the domestically-owned FDI stock invested in OECD countries. Countries with high ratios of net FDI to GDP could be characterised as countries that are the ultimate destination of the inward FDI that are significantly above the average.

The second FDI measure is *gross* inward FDI. Countries with high ratios of gross FDI to GDP include both ultimate destinations (countries with high ratios of net FDI to GDP) and conduits (countries with low ratios of net FDI to GDP) with the inward or flow-through FDI that are significantly above the average.

Both versions of the indicator are presented below and show similar differences between the high-ratio countries and the remaining countries and similar trends.

Rationale: FDI measures cross-border investments among related enterprises. The stock of FDI includes investment related to both BEPS and real economic activity. Significantly high concentrations of FDI to GDP in a country or group of countries may provide an indication of BEPS.

Data source: *OECD Foreign Direct Investment Statistics.* The data is the inward and outward FDI stock from and to OECD countries. The FDI stock data is available for 214 countries identified in the OECD database.

Box 2.1. Indicator 1: Concentration of foreign direct investment relative to GDP

Background: FDI financial flows related to BEPS are expected to result in a relatively high ratio of FDI stocks to GDP.

Description: This indicator compares the average net or gross FDI stocks per euro of GDP in the countries with relatively high ratios of FDI to GDP. In the case of the net FDI calculation, the countries with relatively high ratios are those with ratios over 50% of GDP; for the gross FDI calculation, relatively high ratios are defined as ratios in excess of 200% of GDP. The indicator is the weighted average value of the FDI ratio for the countries with the highest ratios divided by the weighted average ratio for the remaining countries. The countries in the 2012 rankings are used to calculate the prior-year indicator values.

Data used: OECD Foreign Direct Investment Statistics. The FDI stock variables are total inbound and outbound FDI positions to and from OECD countries. The FDI stock is available for 214 countries in the OECD database (in 2012). The source is OECD FDI Statistics 2014. As a result of the transition from the 3rd edition of the Benchmark Definition of FDI (BMD3) to the 4th edition (BMD4), the data on bilateral FDI positions for 2013 and 2014 is not yet available for all OECD countries.

Results:

- Both the net and gross FDI indicators more than doubled between 2005 and 2012 showing similar profiles over the period.
- The 2012 value of the net FDI indicator shows that the amount of net FDI per euro of GDP in the top group of countries was, on average, 99 times higher than the average ratio for the remaining countries. The top group of countries are mostly countries with no or low corporate income tax rates or preferential tax regimes. The top group for the gross FDI indicator also includes countries that are often characterised as conduit countries for FDI.
- The indicator shows a concentration of FDI in a select group of countries that is disproportionate to the real economic activity (as measured by GDP) in these countries. There are 14 countries in 2012 with net FDI/GDP ratios above 50%; 13 countries have gross ratios above 200%.
- The top group of countries in 2012 for the net FDI indicator has an average net FDI stock that is twice as high as GDP; for the gross FDI indicator, the average gross FDI is four times the size of GDP.
- In 2012, the high-ratio countries accounted for 29% of gross FDI positions and 49% of net FDI positions.

Figures 2.2 A and B show the average (weighted by GDP) net and gross FDI to GDP ratios for the countries with relatively high ratios and the remaining countries. The indicator is the ratio of these two figures, shown in the graphs as the height of the two arrows in 2005 and 2012.

Box 2.1. Indicator 1: Concentration of foreign direct investment relative to GDP *(continued)*

Figure 2.2. Indicator 1: Concentration of foreign direct investment relative to GDP

A. Net FDI | B. Gross FDI

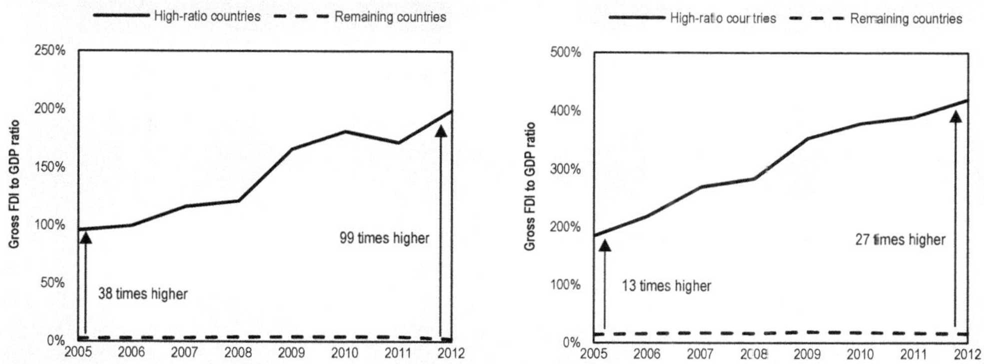

Table 2.1 presents the values for both versions of Indicator 1 for 2005-2012.

Table 2.1. Indicator 1: Concentration of foreign direct investment relative to GDP

Year	Indicator 1 Net FDI	Indicator 1 Gross FDI
2005	37.6	13.0
2006	36.3	13.9
2007	37.4	15.9
2008	31.9	17.4
2009	41.9	18.9
2010	44.9	21.1
2011	43.1	23.4
2012	99.2	26.7

Caveats:

- FDI positions include both real investment and purely financial transactions, including mergers and acquisitions, unrelated to current economic activity. Only a portion of the financial transactions may be related to BEPS. The indicator cannot distinguish between BEPS and other transactions related to real economic activity, but a high indicator may flag potential BEPS.
- The mixture of BEPS and real economic activity may vary between developing and developed countries. For example, developing countries with attractive investment climates may have relatively high FDI stock/GDP ratios. This needs to be taken into consideration in interpreting variations in the indicator across countries.
- FDI stock is not as closely related to BEPS as FDI income, but the FDI income to GDP ratio is much more volatile than the FDI stock to GDP ratio and it is also more affected by the economic cycle.
- The indicator can be refined as new information becomes available, such as the separate reporting of FDI for special purpose entities and mergers and acquisitions.
- Availability of data on bilateral FDI flows is not constant over time.

2.9 Profit rate differentials within top global MNEs

2.9.1 Overview

92. The two indicators in this category are calculated using unconsolidated affiliate and consolidated worldwide group financial statement information. Each of the two indicators is constructed as a *relative* measure. For example, the indicators compare profit rates (defined as a ratio of pre-tax income to a measure of economic activity, such as a firm's assets) of firms or a group of firms in lower-tax and higher-tax locations determined by effective tax rates (i.e. income tax expense divided by pre-tax income).[3]

93. The use of ratios of profit to measures of economic activity recognises that BEPS is characterised by a disconnect between where profit is reported and where the economic activity generating that profit occurs.

94. The denominator in the profit rate, the economic activity variable, could be measured by various inputs (e.g. assets, employment, labour compensation, operating expenditures) or a measure of output (e.g. sales). The indicators presented here use assets to measure economic activity, while recognising that other factors can contribute to economic value added including intangible assets which generally may not be included in reported total assets or may be understated.

Box 2.2. How should economic activity be defined?

There is no single best measure (conceptually or reported) from publicly-available firm data that summarises where the economic activity ("value added") of a firm occurs for use in the profit rate calculations. While value added by a company is the most comprehensive measure of the economic activity of a firm, it can only be calculated indirectly from data available from financial statements. In the public reports, all of the metrics are reported where the entity is incorporated, not where the assets and employment are located, or where the customers are located:

- Assets are most directly related to the use of capital that generates the income subject to the corporate income tax. However, asset measures in financial statements generally tend to significantly understate the value of intangible assets, a major contributor to MNE worldwide income. Firm assets also exclude the value of public infrastructure and other government provided services which are part of a fully-specified production function. Assets include those financed by both equity and debt, while corporate income tax is generally on net equity income.

- Employment and labour compensation are directly related to labour costs, a second component of value added created by the capital and labour used by a firm. However, labour costs are subtracted in determining net income and are not in the taxable corporate net income base.

- Sales may be an indirect measure of the contribution of both labour and capital to value added, but it includes revenue paid to suppliers in addition to the income paid to capital and labour. Sales are the firm's total sales, but are not reported where the customers are located. It should also be noted that the value of sales can be distorted by BEPS through transfer pricing.

- Operating expenditures may be a useful measure of economic functions in some cases such as service industries. The value may be distorted by BEPS through transfer pricing.

95. The indicators in this category differ primarily in the groups of firms used to compare profit rates. The different groups used in the two indicators are: 1) MNE affiliates in higher-tax and lower-tax countries, and 2) combined affiliates in lower-tax countries vs. the MNE's worldwide operations. For each indicator, tax variables are used to either identify groups or to compare profit rates directly to effective tax rates (ETRs) in the calculation of the indicators.

2.9.2 Specific considerations for profit rate indicators

2.9.2.1 Strengths

- Indicators use backward-looking financial ETRs, not headline statutory tax rates which often overstate the marginal tax rate on shifted profits.
- Firm-level data can be used to help control for non-BEPS influences that are specific to an unconsolidated affiliate or entity, although non-tax factors will affect the indicator.
- Using both MNE group and affiliate-level data in calculating an indicator holds many of the MNE-specific, non-tax factors constant, which assists in segregating BEPS effects from real economic effects.
- Based on the theory of profit shifting driven by tax rate differentials across locations, this construct is similar to the approach used in academic studies of income shifting opportunities.

2.9.2.2 Limitations

- Measures are dependent on available financial reporting data, so may not have information for all affiliates and may have limited geographic coverage. Financial statement data is primarily limited to public corporations, not privately-held corporations or partnerships.
- The profit rate is calculated based only on assets, and is not adjusted for functions and risks.
- The calculations of profit rates require information on tax expense, pre-tax income and assets. The availability of this information may vary for MNE affiliates within a single country, as well as across countries due to variations in reporting requirements.
- Information on the economic factors has data issues (e.g. most intangibles are not in total assets).
- The tax variable (average effective tax rates) is calculated from reported financial statement income tax expense (current tax expense plus deferred tax expense), not actual taxes paid or tax liability on current-year income.
- These indicators provide only indirect evidence of BEPS. Reported tax expense (or actual taxes paid, if available) already includes the effects of BEPS and non-BEPS, resulting in lower reported taxes in higher-tax countries and higher reported taxes in lower-tax countries. The net reduction in worldwide taxes of MNEs, either from shifting income among countries with different tax rates or from the net reduction of reported worldwide taxable income, is not directly measured in the indicator.

- Publicly-available information is based on accounting data, not tax variables. Data from the country of incorporation may not align with the country of tax residence.

2.9.2.3 Issues

- Averages may obscure the behaviour of a subset of companies that are undertaking BEPS. Where available, the distribution of the indicator values could be examined for the influence of significant "outliers." Comments on the discussion draft suggested evaluating the databases on a "case-by-case" basis to remove outliers that have relatively large values that distort the indicator measures, but cautioned removing outliers given the somewhat arbitrary methods used to identify and remove outliers.

2.9.2.4 Possible extensions

- Where available, substitute tax data compiled by tax administrations for firm-level financial statement data.
- Expand to a larger list of top corporations.
- Include a random sample of smaller companies from similar sectors. This could provide additional insights into differences in BEPS behaviour by size of firms.
- If data is available, disaggregate by country or industry.
- Conditional on data availability, alternative measures of economic activity, such as labour compensation, employees, operating expenditures or sales could be used in calculating profit rates.
- A significant number of firms in the financial report databases report negative annual profits that produce negative ETRs. The indicator values could be calculated with and without the negative values. When comparing different profit groups, alternative indicators such as the ETRs for each group could be calculated.

Indicator 2: High profit rates of low-taxed affiliates of top global MNEs

Description: This indicator shows the percentage of income earned by affiliates in lower-tax countries with higher profit rates, by comparing the profit rate (i.e. profits/assets) to the ETR (i.e. tax expense/profit) of MNE affiliates for top global MNEs.

For each affiliate, a profit rate differential is compared to the affiliate's ETR differential. The profit rate differential is the difference between the affiliate's profit rate and its MNE group worldwide profit rate; the ETR differential is the difference between the affiliate's ETR and its MNE group worldwide ETR.

"Lower-tax" affiliates are affiliates with ETRs that are less than the MNE group's ETR and "higher-profit" affiliates have profit rates that exceed the worldwide MNE group's profit rates. Indicator 2 focuses on the percentage of total reported income being earned by those lower-tax, higher-profit affiliates.

Rationale: When BEPS occurs, it is expected that the profit rate differential in lower-tax affiliates will be positive. In other words, profit rates of the lower-tax affiliates will exceed the worldwide profit rate of the MNE. In terms of ETRs, it is expected that the

ETR differential will be negative, where BEPS is occurring, because the affiliate's ETR will be less than the MNE's worldwide ETR.

Data source: Unconsolidated affiliate and worldwide consolidated group financial statement information for the top 250 global MNEs reporting information is used to calculate the indicator.

Box 2.3. Indicator 2: High profit rates of low-taxed affiliates of top global MNEs

Background: BEPS involves shifting profits from affiliates in high-tax countries to affiliates in low-tax countries.

Description: This indicator summarises the relationship between the profitability of MNE affiliates in a country and their ETRs. The indicator is equal to the share of total pre-tax income in the sample reported by affiliates in higher-profit, lower-tax countries. In Figure 2.3, the affiliates that are in the lower-tax, higher-profit category are represented by the shaded area in the southeast quadrant of the graph.

Data used: The calculation uses unconsolidated affiliate and worldwide consolidated group financial information on tax expense, pre-tax profits, and assets from financial reports for 250 of the top global MNEs (by sales) and their affiliates. The calculations are done for over 2,300 country-level affiliate groups that include over 10,000 affiliates. Financial groups are not included.

Results:

- In 2011, lower-tax, higher-profit affiliates accounted for 45% of the total income reported by all affiliates in the sample. 45% is the value of the indicator. These affiliates accounted for 33% of total affiliates.
- The affiliate groups in the northwest quadrant, higher ETRs and lower profit rates, accounted for only 7% of the total income. If BEPS is occurring, a portion of the income in this quadrant and in the northeast quadrant may have been shifted to the southeast quadrant (lower-tax, higher-profit affiliates).
- The value of the indicator increased by 32% between 2007 and 2011.

Figure 2.3 explains the indicator in terms of the four quadrants in the diagram. The lower-right quadrant is the area indicating potential BEPS. This is the quadrant that includes affiliate groups with lower ETRs and higher profits, relative to the worldwide MNE measures. The figure also identifies the percentage of total affiliate pre-tax income reported in each quadrant. For example, affiliate groups in the southeast quadrant account for 45% of the total income in 2011.

Box 2.3. Indicator 2: High profit rates of low-taxed affiliates of top global MNEs ***(continued)***

Figure 2.3. Indicator 2: High profit rates of low-taxed affiliates of top global MNEs

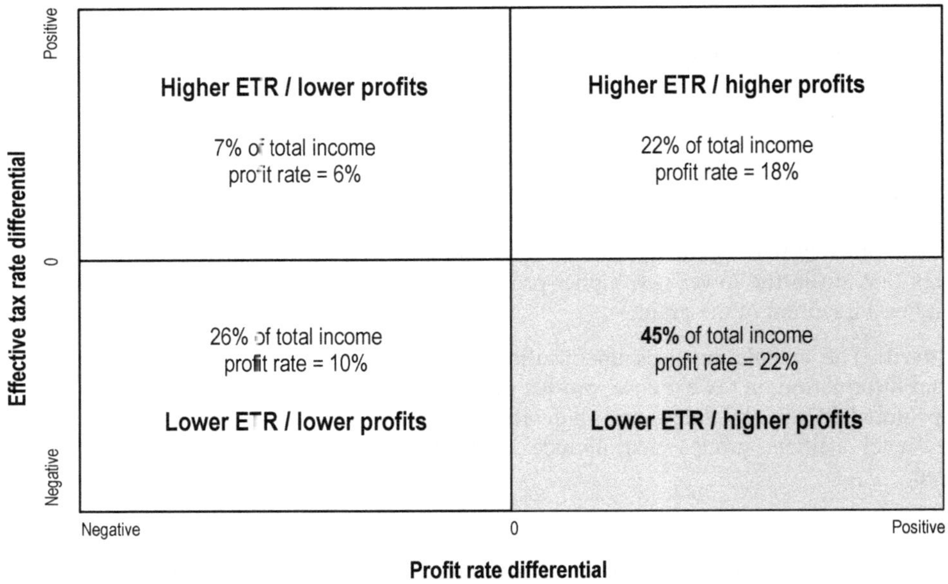

Caveats:

- While the indicator partially controls for differences in the profitability of affiliates, by comparing them to their MNE's worldwide profitability, it cannot differentiate between higher profit rates due to BEPS and higher profit rates possibly needed to ensure competitive after-tax rates of return on investments.
- The indicator does not control for or hold constant other factors that influence BEPS, including variation in affiliate characteristics, such as size and industry.

Indicator 3: High profit rates of MNE affiliates in lower-tax locations

Description: This indicator compares the profit rate (i.e. profits/assets) of top global MNE affiliates in low-tax rate jurisdictions with the MNE's worldwide profit rate. Low-tax countries are defined as countries with the lowest affiliate ETRs, accounting for 20% of the MNE group's worldwide assets.[4]

Rationale: This indicator uses both group and firm-level financial data of the largest global MNEs to show the extent to which reported profits differ between low-tax rate locations and the profit rate of the worldwide group.

An index number above one shows that affiliates in low-tax rate countries have higher reported profit rates than the worldwide rate for their MNE group, which could be an indication that profit shifting into low-tax rate locations is occurring. A higher number is a stronger indication.

Data source: Financial information of top 250 non-financial MNEs and their affiliates.

Box 2.4. Indicator 3: High profit rates of MNE affiliates in lower-tax locations

Background: The presence of BEPS is expected to result in relatively high profit rates in relatively low-tax locations. Indicator 3 defines relatively low-tax locations in terms of the country-by-country distribution of a MNE group's worldwide assets.

Description: This indicator compares the profitability of a MNE's affiliates in lower-tax countries to the profitability of the MNE's worldwide operations. Affiliates' ETRs (weighted by assets) are calculated for each country where a MNE has affiliates; countries are ranked by ETR for each MNE. Profit rates are calculated for lower-tax locations, defined as countries with the lowest ETRs that account for 20% of the MNE group's worldwide assets. The relative profitability of a MNE's affiliates in lower-tax countries is the profit rate in these countries divided by the MNE's worldwide profit rate. The indicator is the weighted (by assets) average profit rate ratio over all MNEs in the sample.

Data used: The calculation uses financial information on tax expense, pre-tax profits, and assets from financial reports for 250 of the top global MNEs and their affiliates. The calculations are done for over 170 MNE groups and their 10 000 affiliates.

Results:

- In 2011 profit rates of affiliates in lower-tax countries of 171 of the largest MNEs were on average almost twice as high as their worldwide MNE group's profit rates (ratio of 2.0).
- For the same year, the top 25% of the MNE affiliates, ranked by relative profit rates, had ratios exceeding 2.4; the ratio exceeded 4.4 for the top 10% of the MNE affiliates.
- The indicator increased by 3% between 2007 and 2011.

Table 2.2 summarises descriptive statistics for 2007 and 2011.

Table 2.2. Indicator 3: High profit rates of MNE affiliates in lower-tax locations

	2007	2011
Indicator 3	**1.9**	**2.0**
Highest 25% have ratios above	1.9	2.4
Highest 10% have ratios above	3.2	4.4

Caveats:

- Relatively high profit rates in lower-tax countries may reflect differences in real economic activity for affiliates in lower-tax countries relative to the MNEs' worldwide operations, but a significantly higher profit rate in lower-tax countries is a potential indication of BEPS.
- There are MNEs in the database that may have relatively low indicator values because of missing affiliates with relatively high profit rates. In these cases, the potential for BEPS may be understated.

2.10 MNE vs. "comparable" non-MNE effective tax rate differentials

96. The indicator in this category compares the backward-looking effective tax rates (ETRs) for large affiliates of MNEs with the ETR of non-MNE entities with similar characteristics. Indicator 4 uses affiliate-level unconsolidated financial statement data.

Indicator 4: Effective tax rates of large MNE affiliates relative to non-MNE entities with similar characteristics

Description: Indicator 4 compares the ETRs of large MNE affiliates with non-MNE entities with similar characteristics in the same country. The indicator measures the extent to which large MNE affiliates have lower ETRs than comparable non-MNE entities.

This indicator shows the estimated ETR differential, due to mismatches between tax systems (e.g. hybrid mismatch arrangements), national preferential tax treatments if MNEs use them to a different extent than non-MNE entities, and/or profit shifting in cases where profit shifting does not proportionally change financial tax expenses and reported pre-tax profits. The estimated ETR differential controls for a number of firm characteristics, including profitability, country, industry, size, patenting activity and position in the corporate group. The ETR equals tax expense divided by reported net income. Large firms are defined as firms with more than 250 employees.

If negative, the indicator would show that large MNE affiliates have lower ETRs than comparable non-MNE entities. This is a possible indication of BEPS.

Rationale: In the presence of some BEPS behaviours, the taxable income of MNE affiliates in high-tax countries is expected to be reduced relative to the affiliates' reported financial income, such as the use of hybrid mismatch arrangements enabling double deductions or deduction with non-inclusion. MNEs may also have the ability to take advantage of domestic tax preferences to a greater degree than domestic-only firms due to strategic location of economic activity. MNEs' profit shifting out of a country may reduce its tax expense proportionately more than the reduction in its reported pre-tax profits. As a result, the MNE's affiliates' taxes (and ETRs) could be lower than the taxes (and ETRs) of non-MNE affiliates that do not have the same opportunities for cross-border tax planning.

Data source: MNE and non-MNE unconsolidated financial information from the ORBIS database.

Box 2.5. Indicator 4: Effective tax rates of MNE affiliates compared to non-MNE entities with similar characteristics

Background: MNEs may have greater opportunities for reducing their taxes due to BEPS than domestic affiliates with similar characteristics. If MNE affiliates are able to take advantage of differences in international tax systems or take greater advantage of domestic tax preferences, then MNE affiliates in a country would have lower reported ETRs (tax expense/assets) than comparable domestic-only firms.

Description: This indicator uses unconsolidated financial data to estimate the difference between the ETR of large MNE affiliates and the ETRs of non-MNE entities with similar characteristics. The indicator is the multi-variate regression coefficient of a dummy variable for large MNEs in an equation estimating ETRs of individual entities. Similar non-MNE entities are based on the multi-variate regression analysis, controlling for company-specific factors, including industry, country, size, presence of patents, and position in the corporate group (headquarters, other parent or non-parent entity)

Data used: Unlike the other indicators, this indicator is estimated using a regression equation for mismatches and preferential tax treatments, described in Annex 3.A1.

Box 2.5. Indicator 4: Effective tax rates of MNE affiliates compared to non-MNE entities with similar characteristics *(continued)*

Results:

- The value of the indicator in 2010 was -3.3. This indicates that, on average, large MNE affiliates had ETRs that were 3.3 percentage points lower than comparable non-MNE entities. The indicator is statistically significant from 0.
- Since 2003, the indicator has shown that, on average, a large MNE affiliate ETR differential over domestic firms with similar characteristics fluctuating around the level of -3 percentage points, with these fluctuations not being significant from a statistical point of view.

Table 2.3 presents the estimates of the indicator for 2000 through to 2010. Figure 2.4 provides a graph of the indicator value over the 2000-2010 period.

Table 2.3. Indicator 4: Effective tax rates of MNE affiliates compared to non-MNE entities with similar characteristics (in percentage points)

Year	Indicator 4
2000	-3.9
2001	-4.5
2002	-3.6
2003	-2.7
2004	-3.2
2005	-3.0
2006	-2.9
2007	-3.2
2008	-3.3
2009	-2.8
2010	-3.3

Box 2.5. Indicator 4: Effective tax rates of MNE affiliates compared to non-MNE entities with similar characteristics *(continued)*

Figure 2.4. Indicator 4: Effective tax rates of MNE affiliates relative to non-MNE entities with similar characteristics (in percentage points)

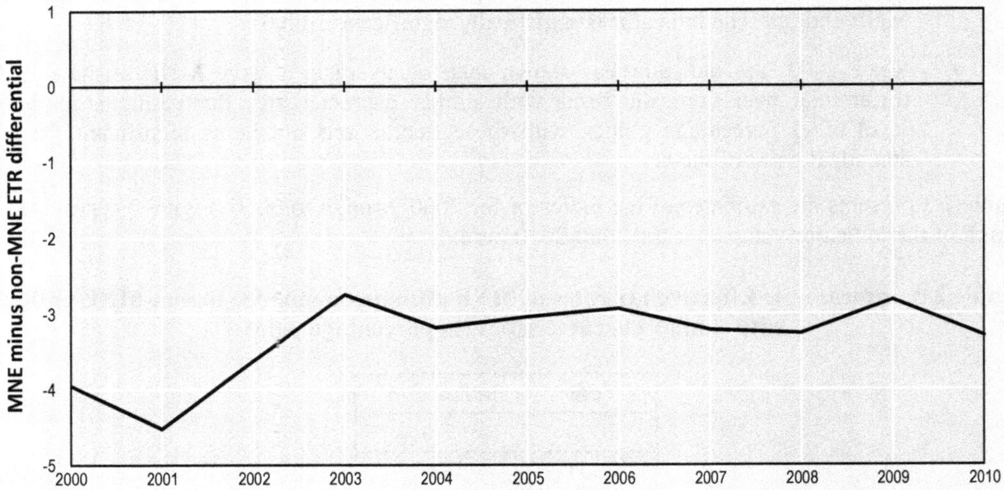

Caveats:

- Unobserved and inherent differences between MNE affiliates and domestic entities that are not related to tax planning (e.g. capital intensity, productivity) may also influence their relative ETRs. In some countries, entities with similar characteristics may not exist to compare to large MNE affiliates operating in the country.
- The indicator includes some non-BEPS behaviours, such as the decision to carry out substantial activity in a country to benefit from certain preferential tax treatments (e.g. R&D tax subsidies, investment tax credits).
- As discussed in Chapter 1, the available firm-level financial data has limitations in terms of country representativeness, the use of financial, rather than actual, tax payment data, and some missing entities and observations with incomplete financial information. The results are dependent on the specific individual firm database used as well as the regression specification.

2.11 Profit shifting through intangibles

97. The indicator in this category provides an indirect measure of BEPS related to intangible property. The indicator is based on macro-data on royalty payments.

Indicator 5: Concentration of royalty receipts relative to R&D spending

Description: This indicator combines balance of payments information on royalty payments received by businesses in a country and information on the country's current R&D expenditures.[5] The indicator compares the average ratio of royalties received to R&D expenditures for a group of high-ratio countries to the average ratio for the other countries in the sample.

Rationale: Transferring intellectual property from a higher-tax country where R&D takes place to a lower-tax country is one channel facilitating BEPS. A high value of the indicator suggests that the income stream from intellectual property received in the high-ratio countries is significantly higher, relative to other countries, than would be expected given the actual R&D expenditures in these countries, which may indicate BEPS.

Data source: Balance of payments and R&D expenditures from the World Bank, *World Development Indicators*.

Box 2.6. Indicator 5: Concentration of royalty receipts relative to R&D spending

Background: The transfer of intellectual property (IP) from high-tax countries where it is developed to low-tax countries after development may facilitate BEPS. It results in lower royalty receipts per euro of R&D spending in the country where the IP was developed and higher receipts per euro of R&D spending in the country to which the IP was transferred.

Description: This indicator compares royalties received to R&D spending in the countries with ratios in excess of 50% to the average ratio in the remaining countries. The composition of the high-ratio countries is based on the 2011 values and kept constant in the other years. Significantly above average royalty/R&D spending values may indicate BEPS.

Data used: Balance of payments and R&D expenditures from the World Bank, World Development Indicators. The data includes 59 countries in 2011 with 4 countries having ratios above 50%.

Results:

- In 2011, the high-ratio countries received EUR 1.04 of royalties per EUR 1 of R&D spending. The remaining countries received only EUR 0.18 of royalties per EUR 1 of R&D spending.
- As a result, the royalties/R&D spending ratio for the top group of countries was almost six times larger than the same figure for the remaining countries included in the sample.
- The indicator value doubled between 2005 and 2012, due to the increase in royalty receipts of the high-ratio countries.
- In 2011, high-ratio country royalties accounted for 3% of royalties for the 59 countries examined. The indicator evidences the existence of BEPS, but is not a measure of the scale of BEPS. Even with the low share of high-ratio countries the indicator still provides evidence of the existence of BEPS.

Figure 2.5 shows Indicator 5 over the 2005-2012 period. The diagram compares the values of the royalties to R&D spending ratios for the countries with the highest royalty/R&D ratios to the same ratio for the remaining countries for which data is available.

Box 2.6. Indicator 5: Concentration of royalty receipts relative to R&D spending *(continued)*

Figure 2.5. Indicator 5: Concentration of royalty receipts relative to R&D spending

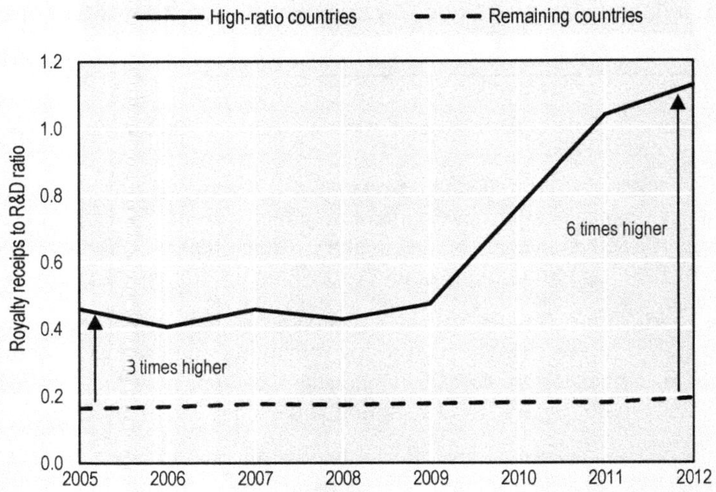

Source: World Bank, World Development Indicators.

Table 2.4 lists the estimated annual indicator values.

Table 2.4. Estimated annual indicator values

Year	Indicator 5
2005	2.8
2006	2.5
2007	2.6
2008	2.5
2009	2.7
2010	4.3
2011	5.8
2012	5.8

Caveats:

- The composition of the group of remaining countries varies as data availability varies over time. The number of countries with data available to calculate this indicator ranged from 32 to 69. However, the value of the indicator does not change significantly if it is calculated only for countries for which data is available in all years in the 2005-2011 period.
- Countries vary in whether they report royalties based on country of incorporation or tax residence. For example, countries with many conduit companies typically do not consider such companies to be part of the domestic economy and do not include data on these companies in their reporting.
- A limitation of this indicator is that current income from intellectual property could be the result of R&D expenditures in prior years. The indicator currently does not

include any adjustment for this time lag.

- Royalties include more than just charges for the use of patents, e.g. they also include payments related to trademarks, copyrights, computer software and cinematographic works. Thus, the royalties do not only come from R&D activities.
- R&D expenditures include both public and private expenditures.

2.12 Profit shifting through interest

98. The indicator in this category measures the use of interest payments on debt of MNEs and their affiliates, which may be a source of BEPS.

<u>Indicator 6</u>: Interest expense to income ratios of MNE affiliates in countries with above average statutory tax rates

Description: This indicator shows the above-average interest-to-income ratio by MNE affiliates with relatively high interest-to-income ratios located in higher-tax countries.

The interest-to-income ratio is defined as interest paid divided by EBITDA.[6] Interest to income ratio differentials are calculated for each affiliate of the top 250 global MNEs. The interest-to-income ratio differential is the difference between an affiliate's interest-to-income ratio (which includes both third-party and related-party interest) and its MNE group's worldwide consolidated interest-to-income ratio. Higher-tax countries are defined as countries with combined national and subnational statutory tax rates (STRs) above the average (weighted by EBITDA) for all included MNE affiliates.

The affiliates are divided into four quadrants based on their interest-to-income ratios and their statutory tax rates. An excess ratio is calculated for each quadrant. This ratio is the difference between the weighted average interest-to-income ratio of affiliates in the quadrant and the weighted average interest-to-income ratio of all affiliates in the sample (i.e. affiliates in all four quadrants). The indicator is the excess ratio in the northeast quadrant (i.e. the excess ratio of affiliates with a high interest-to-income ratio and a high statutory tax rate). When BEPS occurs through interest deductions, it is expected that the interest-to-income ratio differential in countries with STRs above the average will be positive. In other words, the ratio of interest-to-income of the affiliates will exceed the worldwide MNE group's interest-to-income ratio.

Rationale: The strategic allocation of debt to facilitate excessive interest deductions is one of the BEPS channels used by MNEs to reduce their worldwide tax liability. This indicator shows what is the excess ratio of affiliates with positive interest-to-income ratio differentials located in countries with STRs greater than the average STR. Affiliates with relatively high interest-to-income ratios have combined external and internal interest paid to income ratios that exceed the average ratio (with external interest paid only) for the worldwide MNE group. With BEPS, a large share of total interest paid is expected to be reported by affiliates with interest to income ratios above their worldwide group's ratio and located in countries with STRs above the weighted average.

Data source: Unconsolidated affiliate and consolidated MNE group financial statement information was used to estimate the indicator, where information was available.

Box 2.7. Indicator 6: Interest-to-income ratios of MNE affiliates in locations with above average statutory tax rates

Background: The presence of above-average interest-to-income ratios of affiliates located in countries with statutory tax rates (STRs) above the weighted average indicates BEPS through excess interest deductions that shift income from higher-tax to lower-tax countries.

Description: This indicator measures the excess interest-to-income ratio reported by MNE affiliates with relatively high interest-to-income ratios located in countries with STRs above the weighted average.

Data used: The indicator value was calculated using affiliate-level and consolidated financial information on interest paid and EBITDA for over 10 000 affiliates of the top 250 global MNEs. The STRs of the affiliates are from OECD information on national plus subnational statutory corporate income tax rates.

Results:

- For the affiliates with high interest-to-income ratios in higher tax rate countries, the interest-to-income ratio was 29% in 2011. In other words, interest expense accounted for 29% of their pre-tax income before interest, depreciation and amortisation expenses. This ratio exceeds the average interest-to-income ratio of (10%) for all of those affiliates by 19 percentage points, which is the value of the indicator. The affiliates are represented in the shaded, northeast quadrant of Figure 2.6.
- 45% of the total interest expense of all affiliates in the sample in 2011 was attributable to affiliates with interest-to-income ratios in excess of their MNE's worldwide consolidated ratio, and located in countries with STRs above the average.

Figure 2.6. Indicator 6: Interest to income ratios of MNE affiliates in locations with above average statutory tax rates

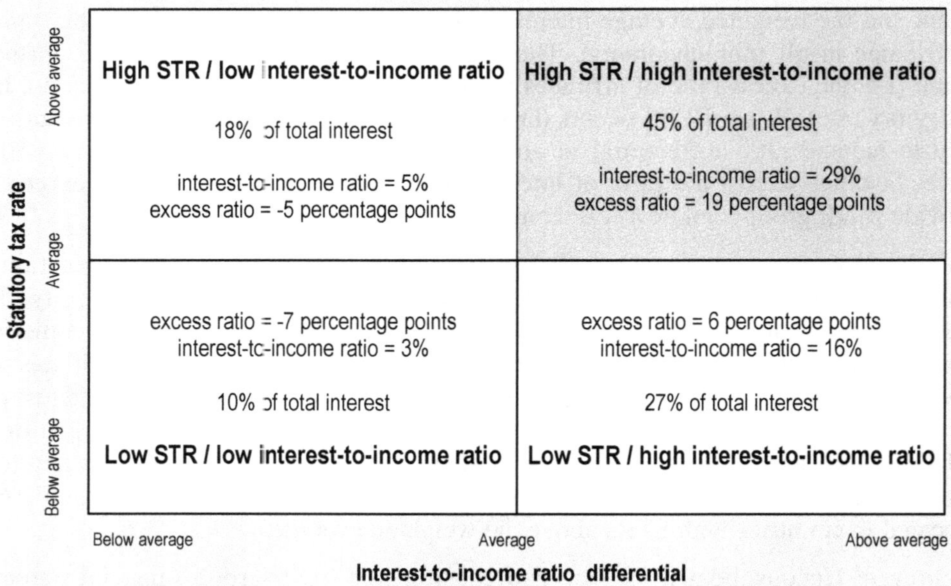

Box 2.7. Indicator 6: Interest-to-income ratios of MNE affiliates in locations with above average statutory tax rates *(continued)*

Caveats:

- The indicator is calculated using gross interest expense as reported in financial statements. If additional data becomes available, net interest expense could be used in the calculation. Financial firms are not included in the calculation of this indicator.
- The interest expense-to-income ratio is designed to measure one channel of BEPS, the use of excess interest expense deductions to shift profits from higher-tax to lower-tax locations. It is not an indicator of other BEPS behaviours.
- The indicator focuses on affiliates' related-party and third-party interest expense relative to their groups' third party interest expense. It does not control for the general corporate tax issue of the double taxation of corporate equity and the deductibility of interest expense.

2.13 Possible future BEPS indicators with new data

99. The six indicators presented in the previous sections are based on currently-available data. Future data sources could be used to estimate additional indicators of BEPS. The following two indicators are examples.

Future Indicator A: Profit rates compared to effective tax rates for MNE domestic (headquarter) and foreign operations

Description: This indicator could compare the profit rate (i.e. profits/assets) differential between the MNE's domestic operations in the jurisdiction of its headquarters and the MNE's foreign operations to the MNE's ETR (i.e. income tax paid/pre-tax profits) differential between domestic and foreign operations.[7] The differentials are measured as the difference between the domestic and foreign values; both differentials can be positive or negative.

Rationale: This indicator could use worldwide consolidated financial statement information for both domestic and foreign operations of the top global MNEs. It could show the extent to which the reported profitability of domestic operations is less than the profitability of the MNE's foreign operations in countries where the ETR on domestic operations is higher than the ETR on foreign operations, and vice versa. A negative correlation between the profit rates and ETRs is an indication of BEPS.

Data source: The profit rates and ETRs could be calculated with improved future MNE data. Currently, different financial reporting requirements on tax expense by country lack consistency, so information is limited to reporting MNEs and varies by country.

Box 2.8. Future Indicator A: Profit rates relative to ETRs, MNE domestic vs. global operations

Example: Illustrative calculations for this indicator have not been made due to current data limitations.

Caveats:

- This indicator requires worldwide financial reporting data for both domestic and foreign MNE operations. Publicly available MNE financial reports vary significantly in how, and if, the worldwide information is reported separately for domestic and foreign operations. This limits the number of MNEs that can be included in this indicator using currently available public financial reports.
- The profitability of domestic and foreign operations will vary by the composition of activities that may involve different degrees and types of capital and labour intensity.

Future Indicator B: Differential rates of return on FDI investment related to special purpose entities (SPEs)

Description: This macro-economic indicator could measure the extent to which FDI inward positions (i.e. cumulative stock of FDI investments in a country owned by foreign investors) are coming from countries with significant outbound FDI through SPEs, serving as investment conduits. These are countries with relatively large shares of FDI outward investment stocks accounted for by special purpose entities (SPEs). SPEs are legal entities that tend to have few employees and real resources located in a country, but are used to raise capital or hold assets and liabilities related to MNE investments in other countries.

Rationale: FDI measures cross-border investments among related enterprises. The expectation is that the more significant are inflows of FDI into SPEs, the greater is the possibility for BEPS. Recent research by the United Nations Conference on Trade and Development (UNCTAD) has found that equity income on the inward stock of FDI is reduced the greater the share of that inward FDI coming through tax havens and SPEs.[8] The share of FDI through SPEs and a lower rate of return on such investment could be an indication of BEPS.

The indicator could compare the rate of return on inward equity FDI in countries with relatively high exposure to FDI from investment conduit countries to the equity rate of return in other countries. The equity rate of return equals the equity income outflows (dividends and reinvested earnings) from the host country to the host country's inward stock of FDI. This is a measure of the profitability of the FDI investment. Investment conduit countries could be defined as those with relatively high percentages of outward FDI stocks accounted for by SPEs.[9]

Data source: *OECD Foreign Direct Investment Statistics.* The data is the inward and outward FDI stock from and to OECD countries. The OECD, *Benchmark Definition of Foreign Direct Investment, 4th Edition*, recommends that countries report FDI investment separately for SPEs to facilitate analysis of capital in transit going through SPEs. However, at this time detailed bilateral FDI data for SPEs is only available for a limited number of countries. This indicator can be estimated when the separate SPE data is reported for a greater number of countries.

Box 2.9. Future Indicator B: Differential rates of return on FDI related to SPEs

Example: Illustrative calculations for this indicator have not been made due to data limitations.

Caveats:

- FDI statistics for SPEs will be reported for an increasing number of countries beginning with data published in 2015. The impact of expanded coverage will affect changes in the value of the indicator unrelated to changes in BEPS. This needs to be recognised in the interpretation of this indicator as a measure of changes in BEPS over time.
- While investment related to BEPS is expected to be a significant portion of SPE investment, there will also be non-BEPS related SPE investment.
- Additional analysis will be needed to determine the criteria for including countries in the top group of home countries that is characterised as investing countries with relatively high ratios of SPE-related FDI.
- The indicator only measures profit shifting that is facilitated by direct investment relationships.

2.14 Indicators considered but not included

100. A number of additional indicators were examined but not included in the indicator dashboard. In addition, there were suggestions for possible indicators that could not be estimated due to the lack of currently available data. Examples of indicators that were considered but not included are:

- Profit rate differentials for global MNEs, high-tax vs. low-tax locations.
- Forward-looking average effective tax rates for representative taxpayers based on financial characteristics of corporate income tax filers. It was not clear how impacts of BEPS on the representative taxpayers could be aggregated to derive an indicator metric.
- Forward-looking average or marginal effective tax rates for hypothetical taxpayers on new investments.
- Concentration of high levels of FDI flows relative to GDP (inflow of FDI owned by OECD foreign investors into a country/the country's GDP).
- Concentration of high levels of FDI income relative to GDP (inflow of FDI income from OECD countries to a recipient country divided by the recipient country's GDP).
- Concentration of high levels of royalty payments (royalty payments received/GDP in receiving country).
- Concentration of FDI leverage.

- Concentration of high levels of patents developed outside of country (patents owned by residents of a country that have been invented in another country/total patents filed in the country).

- Tax gap measures based on the comparison of national income account corporate data and reported taxable corporate income taxes. This measure is currently only available for several countries and includes the impact of significant non-BEPS factors.

- BEPS estimates based on extrapolations of current-law tax audit assessments using a definition of no or low-tax rate countries based on statutory corporate income tax rates.

101. The main reasons these indicators were not included were problems with the data that was available and/or difficulty in distinguishing between real economic effects and BEPS.

2.15 Summary

102. This chapter presents six indicators and a further two potential indicators to assist with the measurement and monitoring of BEPS. These indicators are intended to be viewed like a meter or a gauge, capable of measuring trends and variations over time and acting as "warning lights" that might point to the existence of BEPS. No single indicator is capable of providing the complete picture, but by presenting a "dashboard" of BEPS indicators this report provides new insights regarding the presence and scale of BEPS.

103. As with any gauge, the degree of precision depends on the available information and the accuracy of the measurement tools. Given the state of currently available data, the indicators presented can only provide some general insights into the scale and economic impact of BEPS, but lack the precision that may become possible if more comprehensive and improved data sources, supported by sophisticated statistical analysis, become available in the future.

104. As a dashboard, the indicators provide a signal that BEPS exists, is likely to be increasing in scale, and that better data availability is needed to refine economic analysis of BEPS and the BEPS Action Plan's countermeasures in the future. While the indicators are high-level rather than refined economic analyses, and have significant data limitations and caveats, all six indicators presented in this chapter show the expected sign or trend indicative of the presence of BEPS.

105. The indicators presented include:

- Indicator 1 is based on FDI relative to GDP and shows that both the net and gross FDI stocks relative to GDP of a group of countries with high-ratios (above 50% for net and above 200% for gross) have continued to grow in recent years when compared with the average of all other countries. The net FDI to GDP ratio of those countries increased from 38 times higher than all other countries in 2005 to 99 times higher in 2012.

- Indicators 2 and 3 show that lower ETRs are correlated with higher profit rates amongst affiliates. Indicator 2 shows that 45% of the income of the largest global MNEs was reported by affiliates with below-average ETRs and above average profit rates. These affiliates represented only 33% of total affiliates in the MNE. The value of the indicator increased 32% between 2007 and 2011. Indicator 3 shows that reported profit rates of MNE affiliates in lower-tax countries were, on average, almost twice as high as their group's worldwide profit rate.

- Indicator 4 estimates the ETRs, by calculating the reported tax expense as a percentage of reported profits, of large MNE affiliates relative to non-MNE entities with similar characteristics. Between 2000 and 2010, the ETRs for large MNE entities (with more than 250 employees) was estimated to be between 2.7 to 4.5 percentage points lower than similar non-MNE ETRs.

- Indicator 5 shows that royalties received relative to R&D expenditures in a group of countries with ratios above 50% are six times higher than for the average of all other countries, up from three times higher in 2009.

- Indicator 6 shows the concentration of high interest-to-income ratios in higher statutory tax rate countries. It shows that the largest global MNEs' affiliates with high interest-to-EBITDA ratios, located in high-tax countries have an interest-to-EBITDA ratio almost three times higher than their group's worldwide unrelated-party interest-to-EBITDA ratio.

106. Two additional indicators are also described that could be calculated when new data become available: a comparison of profit rates and ETRs of MNE domestic (headquarter) and foreign operations, and differential rates of return on FDI investment from special purpose entities.

107. Economic analysis of the scale and economic impact of BEPS and the effectiveness of potential BEPS countermeasures are presented in the next chapter, which complement the high level indications of the six BEPS Indicators.

Notes

1. References to the "future state" and "ideal state" are not presented as proposed or inevitable stages, but are designed to highlight that improvements in the data sources available would also lead to improvements in the accuracy of BEPS indicators and economic analyses.

2. The firm-level financial information is for a sample of the 250 largest global non-financial MNEs, as measured by sales. It includes financial information in 2007 and 2011 from both the MNE consolidated and affiliates' unconsolidated financial statements.

3. The tax expense measure includes taxes that are based on income, including corporate income taxes and withholding taxes based on income.

4. Indicators 2 and 3 measure potential profit shifting in different ways. Indicator 2 uses individual affiliate observations in the calculations; Indicator 3 aggregates all of a MNE's affiliates at the country level. The two indicators also differ in how low-tax locations are defined. Indicator 2 defines low-tax as locations of affiliates with ETRs less than the MNE group's worldwide ETR; Indicator 3 defines low-tax as countries with the lowest ETRs accounting for 20% of assets.

5. Research and development expenditures include current (operating) plus capital expenditures (both public and private) for R&D activities performed within a country, regardless of the source of funding. Royalty receipts are payments for the use of property rights (including patents, trademarks, industrial processes and franchises) and licensing charges. Royalties may not be directly related to the measure of R&D spending, such as brands developed from marketing investments.

6. EBITDA is pre-tax income before any deductions for interest paid, corporate income taxes, depreciation and amortization. Net interest expense (interest expense minus interest income) could not be calculated from the available affiliate-level data.

7. Domestic operations include the parent company and its affiliates operating in the same country as the parent.

8. Future Indicator B is a modified version of an indicator suggested by UNCTAD researchers in their Action 11 Public Consultation submission. See UNCTAD draft working paper, *FDI, Tax and Development* (3/20/2015) for a detailed discussion of methods for identifying countries that serve as investment conduits, including tax havens and SPEs. The UNCTAD analysis of the fiscal impact of profit shifting on developing countries used actual bilateral FDI information for SPEs in only four reporting countries.

9. Preliminary data reported in OECD, *How Multinational Enterprises Channel Investments Through Multiple Countries* (February 2015), shows that three out of the nine included countries have *inward* FDI positions accounted for by resident SPEs that exceed 50% of all inward FDI.

Annex 2.A1

Formulas for calculating indicators

Indicator 1A:

1. Year 2012 was chosen as a base year for Indicator 1. OECD FDI Statistics was the source of data on FDI.

2. An inward FDI position of partner country i ($iFDI_i$) is calculated as the sum of outward FDI positions from all available OECD countries to partner country i in 2012 where $oFDIp_{i,j}$ is the outward FDI position reported by OECD country j to partner country i and N is the number of OECD countries[1].

$$iFDI_i = \sum_{j=1}^{N} oFDIp_{i,j}$$

3. An outward FDI position of partner country i ($oFDI_i$) is calculated as the sum of inward FDI positions from all available OECD countries to partner country i in 2012 where $iFDIp_{i,j}$ is the outward FDI position reported by OECD country j to partner country i and N is the number of OECD countries.

$$oFDI_i = \sum_{j=1}^{N} iFDIp_{i,j}$$

4. A net FDI position of partner country i (net FDI_i) is calculated as the difference between its inward FDI position and its outward FDI position.

$$net\ FDI_i = iFDI_i - oFDI_i$$

5. The net FDI to GDP ratio is calculated for each partner country i.

$$net\ FDI\ to\ GDP\ ratio_i = \frac{net\ FDI_i}{GDP_i}$$

6. A group of high-ratio partner countries with a net FDI to GDP ratio above 50% are selected. The weighted average net FDI to GDP ratio for the high-ratio countries (net FDI to GDP $ratio_{high}$) is calculated. The weighted average net FDI to GDP ratio for the remaining partner countries (net FDI to GDP $ratio_{rest}$) is calculated where n is the total number of partner countries reported by OECD countries and m is the number of high-ratio countries.

$$net\ FDI\ to\ GDP\ ratio_{high} = \frac{\sum_{i=1}^{m} net\ FDI_i}{\sum_{i=1}^{m} GDP_i}$$

$$net\ FDI\ to\ GDP\ ratio_{rest} = \frac{\sum_{i=m+1}^{n} net\ FDI_i}{\sum_{i=m+1}^{n} GDP_i}$$

7. The indicator for 2012 is calculated as the ratio of the net FDI to GDP ratio of the high-ratio countries to the net FDI to GDP ratio of the remaining countries.

$$Indicator = \frac{net\ FDI\ to\ GDP\ ratio_{high}}{net\ FDI\ to\ GDP\ ratio_{rest}}$$

8. Steps 2 to 7 are repeated for other years with the same high-ratio countries identified in 2012.

Indicator 1B:

1. Year 2012 was chosen as a base year for Indicator 1. OECD FDI Statistics was the source of data on FDI.

2. An inward FDI position of partner country i ($iFDI_i$) is calculated as the sum of outward FDI positions from all available OECD countries to partner country i in 2012 where $oFDIp_{i,j}$ is the outward FDI position reported by OECD country j to partner country i and N is the number of OECD countries[2].

$$iFDI_i = \sum_{j=1}^{N} oFDIp_{i,j}$$

3. The gross FDI to GDP ratio is calculated for each partner country i.

$$gross\ FDI\ to\ GDP\ ratio_i = \frac{iFDI_i}{GDP_i}$$

4. A group of high-ratio partner countries with a gross FDI to GDP ratio above 200% are selected. The weighted average gross FDI to GDP ratio for the high-ratio countries (gross FDI to GDP $ratio_{high}$) is calculated. The weighted average gross FDI to GDP ratio for the remaining partner countries (gross FDI to GDP $ratio_{rest}$) is calculated where n is the total number of partner countries reported by OECD countries and m is the number of high-ratio countries.

$$gross\ FDI\ to\ GDP\ ratio_{high} = \frac{\sum_{i=1}^{m} iFDI_i}{\sum_{i=1}^{m} GDP_i}$$

$$gross\ FDI\ to\ GDP\ ratio_{rest} = \frac{\sum_{i=m+1}^{n} iFDI_i}{\sum_{i=m+1}^{n} GDP_i}$$

5. The indicator for 2012 is calculated as the ratio of the gross FDI to GDP ratio of the high-ratio countries to the gross FDI to GDP ratio of the remaining countries.

$$Indicator = \frac{gross\ FDI\ to\ GDP\ ratio_{high}}{gross\ FDI\ to\ GDP\ ratio_{rest}}$$

6. Steps 2 to 5 are repeated for other years with the same high-ratio countries identified in 2012.

Indicator 2:

A. For all affiliates of MNE 1 and a given year, profit rate differentials are calculated as follows.

1. For affiliate i, the profit rate (profit $rate_{i,MNE1}$) is calculated as pre-tax income of affiliate i divided by assets of affiliate i.

$$profit\ rate_{i,MNE1} = \frac{pre\text{-}tax\ income_{i,MNE1}}{assets_{i,MNE1}}$$

2. The global profit rate for MNE 1 (profit rate$_{g,MNE1}$) is calculated as MNE's consolidated pre-tax income divided by MNE's consolidated assets.

$$profit\ rate_{g,MNE1} = \frac{pre\text{-}tax\ income_{g,MNE1}}{assets_{g,MNE1}}$$

3. The profit rate differential of affiliate i (profit rate diff$_{i,MNE1}$) is calculated as the difference between the affiliate i's profit rate and MNE 1's global profit rate.

$$profit\ rate\ diff_{i,MNE1} = profit\ rate_{i,MNE1} - profit\ rate_{g,MNE1}$$

B. For all affiliates of MNE 1 and the given year, effective tax rate differentials are calculated as follows.

1. For affiliate i, the effective tax rate (ETR$_{i,MNE1}$) is calculated as affiliate i's tax expense divided by affiliates i's pre-tax income.

$$ETR_{i,MNE1} = \frac{tax\ expense_{i,MNE1}}{pre\text{-}tax\ income_{i,MNE1}}$$

2. The global effective tax rate for MNE 1 (ETR$_{g,MNE1}$) is calculated as MNE 1's consolidated tax expense divided by MNE 1's consolidated pre-tax income.

$$ETR_{g,MNE1} = \frac{tax\ expense_{g,MNE1}}{pre\text{-}tax\ income_{g,MNE1}}$$

3. The effective rate differential of affiliate i (ETR diff$_{i,MNE1}$) is calculated as the difference between the affiliate i's ETR and MNE 1's global ETR.

$$ETR\ diff_{i,MNE1} = ETR_{i,MNE1} - ETR_{g,MNE1}$$

C Steps A and B are repeated for all MNEs in the sample.

D. Affiliates with profit rates differentials greater than zero and ETR differentials less than zero are selected.

E. The indicator for the given year is calculated as the sum of pre-tax income of affiliates selected in step D divided by the sum of pre-tax income of all affiliates where k is the number of all MNEs in the sample, n_i is the number of affiliates of MNE$_i$ and m_i is the number of affiliates of MNE$_i$ selected in step D.

$$Indicator = \frac{\sum_{i=1}^{k}\sum_{j=1}^{m_i} pre\text{-}tax\ income_{j,MNEi}}{\sum_{i=1}^{k}\sum_{j=1}^{n_i} pre\text{-}tax\ income_{j,MNEi}}$$

Indicator 3:

A. For MNE 1 and a given year, the profit rate differential is calculated as follows.

1. For country i where MNE 1 has affiliates, the sum of assets (assets$_{i,MNE1}$), the sum of pre-tax income (pre-tax income$_{i,MNE1}$), and the sum of tax expenses (tax expense$_{i,MNE1}$) of all MNE 1's affiliates in country i are calculated where assets$_{j,i,MNE1}$ is assets of MNE 1's affiliate j in country i (similarly for pre-tax income and tax expense) and n_i is the number of MNE 1's affiliates in country i.

$$assets_{i,MNE1} = \sum_{j=1}^{n_i} assets_{j,i,MNE1}$$

$$pre\text{-}tax\ income_{i,MNE1} = \sum_{j=1}^{n_i} pre\text{-}tax\ income_{j,i,MNE1}$$

$$tax\ expense_{i,MNE1} = \sum_{j=1}^{n_i} tax\ expense_{j,i,MNE1}$$

2. The profit rate of MNE 1' country group of affiliates in country i (profit rate$_{i,MNE1}$) is calculated as the sum of pre-tax income of MNE 1's affiliates in country i divided by the sum of assets in MNE 1's affiliates in country i.

$$profit\ rate_{i,MNE1} = \frac{pre\text{-}tax\ income_{i,MNE1}}{assets_{i,MNE1}}$$

3. MNE 1's global profit rate (profit rate$_{g,MNE1}$) is calculated as MNE 1's consolidated pre-tax income divided by MNE 1's consolidated assets.

$$profit\ rate_{g,MNE1} = \frac{pre\text{-}tax\ income_{g,MNE1}}{assets_{g,MNE1}}$$

4. The effective tax rate of MNE 1's country group of affiliates in country i (ETR$_{i,MNE1}$) is calculated as the sum of tax expenses of MNE 1's affiliates in country i divided by the sum of pre-tax income of MNE 1's affiliates in country i.

$$ETR_{i,MNE1} = \frac{tax\ expense_{i,MNE1}}{pretax\ income_{i,MNE1}}$$

5. The countries where MNE 1 has affiliates are ranked by their effective tax rate. Low-tax countries are defined as countries with the lowest ETRs that account for 20% of the assets of the MNE. The average profit rate (weighted by assets) of low-tax countries is then calculated; m is the number of low-tax countries and n is the number of all countries where MNE 1 has affiliates.[3]

$$\sum_{i=1}^{m} assets_{i,MNE1} = 20\% \times \sum_{i=1}^{n} assets_{i,MNE1}$$

$$profit\ rate_{low,MNE1} = \frac{\sum_{i=1}^{m}(profit\ rate_{i,MNE1} \times assets_{i,MNE1})}{\sum_{i=1}^{m} assets_{i,MNE1}}$$

6. MNE 1's profit rate differential (profit rate diff$_{MNE1}$) is then calculated as the ratio of MNE 1's profit rate in low tax countries divided by MNE 1's global profit rate.

$$profit\ rate\ diff_{MNE1} = \frac{profit\ rate_{low,MNE1}}{profit\ rate_{g,MNE1}}$$

B. Steps 1 to 6 are repeated for all MNEs in the sample.

C. The indicator for the given year is the average profit rate differential (weighted by assets) for all MNEs in the sample where k is the number of MNEs in the sample and assets$_{g,MNEi}$ is consolidated assets of MNE i.

$$Indicator = \frac{\sum_{i=1}^{k}(profit\ rate\ diff_{MNEi} \times assets_{g,MNEi})}{\sum_{i=1}^{k} assets_{g,MNEi}}$$

Indicator 4:

Indicator 4 uses firm-level unconsolidated financial data and ownership information from the ORBIS database compiled by Bureau Van Dijk and processed by the OECD Statistics Directorate.

The sample consists of entities in both multinational and non-multinational groups in 46 countries (all OECD and G20 countries, OECD accession countries Colombia and Latvia as well as Malaysia and Singapore) over 2000-2010. Micro-firms (less than 10 employees), loss-making firms and standalone firms (i.e. firms that are not part of a corporate group) are excluded. The sample has 2 046 838 observations.

Indicator 4 is the regression coefficient β_3 in the following equation estimating ETRs of individual entities in the sample:

$$ETR_{f,c,i,t} = \beta_1 Large\_firm_{f,c,i,t} + \beta_2 Small\_firm_{f,c,i,t} \times MNE_{f,c,i}$$
$$+\beta_3 Large\_firm_{f,c,i,t} \times MNE_{f,c,i} + \beta_4 X_{f,c,i,t} + \delta_i + \delta_{c,t} + \varepsilon_{f,c,i,t},$$

where $ETR_{f,c,i,t}$ is the effective tax rate of entity *f* (operating in country *c* and industry *i* and member of a MNE or domestic group) in year *t*, measured as tax expenses over reported profit. $Large\_firm_{f,c,i,t}$ is a dummy equal to one when firm *f* has more than 250 employees. $Small\_firm_{f,c,i,t}$ is a dummy equal to one when firm *f* has up to 250 employees. $MNE_{f,c,i}$ is a dummy equal to one when a company is part of a multinational group. $X_{f,c,i,t}$ is a vector of firm characteristics, including the position of the firm in the group and a dummy for patenting groups.

The regression analysis based on the whole sample shows that the estimated difference between the ETR of large MNE entities and the ETR of comparable domestic (i.e. non-multinational) groups is 3.3 percentage points (i.e. β_3 = -0.033) and was estimated for each individual year. The adjusted R-squared is 0.186.

Indicator 5:

1. Year 2011 was chosen as a base year for Indicator 6. World Banks's World Development Indicators was the source of data on royalty receipts (charges for the use of intellectual property) and R&D expenditures.

2. For each country i, the ratio of royalty receipts to domestic R&D expenditure was calculated.

$$royalty\ to\ R\&D\ ratio_i = \frac{royalty\ receipts_i}{domestic\ R\&D\ expenditures_i}$$

3. A group of high-ratio countries with a royalty to R&D ratio above 50% are selected. The weighted average royalty to R&D ratio for the high-ratio countries (royalty to R&D ratio$_{high}$) is calculated. The weighted average royalty to R&D ratio for the remaining countries (royalty to R&D ratio$_{rest}$) is calculated where n is the total number of countries for which data is available and m is the number of high-ratio countries.

$$royalty\ to\ R\&D\ ratio_{high} = \frac{\sum_{i=1}^{m} royalty\ receipts_i}{\sum_{i=1}^{m} domestic\ R\&D\ expenditures_i}$$

$$royalty\ to\ R\&D\ ratio_{rest} = \frac{\sum_{i=m+1}^{n} royalty\ receipts_i}{\sum_{i=m+1}^{n} domestic\ R\&D\ expenditures_i}$$

4. The indicator for 2011 is calculated as the ratio of royalty to R&D ratio of the high-ratio countries to the royalty to R&D ratio of the remaining countries.

$$Indicator = \frac{royalty\ to\ R\&D\ ratio_{high}}{royalty\ to\ R\&D\ ratio_{rest}}$$

5. Steps 2 to 4 are repeated for other years with the same high-ratio countries identified in 2011.

Indicator 6:

A. For MNE 1's affiliate 1 and a given year, an interest-to-income ratio differential is calculated as follows.

1. The interest-to-income ratio of affiliate 1 (interest-to-income ratio$_{1,MNE1}$) is calculated as interest expense (to both third parties and related parties) divided by EBITDA (earnings before interest, taxes, depreciation and amortisation).

$$interest\text{-}to\text{-}income\ ratio_{1,MNE1} = \frac{interest_{1,MNE1}}{EBITDA_{1,MNE1}}$$

2. MNE 1's global interest-to-income ratio (interest-to-income ratio$_{g,MNE1}$) is calculated as MNE 1's interest expense divided by MNE 1's EBITDA from consolidated accounts.

$$interest\text{-}to\text{-}income\ ratio_{g,MNE1} = \frac{interest_{g,MNE1}}{EBITDA_{g,MNE1}}$$

3. Affiliate 1's interest-to-income ratio differential (interest-to-income ratio diff$_{1,MNE1}$) is calculated as affiliate 1's interest-to-income ratio minus MNE 1's global interest-to-income ratio.

$$interest\text{-}to\text{-}income\ ratio\ diff_{1,MNE1} = interest\text{-}to\text{-}income\ ratio_{1,MNE1} - interest\text{-}to\text{-}income\ ratio_{g,MNE1}$$

B. For MNE 1's affiliate 1 and the given year, a combined CIT rate differential is calculated as follows.

1. The worldwide average combined CIT rate (weighted by EBITDA) of all affiliates of all MNEs (CIT rate$_w$) is calculated where CIT rate$_{1,MNE1}$ is the combined CIT rate in the country of affiliate 1 of MNE 1, k is the number of MNEs in the sample and n_i is the number of affiliates of MNE i.

$$CIT\ rate_w = \frac{\sum_{i=1}^{k}\sum_{j=1}^{n_i}(CIT\ rate_{j,MNEi} \times EBITDA_{j,MNEi})}{\sum_{i=1}^{k}\sum_{j=1}^{n_i} EBITDA_{j,MNEi}}$$

2. The combined CIT rate differential of MNE 1's affiliate 1 (CIT rate diff$_{1,MNE1}$) is calculated as the difference between the combined CIT rate in the country of MNE 1's affiliate 1 and the worldwide average combined CIT rate.

$$CIT\ rate\ diff_{1,MNE1} = CIT\ rate_{1,MNE1} - CIT\ rate_w$$

C. Steps A and B are repeated for all affiliates and all MNEs in the sample.

D. Affiliates with both the interest-to-income ratio differential and the combined CIT rate differential greater than zero are selected.

E. The indicator for the given year is calculated as the difference between the weighted average interest-to-income ratio of affiliates selected in step D and the weighted average interest-to-income ratio of all affiliates in the sample (both averages weighted by EBITDA) where k is the number of all MNEs in the sample, n_i is the number of affiliates of MNE$_i$ and m_i is the number of affiliates of MNE$_i$ selected in step D.

$$Indicator = \frac{\sum_{i=1}^{k}\sum_{j=1}^{m_i}(interest\text{-}to\text{-}income_{j,MNEi} \times EBITDA_{j,MNEi})}{\sum_{i=1}^{k}\sum_{j=1}^{m_i} EBITDA_{j,MNEi}} - \frac{\sum_{i=1}^{k}\sum_{j=1}^{n_i}(interest\text{-}to\text{-}income_{j,MNEi} \times EBITDA_{j,MNEi})}{\sum_{i=1}^{k}\sum_{j=1}^{n_i} EBITDA_{j,MNEi}}$$

Notes

1. If the partner country is an OECD country, only FDI positions from the other 33 OECD countries are taken into account.
2. If the partner country is an OECD country, only FDI positions from the other 33 OECD are taken into account.
3. The total assets accounted for by low-tax countries, will not be exactly 20%. In that case, the last country to be included in the low-tax countries would cause the sum of low-tax countries' assets exceed 20% of total MNE's assets. The last country is then not assigned a weight equal to its assets. Instead, it is assigned a lower weight. This weight is set such that the sum of assets of all low-tax countries is equal to exactly 20% of the sum of total MNE's assets. For example, the two low-tax countries are A and B. A has an ETR of 11% and assets equal to 15% of total MNE's assets; B has an ETR of 12% and assets equal to 10% of total MNE's assets. In that case, B is assigned a weight of half of its assets equal to 5% of total MNE's assets (15% + 5% = 20%).

Chapter 3

Towards measuring the scale and economic impact of BEPS and countermeasures

Key points:

- There is a large and growing body of evidence of the existence of BEPS, stemming from hundreds of empirical analyses and specific information relating to the tax affairs of certain MNEs that has emerged from numerous legislative and parliamentary enquiries. However, measuring the scale and economic impact of BEPS proves challenging given the complexity of BEPS and the serious data limitations.
- This chapter summarises the available empirical analyses of profit shifting and the effects of previously implemented anti-avoidance countermeasures. Recent research has focused on specific types of BEPS behaviours, mostly on transfer mispricing and debt shifting, but also on treaty abuse, controlled foreign corporation rules, hybrid mismatch arrangements, and disclosure rules, but more empirical analysis is needed in all of these areas.
- No empirical studies comprehensively cover global MNE activity. In particular, most studies are constrained by a lack of data relating to MNE entities in many countries, and where information regarding MNE entities is available it is often incomplete.
- Statistical analyses based upon data collected under the Action 13 Country-by-Country Reports have the potential to significantly enhance the economic analysis of BEPS. However, even with additional data and sophisticated estimation methodologies, researchers of the scale, prevalence and intensity of BEPS will still have difficulty in fully separating BEPS from real economic activity and from non-BEPS tax preferences.
- Several recent studies have presented estimates of the scale of BEPS globally or for individual countries. All of these studies show significant fiscal effects using different types of data and different estimation methodologies. An OECD analysis of financial accounts from a cross-country database estimates the global corporate income tax revenue losses to be in the range of 4% to 10% of corporate income tax revenues, i.e. USD 100 to 240 billion annually at 2014 levels. The studies estimating the fiscal effects on developing countries, as a percentage of their GDP, find that these effects are higher than in developed countries, given the greater reliance on CIT revenues and often weaker tax enforcement capabilities of developing countries, but in some cases these studies also include revenue lost from non-BEPS behaviours.
- BEPS anti-avoidance measures previously implemented by countries have been found to be effective, in countries' fiscal estimates, in academic studies, and in OECD research, to reduce tax planning. Thus, countries with higher statutory corporate tax rates do not necessarily have higher fiscal losses from BEPS if they have strict anti-avoidance rules. International co-ordination of those rules will increase the effectiveness of BEPS countermeasures while reducing the cost of compliance for businesses.

- BEPS causes significant economic distortions. Empirical analyses, including OECD research, find that BEPS involves MNEs manipulating the location of external and internal debt; reduces the effective tax rate on intangible investments, thereby distorting the types of investments made; affects the location of patent registrations, and to a lesser extent actual R&D activity; affects the location of different types and forms of foreign direct investment; and creates tax base and policy spillovers between countries.

- OECD research finds that BEPS reduces the effective tax rate of large MNE entities by 4 to 8½ percentage points on average compared to similarly-situated domestic-only affiliates, providing a competitive advantage in product and capital markets. The reduction in effective tax rates is larger for very large firms and firms with patents. This research also finds that MNE tax planning may allow certain MNEs to increase their market power, resulting in more concentrated markets.

- Analyses of BEPS make comparisons of current business activity with some alternative or "counterfactual." The counterfactual could be a hypothetical "world without BEPS" or a hypothetical "world without co-ordinated multilateral action." When evaluating BEPS countermeasures, the estimated counterfactual of the effects of implementing countermeasures can be compared with current law rules and revenues.

- The extent of BEPS-induced distortions will depend on who currently benefits from BEPS: whether the tax savings from BEPS are passed along in lower consumer prices, higher wages to workers, or to higher returns to capital owners. The reduction in corporate tax liabilities enjoyed by MNEs engaging in BEPS is unlikely to have the same economic effects as a general reduction in corporate income taxes.

- BEPS countermeasures will increase taxes paid by MNEs engaging in BEPS, but other businesses and households will benefit from lower taxes or increased public infrastructure or increased government services, and indirectly through a more level-playing field. The effects on all businesses and households need to be included in analyses of countermeasures. Analysis needs to consider who benefits from BEPS, since if BEPS increases the after-tax economic rents of MNEs engaging in BEPS, countermeasures may not affect some of their investment decisions.

- Additional research on MNEs' investment decisions, determinants of profitability, business tax preferences, and total business taxes is needed to enhance the economic analysis of BEPS and BEPS countermeasures.

3.1 Overview

108. A survey of the academic and empirical literature reveals over one hundred studies have found the presence of BEPS. A recent review of the empirical literature by Dharmapala (2015) does not report a single empirical study not finding some evidence of BEPS. Another review of the academic literature by Riedel (2015) concludes: "Existing studies unanimously report evidence in line with tax-motivated profit shifting (despite using different data sources and estimation strategies)."[1]

109. A common theme of these studies has been the finding that profits are being shifted from high-tax countries to low-tax countries and that there is substantial evidence of a "disconnect" between the jurisdictions where MNEs are recording their taxable profits and the locations where the economic activities that generate these profits are taking place. The studies find empirical evidence of BEPS through various channels, including through: transfer pricing, the strategic location of debt and intangible assets, treaty abuse, and the use of hybrid mismatch arrangements. Government analyses, academic studies, and OECD research presented in Annex 3.A1 have all found that certain measures enacted to address BEPS activity have been effective in protecting the revenue bases of the countries implementing these measures.[2]

110. While the various academic, government and empirical studies undertaken find BEPS is occurring, there is less certainty over the scale or extent to which it is occurring. Scale is defined as the magnitude of the change in overall tax receipts due to BEPS. To date, most studies have focused on individual countries or individual BEPS channels rather than attempt to achieve a comprehensive global estimate of the scale of BEPS activity. Riedel (2015) reports that the estimates of profit shifting range from less than 5% to more than 30% of the income earned by MNEs in high-tax countries being shifted to lower-tax countries. While most of the studies focus on shifting financial profits (not taxable income) and do not include instances of "stateless income",[3] such a large range shows the significant uncertainty surrounding the estimation of the magnitude of BEPS. Due to differences in pre-tax profits reported in financial statements and taxable income, plus tax credits, the percentage change in corporate tax revenues could be even higher than the percentage change in pre-tax reported profits.

111. The two key challenges facing any attempt to undertake an economic analysis of BEPS that arrives at credible estimates relate to the availability of data and the methodology employed for estimating the scale of BEPS. While Chapter 1 discusses the significant limitations of currently available data, this chapter focuses on the methodological issues involved in undertaking economic analyses of the scale and economic impact of BEPS and BEPS countermeasures. It should be noted that few of the academic estimates of profit shifting attempt to estimate the total tax benefits to MNEs or revenues lost to governments from BEPS.

112. Even with the Action 13 Country-by-Country Reports of MNE global taxes and economic activity, measures of the scale of BEPS will require sophisticated estimation techniques to separate BEPS from real economic activity and from non-BEPS tax incentives. Measurement of BEPS and countermeasures will not be available from extracting a single line from a tax return or Country-by-Country Report, but will need to be estimated, and such estimation not only requires better tax and non-tax information, but also requires further refinement of the methodologies applied to future economic analyses.

113. This chapter starts with a discussion of the key issues in measuring BEPS, its economic effects, and the effectiveness of BEPS countermeasures. Significant progress has been made in the last few years in the analysis of BEPS, but given the complexity of BEPS and the serious data limitation, more progress is needed to provide a more precise and a more complete understanding of BEPS behaviours. The chapter outlines what we do know from the empirical studies including some new OECD research, as well as what we do not currently know about the scale and economic impacts of BEPS. The chapter concludes with a number of areas where future economic research with better data will be important in enhancing our understanding of the scale and impact of BEPS and the effectiveness of BEPS countermeasures.

3.2 Key issues in measuring and analysing BEPS

114. Several analytical issues in measuring BEPS are important to consider when evaluating existing empirical analysis of BEPS and how to better monitor BEPS in the future. This section discusses the definition of BEPS, the comparison points against which BEPS is measured, issues of separating BEPS from real economic activity, separating BEPS from non-BEPS government tax incentives, and the appropriate tax rate to use in analysing BEPS.

3.2.1 Defining BEPS

115. For the purposes of empirically analysing the scale of BEPS, it is important to define BEPS behaviours as clearly as possible. It is useful to highlight the description of BEPS from the July 2013 Action Plan on Base Erosion and Profit Shifting[4]:

BEPS relates chiefly to instances where the interaction of different tax rules leads to double non-taxation or less than single taxation. It also relates to arrangements that achieve no or low taxation by shifting profits away from the jurisdictions where the activities creating those profits take place. No or low taxation is not per se a cause of concern, but it becomes so when it is associated with practices that artificially segregate taxable income from the activities that generate it. In other words what creates tax policy concerns is that, due to gaps in the interaction of different tax systems, and in some cases because of the application of bilateral tax treaties, income from cross-border activities may go untaxed anywhere, or be only unduly lowly taxed.

116. The above description helps focus the scope of BEPS. BEPS is about international tax avoidance, i.e. exploiting differences in different countries' tax systems. Tax evasion by individuals or corporate non-compliance with domestic tax rules does not constitute BEPS. Purely domestic tax avoidance is not part of the BEPS project.

117. MNEs taking advantage of differences in countries' tax rates does not amount to BEPS on its own. However, artificial arrangements put in place to exploit these differences do amount to BEPS. With the growing reliance of modern business on intangible property and risk management as part of global value chains, it becomes more difficult to identify where the activities creating profits take place without better data and careful transfer pricing analysis of individual transactions. Working with currently available data and the difficulties of measuring where value is created are both fundamental difficulties associated with measuring the scale of BEPS.

118. If economic functions, assets and risks are effectively relocated to another country to take advantage of a low tax rate or tax credit, this does not constitute BEPS. Such activities are considered to be responses to real economic competition as well as tax

competition where, for example, an entity responds to a tax incentive to invest in a greenfield project that entails building a factory. This is different from, for example, arrangements that highly leverage affiliates in a high-tax rate country to shift profits through related party debt to an affiliate in a low-taxed country. BEPS is often the result of: transfers or acquisitions of intangible or mobile assets for less than full market value; the over-capitalisation of low-tax rate group companies; the excessive-leveraging of high-tax rate group companies; and contractual allocations of risk to low-tax jurisdictions in structures and transactions that would be unlikely to occur between unrelated parties.

119. Many countries have specific legislated domestic tax rules which provide tax credits, tax deductions or tax exemptions for selected activities, such as research and development, investments in alternative energy, and contributions to charitable activities, among many others. These domestic incentives which reduce corporations' average tax rates and which encourage greater activity are not BEPS. However, if domestic incentives are designed to encourage artificial schemes without economic substance, then those schemes would be considered BEPS behaviours.

120. One possible definition of BEPS could refer to the specific BEPS channels identified in the various actions set out in the BEPS Action Plan. By defining BEPS with reference to the individual BEPS channels, the scale would draw upon the consensus reflected in the BEPS Action Plan. Estimation of the scale of each of the BEPS channels would be closely related to what individual governments would estimate for the fiscal and economic impacts of their country's implementation of specific BEPS Actions.

3.2.2 The "counter-factual" for BEPS analysis

121. A second key issue for any analysis of BEPS and countermeasures requires a comparison between an observed world (i.e. current law) and a "counterfactual." When estimating the scale of BEPS, this involves comparing current reported profits, taxes, and economic activity in a world with BEPS with a hypothetical world without BEPS. As no such point of comparison can be observed, empirical analysis must estimate the counterfactual.

122. Three alternative BEPS counterfactuals are described in Box 3.1, being described as: (i) a world today without BEPS, (ii) a future world without co-ordinated multilateral action, and (iii) a future world with proposed countermeasures. Analysing these hypothetical states of the world requires estimating something that cannot be observed. The comparison is only as good as the estimation of the counterfactual.

123. The first counterfactual, a world without BEPS, is used in analysing the scale of BEPS. The other two comparisons can be used to analyse BEPS countermeasures. For example, the revenue effect of a proposed countermeasure is the difference between a world with the countermeasure and the position under current law. When analysing the effect of increased disclosure rules compared to a world without co-ordinated multilateral action where many countries have different disclosure rules, there could be lower compliance costs with co-ordinated disclosure rules, even if there are higher compliance costs compared to current law.

Box 3.1. Alternative points of comparisons - Alternative "counterfactuals"

Analyses will arrive at different estimates of BEPS depending on the comparison point against which they are measured. Several possible counterfactuals are possible when considering BEPS.

"World without BEPS": This is a hypothetical that is not observable and has to be estimated. Many empirical studies estimate the amount of profit shifting as the difference between reported profits and estimated "true" profits. "True" profits are estimated based on available measures of real economic activity, which are described in a later section. To the extent that "true" profits cannot be estimated with precision, then the estimated amount of shifted profits could be biased and lack precision. In this case, the estimate is based on what would have happened today without BEPS.

"World without Co-ordinated Multilateral Action": This is a hypothetical of what would happen in the future if co-ordinated multilateral actions of the type proposed in the BEPS Action Plan did not occur, so BEPS would be unconstrained except by unilateral actions of countries. This requires estimating what MNEs would do without a collective focus and approach to reducing BEPS and what governments would do without consistent adoption of BEPS countermeasures and rules. In this case, the estimate is based on what would be expected to occur in the absence of co-ordinated, multilateral action.

"World with Proposed Countermeasures": This is a hypothetical world of what would happen in the future if the countermeasures are implemented. For estimating the effects of policy changes, analysts generally compare specific proposed BEPS Actions relative to current law. A change in the rules regarding limitations on interest deductions will compare the taxes expected to be collected based on the specific interest limitation proposal with the current tax collections based on a country's current interest deduction rules. In this case, the estimate is based on what would happen in terms of tax collections from a specific BEPS proposal.

3.2.3 Separating BEPS from real economic activity

124. Measuring BEPS requires the identification of the effects of practices that artificially segregate taxable income from the activities that generate it. Companies locate more economic activity in countries with favourable business conditions (e.g. stable social and political environment, access to customers, strong public infrastructure, and low tax rates, etc.). As noted earlier, actions by MNEs taking advantage of differences in countries' tax rates do not amount to BEPS on their own. Thus, simple comparisons of profitability and economic location, including in some of the BEPS indicators, may not fully separate BEPS from the location of real economic activity.

125. However, there are many different and competing perspectives on where profits should be considered to be created for the purposes of differentiating between BEPS and real economic activity. This lack of agreement typically arises over differing views regarding the approach to be taken on two key questions, namely:

- What activity generates profits? and
- Where are the activities that generate profits located geographically?

126. This lack of agreement was recently noted by Doug Shackelford who commented that: "Since we rely on the financial accounting system to guide us about the timing of income and deductions and since accountants cannot measure people, marketing, R&D and similar costs very well, we in the tax community also struggle to recognize income and deductions in an intangibles-based economy. Our problem is magnified because we not only need to know what to recognize and when to recognize it, but we need to know

where to recognize it, i.e. which jurisdiction."[5] This lack of agreement and empirical evidence over where such activity is located is an important source of uncertainty in terms of measuring BEPS.

127. ***What activities generate profits?*** One difficulty that arises from a review of the empirical economic literature is that there is no agreement on what economic activities generate profits, which is critical to measuring BEPS. Some analysts argue that profits are generated where the factors of production (labour and capital) are located, whereas other analysts argue that profits are generated where sales occur. Some other analysts argue that profits are generated based on a combination of labour, capital and sales. Current tax rules generally use a fact specific approach based on a company's functions, assets and risks.

128. The conceptual problem is exacerbated by how capital, sales and labour are typically measured. The value of total assets generally does not include the value of intangible capital assets, which are important generators of value especially in today's economy, but are also highly mobile. Investments in intangible assets, such as R&D expenditures, are generally deducted or 'expensed' in the year of the investment for financial statement accounting, and thus are not included in the value of total assets, except for certain intangibles acquired in an acquisition or purchase. Sales are often measured in the countries where the sales have originated (i.e. origin or production location) rather than where the final consumers are located (i.e. destination or consumption location). Labour is often measured by the number of employees, but this measure may not distinguish between full-time and part-time employees, or differences in productivity or value added per labour hour. A MNE's labour presence may be measured by total employee compensation, but similar to sales, employees often work in multiple jurisdictions during a year, not just in the jurisdiction of incorporation.

129. ***Where are profits generated?*** Just as there is no agreement on the specification of the activities that generate profit, there is considerable disagreement over the key question of where profits are generated. Many of the existing economic studies implicitly define the location "where the activities creating profits take place" in the methodologies employed in their empirical analyses. For example, some economic studies use a profit rate (measured as profit-to-sales, profit-to-employees or profits-to-assets) to test whether financial statement profit is shifted between affiliates based on tax rate differentials.

130. Most of these economic studies use regression analyses to measure BEPS due to tax rate differentials, with other non-tax variables as explanatory variables to explain the creation of real economic profits. The economic studies define real economic profits by reference to the measure used in the profit ratio (e.g. sales or assets) and by the explanatory variables (e.g. tangible capital, size, headquarters location, industry, presence of patents, etc.).

131. To estimate where economic value creation takes place, one has to construct a specification of the production function for the entity. In the case of transfer pricing, consideration of the production function is usually referred to as the functions, risks and capital of the MNE. A production function would not only take into account the usual factors of production: low-skill labour, high-skill labour and physical capital; but research and development (R&D) and other intangible capital, public infrastructure; industry agglomeration effects; and synergies with other entities in the MNE. Thus, the typical empirical specification of profits does not take into account all relevant components of the production function. Omitted variables in the analyses will have at least two effects:

the explanatory power of the regression will be weaker and the estimates of tax shifting responsiveness may be affected by the omitted variables.

132. Additional research is needed in the area of estimating the contributions to real economic contributions to profits, since it is essential to the separation of BEPS from real economic activity. Recent research by Corrado et al. (2012) finds that investment in intangible assets is a significant percentage of companies' total capital expenditures, and a significant contribution to labour productivity. Intangible investments between 1995 and 2009 were 118% of tangible investments in the United States and 62% of tangible investments in the EU15.[6] Better incorporation of intangibles assets (and not just patents or R&D) and also risk management is needed.

3.2.4 Separating BEPS from non-BEPS tax preferences

133. Measuring BEPS also requires separating the effects of MNEs undertaking BEPS from the effects of MNEs using non-BEPS tax preferences. As noted earlier, domestic tax incentives which reduce corporations' average tax rates and which encourage real activity are not BEPS. Many countries provide tax credits or lower rates for R&D and many other socially desirable activities. As long as those tax preferences are not artificial schemes without economic substance, then analyses should attempt to separate the effects of MNEs using non-BEPS tax preferences from the effects of BEPS.

134. This issue is not sufficiently addressed by empirical studies because data limitations are such that most studies use headline statutory tax rates or average effective tax rates. As noted below, tax rate differentials between countries are significantly larger and growing faster when special tax rates are included in the analysis. Currently, information about the magnitude of countries' tax incentives is generally not available to enable analysts to separate the two effects.

3.2.5 Measuring the appropriate tax rate for BEPS analysis

135. Before describing some of the key existing economic studies of BEPS and BEPS countermeasures, it is useful to review the different tax variables used in the analyses. Box 3.2 describes how the many different tax variables are calculated and the different types of analyses they are used for.

Box 3.2. Different tax variables used in BEPS and tax policy analyses

Empirical analyses of BEPS, particularly regression analyses, use tax rate differentials to estimate potential BEPS responses. There are a number of different tax rates used by policy analysts and each of the tax variables has limitations, which are important to understand.

Statutory corporate tax rates are generally thought of as the appropriate measure of the tax incentive for shifting taxable profits between countries. For example, if EUR 100 of taxable income is shifted from a country with a 25% statutory corporate tax rate to a country with a 0% tax rate, then the MNEs tax liability would be reduced by EUR 25. However, in many cases statutory tax rates are not the correct measure of the tax benefit from BEPS. This is because some countries have various tax provisions that may result in a different tax rate from the statutory tax rate being applied to the shifted income. For instance, countries with allowances for corporate equity provide a deduction for notional interest on equity and, therefore, provide less incentive to use interest expense to shift profits. In some cases, countries with high headline statutory tax rates may have significantly lower tax rates on special types of income (e.g. income generated by intangible assets) and this may mean that, even though the country has a high headline statutory corporate tax rate, income may be shifted into the country rather than out of the country. Withholding taxes may also be payable or avoided on flows associated with BEPS.

Box 3.2. Different tax variables used in BEPS and tax policy analyses *(continued)*

Marginal tax rates (MTR) applicable to the shifted income would be the ideal measure for BEPS analysis, but are often not known. In some cases the MTR is the same as the headline statutory tax rate or a special statutory tax rate, but in others it may be a negotiated rate as part of an administrative ruling.

Effective tax rates (ETRs) come in a number of variations and are useful for different types of analyses.

Backward-looking average effective tax rates (AETR) are also used to measure the effects of BEPS, but often are inexact measures of the incentives to shift taxable income. AETRs may be closer to what companies actually pay in tax and reflect all aspects of the corporate tax system. However, they are a backward-looking metric, reflecting historical tax effects (e.g. depreciation from prior investments, loss deductions from prior years taken against current year taxable income, etc.) and non-BEPS tax provisions (e.g. R&D and energy tax credits). AETRs are often computed from financial statement data, and thus identify the country of incorporation not tax residence, and computed from accounting tax expense, rather than tax liability or cash taxes paid, and which can include taxes paid in other countries, as described in Chapter 1.

Forward-looking marginal and average effective tax rates (FL-METRs and FL-ATRs) are calculated using hypothetical companies to illustrate the tax on a future investment. FL-METRs are used to analyse domestic investment incentives at the margin, but are increasingly recognised as inappropriate for measuring MNEs' decisions on the location of high-return intangible assets.[7] FL-ATRs illustrate the tax on the total return or economic profit of an investment, particularly for investments earning above a competitive return, for purposes of considering the location of that investment across different countries. Hypothetical companies are fact-specific and difficult to weight to be representative of the whole economy, plus they do not capture all of the important tax aspects of the corporate tax structure, particularly international tax rules.

Other tax rates. In evaluating the level of taxes paid by selected groups of taxpayers or specific taxpayers, some analyses and press articles report a ratio of taxes paid to sales, and may even call it an effective tax rate. Sometimes a low ratio is the basis for concluding that a MNE is artificially shifting profits out of a country. This interpretation illustrates the confusion caused by mixing tax base concepts. The corporate income tax is a tax on a company's equity income, not a tax on sales (consumption). The appropriate measure for evaluating the burden of an income tax is taxes divided by income, not the ratio of taxes to sales. A low ratio of taxes to sales may simply reflect the fact that a firm operates in a low profit margin industry, where sales are high relative to profits. In contrast to net income, the amount of sales has to cover payments to labour and lenders, as well as intermediate purchases from other firms.

Tax policy analysts are still grappling with which tax rate(s) should be used to empirically estimate the effects of BEPS. Sensitivity analysis, such as running regressions with different tax rate measures, can be used to determine if the choice of tax rate makes a significant difference.

136. In addition to the tax rate used in the analysis, another methodological issue relates to the question of determining the appropriate way to calculate the tax rate differential (i.e. the differential between one MNE entity's tax rate compared to the average tax rate of other entities in the MNE group). A number of empirical studies compare affiliates' tax rate to the MNE parent's tax rate. That captures shifting between parents and affiliates. Other studies compare an affiliate's tax rate to the tax rate of the group. That captures inter-affiliate shifting but in some cases does not include shifting with the parent. Some of the studies compare the entity's tax rate to the other related entities' average tax rate, either a simple unweighted average or weighted by revenue, but shifting may be disproportionately undertaken with the lowest tax rate affiliates. In fact, all of the shifting may be undertaken with one entity based in a zero tax rate country. This

issue requires additional exploration to improve the measurement of BEPS tax rate differentials.

3.3 What we know about BEPS and the effect of countermeasures

137. This section describes the empirical analyses of overall profit shifting, estimates of the fiscal effects of BEPS, the empirical analyses of the effects of BEPS countermeasures and particular channels of BEPS, and the economic impacts of BEPS and countermeasures.

3.3.1 General profit shifting analyses

138. A burgeoning empirical literature on BEPS is continuing and reports significant BEPS occurring due to tax rate differentials. The bibliography has a select listing of articles and reports. Recent surveys of the literature on profit shifting by Dharmapala (2014) and Riedel (2014) and a meta-analysis of profit shifting by Heckemeyer and Overesch (2013) analysing prior empirical studies report significant BEPS among MNEs. A review of the various general profit shifting analyses illustrates the range of databases, tax and other variables, and methodologies used.

139. The range of studies previously undertaken use many different types of data, including individual firm-level financial statement data, national aggregate statistics, confidential government company surveys, export and import pricing data, and in some cases corporate tax returns. Recent studies have increasingly examined specific BEPS channels, such as interest deductibility and transfer pricing.

140. Most of the analyses are limited to a single country or MNEs headquartered in a single country, where access to company surveys, corporate tax returns, or company trade data are made available to researchers on a confidential basis, or based on analyses of MNE affiliates in multiple countries from a limited number of financial databases. For instance, a number of studies have used confidential information from MNEs headquartered in Germany and the United States and their global affiliates, based on mandatory investment surveys from the German Bundesbank and the United States Bureau of Economic Analysis. Similar data unfortunately is not available for other countries, and thus the results from these studies are specific to those countries' MNEs, and would not necessarily be representative for other countries due to differences in tax rates and tax rules, differences in the industry mix and other country differences.

141. Several studies of customs and trade data identify non-arms' length intra-group pricing, but those have also been with individual country data. Extrapolation of the BEPS found in those studies beyond the specific countries the subject of the analyses rests on a critical assumption that the BEPS behaviours studied are of similar magnitude in other countries.

142. Academic studies have also taken advantage of the availability of cross-country databases of company financial records. Many economic analyses have used the Amadeus database which is limited to European companies. Similar to individual country analyses, the results from these studies are specific to Europe, and are unlikely to be representative for other countries. More recently, a number of academic studies have turned to global databases such as ORBIS. These have the advantage of including more than just European countries, but as described in Chapter 1 the coverage while large in total number of entities is significantly limited in the countries covered and the entities with full financial information. Various analyses have taken different approaches, with

some analysing profit shifting from parents to affiliates and others analysing profit shifting between unconsolidated affiliated entities.

143. While academic studies have increasingly focused on individual company data, several international organisations have used macroeconomic data to estimate the effects of BEPS. These studies focus on the effects of "tax haven" countries and FDI through special purpose entities. Although macroeconomic data cannot capture detailed firm-level behaviour, it can capture some dimensions of BEPS which may not be reflected in micro-data due to its incomplete coverage. One limitation with using macro data, such as foreign direct investment data, is it includes the impact of taxes on both real economic activity and BEPS.

144. Most academic studies have not applied their estimates of profit shifting based on the sample data to provide an estimate of the fiscal effects. Fiscal estimates require significantly more information than just the average responsiveness of financial profits to a change in tax rates. Financial statement profits generally differ from taxable income due to differences in accounting and tax rules. Companies with negative taxable income in a given year generally cannot receive a tax refund in that year, but must carry forward any tax losses to future years. Further, the relationship between income and tax liability is not proportional due to the extensive use of tax credits in many countries.

145. Two recent studies provide useful summaries of the empirical analysis of BEPS. Dharmapala (2014) summarises the empirical literature of profit shifting analyses and reports that the more recent empirical literature finds the estimated magnitude of BEPS to be smaller than that found in earlier studies. The change seems mainly due to the increasing recent use of micro firm level data, which is able to hold more non-tax factors constant, compared to aggregate data across countries. Riedel (2015) reports that existing studies unanimously report evidence in line with tax-motivated profit shifting, but there is a wide range of profit shifting estimates from 5-30% of MNE profits.

146. Notable examples of general analyses of profit shifting using firm-specific data are Grubert (2012), Huizinga and Laeven (2008), Heckmeyer and Overesch (2013), OECD Annex 1, and Dowd, Landefeld and Moore of the United States Congressional Joint Committee on Taxation (JCT) (2015). Grubert (2012) uses a sample of United States corporate tax return data of large non-financial United States-based MNEs to investigate the role of taxation in the large increase in the foreign share of total income of United States MNEs between 1996 and 2002. The paper finds that companies with lower foreign effective tax rates have higher foreign profit margins and lower domestic profit margins. The analysis finds that introduction of the "check-the-box" regulation in 1997 accounted for a significant fraction of the reduction in the foreign effective tax rates. The analysis shows that R&D intensity reduces foreign effective tax rates, indirectly indicating that the strategic location of intangible assets can facilitate BEPS.

147. Huizinga and Laeven (2008) analyse the Amadeus database of European MNEs unconsolidated affiliate financial account information to investigate profit shifting incentives due to international tax differences. They were the first to take a portfolio approach to MNE behaviour, using as a tax variable the average of bilateral differences in statutory tax rates between companies in the same group. The analysis uses earnings before interest and taxes as the dependent variable. Considering both tax differentials among foreign affiliates and tax differentials between parents and foreign affiliates, they find evidence of profit shifting, both among foreign subsidiaries and between parent companies and their affiliates abroad. Finally, they estimate the associated revenue implications for each country by comparing the actual profit shifting outcome to a

theoretical benchmark without profit shifting. They find a semi-elasticity of reported profits with respect to the top statutory tax rate of -1.3.

148. Heckemeyer and Overesch (2013) conduct a "meta-analysis" of available profit shifting analyses and report a tax semi-elasticity of subsidiary pre-tax profits of -0.8, where a 10 percentage point increase in the tax variable reduces financial statement profits by 8 percent. The analysis uses multiple estimates from individual studies and is heavily weighted to studies of European companies. The analysis does not separately estimate the effects of the different types of data, such as financial account, investment survey, and tax return data.

149. New research in Annex 3.A1 uses the ORBIS database of unconsolidated affiliate's financial accounts to analyse profit shifting and differences between MNE affiliates and similarly-situated domestic companies. The analysis finds that between 2000 and 2010 an affiliate's statutory headline tax rate that is one percentage point above its MNE group average is associated with a lower reported profit by about 1 percent on average, a semi-elasticity around -1.0. A second analysis finds that large MNE entities (with more than 250 employees) have an estimated 2½ to 5 percentage points lower effective tax rate on average than comparable domestic-only companies, which reflects the exploitation of mismatches between tax systems and the relative use of domestic tax preferences. Combining the two estimates, BEPS is found to reduce the ETR of large MNEs entities by a range of 4 to 8½ percentage points. The analysis also finds that existing tax anti-avoidance rules have a positive effect on reducing profit shifting.

150. Dowd, Landefeld, and Moore (2015), three economists of the United States Joint Committee on Taxation, analyse United States tax return data for foreign controlled corporations of United States parent MNEs and find significant non-linear effects of profit-shifting. They find a linear estimate of the semi-elasticity is -1.3, but the study also finds 4 to 7 times higher elasticities for profit shifting to low-tax affiliates. Despite working with actual tax return data, missing data[8] and consolidation issues (e.g. affiliates in zero tax rate countries report some taxes paid to other countries) could affect the results.

151. Dharmapala (2014) has noted that the estimates of tax responsiveness from academic studies often seem small relative to the large fraction of net income in tax havens. These are not necessarily contradictory, since the former measure the effects of small marginal changes (i.e. in tax rate differentials) rather than the absolute levels of tax rate differences of 20% or 30% compared to 0%.[9] Thus, econometric estimates of marginal changes may understate the actual effects of large tax rate differentials.

152. Table 3.1 presents a number of profit shifting economic analyses using individual company information. All of these empirical studies are attempting to measure the effect of profit shifting due to tax rate differentials, separating profit shifting from the effects of real economic activity. Differences in the data, variables used, and methodology used (Box 3.3) explain why good empirical analyses yield different results, but all show strong evidence of profit shifting. The median elasticity among the 20 studies is -1.0.

Box 3.3. Different approaches used to estimate profit shifting

Since the seminal articles on estimating profit shifting by Grubert and Mutti (1991) and Hines and Rice (1994), an increasing number of empirical analyses of profit shifting have been conducted with individual company (micro-level) data. Analysis of micro data enables researchers to avoid aggregation issues and more importantly to better take account of firm level measures of economic factors explaining company profitability. The estimates of profit shifting attributable to tax differences from analyses since 2007 show a wide range of semi-elasticities from -0.4 to -3.7. The analyses suggest that a 10 percentage point lower corporate tax rate could reduce profit shifting by 4% to 37%, holding all other factors constant and these studies do not take into account countries' current anti-avoidance rules.

Although a common general approach is taken, the statistical regression analyses use different data sources, different data variables and different estimation techniques. Differences in the results can be due to any number of these factors.

Type of data: The micro-data empirical analyses use three types of data: financial accounts, confidential company investment surveys, and tax return data. Financial account data reports tax expense rather than actual taxes paid, which can differ due to deferred taxes and includes taxes paid to countries other than the country of incorporation.

Coverage by country: Depending on the database used, MNE entities analysed differ across studies. Many studies use a European entity database, so only include European affiliates of worldwide parents. Several studies analyse entities around the world, but only affiliates of United States parent MNEs, while Weichenrieder analyses German affiliates of foreign parent MNEs. Recently several studies have analysed entities worldwide through the use of the ORBIS database, but as noted in Chapter 1, this database is not comprehensive particularly outside of Europe and is especially weak in developing countries.

Coverage by MNE relationships: Studies differ in the type of MNE entities included. Some limit the analysis to unconsolidated entities, while others include both affiliates as well as parents. The OECD analysis takes advantages of ownership links to affiliated companies to include the statutory tax rate of the linked affiliates, even if the linked entities do not have financial information included in the database.

Estimated profit variable: Most studies use some variant of profit as the dependent variable, while a few use broader capital income measures such as return on assets and total factor productivity. The measures of profits include pre-tax profit, post-tax profit, and earnings before interest and taxes (EBIT). Some studies normalise pre-tax profits as a ratio of sales or assets.

Tax rate variable: A key predictive variable is the tax rate. Most studies use either the statutory headline tax rate or an average effective tax rate. Often the top marginal tax rate is the incentive at the margin for shifted income, but in many countries special lower tax rates apply to certain types of income, especially highly mobile income. Other studies use average effective tax rates to reflect special lower rates as well as other tax incentives or negotiated rates which can significantly reduce the applicable tax rate below the headline statutory tax rate. Several studies use a composite tax rate variable that weights tax rate differentials by revenue to control for different opportunities to shift income.

Tax rate differential variables: Profit shifting depends on differences in tax rates across countries. Profit shifting can also occur between countries with similar statutory tax rates where one entity has tax losses, and thus a lower effective tax rate. Some studies calculate tax rate differentials between the affiliates and the parent; others calculate the differential between affiliates using an average rate for the other affiliates; while other studies simply use the absolute tax rate of the entity.

Box 3.3. Different approaches used to estimate profit shifting *(continued)*

Explanatory economic variables: Separating profit shifting from real economic activity contributions to reported profits is important. Most studies include a variety of measures of real economic activity to isolate the tax effect. Most studies use available metrics of capital and/or labour, additional variables such as population, unemployment, inflation, trade and corruption indices, and GDP related measures to account for macroeconomic differences in the countries in which the MNE entities are operating. The capital measure only includes reported total assets or tangible/fixed assets, and thus does not include other potential contributors to firm profit, such as intangible assets of the MNE group, public infrastructure, social capital, etc. It should be noted that the explanatory economic variables used are quite different from the arm's length pricing measures based on functions, risks and assets of the MNE entities or uncontrolled comparable prices. No studies to date have used both affiliate and group data to estimate the entities' shares of the MNE group profit due to data limitations.

Fixed effects (dummy) variables: Most of the empirical studies use fixed effects variables to hold constant factors unique to the individual entity, individual year, industry or country. Ideally, the regressions would include specific economic measures for these dimensions, but due to data or conceptual limitations, simple one-zero dummy variables are often used to capture those important effects.

Linear vs. non-linear tax effects: Analysts must choose a specification of the regression equation of how tax rates affect profit shifting. Most analysts choose a semi-log elasticity measure where the percentage change in profits is a function of a percentage point change in the chosen tax rate variable. Alternatively, the estimate can be calculated with a simple elasticity, where the percentage change in profits is a function of the percentage change in the chosen tax rate. The two types of estimates can be presented as equivalents by calculating the semi-log elasticity equivalent for the simple elasticity at the average of the tax rate. The Hines/Rice analysis suggested that a non-linear specification could be used, but most empirical analyses have conducted linear specifications. The United States JCT economists' analysis cites a -1.3 linear semi-elasticity, but their preferred speciation is non-linear and ranges from -0.8 to -9.5 depending on the level of the effective tax rate faced by the affiliate.

Semi-elasticity vs. elasticity: Most analyses use a semi-elasticity measure (based on a log-linear specification) where the percentage change in profits is a function of a percentage point change in the chosen tax rate variable. Alternatively, the estimate can be calculated with a standard elasticity (based on a log-log specification), where the percentage change in profits is a function of the percentage change in the chosen tax rate. The main advantage of the semi-elasticity is that it is straightforward to interpret; an x percent change in profits for a one percentage point change in the tax rate. Elasticity specifications can capture a changing responsiveness depending on the absolute level of the tax variable. A semi-elasticity equivalent can be calculated for the elasticity specification at the average of the tax rate.

Cost of tax planning / Linear vs. non-linear tax effects: Economic theory suggests two reasons for a non-linear relation between tax rates and profit shifting: fixed cost of tax planning and convex concealment costs. These effects are not mutually exclusive. Convex concealment costs arise when the cost of shifting increases with the absolute amount of profits shifted. This implies that the effect on pre-tax profits will be smaller at higher absolute levels of the tax rate differential. If tax planning is associated with fixed costs, higher tax semi-elasticities would be expected at higher absolute levels of the tax rate differential. Although Hines and Rice (1994) found evidence of a non-linear relationship, most subsequent empirical analyses have reported only linear specifications. Grubert and Mutti (1991) found evidence of fixed tax planning costs. Dowd, Landefeld and Moore (2015) find a strong non-linear relationship with semi-elasticities ranging from -0.8 to -9.5 depending on the level of the effective tax rate faced by the affiliate, which provides empirical support of fixed costs of tax planning and for testing non-linear specifications.

Box 3.3. Different approaches used to estimate profit shifting *(continued)*

Methodologies: Given the significant differences in the empirical analyses of profit shifting, recent research has included "meta" analyses which use other studies' results and differences as described above to attempt to summarise the available analyses. One meta-study reports significant profit shifting responses, but the results are dependent on the underlying data used and the particular methodologies of the underlying studies. Some studies are included multiple times because different variants of the same data and approach are included, and the majority of studies are based on European entities and financial statement information. An alternative methodology based on a temporary change in profits, rather than tax rate differentials, by Dharmapala and Riedel (2013) has been used, but they note that the methodology is unlikely to capture longer-term planning opportunities, such as transfer pricing.

Time period: Huizinga and Laeven analyse a single year, 1999, while most analyses use multiple years but with different time periods, such as Weichenrieder (1996-2003) and Beer and Loeprick (2003-2011). If BEPS is changing over time, the time period used will affect the estimated responsiveness.

Many of the studies in Table 3.1 include a number of sensitivity analyses and alternative specifications, providing important additional insights beyond just a single tax rate elasticity. For example, the OECD profit shifting analysis in Annex 3.A1 tested the sensitivity of different dependent variables (i.e. pre-tax profit to employment, operating profit to total assets) and different fixed effects (i.e. country and country interacted with time fixed effects), and the profit shifting elasticity was found to be robust.

Table 3.1 Data sources, estimation strategies and results from recent profit shifting studies

Authors	Year	Semi-elasticity	Dependent Variable	C	L	GDP	ADD	Fixed Effects				Tax variable	Tax rate differential	R-squared	Time Period	Coverage	Data
								Firm	Time	Ind.	Ctry.						
Dischinger	2007	-0.7	pre-tax profit	x	x	x	x	x	x			STR	affiliate to parent	0.76	1995-2005	EU entities	FS
Huizinga and Laeven	2008	-1.3	pre-tax profit	x	x	x				x	x	STR	affiliate to parent	0.68	1999	EU entities	FS
Azemar	2010	-1.0	pre-tax profit			x	x					US-STR and foreign ETR	no	0.81	1992-2000	foreign aff. of US parents	TR
Becker and Riedel	2012	-0.7	pre-tax profit	x		x	x	x	x	x		STR	affiliate to parent	N/A	1995-2006	EU entities	FS
Blouin, Robinson and Seidman	2012	-0.5	pre-tax profit	x	x	x		x	x	x		STR	foreign aff. to US parent	0.60	1982-2005	foreign aff. of US parents	IS
Dischinger, Knoll and Riedel	2013	-0.5	pre-tax profit	x	x	x	x	x				STR	affiliate to parent	0.14	1995-2005	EU entities	FS
Dharmapala and Riedel	2013	-1.1	pre-tax profit	x		x	x	x	x	x		STR	no	0.21	1995-2005	EU entities	FS
Markle	2015	-0.9	pre-tax profit	x	x	x		x	x			composite var. based on STR	affiliate to group	0.83	2004-2008	worldwide entities	FS
Dowd, Landefeld and Moore at United States Joint Committee on Taxation	2015	-1.3	pre-tax profit	x	x	x	x	x	x			STR and ETR	no	0.46	2002-2010	foreign aff. of US parents	TR
Clausing	2015	-2.4	pre-tax profit			x		x				ETR	foreign aff. to US parent	0.64	1983-2011	foreign aff. of US parents	IS
Schwarz	2009	-3.5	pre-tax profit to sales			x	x				x	ETR	no	0.28	1999-2001	foreign aff. of US parents	IS
Grubert	2012	-1.6	pre-tax profit to sales				x					change in foreign ETR	no	N/A	1996, 2004	foreign aff. of US parents	TR
OECD	2015	-1.0	pre-tax profit to assets	x		x	x		x	x		STR	affiliate to group	0.03	2000-2010	worldwide entities	FS
Loretz and Mokkas	2011	-1.1	post-tax profit	x	x	x	x	x	x			STR	no	0.01	2002-2009	EU entities	FS

Table 3.1 Data sources, estimation strategies and results from recent profit shifting studies *(continued)*

Authors	Year	Semi-elasticity	Dependent Variable	C	L	GDP	ADD	Fixed Effects Firm	Time	Ind.	Ctry.	Tax variable	Tax rate differential	R-squared	Time Period	Coverage	Data
Lohse and Riedel	2013	-0.4	EBIT	x	x	x	x	x	x	x		STR	affiliate to parent	0.16	1999-2009	EU entities	FS
Beer and Loeprick	2013	-1.0	EBIT	x	x	x		x	x	x		STR	affiliate to group	0.06	2003-2011	worldwide entities	FS
Beuselinck, Deloof and Vanstraelen	2014	-1.6	EBIT	x	x	x		x		x	x	composite var. based on STR	affiliate to parent	0.71	1998-2009	EU entities	FS
Maffini and Mokkas	2011	-1.0	total factor prod.					x	x		x	STR	no	0.10	1998-2004	worldwide entities	FS
Weichenrieder	2009	-0.5	return on assets	x	x		x	x	x			STR	German affiliate to parent	0.52	1996-2003	German aff. of foreign par.	IS
Heckemeyer and Overesch	2013	-0.8	pre-tax profit and EBIT	-	-	-	-	-	-	-	-	STR and ETR	various	N/A	various	various	meta

Note: Studies estimating tax semi-elasticities of profit shifting published after 2006. In case of no preferred estimate, the baseline specification was used. "C" stands for tangible capital, "L" for employee compensation, "ADD" for additional variables; a "x" indicates that corresponding control variables have been included. In the last column "FS" indicates financial statement data, "IS" investment survey, and "TR" tax return data.

3.3.2 Incentives for BEPS

153. Much of the discussion of BEPS has focused on tax elasticities of profit shifting or on the declining corporate tax rates among OECD countries over the last twenty years. This might lead some to conclude that the incentive to engage in BEPS behaviours has declined. However, profit shifting is based on tax rate differentials between MNE entities in two countries, not the level of CIT rates. The incentive to shift income from an entity in a country with a 40% tax rate to a related entity in a country with a 20% tax rate is the same as the incentive to shift income from an entity in a country with a 30% tax rate to a related entity in a country with a 10% tax rate. In both cases, there is a tax avoidance of 20% of the amount of profit shifted.

154. Tax rate differentials can be measured by the statistical concept of standard deviation, reflecting the distance of individual countries' CIT rates from the average CIT rate. Figure 3.1. shows the average CIT rate and the standard deviation of CIT rates in OECD countries between 1998 and 2013. The tax rates and standard deviation are weighted by foreign direct investment to focus the analysis more closely on MNE cross-border activity and BEPS. The average OECD CIT rate declined on average from 34.5% in 2003 to 30.1% in 2013. In contrast, the standard deviation of CIT rates increased from 5.6 in 2003 to 7.0 in 2013, i.e. by 25%.

Figure 3.1. Incentive to engage in BEPS: Corporate income tax rate variation within OECD countries

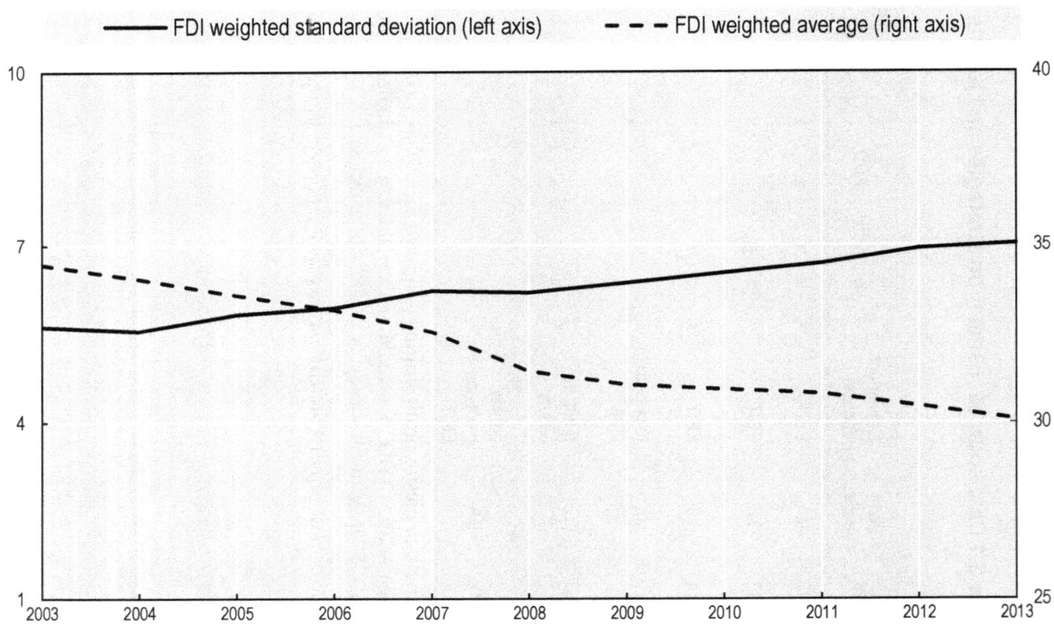

Weighted by the average inward and outward FDI position. Source: OECD Tax Database, OECD FDI Statistics.

155. Most empirical studies analyse the effects of statutory headline tax rates. The incentives for BEPS are based not only on headline statutory CIT rate differentials. Many countries have preferential tax treatment for certain types of income. For example, the strategic location of intangibles is a significant BEPS strategy, and the incentives to

engage in BEPS behaviour are increased when there are preferential tax rates on patent income without economic nexus requirements. Figure 3.2. shows the average CIT rate on patent income and the standard deviation in OECD countries. In 2013, eight OECD countries had patent boxes. The remaining OECD countries applied their headline CIT rates on patent income. Again, the tax rates are weighted by FDI to narrow the focus towards MNE cross-border activity and BEPS.

156. The average CIT rate on patent income is lower and declined more than the average headline CIT rate. The standard deviation of CIT rates on patent income is higher and increased more than that of CIT headline rates. The standard deviation increased sharply in 2007 when Belgium and the Netherlands introduced their patent boxes. The weighted standard deviation of CIT rates on patent income in OECD countries increased from 8.6 in 2003 to 11.8 in 2013, i.e. by 38%.

Figure 3.2. Incentive to engage in BEPS: Corporate income tax rate on patent income variation within OECD countries

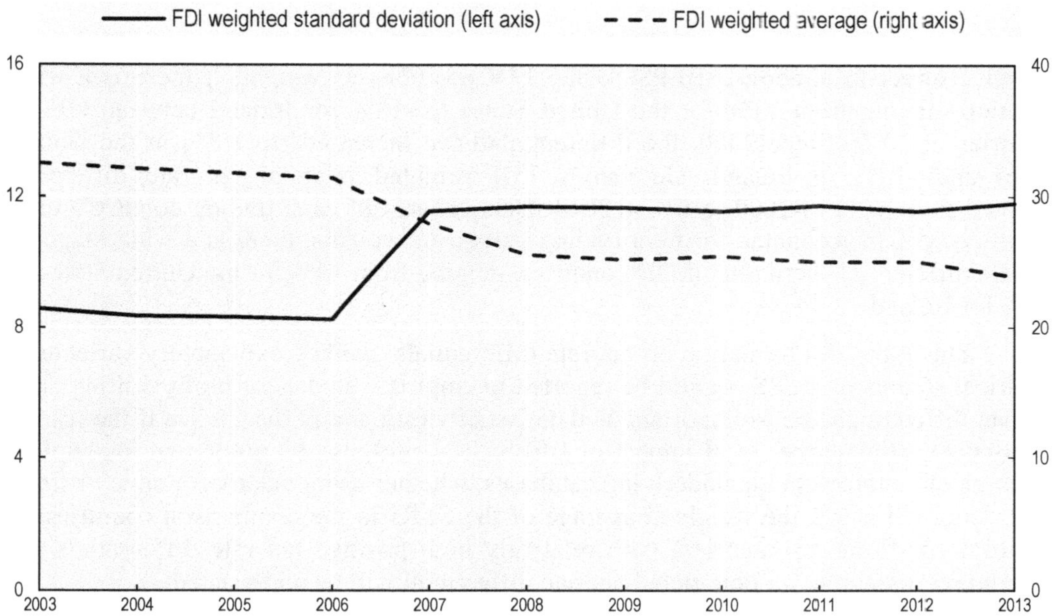

Weighted by the average inward and outward FDI position.

Source: OECD Tax Database, OECD FDI Statistics. European Commission (2015)

157. Further refinement of these measures is possible, but they clearly show the incentives for engaging in BEPS behaviours, such as the strategic location of intangibles, has been increasing over the past 11 years. Finally, the incentive to shift profits to countries with zero tax rates still remains strong even with lower average tax rates. Reducing taxes to zero from 10% or 20% still creates a large tax rate differential effect, which is why there is BEPS shifting to zero rate countries from all positive tax rate countries.

158. When analysing BEPS it is important to refine the measurement as closely as possible to the affected economic activity. Table 3.2 shows that a simple unweighted standard deviation of statutory tax rates in OECD countries does not show an increase in

the incentive for BEPS. However, when the tax rate differentials are weighted by GDP they show a significant increase. When they are weighted by FDI and trade, both measures of MNE activity, they are even higher and the percentage change over the past eleven years is also higher.[10] The standard deviation of CIT rates on patent income is much higher than simply using the statutory headline tax rate.

Table 3.2. Standard deviation of OECD tax rates, 2003 and 2013

	Unweighted	GDP weighted	FDI weighted	Trade weighted
		Statutory headline tax rates		
2003	6.5	4.7	5.6	5.6
2013	5.8	6.6	7.0	6.6
		CIT rates on patent incomes		
2003	8.5	7.2	8.6	8.3
2013	8.4	10.0	11.8	10.7

159. A similar analysis using bilateral tax rate differentials shows a similar large incentive effect to undertake BEPS. Using FDI positions as weights[11], there is a wide variation ranging from 11% for the United States to -18% for Ireland between OECD countries in 2012. Since 2000, the differentials have increased from 3% in the United States and -13% in Ireland. Germany's FDI-weighted bilateral tax rate difference declined from 16% in 2000 to 0% in 2014. Using shares of each trading country's total exports of goods accounted for by a trading partner as weights, there is a wide range of tax rate differentials between OECD countries, ranging from 14% for the United States to -16% for Ireland.

160. This type of information on tax rate differentials, the key explanatory variable in empirical studies of BEPS, should be reported in empirical studies of profit shifting. The tax rate differentials are as important as the elasticity estimate in the studies if the results are used to estimate the fiscal impact of BEPS. It should also be noted that incomplete coverage of countries in the underlying databases, whether using macroeconomic or firm-level data, will affect the weighted average of the STRs in the comparison countries. If countries (or firms in countries) with relatively high positive tax rate differentials are underrepresented, the implicit global tax rate differential will be understated.

3.3.3 BEPS and developing countries

161. Due to limitations of the available data, both in terms of quality and quantity, as noted in Fuest and Riedel (2010), empirical research of profit shifting in developing countries is quite limited. Attempting to fill the gap on developing country studies of BEPS, Fuest, Hebous and Riedel (2011) empirically examine income shifting from developing countries by focusing on related party loans. Distinguishing between German MNE affiliates in developed and developing countries, the results show that related party debt in developing countries is significantly more sensitive to changes in corporate tax rates than in developed countries. The study concludes that profit shifting, measured relative to current CIT collections, is about twice as large in developing countries as in developed economies. The IMF (2014) study on international tax spillovers uses a rough comparison of corporate tax efficiency, which suggests that revenue losses as a percent of CIT revenues in developing countries could be several multiples of those in developed countries, due to weaker enforcement resources.

162. Many studies focusing on developing countries do not separate the revenue lost from BEPS behaviours from individual tax evasion and illicit financial flows. Developing countries have higher ratios of CIT to GDP, so their revenue base is potentially more at risk from BEPS behaviours than developed countries, and loss of CIT revenue could lead to critical underfunding of public investment that could help promote economic growth. In a report by the African Tax Administration Forum, African tax administrations find that transfer-pricing abuse is a major obstacle not only to effective revenue mobilisation, but also to development and poverty alleviation, and that most countries lack the necessary skills to identify and analyse complex cases.[12] Better understanding of the economic effects of BEPS on developing countries is important for the design of tax policies that account for country differences in tax systems and levels of enforcement capabilities.

163. A recent working paper by UNCTAD[13] provides a tax and investment perspective on the tax consequences of FDI for developing economies. Investment is important to sustainable growth of developing countries, which must be considered when reducing profit shifting out of those economies. Again, how the potential additional tax revenues from reducing BEPS behaviours are used by developing counties will be important to the future effects of countermeasures on their inbound FDI.

164. The UNCTAD empirical analysis investigates the role of investment as one of the enablers of tax avoidance, highlighting the use of special purpose entities (SPEs), tax havens and the role of offshore investment hubs as major players in foreign direct investment in developing countries. It states: "The root-cause of the outsized role of offshore hubs in global corporate investments is tax planning." The analysis is based on an approach which maps aggregate corporate international investments between direct investor and recipient jurisdictions based on bilateral flows in or coming from SPEs and tax havens. It finds a relatively larger effect of SPE and tax haven investment in developing countries.

3.3.4 Estimating the scale (fiscal effects) of BEPS

165. In addition to existing data limitations, the need to develop a clear methodology for measuring BEPS was the second most cited problem facing government tax policy analysts, according to the country survey conducted by the CFA's WP2, and by numerous commentators on the Action 11 discussion draft. All studies of the scale of BEPS attempt to measure how the actual amount of corporate tax paid across countries differs from the counterfactual of a world without BEPS behaviours.

166. A number of studies have sought to compare the geographic location of profits reported by MNEs, which are affected by BEPS behaviours, with a "counterfactual" of a world without BEPS, where the location of profits is aligned with the location of the economic activity that generated those profits. Without specifying individual BEPS behaviours, these studies take an aggregate approach (not based on specific BEPS channels) and examine the effect of profit shifting due to differences in tax rates, which are not otherwise explained by the available measures of real economic activity. These studies were initially undertaken with country macroeconomic variables, but now increasingly take advantage of available firm-level data, enabling closer linkage of differences in profitability across firms based on firm-specific tax and non-tax factors, albeit with the significant data limitations of currently available firm-level data.

167. Analyses estimating the effect of tax rate differentials without refining the estimates for BEPS behaviours (i.e. artificial strategies segregating taxable income from

the activity that generates it) will have a tendency to overestimate the scale of BEPS. This is because BEPS is not due to tax differentials per se, but rather to specific taxpayer strategies segregating taxable income from the activities that create that value. Tax rate differentials using AETRs reflect non-BEPS tax reductions, such as from R&D tax credits or accelerated depreciation, thus resulting in an overestimate of the scale of BEPS. Implementation of transfer pricing rules allows a range (acceptable within inter-quartiles) within which acceptable prices can be set, which are not reflected in tax rate differentials. Due to other factors, particularly data limitations and incomplete specification of the underlying production function, estimates from tax rate differences may underestimate the scale of BEPS.[14]

168. Another approach uses aggregate macroeconomic country measures to take into account tax rate differences or institutional differences. These studies take advantage of country-specific details, such as the amount of country FDI from SPEs or tax havens, or the statutory tax rates of tax havens and other countries. These studies are unlikely to fully separate BEPS from real economic activity and non-BEPS tax preferences.

169. Another approach measures specific BEPS behaviours. A recent survey of the academic literature by Riedel (2015) states: "The most convincing empirical evidence has been presented by academic studies that investigate specific profit shifting channels as their empirical tests are more direct and offer less room for results being driven by mechanisms unrelated to income shifting."[15] Examples include quantifying the effects of non-arm's length transfer pricing, excessive interest deductions, and treaty abuse. Measuring specific BEPS behaviours enables researchers to use different types of data sources, such as trade data to analyse transfer pricing, leverage rates of affiliated companies to analyse excessive interest, or bilateral investment flows to analyse treaty abuse. BEPS behaviours are driven by differences in tax rates and/or differences between tax systems that can be exploited to reduce taxation through artificial schemes.

170. While measuring specific BEPS Actions is a more direct approach, many of the same data and methodological issues arise. Estimating the revenue effects of specific BEPS Actions requires consideration of the interactions between different BEPS channels (e.g. possible overlap or complementarities) in producing a total BEPS estimate. For example, the tax challenges of the digital economy (Action 1) are being addressed through the other Actions, in particular the work on artificial avoidance of permanent establishment, transfer pricing and CFC rules.

171. At the individual country level, the BEPS Actions approach may be estimated by governments using their own administrative databases, which will often include tax return data. Proposed BEPS countermeasures are not expected to eliminate 100% of the impact of BEPS behaviours out of consideration of administrative costs for tax administrations and businesses. See Annex 3.B1 for a description of how governments could use this approach to measure individual BEPS Actions.

172. There are a limited number of other estimates of global fiscal effects of BEPS or the fiscal effects of BEPS for developing countries. A recent study[16] uses aggregate country data on investment through offshore investment centres and tax havens to estimate the fiscal effects for developing countries and globally. Several non-government organisations (NGOs) have published figures which are often multi-year estimates based on trade or total corporate tax numbers, but do not attempt to separate real economic activity from BEPS behaviours, and often include estimates of individual income tax evasion or non-compliance.

173. Given the many uncertainties associated with global estimates of the scale and economic impacts of BEPS, no single empirical estimate will be definitive, but such estimates are generally of more value for policymakers than extrapolating from more narrow studies involving a limited number of companies or countries. By laying out the approaches taken, the research can be further refined as improvements in available data and methodologies become available.

174. Table 3.3 shows the range of global estimates from a new OECD estimate of the global revenue loss from BEPS (described below), as well as from two other analyses. The estimates range from 4% to 10% of global CIT revenue for the global revenue loss, and from 7.5-14% of developing countries' CIT revenue. It should be noted that the UNCTAD estimates do not include the full effects of trade mispricing.[17]

Table 3.3. Estimates of global and developing country fiscal effects from BEPS

Fiscal estimate approach	Scope	Range USD (billions)	Year (level)
OECD aggregate tax rate differential	Global	100-240 (4-10% of CIT)	2014
Other Estimates			
IMF CIT efficiency 2014	Global	5% of CIT	
UNCTAD offshore investment matrix 2015	Global	200 (8% of CIT)*	2012
IMF CIT efficiency 2014	Developing countries	13% of CIT	
UNCTAD offshore investment matrix 2015	Developing countries	66-120 (7.5-14% of CIT)*	2012

* Only includes investment-related BEPS: not trade mispricing.

3.3.5 Global estimate of the revenue loss from BEPS

175. Annex 3.A1 presents a global estimate of the revenue loss from BEPS based on both an analysis of profit shifting due to tax rate differentials and an analysis of differences in effective tax rates between large MNE affiliates and comparable domestic companies reflecting mismatches between tax systems and tax preferences. The analysis is based on data from the ORBIS database of financial accounts from 2000 to 2010. The ORBIS database has the largest set of financial accounts, with the limitations described in Chapter 1.

176. The global revenue analysis starts with two key empirical findings. First, the analysis estimates the semi-elasticity of reported profits to tax rate differentials between unconsolidated affiliates' statutory headline tax rates and their MNE group average tax rate (taking the unweighted average of the other affiliates' statutory tax rate). The analysis extends prior analyses of the ORBIS database by taking into account ownership linkages, including linkages with affiliates that do not report financial information but have information on the affiliates' country of incorporation, so can include their statutory tax rate. This enables the inclusion of many low-tax rate country affiliates as part of the unweighted group average tax rate. The analysis finds a semi-elasticity of reported profits to the tax rate differential on average of about -1.0. The analysis is based on 1.2 million records between 2000 and 2010, although coverage is limited in a number of countries.

177. Second, the analysis estimates that average effective tax rates of large MNEs (with more than 250 employees) are on average 2½ to 5 percentage points lower than comparable entities in domestic-only (i.e. non-multinational) groups. This difference could be due to MNEs' ability to exploit mismatches between tax systems, such as hybrid mismatch arrangements, and a greater ability to take advantage of preferential tax treatment to reduce their tax liability, such as tax concessions to attract foreign direct

investment by MNEs. The analysis is based on 2.0 million records between 2000 and 2010. As a result of both profit shifting, mismatches between tax systems and relative use of domestic tax preferences, the ETR of large MNE entities is estimated to be lower on average by 4 to 8½ percentage points compared to similarly-situated domestic-only affiliates. This differential is even higher among very large firms and MNEs with patents.

178. A revenue loss estimate requires a number of important parameters and assumptions to extrapolate from one database to a global estimate. As the available data have limitations in representativeness and coverage in a number of countries, only a global estimate based on global parameters was produced. The revenue loss arises from two effects: profit shifting due to tax rate differentials and differences in average effective tax rates for large affiliates due to mismatches between tax systems and tax preferences. The combination of the two effects results in estimates of the net[18] global corporate tax revenues lost from BEPS at 4-10% of corporate tax revenues, or USD 100-240 billion at 2014 levels. These estimates are based on the specific database, methodology and assumptions used as described below and in more detail in Annex 3.A1.

179. The estimate of profit shifting is calculated on the following equation:

$$\begin{aligned}&CIT\ revenues\ lost\ from\ profit\ shifting\\&= A\ worldwide\ responsiveness\ of\ profit\text{-}to\text{-}asset\ ratio\ to\ tax\ rate\ differentials\\&\times average\ asset/profit\ ratio \times average\ tax\ rate\ differential\\&\times MNEs'\ average\ share\ of\ total\ profits \times estimated\ global\ CIT\ revenue\end{aligned}$$

180. The key parameters used are the responsiveness of the profit-to-asset ratio to tax rate differentials estimated from the ORBIS database with a particular regression specification for profitable entities (-0.1); the average profit-to-asset ratio (6.2%) from ORBIS data; an average tax rate differential between affiliates (3.6%) from ORBIS data; MNEs' share of profits (59%) with the ORBIS data and supplemented with aggregate tax return tabulations for several countries; tax credits as percent of before-credit corporate tax collections (19%) from an OECD survey[19]; and an estimate of USD 2.3 trillion of after-credit corporate tax collections in 2014, adjusted for expected growth from 2011.

181. The estimate is based on a number of assumptions. The estimated semi-elasticities of reported profits to tax rate differentials of -1.0 for all MNE entities and -1.6 for profitable MNE entities is assumed to be the same for the MNEs outside the ORBIS sample as the MNEs in the sample; the tax variable is assumed to accurately capture profit shifting, based on the specification of the regression and the variables used; tax revenue changes are assumed to be proportional to the amount of profit shifting; non-corporate businesses are assumed not to be engaged in BEPS; ORBIS relationships for tax rate differentials and asset/profit ratio are assumed to be the same for MNEs outside the ORBIS sample as the MNEs in the sample; differences in any of these relationships across countries are assumed to not significantly affect the global estimate; and the average profit shifting response to tax rate differentials between 2000 and 2010 is assumed to be the same for 2014.

182. The estimate of the mismatches between tax systems and the relative use of domestic tax preferences is calculated by the following equation:

CIT revenue lost from MNE mismatches between tax systems and preferential tax treatment = Average ETR difference between large MNE entities and comparable domestic entities ×MNEs' share of total profits × Share of large MNEs × estimated global CIT revenues

183. The key variables different from the profit shifting equation are the average ETR difference between large MNE entities and comparable domestic entities estimated from the ORBIS database with a particular regression specification (3.25%) and the share of large MNEs as a percentage of all MNEs in the ORBIS sample (93%).

184. The estimate is based on some additional assumptions. The estimate of a ETR differential between large MNEs and comparable domestic entities is assumed to be the same for the MNEs outside the ORBIS sample as the MNEs in the sample; the differential tax rate variable is assumed to not include non-BEPS tax preferences available to both MNEs and domestic companies; tax revenue changes are assumed to be proportional to the amount of the estimated ETR differential; and the average ETR difference between 2000 and 2010 is assumed to be the same for 2014.

185. Some factors may lead to an underestimation of the revenue loss (e.g. missing entities engaged in significant BEPS, different weighting in estimation[20]), while other factors may lead to an overestimate (e.g. not controlling for country-fixed effects[21]). Recognising these uncertainties, a range of the global revenue estimates is presented. The range from 4% to 10% of CIT revenues takes into account a 95% confidence interval around the tax sensitivity estimates[22] and the upper bound assumes that firms outside the sample have a 50% higher tax planning intensity than firms in the sample. The coverage rate of ORBIS with the OECD STAN Business Demography Statistics was an average 32%, weighted by corporate tax collections.

3.3.6 Some other fiscal estimate studies

186. As described earlier, three other studies have estimated the fiscal effects of BEPS on a global basis and also for developing countries, while other studies have estimated the fiscal effects for different groups of countries. Their results were included in Table 3.3 and are briefly described in Box 3.4.

187. Individual countries have made government fiscal estimates of prior legislation enacting unilateral BEPS countermeasures. In most cases, the fiscal estimates are ex ante estimates made at the time of the legislative enactment, rather than ex post analyses of the enacted legislation, and may not include behavioural effects. In several countries, recent limitations on excessive interest deductions were estimated to increase corporate income tax revenues by 3-9 percent.

188. A number of countries do not estimate the fiscal effects of "base protection" measures, since they are intended to preserve existing revenue rather than to increase revenue above prior projections. This is another example of the key issue of what the "counterfactual" comparison should be. If the BEPS-type countermeasure is not enacted, then the revenue base would not be protected and revenue would decline. Once the projected revenue is reduced for the uncorrected BEPS problem, then countermeasure legislation would result in higher revenue. Under either scenario, BEPS countermeasures are important for ensuring corporations reduce their BEPS-related tax planning activities through artificial arrangements which separate taxable income from where the value is created.

189. Academic researchers have general chosen not to extend their estimates of the profit shifting responses to producing fiscal estimates. Bach (2103), Clausing (2009) and Vicard (2015) are exceptions that have taken the additional steps to extend empirical estimates of elasticities to the magnitude of revenue foregone by governments.

Box 3.4. Other empirical analyses of BEPS fiscal effects

International Monetary Fund. The IMF in 2014 as part of their Spillover of International Taxation report estimated the spillover effects of profit shifting, and reports an unweighted average revenue loss across all countries in the sample of 5 percent of current CIT revenue, but almost 13 percent in the non-OECD countries.[23] The calculation is based on differences in countries' corporate income tax efficiency ratio (i.e. a country's estimated tax base relative to a measure of capital income from national accounts) compared to the average ratio in the sample countries. The analysis assumes that all of the variation in cross-country CIT efficiency ratios is attributable to profit shifting. The estimate does not separate non-BEPS tax incentives or adjust for differences in compliance or enforcement, nor does it include tax haven countries. Counterintuitively, the calculation estimates that the United States is a beneficiary of corporate income tax profit shifting.

UNCTAD. In the World Investment Report 2015, UNCTAD estimates the revenue losses for developing countries due to profit shifting range from USD 66 billion to USD 122 billion in 2012. The rate of return on FDI is estimated to be 1-1.5 percentage points lower for each 10% share of inward investment stock originating from offshore investment hubs and tax havens. The report cites the "massive and still growing use of offshore investment hubs by MNEs." The estimated shifted profits from offshore investment hubs multiplied by an average tax rate provide an estimate of potential revenue loss. The shifted profits are estimated to be around 50% of the currently reported profits of MNEs.[24] When extending the analysis to all countries, the estimated revenue loss is USD 200 billion, or approximately 10% of current CIT revenue. The report notes that the estimated revenue losses are mostly confined to those associated with tax avoidance schemes that have a direct investment relationship, and states that "Trace mispricing does not require a direct investment link." The results do not include several key BEPS channels.

United States Congressional Joint Committee on Taxation (JCT). The JCT in modelling a major United States tax reform proposal calibrated their dynamic general equilibrium model for corporate profit shifting. They set the level of current profit shifting at approximately 20% of the corporate tax base in 2013, 'consistent with the middle point of estimates of this shifting under present law."[25] Since tax collections are not proportional to the tax base due to tax credits, the effect on corporate taxes would be larger than the 20% or USD 70 billion.

United States JCT economists. Using United States tax returns for foreign affiliates of United States parents, the analysis not only estimated the tax responsiveness of profit shifting to tax rates, but also did a simulation of the effects on reported profits if six countries with low tax rates increased their rates to 17%.[26] The study estimates that over USD 110 billion of reported profits would no longer be reported in those six low tax countries as a result of reduce profit shifting by United States affiliates in these countries.

MSCI. MSCI updated an analysis of the largest global companies and the difference between their reported taxes and an estimate of the tax liability based on where they generate revenues.[27] The report found that 22% of the companies had effective tax rates 10 percentage points below the weighted average statutory tax rate of the countries in which they generate revenues. Between 2009 and 2013, the analysis estimates that just 243 companies paid USD 82 billion annually less taxes that "their peers on the MSCI World Index" and also below the average statutory tax rate of the countries in which they generate revenues. The analysis did not attempt to separate non-BEPS tax incentives which reduce companies' ETRs, and the analysis uses sales to allocate financial report income between countries.

Box 3.4. Other empirical analyses of BEPS fiscal effects *(continued)*

Christian Aid. In 2009, Christian Aid estimated that trade mispricing in non-EU countries reduced tax revenues by USD 122 billion per year.[28] Trade mispricing is defined to include mispricing between both MNEs and unrelated parties that shifts income out of developing countries. The estimate is based on bilateral trade data, at the product level, for the EU countries and the United States Mispricing is calculated using reported prices that fall outside of the inter-quartile range (assumed to represent arm's length prices) in the data. These price differences are summed for exports and imports from and to developing countries to estimate the capital (income) shifting from non-EU countries to EU countries and the United States. The CIT revenue loss for developing countries is calculated using the top marginal tax rate. The analysis does not include any adjustments for possible quality differences in bilateral product trades and does not incorporate information on special tax rates that may apply in developing countries on specific activities. The analysis does not include mispricing between EU countries and the United States that could be shifting income into a developing country in response to tax rate differentials. The analysis does not separate developing country revenue loss estimates for trade among MNE entities, the type of mispricing classified as BEPS.

Oxfam. Oxfam estimates that African countries lost USD 11 billion in CIT tax revenue in 2010 due to trade mispricing.[29] The estimate, which is based on a study by the High Level Panel on Illicit Financial Flows, found MNEs were responsible for around USD 40 billion of trade mispricing in Africa. Trade mispricing is not only due to tax avoidance, but also tax evasion, avoiding customs duties, or money laundering.

Bach: A 2013 German business income study compares the German corporate income tax base derived from the national accounts with the tax base reported in the tax statistics to provide an estimate of the possible erosion of the corporate income tax base.[30] The study makes a number of detailed adjustments in the national accounts profit figures to derive a modified corporate income base. The modifications reflect the institutional details of the German business income tax system, as well as the differences between corporate tax and national accounts concepts. The study calculates the difference between the tax base measure reported in the tax statistics and the modified national account tax base to examine possible tax base erosion. For taxpayers with positive income, the comparison suggests that the tax statistics base is 21% lower than the corresponding national accounts income. The author is careful to point out that the measured difference in the tax bases cannot be interpreted as largely due to BEPS behaviours. Additional analysis using empirical studies of BEPS and country-specific information on trade, interest and balance of payments flows is needed to determine what percentage of the tax base difference is related to international profit shifting.

Clausing. A regression analysis is used to estimate the semi-elasticity (responsiveness) of gross profits reported by United States MNE entities in foreign countries to effective tax rate differentials between foreign affiliates and their United States parent, based on survey data on foreign activities of United States MNEs aggregated at the country level.[31] The estimated semi-elasticity (-3.3) is used to eliminate the influence of the tax rate differential on overseas profitability. The difference in reported and adjusted profitability is assumed to be the effect on overseas profits due to profit shifting. A portion of this change is attributed to the United States using estimates of United States and foreign activities of the MNEs. Multiplying the resulting change by an effective United States tax rate produces a "best estimate" USD 90 billion lost from profit shifting from United States MNEs in 2008, which represents 30% of United States federal corporate income tax collections. A lower bound estimate, using a different data series, found a USD 57 billion loss, or 19% of CIT revenues.

Box 3.4. Other empirical analyses of BEPS fiscal effects *(continued)*

Vicard. The study estimates profit shifting through transfer pricing for French MNEs.[32] Firm-level export and import data from customs trade data, combined with ownership information for MNE entities, is used to estimate intra-firm trade and price differentials between transactions between related affiliates and unrelated parties. The estimates are done by product and destination country. A regression analysis explaining these price differentials finds that a one percentage point increase in the relative statutory tax rate in France reduces (increases) relative export (import) prices to related parties by 0.22% (0.24%). Based on these semi-elasticity values, the study estimates that mispricing of MNE trade with related parties reduced French CIT payments of these MNEs by an average of 10%, or USD 8 billion in 2008. The study also finds that the lost revenue has increased over time as the tax rate differential has widened.

3.3.7 The extent of BEPS behaviours and possible dynamic effects if not curtailed

190. Another dimension to the scale of BEPS is the question of "How widespread is BEPS activity among corporations?" A number of studies have found evidence that profit shifting is widespread across the corporate MNE sector, but several recent papers (Davies et al., 2014; Egger et al., 2014) report significant BEPS behaviours by a limited number of large MNEs with affiliates in a small number of jurisdictions. The answer to this question has implications for the design of BEPS countermeasures. More research is needed in this area.

191. Another aspect is the dynamic nature of BEPS. Even if BEPS is not widespread now, it could become much more widespread if nothing is done on an internationally-co-ordinated basis. Competitive pressures through pricing and acquisitions give MNEs using BEPS an advantage in lower costs to take market share from companies or acquire companies that do not use BEPS to lower their costs. As seen recently in the case of corporate inversions, a significant change in corporate tax behaviour minimising taxes can occur suddenly even when legal arrangements under current law had existed for years.

3.3.8 Effects of BEPS countermeasures

192. A number of empirical studies are focusing on individual BEPS issues and the effects of existing BEPS countermeasures. These studies often provide some insight into the scale of the particular BEPS channel, but also the effects of current or proposed BEPS countermeasures. The existing countermeasures are unilateral, individual country, anti-avoidance rules, which would have different effects than a uniform multilateral countermeasure.

193. It is important in assessing the effectiveness of the BEPS countermeasures (described below) to take into account the level of enforcement. Some countries may choose not to enforce certain regulatory rules strongly for tax competitiveness reasons. Other countries may not have the resources or capacity to fully enforce their existing laws and regulations.[33]

Neutralising the effects of hybrid mismatch arrangements (Action 2)

194. Hybrid mismatch arrangements have been discussed descriptively in a number of papers, but have not been empirically estimated. Grubert (2012) attempted to evaluate the effect of check-the-box and hybrid structures on foreign effective tax rates. The hybrid variable was based on whether a CFC owned a disregarded entity or not. Several countries have estimated the effects of proposed legislation addressing hybrids, although the estimates are relatively small due to behavioural effects of shifting activity to other tax minimisation strategies. The OECD analysis in Annex 3.A1 finds that affiliates of large MNEs have average effective tax rates 2½ to 5 percentage points lower than similarly situated affiliates of domestic-only groups in the same country, which could be partially attributable to hybrid mismatch arrangements. The analysis does not find statistically significant different effective tax rates between small (defined as affiliates with less than 250 employees) MNEs and similar small domestic affiliates.

Strengthening CFC rules (Action 3)

195. Two recent empirical studies examine the effect of consolidated foreign company tax rules on MNE behaviour.

196. Ruf and Weichenrieder (2013) use the German Micro-database Direct Investment (MiDi) data on German MNEs to investigate the effect of the change of Germany's CFC legislation in response to a decision by the European Court of Justice (ECJ). The ECJ ruled that German CFC legislation infringed on the freedom of establishment within the European Union, and thus could not be applied to CFCs in EU countries. The analysis found that after the liberalising CFC legislation, passive investments in low-tax European countries increased compared to low-tax non-European countries, signalling that the prior CFC rules limited shifting of passive investments of German MNEs.

197. Markle and Robinson (2012a) investigate whether CFC rules, bilateral tax treaties and withholding taxes affect the tax behaviour of MNEs. Using ORBIS and COMPUSTAT data, they find that CFC legislation as well as other measures reduces the activity of affiliates in "tax haven" countries. Markle and Robinson (2012b) find 44 percent of the 7,600 MNEs in their global sample have a tax haven subsidiary. They find that the existence and scope of CFC rules is associated with lower tax haven use in those countries.

Limit base erosion via interest deductions (Action 4)

198. Several studies have found that MNEs' strategic placement of debt and the associated interest deductions are sensitive to tax differentials and tax interest limitations.

199. Desai, Foley and Hines (2004) use United States Bureau of Economic Analysis investment survey data to identify the determinants of the capital structure of foreign affiliates of United States MNEs. They find that higher tax rates increase the use of both external and internal debt for United States foreign affiliates, with a more intense effect on internal debt. They control for a credit market imperfection proxy, as companies might increase their internal debt to total debt ratio, not only with the objective of shifting profit through interest expenses, but also in order to overcome credit market imperfections. They find that companies in countries with a less developed credit market borrow relatively more from related parties (in particular from parent companies). They find that "Ten percent higher local tax rates are associated with 2.8% higher debt/asset ratios, with

internal borrowing being particularly sensitive to taxes". Using German firm-level data, Moen et al. (2011) find evidence of both internal and external debt shifting and estimate that they are of about equal relevance.

200. Huizinga, Laeven and Nicodème (2008) use the European Amadeus database to test whether differences in taxation among countries have a statistically significant effect on the firm's capital structure and on internal debt. They include both marginal effective tax rates and an indicator of the tax incentive to shift debt (calculated as the sum of international tax differences weighted by local assets), and find a statistically significant effect on firm's leverage, indicating that debt shifting might occur, not only between parent and subsidiaries, but also among foreign subsidiaries. They find "an increase of the effective tax rate by 0.06 in the subsidiary country has a positive 'international' effect on leverage in the subsidiary country of 0.4%".

201. Weichenrieder (2015) describes the growing literature on rules limiting the deductibility of interest, including studies of German inbound FDI (Weichenrieder & Windischbauer (2008) and Overesch & Wamser (2010)); German outbound FDI (Buettner et al. (2012)), and United States outbound FDI (Blouin et al. (2014)). Two papers evaluated the German interest barrier rule introduced in 2008, which limits the deductibility of interest generally to 30% of EBITDA. Using the DAFNE database for German companies, Buslei and Simmler (2012) consider how the rule affected firms' capital structure, investment and profitability. The results show a strong behavioural response by firms to avoid the limited deductibility of interest expenses, successfully broadening the tax base in the short-term. Affected firms decreased their debt-to-assets ratios and there was no evidence of a negative (short-term) effect on investment. Dreßler and Scheuering (2012) analysed how German firms subject to the interest barrier rule adjusted their debt-to-assets ratios and their net interest payments compared to a control group. Their analysis shows that the interest barrier resulted in firms lowering their debt-to-assets ratios and their net interest payments, but principally by reducing external debt rather than related party debt.

202. The OECD analysis in Annex 3.A1 finds evidence of strategic placement of external (third-party) debt in MNE consolidated groups due to tax rate differentials within the group. A one percentage point higher statutory corporate tax rate of an affiliate than the average in the MNE group is associated with a 1.3% higher external debt/equity ratio for that affiliate. The analysis does not include the location of intra-group debt.

Prevent treaty abuse (Action 6)

203. Empirical analyses of tax treaty issues are limited and often are included with other BEPS behaviours or are specific to particular countries. One recent simulation analysis, Van't Reit and Lejour (2014), shows the potential reduction in withholding taxes due to treaty shopping, but the analysis is not based on actual taxpayer behaviour.

204. The analysis examines bilateral tax rates on cross-border dividends between 108 countries (3,244 country pairs) and shows that indirect routes (treaty shopping) are cheaper than direct routes for 67% of the country pairs. 21% of the country pairs have a zero effective tax rate without treaty shopping, but 54% when treaty shopping is possible. Treaty shopping is estimated to reduce the withholding effective tax rate by more than 5 percentage points from nearly 8% to 3%. A simulated removal of tax havens from any double tax relief (other than foreign tax credit) shows an increase in the world average effective withholding tax rate by 0.14 percentage points.

Assure that transfer pricing outcomes are in line with value creation (Actions 8-10)

205. Transfer pricing has been identified as a major BEPS issue with four actions identified in the BEPS Action Plan specifically dedicated to addressing BEPS through this channel. Transfer pricing, particularly through the shifting of intangible assets, is discussed in the general BEPS analyses. Four key studies focus specifically on transfer pricing.

206. Clausing (2003) investigates the effect of host country statutory and effective tax rates on inter-company trade in goods. Using data on intra-firm transactions from the United States Bureau of Labor Statistics, the analysis finds that low foreign statutory tax rates are correlated with lower export prices and higher import prices relative to third-party transactions. The analysis finds a "tax rate 1% lower in the country of destination/origin is associated with intra-firm export prices that are 1.8% lower and intra-firm import prices that are 2.0% higher, relative to non-intra-firm goods". Several other studies using price-based comparisons of related-party and third-party imports and exports show significant tax effects, including a recent study of French 1999 trade data by Davies et al. (2014).

207. Grubert (2003) analysing data from United States MNEs' tax returns for United States MNEs finds that United States controlled foreign corporations (CFCs) located in countries with relatively low and relatively high statutory CIT rates engage in significantly greater volumes of inter-affiliate transactions. This is consistent with BEPS related activity. The analysis finds that R&D intensive companies engage in greater volumes of such intra-company trade.

208. Mutti and Grubert (2009) analyse United States MNEs' tax return data to investigate whether the United States "check-the-box" regulation has encouraged the relocation of intangible assets abroad. They provide evidence of a substantial migration of intangible assets abroad, in particular to low tax countries through hybrid entities and cost-sharing agreements. Moreover, descriptive statistics show that royalty payments among foreign affiliates increased sharply in the period considered, from entities in high-tax countries to entities in low-tax countries.

209. Karkinsky and Riedel (2012) focus on the effect of statutory tax rates and other tax-related variables (such as binding CFC rules and withholding tax on royalties) on the number of MNEs' patent applications. They build a unique dataset of European firms merging Amadeus financial statement database with PATSTAT information. They find that low tax rates increase the probability that the firm applies for a patent in low-tax locations. This result is similar to a study by Griffith, Miller and O'Connell (2011).

210. The OECD analysis in Annex 3.A1 finds that the tax sensitivity of profit shifting is almost twice as large among MNE groups with patents as for non-patenting MNE groups, controlling for a number of factors affecting firms' profitability. A separate analysis, which uses combination of data on patents from PATSTAT and firm characteristics from ORBIS financial account data, suggests that preferential tax treatment of patents increases both patents invested in other countries as well as R&D activities.

Benefits of better disclosure (Actions 5, 11, 12 and 13)

211. Hoopes (2015) provides a survey of a number of studies that have analysed the effects of disclosure issues. A paper by Dyreng, Hoopes and Wilde (2014) finds empirical

evidence suggesting that U.K. public companies decreased tax avoidance and reduced the use of subsidiaries in tax haven countries when there was increased public disclosure. Several studies (Lohse et al., 2012; Lohse and Riedel, 2012; Annex 3.A1) find empirical evidence of reduced profit shifting from tougher transfer pricing documentation rules. Increased transparency of government tax rules (Action 5) will reduce a non-tax rate competition, with greater disclosure of government rulings involving potential base erosion.

212. Announcements of future legislative changes can affect corporate taxpayer behaviours even before specific legislative measures have been enacted. Some corporations are already changing their international tax structures due to the progress of the BEPS Project and expected changes by governments.[34]

3.3.9 Impact of existing unilateral BEPS-related countermeasures

213. Several academic studies find that anti-avoidance countermeasures have reduced profit shifting through transfer pricing documentation (Lohse and Riedel, 2012) and interest limitations (Blouin et al., 2014). These studies show positive effects of current law unilateral measures, which could be shifting BEPS behaviours away from the countries with anti-avoidance rules to countries without the anti-avoidance rules. The OECD analysis in Annex 3.A1 combines four anti-avoidance measures (different levels of transfer pricing documentation, different levels of interest limitations, the presence of controlled foreign corporate (CFC) rules, and the presence of general anti-avoidance rules (GAAR)), as well as the level of withholding taxes (taking into account tax treaties), in a single metric. The analysis uses the metric in 2005 for an analysis of profit shifting across OECD and G20 economies over the 2000-2010 period and finds that profit shifting is negatively correlated with the metric. These analyses suggest that countries with higher statutory tax rates do not necessarily have higher fiscal losses from BEPS if they have strict anti-avoidance measures.

3.3.10 Economic impacts of BEPS and BEPS countermeasures

214. The scale of BEPS, in terms of the fiscal effects on government revenues, is important, but there are other economic effects of BEPS. The scale of the fiscal effects is an important intermediate input to the analysis of the other economic effects. Changes in corporate income taxes due to BEPS behaviours and countermeasures result in real economic effects, including effects on the incidence (or economic burden) of taxes, debt bias and strategic location of debt, differential taxation of companies, investment and economic growth, and tax competition between countries (spillover effects).

3.3.11 Important considerations in the economic analysis of BEPS and BEPS countermeasures

215. By definition, BEPS behaviours involve artificial shifting of taxable income from the location where the activities creating those profits takes place, and when the interaction of different tax rules leads to double non-taxation or less than single taxation. In some cases, MNEs may undertake minimal economic activity as part of artificial arrangements that shift profits away from where the value is created simply to claim tax benefits under current national tax rules.

216. Addressing BEPS will increase effective tax rates of tax aggressive MNEs, which can have economic effects on the location of economic activity. Effective tax rates of those companies will be closer to countries' statutory corporate tax rates when BEPS

countermeasures are implemented. Differences in countries' statutory and effective corporate tax rates will continue to exist after the BEPS Project, but they will not be reduced due to artificial BEPS arrangements. When evaluating the economic effects of BEPS, several important issues need to be factored into any analysis.

217. First, the economic effects of unilateral tax policy changes by an individual country are very different from the economic effects of internationally co-ordinated multilateral changes, such as those proposed under the BEPS Action Plan. If all countries (or the vast majority of countries where real economic activity takes place) adopt similar countermeasures, then MNEs will not be able to change the location of their BEPS-related activities to avoid them. Currently, if one country were to adopt tough BEPS countermeasures, then MNEs could move their activities to continue BEPS behaviours elsewhere.

218. Second, economic analyses of BEPS countermeasures should be considered in a budget-neutral context. For purposes of a budget-neutral analysis, any potential additional tax revenues from BEPS countermeasures could be assumed to lower taxes on other economic actors or be used to invest in public infrastructure or services. Any tax increase will have some adverse effects, but BEPS is a structural, not a macroeconomic, tax policy change: BEPS countermeasures are designed to close unintended loopholes, not to change GDP. Adverse effects from companies experiencing tax increases could be offset by positive effects from companies, investors, and consumers experiencing tax decreases or benefits from increased public infrastructure or services. Budget-neutral assumptions are used in many tax policy analyses to isolate structural tax effects. Similarly, the effect on one group of businesses is only part of the overall effect, since other businesses and households will benefit when BEPS is corrected.

219. Third, the effects of BEPS countermeasures are different than changes in corporate tax rates or other general tax changes. Increasing corporate income taxation by ending artificial schemes by a "self-selecting" group of tax aggressive MNEs is not necessarily adverse to economic growth since it would reduce differential taxation across businesses and eliminate tax-induced competitive advantages. Individual MNEs' abilities to achieve significant corporate tax reductions due to BEPS behaviours distorts a number of resource allocation margins, and shifts talent to tax planning rather than more productive activities.[35] Depending on market conditions, much of the tax benefits from BEPS behaviours for many companies may simply be a product of "rent-seeking", rather than a reduction in the marginal cost of investment capital.[36]

220. Fourth, the prevalence of BEPS behaviours among MNEs will affect the degree and types of distortions caused by BEPS. The MNE sector is heterogeneous, and is also likely to be with respect to engaging in BEPS. If BEPS is engaged in by most MNEs, the economic effects will be more widespread than if BEPS is principally concentrated and most intensively used by a small group of MNEs or in particular industries. The economic effects of BEPS, if limited to a select group of MNEs versus being more prevalent, will cause additional distortions between companies (even within the MNE sector), across industries, and across types of investment. Distortions from tax rate differentials are often ranked by the ease of responding to tax rate differentials: tax planning taking into account timing issues such as around fiscal years or tax rate changes is easiest, followed by tax planning involving financial accounting and mobility of legal contracts (which includes BEPS), then mobility across jurisdictions of real economic activity, and the most difficult changes are in the level of total economic activity.[37] Shifting profits is much easier than shifting or increasing real economic activity.

221. Fifth, economic analyses and estimates of BEPS and BEPS countermeasures are subject to significant uncertainty, given the difficulty of disentangling BEPS activity from MNEs' real economic activity and non-BEPS tax preferences, plus the significant limitations of currently available data. Multiple approaches finding large magnitudes provide greater certainty of the general scale of BEPS than individual studies using one methodology and relying upon a single data source. Any statistical estimate has a range of error given the sample used and the unexplained variance of the underlying economic activity. Extrapolation beyond the sample from which an analysis is conducted is a further source of bias since it is not known whether the missing companies have the same behaviours as the included companies.

222. Sixth, although the incidence of corporate taxes is still widely debated, most analyses conclude that corporate income tax falls on both capital and labour, varying in the degree of capital mobility, openness of the economy, and the extent to which the corporations are earning competitive returns or economic rents.[38] Since BEPS is not a general CIT rate reduction, but a self-selected tax reduction of some MNEs, the burden of BEPS countermeasures would not be the same as the burden of a general corporate tax policy change. Not all of the corporate tax increase on MNEs engaging in BEPS will affect their investment decisions, since some could fall on economic rents or be passed forward or backward to other economic actors.

223. Seventh, it is important to account for taxpayer behaviours. If the BEPS countermeasures are not adopted by most countries or if there are other tax avoidance mechanisms not addressed by the BEPS countermeasures with which MNEs could avail themselves, then the positive gains from the BEPS Project would be reduced. If BEPS is reduced, tax rate differentials for some MNEs could increase resulting in shifts of real economic activity, plus tax competition affecting real economic activity could increase. Additional economic research on the mobility of real economic activity (research and expenditure, physical investment, employees) is needed, since current measures of mobility are often on the mobility of income, which reflects significant BEPS behaviours.

224. Finally, a comprehensive analysis of the economic impacts of BEPS countermeasures would also include an evaluation of the net change in the taxpayer compliance costs, the effectiveness of tax administration enforcement. The analysis would identify any unintended double taxation from inconsistent implementation of tax treaties and improvements in dispute resolution through the mutual agreement procedure.

225. The global fiscal and economic impacts of BEPS and BEPS countermeasures are important, and initial estimates based on currently available data, tools and methodologies are helpful to policymakers. While current modelling of BEPS and countermeasures is not done comprehensively or with a full general-equilibrium model due to data and conceptual limitations, the economic impact analyses show BEPS distorts many business decisions. Analyses by each country's tax policy and statistical offices using more detailed information about their economies and tax systems will be necessary to fully assess the effects of the BEPS Action Plan on individual countries.

3.3.12 Expected incidence of CIT changes in response to BEPS countermeasures

226. The economic effects of BEPS and BEPS countermeasures will depend on the difference in the distribution of income tax burdens with current BEPS behaviours and after the potential BEPS countermeasures are adopted. This analysis focuses on the change in tax burdens due to the potential BEPS countermeasures.

227. Tax incidence analysis is designed to determine who bears the burden of a tax. The burden of a tax is defined to be the ultimate resting point of the tax after recognising any tax shifting that might occur after the tax is imposed. Tax shifting is the process by which taxpayers bearing the legal responsibility for paying the tax ("legal incidence") alter their behaviour and, as a result, shift the burden of the tax to other parties (e.g. consumers, workers and capital owners) through changes in output or input prices. The final resting point for a tax is the "economic incidence" of the tax. Thus, the economic incidence or burden of a tax can be very different than the initial legal incidence of the tax.[39]

228. The extent of tax shifting from BEPS countermeasures will depend on a number of factors, including how the additional tax revenues from the BEPS countermeasures are used by the government: which taxes are changed, what type of spending is changed, and/or the extent to which governments' budget balances are changed. The extent of tax shifting also depends on the market conditions faced by MNEs engaging in BEPS: how sensitive consumers are to price changes, the presence of competition, and how responsive the supply of labour and capital are to changes in compensation and the return on investment.[40]

229. There are several assumptions used in this analysis to identify the economic incidence of changes in global corporate income taxes as a result of the implementation of the BEPS countermeasures. Any analysis of the economic incidence of BEPS countermeasures requires making assumptions about these issues.

- All countries adopt the recommended BEPS countermeasure. If a significant amount of economic activity is not subject to the countermeasure, then the conclusions would be different. This is consistent with a longer-run perspective on the incidence of the tax changes.
- Capital is mobile across industries within a country and between countries in the medium term (3-10 years), while labour is less mobile.
- The impact on global economic activity from the implementation of the BEPS countermeasures will depend primarily upon the average worldwide change in total CIT collections and the global after-tax rate of return on capital investment.
- The impact on economic activity in any single country will depend on how the after-tax rate of return in the country initially changes relative to the worldwide after-tax rate of return as a result of the BEPS countermeasures.
- Countries' CIT rates remain constant.

230. Based on the fiscal impact estimates of the impact of the BEPS countermeasures, there will be a net worldwide increase in corporate income tax collections. However, while most countries will have higher corporate tax collections from the BEPS countermeasures, some countries could experience decreases in CIT collections as a result of BEPS countermeasures that align taxable income with the location where the economic activity generating that income is located. Given the global net CIT tax increase, the following discussion describes the tax shifting process in terms of where the burden of any additional taxes collected will fall.

231. In the short run, the net increase in CIT revenues will lower the after-tax rate of return on capital investments of the firms currently engaging in BEPS behaviours. An important question relates to the extent to which capital would be reallocated in response

to reducing BEPS and its effect on the after-tax rate of return of companies that have been engaging in BEPS. The answer depends upon the extent to which BEPS behaviours have increased their after-tax rates of return (relative to what they would be without BEPS), as well as the market conditions in which they operate.

232. MNEs that have used BEPS to reduce their CIT revenues have been able to reduce, on average, effective tax rates in those countries (most often in countries with weak anti-avoidance rules and above-average statutory or effective tax rates). While MNEs take these ETRs into consideration when making initial location investment decisions, BEPS can result in increases in the after-tax rates of return of those companies without necessarily increasing the level of their existing capital investments. OECD research presented in Annex 3.A1 finds in industries with a high concentration of MNEs with affiliates in no-tax countries the responsiveness of investment to tax rates is less than other firms' investments. This is because tax-planning MNEs can achieve lower taxes through artificial arrangements without changing the location of the value-creation and real economic activity. With BEPS countermeasures, the availability of this form of "do-it-yourself" tax relief will be substantially reduced. As a result, the after-tax rates of return of those companies will be reduced.

233. If after-tax rates of return are reduced of companies engaging in BEPS in some countries as a result of the BEPS countermeasures, what will be the impact on real investment and economic activities in those industries and those countries? The answer to this question is complicated, and depends, to a significant degree, on whether the affected MNEs are operating in competitive or imperfect markets and on the time horizon for the analysis.

234. If the MNEs paying higher taxes are operating in competitive markets (i.e. earning just the required rate of return on their capital at the margin, which means zero economic rent), the standard CIT incidence analysis would predict that in the long run they will reallocate capital from the high-tax industries and countries with lower after-tax rates of return to other industries and countries that now offer higher after-tax rates of return. In the process there will be less real economic activity in the relatively high-tax industries and countries and more real economic activity in the lower-tax industries and countries. The shifting process will end when the after-tax rate of return is equalized at the new, lower after-tax rate of return on all worldwide capital that reflects the higher global CIT tax "wedge" due to the net increase in global CIT taxes from implementing the BEPS countermeasures.

235. In the competitive market case, in the long run after sufficient time for real capital to be reallocated, the expected impact of the higher global CIT is:

- Capital owners will bear most of the burden of the average global *net* tax increase due to the adoption of BEPS countermeasures. In the adjustment process, capital may be reallocated across industries and countries with associated impacts on consumer prices and labour compensation. However, the burden of the overall net increase will be borne by capital owners located in all countries and all industries because reallocations of capital cannot avoid this incremental burden.[41] To the extent the increase in corporate tax reduces the after-tax rate of return to all capital, a lower return to saving and investment in the long run could reduce overall global capital investment and thus the productivity of labour with some proportion shifted to labour in the form of lower wages.

- Industries and countries with above-average corporate income tax increases may experience lower levels of capital investment needed to offset any reduction in the after-tax rates of returns that exceed the worldwide average reduction.
- The burden of this differential CIT increase will be borne primarily by labour through wages, consumers through higher prices for goods and services due to the reduction in the industries' or countries' capital stock and level of production, and capital owners of land.
- Industries and countries with below-average CIT increases may experience higher levels of capital investment as they gain capital relative to the industries and countries with above average CIT increases. Labour in those industries and countries will benefit from higher wages and lower consumer prices for goods and services as the capital stock and output is expanded.[42]

236. There are several reasons why the theoretical incidence analysis of BEPS countermeasures may overstate the potential real economic impacts over the medium term.

- The simplified, theoretical tax incidence model assumes the time horizon is long enough to allow the reallocation of real capital across borders. In fact, it takes many years for the reallocation of real economic resources to occur across industries or countries. Capital mobility is high when capital is measured in terms of legal contracts or ownership claims, but capital mobility is much lower and slower when it involves actual geographic relocation of research scientists and physical capital. Tax incidence models have little to say about the dynamics of the adjustment process over time, and measures of the speed of mobility of real capital and specialised labour between countries are lacking in the empirical literature. In the transition to reallocation, the capital owners who previously benefited from the lower effective tax rates achieved by BEPS behaviours in countries will bear the burden of the CIT increase. In other words, while the elasticity of investment to changes in after-tax rates of return increases the longer the time period, there is limited empirical evidence on how the elasticity changes over time.
- Many MNEs engaging in BEPS do not operate in perfectly competitive markets. An important reason for this is the increasing importance of the contribution of intangible property to MNE net income.[43] Unique intangible capital, not only intellectual property but also brands and economic competencies, can generate excess economic returns over a long period of time.[44] Due to these excess returns to capital, MNEs facing lower after-tax rates of return may still be earning more than the next-best alternative investment after the adoption of the BEPS countermeasures. Thus, the tax increases from BEPS countermeasures may have little or no effect on those companies' marginal investment decisions.[45]
- If MNEs are earning excess economic returns, there will be minimal reallocation of real investments in response to the BEPS countermeasures.[46] As a result, there would be little shifting of the burden to consumers or labour. In this specific case, capital would bear almost all of burden of the tax on

economic rents over a long period of time and there would be no significant reallocation of capital among countries.

237. Economic incidence, particularly of the CIT in a global economy, is still an unresolved issue for economists. The economic incidence of unilateral measures increasing the cost of capital for business in one country relative to other countries with mobile capital in competitive markets would fall on the fixed factors. The economic incidence analysis of co-ordinated, multilateral BEPS countermeasures in the presence of imperfect competition, however, may lead to significantly different conclusions compared to the analysis of unilateral measures in competitive markets.

3.3.13 Economic efficiency and growth

238. Economic efficiency and growth are critically important to all countries. This section discusses the effects of BEPS on capital structures, tax differentials between companies, effects on investment decisions, effects on patent registrations and R&D spending, and effects from uncertainty and compliance costs.

239. The OECD's *Tax Policy Reform and Economic Growth* (2010) ranked corporate income tax as the most harmful to economic growth. Some have expressed concern that BEPS countermeasures would increase effective corporate tax rates on some MNEs, with adverse economic effects resulting. The BEPS project proposes structural tax reforms that close unintended interactions of different country tax rules with internationally-co-ordinated rules. Any additional corporate tax revenue from BEPS countermeasures would enable the lowering of taxes on taxpayers or increased government spending, if the specific tax effects on macroeconomic growth are a concern.

240. In the presence of BEPS, effective tax rates are reduced relative to statutory tax rates. With BEPS countermeasures, ETRs of MNEs engaging in BEPS will move closer to applicable statutory tax rates. The change in these companies' ETRs can impact their real economic activity at different margins, but depends on a number of factors, including the economic incidence of the BEPS countermeasures, the use of the revenues, and the responsiveness of real economic activity to both effective marginal tax rates and effective average tax rates. The effect of curtailing BEPS profit shifting will vary among countries depending upon the relative importance of BEPS-engaging MNEs, current anti-avoidance rules, the structure of the economy and the degree of cross-border intra-firm transactions.

241. The above discussion of the economic incidence of CIT in a global economy with less than competitive markets due to unique intangibles, and in particular the benefits of self-help CIT reductions from BEPS behaviours, suggests that just because CIT increases for MNEs engaging in BEPS does not mean their marginal cost-of-capital for investment will increase proportionally. Further, CIT is not the only business tax affecting FDI and investment; other source based taxation, include withholding taxes, property taxes, non-refundable or deferred value added tax refunds on business inputs, environmental taxes, etc. factor in companies' location decisions. Thus, a 10% increase in corporate income tax will have less than a 10% increase in total source-based business taxation of the MNE's activity. Standard cost-of-capital calculations do not include other source-based business taxes, often have relatively low real rates of return for equity capital investments, and assume no economic rents.

242. ***Differential tax rates across companies***. Economic distortions occur when the tax rules create an uneven playing field across industries and companies. Many countries report backward-looking ETRs which vary significantly across different industries due to

tax rules which are used more by certain industries, such as accelerated depreciation or research and development tax credits, or which have special industry tax rules. Tax revenue reductions from BEPS are also likely to vary from industry to industry. For example, the ability to move intangible assets and the income associated with intangible assets without changing the location of where the value was created is a significant source of BEPS and is likely to occur in some industries more than others. This can create economic distortions across industries from varying ETRs. Many of the empirical analyses find stronger profit shifting responses to taxes for companies that have patents, where the MNE has intangibles, or are in industries with extensive intangibles. Annex 3.A1 shows that the ETR differential is higher among MNEs with patents, since they have a higher profit-shifting intensity and can take greater advantage of tax preferences, such as for R&D, than domestic firms by the strategic placement of R&D and patents.

243. MNEs can take advantage of both domestic tax planning and BEPS to lower their effective tax rates below the rates of domestic competitors, providing them with an advantage in gaining market share through lower consumer prices or their ability to acquire domestic companies. Egger, Eggert and Winner (2010) and Annex 3.A1 find effective tax rates of MNEs or their affiliates are lower than comparable domestic corporations or their affiliates. Annex 3.A1 estimates that BEPS reduces the effective tax rate of large affiliates of MNEs by 4 to 8½ percentage points on average compared to similarly-situated domestic-only affiliates, due to both profit shifting, mismatches between tax systems and domestic tax preferences.[47] The differential is larger for MNEs affiliates with more than 1,000 employees and MNEs with patents. Identifying comparable MNE and domestic-only companies may not be possible given inherent differences between companies operating multi-nationally and those operating only domestically.[48] Identifying even somewhat comparable companies is a challenge, particularly for smaller countries, but statistical techniques, such as propensity score matching and regression analysis, have been used.

244. Academic studies have generally not analysed the economic implications of tax planning on competition between companies. The OECD analysis in Annex 3.A1 assesses if industries with a strong presence of tax-planning MNEs are more concentrated and if MNE groups engaged in tax planning obtain different price mark-ups as compared to other firms with similar characteristics. The empirical analysis suggests that industries with a strong presence of MNEs are more concentrated. The empirical analysis also finds that MNE groups with an affiliate in a no-corporate-tax-country are associated with higher price mark-ups (pre-tax operating profit divided by turnover), controlling for other factors affecting mark-ups such as size, productivity, leverage, presence of patents and exposure to foreign competition. Sikes and Verrecchia (2014) find a negative effect on firms' cost of capital in economies where a significant proportion of firms engage in tax avoidance, with the most burdensome effect on firms that do not engage in tax avoidance.

245. ***BEPS-induced distortions in the location of corporate debt.*** Economic efficiency is also affected by BEPS effects on MNEs' capital structure. A number of studies show BEPS occurring through excessive interest deductions, with both related-party and external debt. As interest deductions are taken in high-tax rate countries, and interest income is attributed to in low or no-tax countries, the after-tax cost of debt is reduced. Differences in the tax treatment of debt and equity can be exploited in the cross-border context. Thus, debt shifting exacerbates the existing tax bias towards corporate debt financing.

246. A bias toward corporate debt and a bias against corporate equity already exist in most corporate tax systems. Corporate interest is deductible and generally taxed at the interest recipient level. Corporate equity income in the form of retained earnings and dividends are taxed at the entity level and generally again at the investor level, although a number of countries provide reliefs to dividends and capital gains. Debt shifting by MNEs exacerbates the corporate tax bias by effectively increasing the tax benefit from interest deductions through the strategic location of both external and internal debt to high-tax countries. Use of hybrid mismatch arrangements can result in multiple layers of borrowing within a MNE group with multiple interest deductions, or deductions of interest in one country but the payment is treated as an exempt dividend in another country. Increased external and internal debt shifting thus increases the overall level of debt bias.

247. Proposals to reduce the debt bias through notional allowances for corporate equity (ACE) have been implemented in several countries. MNEs can shift their capital structure to maximise tax benefits from external and internal debt in high tax countries without interest limitations, while increasing their equity contributions in countries with an ACE system.

248. ***BEPS-induced distortions in the location of patents***. Numerous studies show that BEPS affects the location of FDI and patents, since taxable income can be segregated from where the value is created. This can affect the location of some employment and physical capital to justify claims for the desired tax treatment. This varies depending on the tax treatment, generally in the form of a preferential IP regime, on offer, and the activity requirement needed to qualify for such treatment. The analysis in Annex 3.A1 which uses a combination of data on patents from PATSTAT and firm characteristics from the ORBIS database, finds tax rate differences affect the location of patent registrations. A recent European Commission study finds that lower tax rates on certain intangible income encourages greater connection between residence of inventors and the location of registration of patents if the rules require such connection. Otherwise the lower tax rate encourages shifting of patent registrations and taxable income without a significant shift in real economic activity.[49]

249. Future studies of the effects of taxes on the location of real R&D investment expenditures and research engineers and scientists are needed. Studies examining R&D effects have looked at the location of the registration of patents and whether an investor associated with the patent resides in the country, but have not analysed actual R&D activity.[50] Such studies would need to account for existing R&D tax credits and deductions of more than 100% of R&D expenditures, plus personal income taxes on the inventors as well as non-tax factors such as agglomeration effects and countries' public R&D investments.

250. ***Effects on the location of real economic activity.*** Taxes matter in location decisions as shown in a number of empirical analyses. De Mooij (2008) did a meta-analysis of which finds that effective marginal tax rates and average marginal tax rates, rather than statutory tax rates, have significant effects on FDI. He reports a -0.4 semi-elasticity of effective marginal tax rate effect on the intensive margin of FDI (increases within an individual country), while finding a -0.65 semi-elasticity of the effective average tax rate on the extensive margin of FDI (changes between countries). It should be noted that FDI includes more than just greenfield investments and business expansions, but also reinvested earnings and merger and acquisitions. Estimates of the responsiveness

of real economic activity could be understated if companies can currently achieve tax benefits without moving real economic activity.

251. Linking real economic activity to tax benefits for patent income or for any type of income or economic activity will more closely align taxable income with actual economic activity. Providing tax benefits associated with a type of income or behaviour without any such requirement that real or substantial activity occur is likely to achieve a country's policy goal of generating significantly more of the economic activity in their country, but is likely to result in MNEs engaging in BEPS. Increasing the link through measures to counter harmful tax practices and through assuring transfer pricing outcomes are in line with value creation will result in higher taxes on companies currently doing profit shifting. Aligning taxable income with real economic activity will result in more taxable income being reported by companies currently engaging in profit shifting in the jurisdictions where the economic activity giving rise to that income actually occurs. Aligning taxable income with real economic activity will not mean that companies will pay less attention to countries' statutory tax rates, but instead tax rates will be taken into account when decisions about the actual location or relocation of the real activities and function that generate income are being made. The analysis in Annex 3.A1 finds support for the hypothesis that tax planning MNEs' investment is currently less sensitive to tax rates than other firms' investment since tax planning MNEs can reduce their ETRs through artificial arrangements without changing the location of their real economic activity.

252. While taxes affect location and investment decisions, they are not the only factor MNEs take into account. It is important for researchers to estimate the effects of all business taxes, not just corporate income taxes, and taking into account the effects of non-tax factors. Table 3.4 summarises key factors determining the location of MNE operations from two business surveys. The right column shows the ranking from a World Bank survey of almost 200 decision makers of the largest MNEs. The left column shows the ranking from a recent EY report of European decision-makers.

Table 3.4. Ranking of key location factors of MNE operations

	Europe 2014	Worldwide 2002
Stable social and political environment	1	2
Access to customers	2	1
Ease of doing business	-	3
Potential productivity increase for their company	3	-
Cost of labour	4	8
Reliability and quality of infrastructure and utilities	5	4
Ability to hire technical professionals	6	5
Ability to hire management staff	6	6
Ability to hire skilled labourers	6	10
Crime and safety	7	9
Level of corruption	-	7
National taxes	8	11
Local taxes	8	17
Telecommunications infrastructure	9	-
Labour relations and unionisation	10	19

Note: The ranking for Europe comes from the EY Attractiveness Survey 2014 and the worldwide from the Foreign Direct Investment Survey by the World Bank 2002. "Local labour skill level" was number 6 and "corporate taxation" number 8 in the EY survey. Factors that could not be matched are marked with a minus sign.

165. The table shows similar rankings about key location factors of MNE operations in Europe and worldwide. A "stable social and political environment" and "access to customers" rank at the top of both lists. The cost of labour and the qualification of potential employees are also very important. National and local taxation are ranked 8th or lower, and do not appear to be as important as many other factors.[51] Nonetheless, when tax differences are large or when other factors are fairly similar across locations, taxes will affect business location decisions, as reflected in the empirical studies.

166. ***BEPS-induced distortions of types of investment.*** BEPS distorts the allocation of investment and capital resources, favouring types of capital that are most conducive to BEPS behaviours.[52] Table 3.5 shows an illustrative marginal effective tax rate calculation for knowledge based capital (KBC) from the OECD *Supporting Investment in Knowledge Capital, Growth and Innovation* (2013). The analysis calculated a tax wedge, difference between the pre-tax required "hurdle" rate of return on R&D at the margin and the after-tax required rate of return to the investor. The R&D tax wedge for domestic licensing and production, or for a company's own-use in production, is 16 percentage points. The R&D tax wedge becomes a negative 32 percentage points with the transfer of the KBC to an offshore holding company with a substantially lower effective tax rate. Instead of the income from the KBC investment bearing some tax, albeit much lower than the statutory tax rate, the tax treatment of the income from the KBC becomes a significant subsidy as a result of BEPS behaviours.

Table 3.5. Summary R&D tax wedge with MNE tax planning

		R&D tax wedge No R&D tax credit (percentage points)	**R&D tax wedge 5% R&D tax credit (percentage points)**
1	Own-use / Domestic license and production	16.2	6.1
2	Foreign license and production (territorial system)	11.7	2.0
3	Transfer of KBC to offshore holding company, foreign production, 80% domestic inclusion	-3.0	-11.5
4	Transfer of KBC to offshore holding company, foreign production, 20% domestic inclusion	-32.4	-38.4
5	R&D cost-sharing agreement with offshore holding company, foreign contract manufacturing, domestic tax base shifting of 200% of production costs	-14.5	-17.3

Source: OECD (2013b). Key assumptions.

167. Another economic distortion and economic efficiency effect occurs when the tax system favours one type of company over another. This results when MNEs engaging in BEPS are able to reduce their ETR due to BEPS compared to MNEs not engaging in BEPS and compared to domestic-only companies. MNEs have an inherent advantage over domestic-only companies in being able to strategically place activity in jurisdictions that offer special domestic tax incentives, such as R&D investment expenditures. Those differences, which can result in differential effective tax rates, are not BEPS behaviours.

168. MNEs can take advantage of BEPS behaviours to artificially segregate taxable income from the activity creating that income to reduce the MNE group's overall effective tax rate (i.e. the affiliate in a country will face the same statutory tax rate as a domestic only group, but will have less or more taxable income in that country due to profit shifting).[53] The overall group's effective tax rate can be lowered, which can provide a potential competitive advantage in terms of cost savings compared to less aggressive tax planning MNEs or domestic only companies without multinational tax planning opportunities. The tax savings from BEPS behaviours can enable tax planning MNEs to have a competitive advantage in obtaining favourable financing, in making acquisitions, and in lowering product prices.

3.3.14 Increasing government competition on tax bases and attracting economic activity

169. The BEPS project proposes a structural reform of the international corporate tax system. The set of reforms, as recommended by the Action Plan, represent a multilateral effort to address unintended interactions among national corporate tax systems. While the implementation of the BEPS countermeasures will increase net global corporate tax revenue, individual countries may be affected differently. It is therefore important to understand how fiscal externalities or spillover effects from one jurisdiction's tax rules and practices affect other countries' tax revenues and domestic tax policies.

170. Countries compete for FDI and employment through domestic government policies including tax policy. They compete not only on headline statutory tax rates, R&D tax credits, but increasingly on tax base changes.[54] Revenue losses from BEPS arise from both aggressive tax planning by some MNEs and tax competition between some governments. The tax competition and spillover economic literature is increasing as countries both compete for their national interest as well as find situations, such as BEPS, where multilateral co-operation is important.[55]

171. National corporate tax policies can have a fiscal impact on other countries through several interrelated channels. As highlighted by BEPS related research reviewed previously, significant cross-border fiscal effects may arise through tax-induced changes in FDI patterns and financing structures of MNEs. On the one hand, this leads to *direct* tax base fiscal spillover effects as changes in real economic activity and profit shifting affect other countries' corporate tax bases. However, the anticipation of adverse fiscal effects may also induce governments' *strategic* tax policy changes as a response to tax policies in other countries. Strategic tax spillover effects may lead, in the worst case, to excessive tax competition ('race to the bottom') and corresponding reductions in revenue and government services and public investment.

172. A 2014 IMF paper assesses the fiscal effects from direct and strategic spillovers by linking tax bases and statutory CIT rates for 103 countries over the period 1980 to 2013. Results from a panel data analysis show strong and significant evidence for direct tax spillovers, implying that a one percentage point reduction in the CIT rate of all other countries reduces a country's tax base on average by 3.7 percent. While these effects account only for real economic activity, disentangling the effects from profit shifting yields results of similar magnitude and even higher significance. A separate analysis for developing countries shows that direct spillover effects are two to three times larger than in OECD countries.

173. To quantify strategic spillover effects, the IMF analysis applies the approach of Devereux et al. (2008), relating foreign statutory (or effective) CIT rates to domestic

rates. While the estimates based on *effective* tax rates do not provide statistically significant results, strategic setting of *statutory* tax rates is supported by the evidence. The analysis confirms the negative effect of foreign CIT statutory rates on domestic tax bases. Specifically, a one percentage point reduction in CIT statutory rates in all other countries yields a 6.5 percent decrease in the CIT base of the average country and a simultaneous reduction in the domestic CIT rate by 0.5 percentage points. This strategic decrease of the CIT rate leads to an increase in the CIT base by 4 percent and a net base loss of 2.5 percent.

174. The presence of fiscal externalities implies that unilateral approaches to international tax policy issues are likely to lead to inefficient outcomes at the global level. Countries enacting unilateral countermeasures may protect their tax bases, while shifting base erosion activity to other countries.[56] Countries that encourage tax base shifting with BEPS-facilitation attributes, such as lack of transparency, combined with a low or no corporate tax,[57] can reduce tax revenues in other countries and overall through both direct and strategic spillover effects.

3.4 Future areas for economic research to better measure the scale and economic impact of BEPS with better data

175. The mandate for Action 11 included developing an economic analysis of the scale and impact of BEPS (including spillover effects across countries) and actions to address it. This chapter summarises the current understanding of the scale and impact of BEPS based on academic studies, other international organisations' analyses, as well as some new OECD research. Progress is being made in better understanding BEPS and countermeasures, and the economic analysis show that BEPS is significant and affects many economic decisions of both taxpayers and governments. The issue of BEPS and appropriate geographic allocation of income and expenses relative to measures of value creating activities is important not only to the current corporate income tax, but also would affect other taxes proposed by some academics such as a business cash-flow tax or a comprehensive business income tax.

176. The current body of empirical research into the fiscal and economic impacts of BEPS demonstrates that the stakes are high, but there is still much further research needed to be undertaken. Chapter 1 has illustrated how currently available data is affected by many limitations, and this chapter outlined many methodological challenges confronted by BEPS researchers. Chapter 2 includes BEPS Indicators that can be refined with better data and more sophisticated analysis of that data. Annex 3.A1 provides empirical estimates of the economic effects of tax planning based on financial account data, which could be refined with better data. Annex 3.A2 provides a toolkit for analysing the fiscal effects of specific BEPS countermeasures, which is often a strong starting point for analysis of other economic effects. Chapter 4 makes recommendations on how better use could be made of current and future data and recommends tools to monitor and evaluate the effectiveness and economic impact of the actions taken to address BEPS in the future. This chapter identified a number of areas for future BEPS analysis that have not been undertaken or that are limited by current data. A number of areas for future research beyond the Action 11 mandate but which will add to the understanding of BEPS and MNEs are highlighted, since better data alone will not be sufficient for the best possible analysis of BEPS.

177. The following are some of the areas where additional analysis is needed:

- The prevalence and intensity of BEPS. How pervasive are BEPS behaviours? Is BEPS limited to a small number of MNEs or more widespread? Are some MNEs more intensively exploiting BEPS than other MNEs, and if so why (e.g. costs of tax planning, corporate governance, risk profile)?[58] Would largely unrestricted BEPS encourage smaller MNEs to start engaging in BEPS and encourage domestic companies to go global for the BEPS tax benefits?

- Differences in the profitability of MNEs vs. comparable domestic entities. Are there inherent economic differences between MNEs and domestic entities which make comparisons of ETR difficult? If so, how can competitiveness between MNEs and domestic entities be evaluated?

- Factors contributing to group profitability. What contributes to the profitability of a global consolidated MNE? How much can be explained by tangible capital, labour and/or sales compared to other factors such as different types of intangible assets, public infrastructure, country risk diversification, etc.

- Factors contributing to affiliate profitability. What contributes to the profitability of individual MNE entities? How can functions, assets and risks be incorporated in future analyses of BEPS, since they are the basis of arm's length pricing? How much can be explained simply by tangible capital, labour and/or sales compared to other factors such as the intangible assets of their global MNE, public infrastructure, labour force qualities and stability in a country, etc.? How can these other factors which may change over time be incorporated more fully than just dummy variables?

- Other tax factors in location decisions. Corporate taxes are only one source-based tax affecting location decisions. How do these other business taxes affect MNEs' tax decisions? How can measures of profit shifting separate the effects of non-BEPS tax preferences from BEPS?

- Effects of uncertainty, reputation and compliance costs, and disclosure. Companies face the equivalent of implicit taxes from uncertainty, reputation[59] and compliance costs. Can these be measured and included in the economic analysis of taxes and BEPS? What effects do disclosures to tax administrations have?[60]

- Mobility of different types of labour and capital. How mobile are different forms of real economic activity, such as top level executives, R&D scientists, production workers, back-office workers, buildings, equipment, different types of intangible assets, etc.?

- Governments' strategic behaviours. How do different institutional settings affect countries' co-operative versus competitive behaviours? How multilateral do agreements need to be to achieve effective co-operative outcomes?

178. The analysis of BEPS and countermeasures has advanced since 2013, providing more evidence of BEPS and insights into specific BEPS channels and potential effects of BEPS countermeasures. As analysts can only observe the current world with BEPS, any analysis of BEPS and countermeasures must estimate a comparison point, whether it be a

world without BEPS, a future world without co-ordinated multilateral action, or a future world with proposed countermeasures. Future analysis of BEPS, MNEs' BEPS behaviours, and tax competition with improved estimation methodologies are needed to complement improvements in the available data relevant for analysing BEPS and BEPS countermeasures.

Bibliography

Acciari, P., F. Tomarelli, L. Limosani, and L. Benedetti (2015), "Measurement of Base Erosion and Profit Shifting Phenomena through the Analysis of FDI Stocks", Italian Ministry of Economy and Finance – Department of the Treasury Working Papers. www.dt.mef.gov.it/export/sites/sitodt/modules/documenti_en/analisi_progammazione/working_papers/WP_3.pdf

Akcigit, U., S. Baslandze, and S. Stantcheva (2015), "Taxation and the International Mobility of Inventors", National Bureau of Economic Research Working Paper 21024.

African Economic Outlook (2010), "Direct taxation in Africa", Public Resource Mobilisation & Aid. www.africaneconomicoutlook.org/en/theme/public-resource-mobilisation-and-aid/the-state-of-public-resource-mobilisation-in-africa/direct-taxation-in-africa/.

Armstrong, C. S., J. L. Blouin, A. D. Jagolinzer and D. F. Larcker (2015), "Corporate governance, incentives and tax avoidance", Journal of Accounting and Economics, Vol. 60, Issue 1, pp. 1-17. DOI: http://dx.doi.org/10.1016/j.jacceco.2015.02.003.

Australia (2014), Parliament of Australia: Inquiry into Tax Disputes, www.aph.gov.au/Parliamentary_Business/Committees/House/Tax_and_Revenue/Inquiry_into_Tax_Disputes (accessed 19 December 2014).

Azémar, C. (2010), "International corporate taxation and U.S. multinationals' behaviour: An integrated approach", Canadian Journal of Economics, Vol. 43, No. 1, pp. 232–253.

Bach, S. (2013), "Has German business income taxation raised too little revenue over the last decades?" DIW Berlin.

Becker, J. and N. Riedel (2012), "Cross-border tax effects on affiliate investment — Evidence from European multinationals", European Economic Review, Vol. 56, pp. 436–450.

Beer, S. and J. Loeprick (2013), "Profit shifting: Drivers and potential countermeasures", WU International Taxation Research Paper Series, No. 2013-03, DOI: http://dx.doi.org/10.2139/ssrn.2271539.

Beuselinck, C., M. Deloof, and A. Vanstraelen (2014), "Cross-jurisdictional income shifting and tax enforcement: Evidence from public versus private multinationals", Review of Accounting Studies, Vol. 20, No. 2, pp. 710-746.

Blouin, J., L. Robinson and J. Seidman (2011), "Co-ordination of transfer prices on intrafirm trade", Working Paper.

Blouin, J. et al. (2014), "Thin capitalisation rules and multinational firm capital structure", IMF Working Paper, No. 14/12.

Buettner, T. et al. (2012), "The impact of thin-capitalization rules on the capital structure of multinational firms", Journal of Public Economics 96, 930-938.

Bureau Van Dijk, ORBIS Database, Bureau Van Dijk Electronic Publishing.

Buslei, H. and M. Simmler (2012), "The impact of introducing an interest barrier: Evidence from the German corporation tax reform 2008", DIW Berlin Discussion Paper No. 1215.

Cederwall, E. (2015), "Marking sense of profit shifting: Jack Mintz", Tax Foundation, http://taxfoundation.org/blog/making-sense-profit-shifting-jack-mintz.

Chen, D. and J. M. Mintz (2008), "Taxation of Canadian inbound and outbound investments", Research Report Prepared for the Advisory Panel on Canada's System of International Taxation.

Christian Aid (2009), "False profits: Robbing the poor to keep the rich tax-free", www.christianaid.org.uk/Images/false-profits.pdf.

Clausing, K. A. (2003), "Tax-motivated transfer pricing and US intrafirm trade", Journal of Public Economics 87(9-10), 2207-2223.

Clausing, K.A. (2009), "Multinational firm tax avoidance and tax policy", National Tax Journal, Vol. 62, No 4.

Clausing, K. A. (2011), "The revenue effects of multinational firm income shifting", Tax Notes, Tax Analysts, Available at SSRN: http://ssrn.com/abstract=2488860.

Clausing, K. A. (2012), "In search of corporate tax incidence", Tax Law Review, Vol. 65, pp. 433-472.

Clausing, K. A. (2013), "The future of corporate tax", Tax Law Review, Vol. 66, No. 4.

Clausing, K. A. (2015), "The nature and practice of capital tax competition", DOI: http://dx.doi.org/10.2139/ssrn.2489224.

Corrado, C., J. Haskel., C. Jona-Lasinio and M. Iommi (2012), "Intangible capital and growth in advanced economies: Measurement methods and comparative results", Institute for the Study of Labor discussion paper series, No. 6733.

Corrado, C., C. Hulton and D. Sichel (2009), "Intangible Capital and U.S. Economic Growth," Review of Income and Wealth, Series 55, No. 3.

Cronin, J. A., E. Y. Lin, L. Power and M. Cooper (2012), "Distributing the corporate income tax: revised U.S. Treasury methodology", United States Treasury Office of Tax Analysis, Working Paper No. 5.

Davies, R.B. et al. (2014), "Knocking on tax haven's door: Multinational firms and transfer pricing", CEPII Working Paper, No. 2014-21.

De Mooij, R. A. (2011), "Tax biases to debt finance: Assessing the problem, finding solutions", IMF Staff Discussion Note.

De Mooij, R. A. and S. Ederveen (2008), "Corporate tax elasticities: a reader's guide to empirical findings", Working Paper 8/22, Oxford University Centre for Business Taxation.

Desai, M.A., F. Foley and J.R. Hines (2004), "A multinational perspective on capital structure choice and internal capital markets", The Journal of Finance, Vol. 59, No. 6.

Devereux, M. and R. Griffith (1998), "Taxes and the location of production: evidence from a panel of US multinationals", Journal of Public Economics, 68(3), pp. 335-367.

Devereux, M., B. Lockwood and M. Redoano (2008), "Do countries compete over corporate tax rates?" Journal of Public Economics, Vol. 92, pp. 1210–35.

Dharmapala, D. and N. Riedel (2013), "Earnings shocks and tax-motivated income-shifting: Evidence from European multinationals", Journal of Public Economics, Elsevier, vol. 97(C), pp. 95-107.

Dharmapala, D. (2014), "What do we know about base erosion and profit shifting? A review of the empirical literature", Fiscal Studies, Vol. 35, pp. 421–448.

Dharmapala, D. (2015), "Base erosion and profit shifting: A simple conceptual framework", CESifo DICE Report, Vol. 12, Issue 4, pp. 8-14.

Dischinger, M., B. Knoll and N. Riedel (2014), "The role of headquarters in multinational profit shifting strategies", International Tax Public Finance, Vol. 21, No. 2, pp. 248-271. DOI: 10.1007/s10797-012-9265-5.

Dowd, T. P. Landesfeld and A. Moore (2015), "Profit shifting of U.S. multinationals", Joint Committee on Taxation working paper.

Dreßler, D. and U. Scheuering (2012), "Empirical evaluation of interest barrier effects", ZEW Discussion Paper, No. 12-046.

Dyreng, S., J. L. Hoopes and J. H. Wilde, (2014), "Public pressure and corporate tax behaviour", Working Paper available at SSRN: http://ssrn.com/abstract=2474346 or http://dx.doi.org/10.2139/ssrn.2474346.

Dyreng, S. and K. Markle (2014), "The effect of financial constraints on tax-motivated income shifting by U.S. multinationals", Working paper, Duke University.

Egger, P., Eggert, W. and Winner, H. (2010), "Saving taxes through foreign plant ownership", Journal of International Economics, 81, S. 99-108.

Egger, P. et al. (2014), "Corporate taxes and internal borrowing within multinational firms", American Economic Journal: Economic Policy, 6 (2), 54-93.

Ernst and Young (2014), "European attractiveness survey 2014 - Back in the game", www.ey.com/GL/en/Issues/Business-environment/european-attractiveness-survey.

European Commission (2014), "A study on R&D tax incentives", Working Paper No. 52-2014.

European Commission (2015), "Patent boxes design, patents location and local R&D", IPTS Working Papers on Corporate R&D and Innovation, No. 6/2015.

Fryt, M. D., A. Lyon, W. McBride, D. Shackelford and T. Treichel (2015), "Session 3: Evaluating the U.S. corporate income tax", The Tax Magazine, June 2015.

Fuest, C. (2015), "Who bears the burden of corporate income taxation?," mimeo for the European Tax Policy Forum, www.etpf.org/papers/PP001CorpTax.pdf.

Fuest, C. and N. Riedel (2010), "Tax evasion, tax avoidance and tax expenditures in developing countries: A review of the literature," Report prepared for the U.K. Department for International Development (DFID), Oxford University Centre for Business Taxation.

Fuest, C., S. Hebous and N. Riedel (2011), "International debt shifting and multinational firms in developing economies", Economics Letters, pp. 135-138.

Fullerton, D. and G. E. Metcalf (2002), "Tax incidence", Handbook of Public Economics, A.J. Auerback and M. Feldstein (ed.), Elsevier, Edition 1, Vol. 4, Chapter 26, pp. 1787–1872.

Gravelle, J. C. (2010), "Corporate tax incidence: Review of general equilibrium estimates and analysis," Working Paper 2010-03, United States Congressional Budget Office, pp. 30-33.

Genschel, P. and P. Schwarz (2011), "Tax competition: A literature review", *Socio-Economic Review, No. 9, pp.* 339-370.

Griffith, R., H. Miller and M. O'Connell (2011), "Corporate taxes and the location of intellectual property", CEPR Discussion Papers 8424.

Grubert H. (2003), "Intangible income, intercompany transactions, income shifting, and the choice of location", National Tax Journal, Vol. 56, No. 1, Part 2, pp. 221-242.

Grubert, H. (2012), "Foreign taxes and the growing share of U.S. multinational company income abroad: profits, not sales, are being globalized", National Tax Journal 65(2): 247-282.

Grubert, H. and J. Mutti (1991), "Taxes, Tariffs and Transfer Pricing in Multinational Corporate Decision Making", The Review of Economics and Statistics, Vol. 73, No. 2, pp. 285-293.

Hanlon, M. and S. Heitzman (2010), "A review of tax research", DOI: http://dx.doi.org/10.2139/ssrn.1476561.

Harberger, A. C. (1995), "The ABCs of corporation tax incidence: Insights into the open-economy case," Chapter 2, American Council for Capital Formation, Policy and Economic Growth.

Harberger, A. C. (2006), "Corporate tax incidence: reflections on what is known, unknown and unknowable", www.econ.ucla.edu/harberger/ah-corptax4-06.pdf.

Hebous, S. and M. Ruf (2015), "Evaluating the effects of ACE systems on multinational debt financing and investment", CESIFO Working Paper No. 5360.

Heckemeyer, J. H. and M. Overesch (2013), "Multinationals' profit response to tax differentials: Effect size and shifting channels", ZEW Discussion Paper No. 13-045.

Hines, J.R, and E.M. Rice (1994), "Fiscal paradise: Foreign tax havens and American business," The Quarterly Journal of Economics, MIT Press, 109(1), pp. 149-82.

Hoopes, J. (2015), "Taxes and disclosure: A brief summary of the research."

Huizinga, H. and L. Laeven (2008), "International profit shifting within multinationals: A multi-country perspective", Journal of Public Economics, 88(6), pp. 1149-1168.

Huizinga, H., L. Laeven and G. Nicodème (2008), "Capital structure and international debt shifting", Journal of Financial Economics, 88, pp. 80–118.

IMF (2014), "Spillovers in International Corporate Taxation", IMF Policy paper.

Karkinsky, T. and N. Riedel (2012), "Corporate taxation and the choice of patent location within multinational firms", Journal of International Economics, 88, 176-185.

Keen, M. and K. Konrad (2012), "The theory of international tax competition and co-ordination", Max Planck Institute for Tax Law and Public Finance, Working paper No. 2012-06. DOI: http://ssrn.com/abstract=2111895.

Kleinbard, E. (2011), "Stateless Income", Florida Tax Review, Vol. 11, No. 9. DOI: http://ssrn.com/abstract=1791769.

Liu, L. and R. Altshuler (2013), "Measuring the burden of the corporate income tax under imperfect competition", National Tax Journal, Vol. 66, No. 1, pp. 215-237.

Lohse, T., N. Riedel and C. Spengel (2012), "The increasing importance of transfer pricing regulations: A worldwide overview", Oxford Center for Business Taxation Working Paper, No. 12/27.

Lohse, T. and N. Riedel (2012), "The impact of transfer pricing regulations on profit shifting within European multinationals", FZID Discussion Paper, No. 61-2012, https://fzid.uni-hohenheim.de/71978.html.

Lohse, T. and N. Riedel (2013), "Do transfer pricing laws limit international income shifting? Evidence from European multinationals", Oxford University Centre for Business Taxation Working Paper, No. 13/07.

Loretz, S. and S. Mokkas (2011), "Evidence for profit shifting with tax sensitive capital stocks", Working papers 1116, Oxford University Centre for Business Taxation.

McDonald, M. (2008), "Income shifting from transfer pricing: Further evidence from tax return data", United States Department of the Treasury, Office of Tax Analysis, OTA Technical Working Paper 2.

Maffini, G. and S. Mokkas (2011), "Profit shifting and measured productivity of multinational firms", Oxford Bulletin of Economics and Statistics, Vol. 73, Issue 1, pp. 1–20.

Markle, K.S. (2015), "A comparison of the tax-motivated income shifting of multinationals in territorial and worldwide countries", http://dx.doi.org/10.2139/ssrn.1764031.

Markle, K. S. and L. Robinson (2012), "Tax haven use across international tax regimes".

Markle, K. S. and D. Shackelford (2012), "Cross-country comparison of corporate income tax", National Tax Journal 65:3, pp. 493-527.

Mieszkowski, P. and G.R. Zodrow (1986), "The new view of the property tax: A reformulation", Regional Science and Urban Economics, 16 (3), pp. 309–327.

Mintz, J. M. and V. B. Venkatachalam (2015), "The problem with the low-tax backlash: Rethinking corporate tax policies to adjust for uneven reputational risks", University of Calgary School of Public Policy Research Paper, Vol. 8, Issue 24.

Møen, J., D. Schindler, G. Schjelderup and J. Tropina (2011), "International debt shifting: Do multinationals shift internal or external debt?" CESIFO Working Paper, No. 3519.

Monkam, N. (2012), "ATAF Regional studies on reform priorities of African tax administrations: Africa-wide report", African Tax Administration Forum. DOI:

http://10.100.15.87:15871/cgi-bin/blockpage.cgi?ws-session=18446744072250628799.

MSCI (2015), "Re-examining the tax gap", www.msci.com/documents/10199/4043da8b-4d49-4449-ac0e-28b09df3b220.

Mutti, J. and H. Grubert (2009), "The effect of taxes on royalties and the migration of intangible assets abroad", in M. Reinsdorf and M. Slaughter (ed.) International Trade in Services and Intangibles in the Era of Globalization, University of Chicago Press.

Nicodème, G. (2008), "Corporate income tax and economic distortions", CEB Working Paper, No. 08-033.

OECD (2010), *Tax policy reform and economic growth*, OECD Publishing, Paris, http://dx.doi.org/10.1787/9789264091085-en.

OECD (2013), *Action Plan on Base Erosion and Profit Shifting*, OECD Publishing, Paris, http://dx.doi.org/10.1787/9789264202719-en.

OECD (2013), *Supporting investment in knowledge capital, growth and innovation*, OECD Publishing, Paris, http://dx.doi.org/10.1787/9789264193307-en.

OECD (2014), "Part 1 of a report to G20 Development Working Group on the impact of BEPS in low income countries", OECD, Paris, www.oecd.org/tax/part-1-of-report-to-g20-dwg-on-the-impact-of-beps-in-low-income-countries.pdf.

Overesch and Wamser (2010), "The effects of company taxation in EU accession countries on German FDI", Economics of Transition 18, pp. 429-457.

Oxfam (2015), "Africa: Rising for the few", www.oxfam.org/sites/www.oxfam.org/files/world_economic_forum_wef.africa_rising_for_the_few.pdf.

Randolph, W. C. (2006), "International Burdens of the Corporate Income Tax", Congressional Budget Office, Washington, D.C.

Riedel, N. (2015), *Quantifying international tax avoidance: A review of academic literature*, European Tax Policy Forum Policy Paper No. 2, www.etpf.org/papers/PP002QuantAvoid.pdf.

Ruf, M. and A. J. Weichenrieder (2013), "CFC legislation, passive assets and the impact of the ECJ's Cadbury-Schweppes decision", CESifo Working Paper, No. 4461.

Schwarz (2009), *Tax-avoidance strategies of American multinationals: An empirical analysis*, Managerial and Decision Economics, Vol. 30, pp. 539–549, http://dx.doi.org/10.1002/mde.1471.

Scottmay, M., "Amazon to stop funnelling European sales through low-tax haven", The New York Times, 24 May 2015.

Sikes, S. and R. Verrecchia (2014), *Externalities of corporate tax avoidance*, University of Pennsylvania working paper, www.mccombs.utexas.edu/~/media/Files/MSB/Departments/Accounting/TARC/2014/Sikes%20Verrecchia%20Paper.pdf.

Slemrod (2010), "Location, (real) location, (tax) location: An essay on mobility's place in optimal taxation", National Tax Journal, Vol. 63 (4, Part 2), pp. 843-864.

Slemrod and Wilson (2009), "Tax competition with parasitic tax havens," Journal of Public Economics, Elsevier, Vol. 93(11-12), pp. 1261-1270.

UNCTAD (2015), "FDI, tax and development", UNCTAD Investment and Enterprise Division Working Paper.

UNCTAD (2015), *World Investment Report 2015: Reforming international investment governance*, UN Reference: UNCTAD/WIR/2015.

United States Joint Committee on Taxation (2014), "Technical explanation, estimated revenue effects, distributional analysis, and macroeconomic analysis of the Tax Reform Act of 2014: A discussion draft of the Chairman of the House Committee on Ways and Means to reform the Internal Revenue Code", United States Government Printing Office, Reference No. JCS-1-14.

Van't Riet, M. and A. Lejour, (2014), "Ranking the stars: Network analysis of bilateral tax treaties", CPB Discussion Paper, No. 290.

Vicard, Vincent (2015), "Profit shifting through transfer pricing: Evidence from French firm level trade data", Banque de France Working Paper No. 555, http://dx.doi.org/10.2139/ssrn.2614864.

Voget, J. (2015), *The effect of taxes on foreign direct investment: A survey of the empirical evidence*, European Tax Policy Forum, Policy Paper No. 3, www.etpf.org/papers/PP003FDI.pdf.

Weichenrieder, A.J. (2009), *Profit shifting in the EU: Evidence from Germany*, International Tax Public Finance, Vol. 16, pp. 281–297, http://dx.doi.org/10.1007/s10797-008-9068-x.

Weichenrieder, A.J. (2015), *Does exchange of information between tax authorities influence multinationals' use of tax havens?*, ZEW Discussion Paper, No. 15-015.

Weichenrieder, A.J. and H. Windischbauer (2008), "Thin-capitalization rules and company responses: Experience from German legislation", CESifo Working Paper, No. 2456.

World Bank, (2002), "Foreign direct investment survey", Washington, DC: World Bank. http://documents.worldbank.org/curated/en/2002/01/2524561/foreign-direct-investment-survey.

Notes

1. Several commentators on the discussion draft noted the possibility of academic "publication bias", where empirical studies not finding statistically significant effects of profit shifting are not published in academic journals.

2. Several of the studies referred to later in the chapter describe the effects of some existing BEPS counter-measures, including interest limitations. Several countries reported in the survey by the OECD CFA Working Party No.2 revenue from interest limitations ranging from 3-9% of corporate income tax revenues.

3. Kleinbard (2011).

4. OECD (2013), page 10.

5. See Fryt et al. (2015).

6. Corrado et al. (2012).

7. Devereux and Griffith (1998).

8. A number of tax returns are not included in the analysis because the compilation of the database did not distinguish between zeros and not reported. Thus, some "cash boxes" with no employees or tangible assets could have been excluded from the analysis due to missing data.

9. Dharmapala (2014), pp. 28-29.

10. The FDI weighted standard deviation presented has the FDI weights changing each year as FDI changes. Using the 2003-2013 average FDI positions as a constant weight for all years shows the same trend.

11. FDI includes both real economic activity and BEPS, so is not an ideal measure, but information about special purpose entities and other conduit financing and the ultimate destination of some FDI is not available.

12. Monkam, N. (2012).

13. UNCTAD (2015), World Investment Report.

14. Different methodologies, variable used and data sources can explain different estimates. Some microdata profit shifting studies explain a very small amount of the variation in profitability across affiliates.

15. Riedel (2015).

16. UNCTAD (2015).

17. UNCTAD (2015), World Investment Report (pp. 201): "The profit shifting and tax revenue losses estimated here are mostly confined to those associated with tax avoidance schemes that exploit a direct investment relationship through equity or debt." "Trade mispricing does not require a direct investment link: MNEs can shift profits between any two affiliates based in jurisdictions with different tax rates."

18. Tax rate differentials are both positive and negative so BEPS involves some redistribution of revenue across countries. Because BEPS involves shifting of profits from entities subject to marginal tax rates higher than to the entities receiving the shifted income, profit shifting is not a zero-sum game: it involves significant global revenue losses. Individual country estimates are not done due to data limitations and the complexity of individual countries' tax rules.

19. Averages are weighted by share of corporate tax collections after tax credits in 2005-2010 among the countries included in the analysis. For the final profit shifting fiscal estimate, actual corporate tax collections after tax credits are adjusted upward by 23% to more accurately reflect the taxable income base affected by profit shifting, based on a CFA/WP2 survey of corporate tax credits, principally at 2011 levels.

20. A sensitivity test shows the effect of an alternative tax rate differential and weighting factor. The tax rate differential calculated for the MNE entities in the ORBIS database could be changed to the tax rate differential between countries weighted by their macro-level goods export trade. Bilateral trade in goods exports is an important area of transfer mispricing, although comparable data for related party exports are not available for many countries. Services including royalties have larger tax rate differentials, but service export data are not comprehensive. A second adjustment could weight country tax rate differentials by corporate taxes before credits, rather than corporate taxes after credits. Those two adjustments result in the global corporate tax revenue loss ranging from 6% to 14% of CIT. Leaving the revenue loss from mismatches and tax preferences aside, the two changes produce an estimate of corporate revenue loss just from profit shifting in the same range as the base case.

21. The analysis in Annex 3.A1 tested the sensitivity of the profit shifting tax responsiveness for country fixed effects. The regression coefficient was one-third lower than the baseline estimate. Country fixed effects are used to hold non-tax factors constant across counties, but the estimates of the tax relationship is then based only on variation in tax rates *within* countries over time, since *between* country variation in tax rates are captured by the country fixed effects. When using the profit shifting estimate with country fixed effects, the global corporate tax revenue loss ranges from 3% to 8% of CIT. Country fixed effects are already used in the mismatches and tax preferences regression estimate.

22. The 95% confidence interval is roughly two standard deviations from the mean. The profit shifting estimate's standard error is 0.0164 and the ETR differential estimate's standard error is 0.0026.

23. IMF (2014), pp. 20 and 61-65.

24. UNCTAD, World Investment Report (2015), pp. 201-204 and Annex II pp. 24-26.

25. United States Joint Committee on Taxation (2014).

26. Dowd, Landefeld and Moore (2015).

27. MSCI (2015).

28. Christian Aid (2009).

29. Oxfam (2015).

30. Bach (2013).

31. Clausing (2011).

32. Vicard (2015).

33. Annex 3.A1.

34. Scottmay (2015).

35. Slemrod and Wilson (2009) and Dharmapala (2014).

36. Cederwall (2015).

37. Slemrod (2010).

38. See Fuest (2015).

39. See Clausing (2012), Gravelle (2010), Harberger (1995) and Harberger (2006).

40. The standard corporate income tax incidence analysis is based on the "Harberger Model" of the incidence of changes in a general corporate income tax. For a fairly easy-to-follow explanation of the model, see Harberger (1995). In this article, Harberger explains how his original closed-economy model has to be modified to analyse CIT incidence in the international setting. Randolph (2006) provides a more detailed analysis of the expected incidence of the general corporate income tax.

41. It has been noted that the incidence effects outlined in this section are similar in nature to the "new view" of the incidence of a property in open-border local economies. See Mieszkowski and Zodrow (1986). In this view, property owners bear the burden of an average tax rate across jurisdictions with above and below-average tax rates creating "excise tax" effects in different jurisdictions that shift the remaining portion of the burden to households. See Gravelle (2010).

42. This result under perfect competition is fundamentally the same result that would be expected from an increase in the CIT in a closed-border economy, except that the reallocations of capital occur between the corporate and non-corporate sectors only, not across borders. Harberger (2006) made this point, noting: " if all countries (or a set of big countries making up most of the world economy) choose to move their CIT rates in more-or-less parallel fashion, then the appropriate [incidence] model is one of a closed economy." (p.7).

43. Corrado et al. (2009) and Corrado et al. (2012).

44. Cronin et al. (2012) estimate that 63% of the total returns to capital is excess profits, while only 37% is a "normal" return.

45. Clausing (2012) discusses how the presence of economic rents would increase the burden of CIT on owners of capital. She also notes empirical studies of the incidence of the CIT in the international setting are "tainted" by the presence of BEPS as MNEs can reduce effective tax rates through the shifting of profits unrelated to changes in the international allocation of capital. In this case, there may be a minimal tax burden on capital to be shifted. Voget (2015) cites some empirical studies that "could imply that some of the multinationals' rents are location specific and relatively immobile".

46. Devereux and Griffith (1998) note that MNEs facing discrete investment choices with finite capital will choose location decisions based on the average effective tax rate, rather than the marginal effective tax rate on investment. This incidence analysis assumes companies have access to capital when earning excess returns, and thus would still be earning more than the next-best alternative investment.

47. The estimated range includes two effects: 1) a range of -2.5% to -5.0% around the estimated average -3.25% lower effective tax rates due to mismatches between tax systems and domestic tax preferences, and 2) a range of -1.5% to -3.5%% due to profit shifting of all MNEs. The latter estimate multiples the estimated -2.8% to -7.5%

reduction in global CIT revenue from profit shifting alone times the estimated 59% of MNEs' share of profits divided by the average weighted effective tax rate of 30% in the countries included in the analysis.

48. Several studies do not report finding statistical differences, although the studies differ in the companies analysed and have different methodologies. See Markle and Shackelford (2012), Dyreng and Markle (2014) and UNCTAD (2015). The Annex 1 estimate finds a statistically significant difference between large MNEs and similarly situated domestic-only large affiliates. It does not find a statistically-significant difference between large MNEs, small MNEs and small domestic-only affiliates.

49. European Commission (2015).

50. Akcigit et al. (2015) analyse the international mobility of inventors and personal income taxation, and report inventors who are employed by MNEs are more likely to take advantage of personal income tax differentials.

51. It is possible that company officials place less importance on national taxes currently due to the availability of BEPS.

52. Chen and Mintz (2008).

53. Hanlon and Heitzman (2010) discusses how many tax planning activities reduce both financial reported profits and taxable income ("conforming" planning), and thus do not affected measured ETRs. Only "non-conforming" planning where taxable income or taxes are reduced but reported profits are not results in lower ETRs. For instance, increased interest deductions reduce both reported profits and taxable income, while exempt dividends do not affect reported profits, but reduce taxable income.

54. European Commission (2015).

55. See Genschel and Schwarz (2011) and Keen and Konrad (2014).

56. De Mooij (2011).

57. Hebous and Ruf (2015).

58. The tax accounting literature has begun work in this area but limited by available financial statement information. For example, see Armstrong et al. (2015).

59. Mintz and Venkatachalam (2015).

60. See Hoopes (2015) for current summary of literature.

Annex 3.A1

Economic implications of multinational tax planning

Box 3.A1.1. Summary of main findings

This annex provides robust evidence of tax planning by multinational enterprises (MNEs). The analysis is based on a sample of data that are considered to be the best available cross-country firm-level information. Yet, the data have significant limitations in their representativeness in some countries, do not include all MNE entities and are based upon financial accounts rather than tax returns.

The focus of this annex is broader than the OECD/G20 Base Erosion and Profit Shifting (BEPS) Project.[1] The BEPS Project focuses on "instances where the interaction of different tax rules leads to double non-taxation or less than single taxation" and it also relates to "arrangements that achieve no or low taxation by shifting profits away from the jurisdictions where the activities creating those profits take place". The analysis contained in this study assesses the fiscal and economic implications of international differences in statutory and effective corporate tax rates and as such it also covers domestic tax incentives.

Tax planning is widespread among MNEs and entails tax revenue losses.

- **Robust empirical evidence shows that MNEs engage in international tax planning.** MNEs shift profit from higher to lower-tax rate countries. Large MNEs also exploit mismatches between tax systems (e.g. differences in the tax treatment of certain entities, instruments or transactions) and preferential tax treatment for certain activities or incomes to reduce their tax burden.
- **Transfer price manipulation, strategic allocation of intangible assets and manipulation of internal and external debt levels are important profit shifting channels.**
- **The empirical patent analysis suggests that preferential tax treatment of intellectual property (IP) influences the location of intangible assets.** Preferential IP regimes attract research activities and the ownership of patents invented in other countries. Preferential regimes may also encourage the relabeling of certain incomes to benefit from the regime.
- **Tax planning reduces the effective tax rate of large MNEs by 4-8½ percentage points on average.** The reduction is even greater for very large firms and firms intensive in the use of intangible assets. Small MNEs also engage in tax planning but to a lesser extent.
- **The net tax revenue loss from tax planning is estimated at 4-10% of global corporate tax revenues.** These estimates based on 2000-10 data are surrounded by uncertainty and should be interpreted with caution.

Box 3.A1.1. Summary of main findings *(continued)*

- **Strict anti-avoidance rules reduce tax planning.** Strict anti-avoidance rules, such as transfer pricing, interest deductibility, GAARs and CFCs rules, are found to reduce profit shifting. However, complex rules generate compliance costs for all firms, hampering profitability, as well as administrative and enforcement costs for tax authorities. These costs could be reduced by international co-ordination.

Tax planning effects on economic efficiency are unclear.

- **Tax planning may allow certain MNEs to increase their market power**, resulting in more concentrated markets. The reduced competitive pressure may entail welfare losses. However, these losses may be partially offset by the associated reallocation of resources to high-productivity MNEs.
- **The possibility to manipulate the location of internal and external debt lowers the cost of debt for MNE groups and can compound the "debt-bias" present in most tax systems.** Even so, domestic firms have on average higher external leverage than MNE groups. Information on internal debt is not available.
- **International tax planning reduces effective tax rates and the effect of cross-country corporate tax differences on the location of investment by tax planning MNEs.** However, this is achieved at the cost of additional distortions (e.g. uneven playing field between tax-planning MNEs and other firms) as compared with a situation in which corporate tax rates were cut across the board.

Introduction

The design of corporate tax systems influences the behaviour of multinational enterprises (MNEs). International differences in taxation can lead MNEs to locate a larger share of their economic activity in lower-tax countries. In addition, it can lead to international tax planning by MNEs to reduce their tax burden. MNEs may locate profits in lower-tax countries, independently of where the profit-generating activity takes place, for example by manipulating the price of intra-group transactions or the location of external and related-party debt. They may also exploit differences in the tax treatment of certain entities or instruments (henceforth called mismatches between tax systems) or preferential tax treatment for certain activities or incomes to reduce their tax burden. In some cases, MNEs may also defer repatriation of profits from abroad indefinitely to avoid taxes. This raises a number of fiscal, redistributive and economic efficiency concerns, which are discussed in this study (see Figure 3.A1.1 for an overview).

Figure 3.A1.1. Issues covered by the analysis

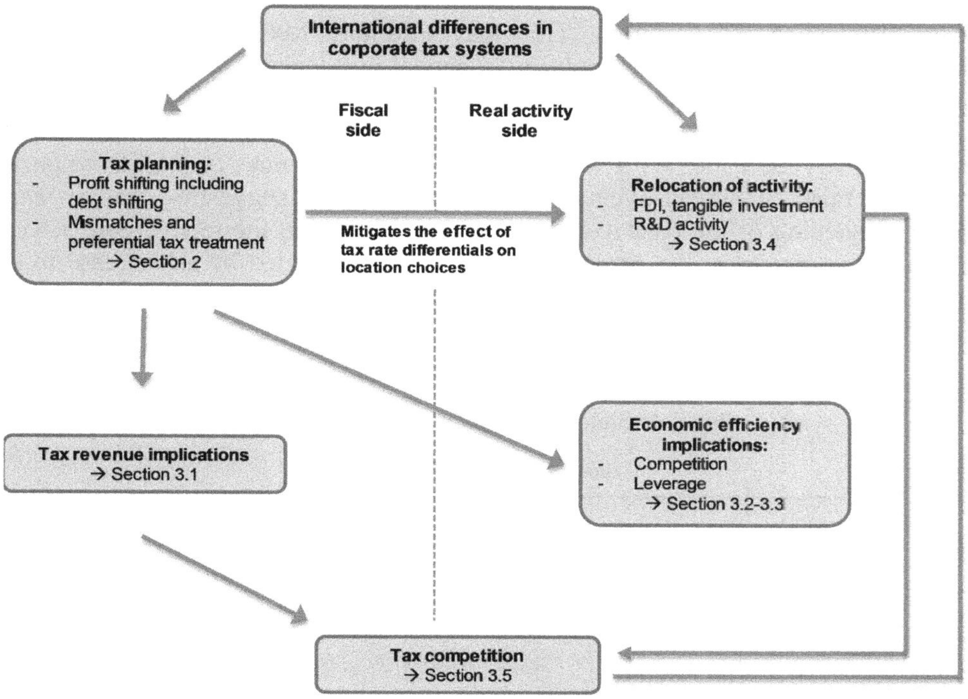

This annex provides an estimate of tax planning based on financial account data from the largest commercially-available firm-level database (ORBIS).[2] The study estimates the relationship between tax rate differentials and profit shifting using financial account data. It is well known that the legal accounting standards for firms differ between public financial accounting and confidential tax accounting (e.g. Lisowsky, 2010) and improved access to data, especially tax return data, would enable refined estimates of the effects of tax planning. In the absence of such data, this study relies on the best cross-country firm-level financial account data currently available.

The study looks at both fiscal and efficiency issues related to tax planning behaviour by MNEs. Tax planning affects the distribution of tax bases and revenues among countries, thereby entailing fiscal considerations. By reducing the effective corporate tax rate of certain MNEs relatively to other MNEs and domestic firms, tax planning may also distort competition and lead to efficiency losses (e.g. if domestic firms are hindered from growing). Tax planning opportunities may also be one factor altering firms' financing decisions by reinforcing the debt bias present in most countries' tax system at the expense of equity financing, with potential effects on firms' investment choices and bankruptcy risks at the MNE group level.

The location of MNE investments in tangible and intangible assets depends, among other factors (e.g. labour taxation, regulations, access to market, agglomeration effects, labour force skills, quality of infrastructure, etc.), on corporate taxation. All else equal, countries with lower tax rates or preferential tax regimes for certain investments attract more foreign investment including R&D investments than higher-tax countries. These investments can create technological spillovers, with positive effects for productivity and growth (and in turn reduce such positive spillovers in higher-tax countries) (e.g. Blomström and Kokko, 1998; Markusen and Venables, 1999). They can also influence trade patterns (Dahlby, 2011).

Globalisation and the ongoing integration of world capital markets may further increase the mobility of corporate tax bases and the sensitivity of investment to international tax differences (Braconier et al., 2014). This may intensify tax competition. Indeed, evidence suggests that an increasing mobility of capital is associated with lower statutory corporate tax rates (Devereux et al., 2008; OECD, 2009; Arnold et al., 2011; IMF, 2014), which is consistent with the reduction in corporate tax rates that occurred over the past decades (Figure 3.A1.3, Panel A). Even so, corporate tax revenues of OECD countries have remained fairly stable on average as a share of GDP, suggesting that in many countries a broadening of the base has accompanied the cuts in the rate (Figure 3.A1.2, Panel B). In some countries, the corporate tax base was supported by an increase in the profit rate and also possibly by substitution effects between personal and corporate income tax.

Figure 3.A1.2 Corporate tax rates and tax revenues

Panel A: Statutory corporate tax rate, %[3]

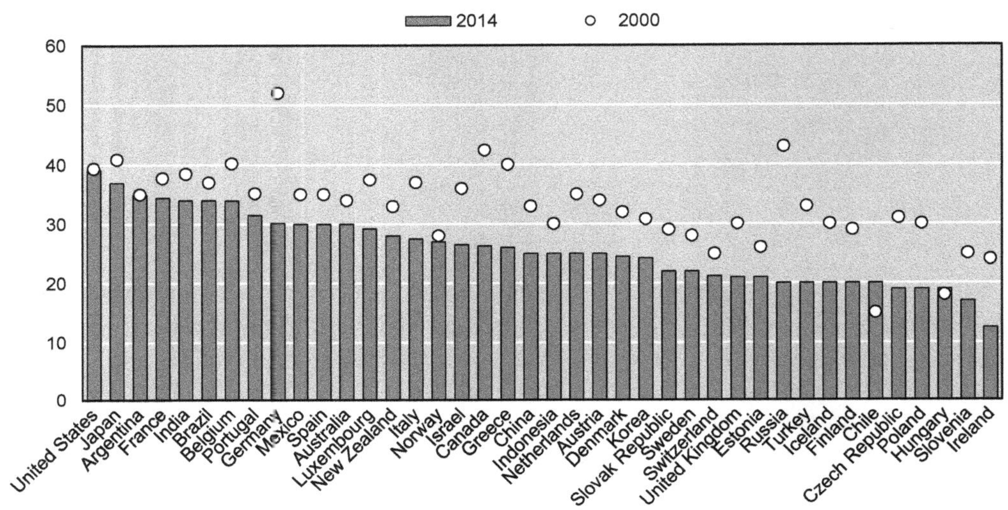

Panel B: Corporate tax revenues in OECD countries, % of GDP[4]

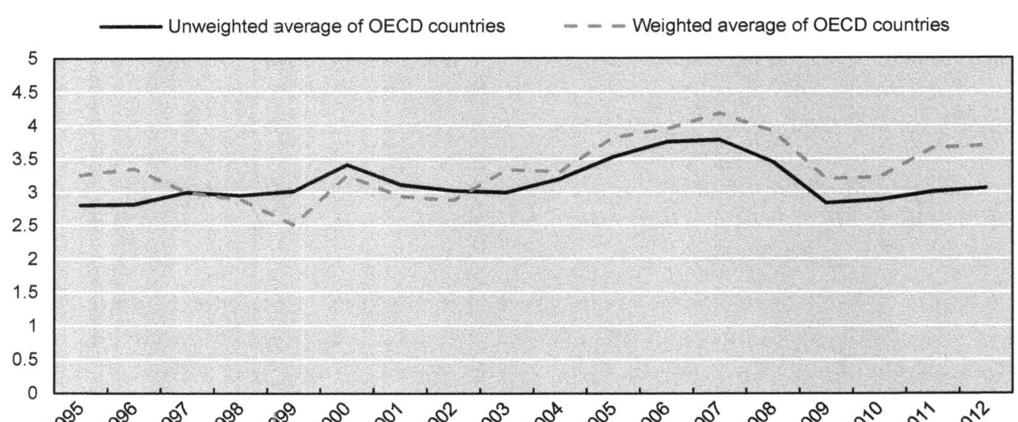

Source: OECD Tax Database and KPMG.

Assessing tax planning of MNEs

Main tax planning channels

Tax planning, as defined in this annex, is somewhat broader than BEPS behaviours identified in the OECD/G20 BEPS Action Plan (OECD, 2013). The BEPS project focuses on *"instances where the interaction of different tax rules leads to double non-taxation or less than single taxation"* and it also relates to *"arrangements that achieve no or low taxation by shifting profits away from the jurisdictions where the activities creating those profits take place"* (OECD, 2013).

In this study, tax planning refers to situations in which there is a disconnection between the location of profits and the real activity generating them. It also includes situations where the effective tax rate (ETR) of MNEs is artificially reduced – compared to that of similar domestic firms – due to exploitation of tax planning schemes involving loopholes in tax systems and preferential tax treatment. Some behaviours included in the measure of tax planning in this study are not BEPS behaviours, such as the decision to carry out substantial activity in a country to benefit from certain preferential tax treatments (e.g. R&D tax subsidies). This reflects the limitations of the available data, which make it impossible to disentangle certain BEPS from non-BEPS behaviours. Still, most tax planning channels covered by the analysis in this study overlap with BEPS behaviours and represent artificial financial flows that are not related to the location of real activity. Below is a non-exhaustive and simplified description of the tax planning channels covered in the analysis in this study:

- **Profit shifting channels:** MNEs have different ways to reduce their corporate tax burden by locating in lower-tax rate countries their profit generated in higher-tax rate countries.[5]

  - **Transfer price optimisation:** Optimising the price of transactions between related entities within the range of possible market-based so-called "arm's length" prices to achieve tax advantages. For example, by selecting a low price in the range for rights, products and services transferred from high to low-tax entities or *vice versa*.

  - **Allocation of intangibles, assets and risks:** Allocating through intra-group arrangements the ownership of income producing intangibles, assets and risks in low-tax countries to divert profit from high-tax countries. Operational functions are more difficult to re-locate and the main value-creating activities which manage and exploit those intangibles, assets and risks may be performed in higher-tax locations under contract to the legal owner.

  - **Manipulation of the location of debt:** Interest payments on debt are generally deductible from taxable income. Locating MNE external and internal debt (and the associated interest payments) in an entity in a higher-tax rate country allows offsetting profits and reducing tax payments of this entity.

- **Mismatches between tax systems, including preferential tax treatment and negotiated tax rates:** MNEs may exploit differences in the tax treatment of entities, instruments, or transfers between countries to reduce their corporate tax burden (OECD, 2014b). This is possible even in the absence of a difference between statutory tax rates. MNEs may also be able to reduce their tax burden via preferential tax treatment and negotiated firm-specific reduced tax rates.

- **Hybrid instruments and transfers:** Instruments which are treated differently in two countries, for example as debt in one country and as equity in another country. This can result in an interest deduction in the first country and non-taxable income in the second country (as the income is treated as a tax-exempt dividend).

- **Hybrid entities:** The same entity can be treated differently in two countries for tax purpose. For instance, an entity may be considered as tax resident by no country (so called "stateless entities") and in this way achieve double non-taxation of profit. Alternatively, an entity can be treated as a non-taxable entity such as a partnership (where the partners are taxed instead of the entity itself) in one country and a taxable entity in another. This can result in a deduction in the first country and non-inclusion of the income in the second country.

- **Preferential tax treatment:** MNEs may shift certain incomes to benefit from special tax treatment offered by some countries (or areas within them), such as for intellectual property (e.g. patent boxes) or financial services. Domestic firms can also benefit from preferential tax treatment, but to a lesser extent than MNEs since they cannot shift incomes across borders to enjoy these treatments on a larger scale.[6]

- **Negotiated tax rates:** Firm-specific reduced tax rates for individual MNEs through negotiation between the MNE and the tax authority.

Tax planning schemes are often complex and can involve several of these channels in combination. To take this complexity into account, this study relies on a systematic top-down approach. It first focuses on where profits of MNEs are reported (profit shifting), and second it assesses the effective taxation of reported profits in each country (mismatches between tax systems, including preferential tax regimes). This ensures consistency and that there is no double-counting between the two. The exploitation of preferential tax regimes and negotiated tax rates are included in the mismatches analysis since they cannot be disentangled from them with the available data.

The approach also takes into account potential interactions between profit shifting and mismatches between tax systems. For instance, if profits are shifted to a country to enjoy a preferential tax treatment, the ETR differential resulting from this treatment is applied to the complete tax base (i.e. including the shifted profits) when assessing the fiscal implications of tax planning.

MNEs engage in international tax planning

The empirical analysis, covering a large sample of firms from 46 countries (mainly OECD and G20) based on financial accounts data, supports the hypothesis that MNEs engage in international tax planning. This confirms the existing anecdotal insights, case studies of specific firms and findings from other firm-level studies. These studies most often cover only one specific country – or only European countries – and are based on much smaller samples of firms (e.g. Huizinga and Leaven, 2008; Clausing, 2009; Fuest and Riedel, 2010; Heckemeyer and Overesch, 2013). Both profit shifting and the exploitation of mismatches between tax systems (including the exploitation of preferential tax treatment) are found to be important tax planning strategies.[7]

Profit shifting analyses in the literature rely either on financial account data (e.g. the ORBIS database or its regional subsamples) or tax returns (e.g. Grubert, 2012 for the United States), the latter being only available at the country level and on a non-harmonised and confidential basis (Dharmapala, 2014). The analysis in this report is based on commercially-available financial account data that offers the advantage of wide cross-country coverage and largely consistent accounting rules across countries (see Box 3.A1.2 for details on the data). However, one caveat is that reported profits in financial accounts may differ from taxable profits due to divergence in accounting standards and tax planning.[8] More specifically, reported profit can differ from taxable profit due to differences in the timing of recognition of income and expenses (e.g. different capital depreciation rules), in the definition of income (e.g. Hanlon, 2003; Boynton et al., 2014), because taxable profit may reflect past losses being carried forward or because tax residence of an affiliate is different from its country of incorporation. Nevertheless, profit reported in financial accounts and taxable profit is expected to be generally affected in the same direction by profit shifting, justifying the use of reported profit as a proxy for taxable profit. Still, differences in profits and taxes reported in financial accounts and tax returns are a limitation of currently available firm-level information.

Box 3.A1.2. Disclaimer on the data used in the empirical analysis

Measuring tax planning of multinationals poses a number of data challenges. Data from tax reports are confidential and not available on a cross-country basis. In addition, in most countries tax data do not include information on group activities, profits and tax payments abroad, which is necessary to properly assess profit shifting. In the absence of consistent tax data, this study relies on the ORBIS database (commercialised by Bureau Van Dijk), which is generally considered as the most comprehensive commercially-available data on (listed and non-listed) firms' financial accounts and ownership structures (Fuest and Riedel, 2012; Dharmapala, 2014).

The ORBIS database and coverage of the sample

The ORBIS data is based on financial accounts of firms as reported to institutions such as business registers, chambers of commerce or local credit institutions. These data have been cleaned and checked by the OECD Statistics Directorate to ensure consistency across countries (Ragoussis and Gonnard, 2012) and further reviewed for this project by removing implausible values and outliers. The final sample consists of 1.2 million observations of unconsolidated MNE accounts over the period 2000-2010 in 46 countries. Although the economies themselves cover about 90% of world GDP, the coverage in the sample varies meaningfully across countries. Hence a smaller fraction of the activity is likely to be accounted for in countries with low representation. See below for more details on coverage. Additionally, MNEs' links to countries outside of the sample (including no-corporate-tax countries) are also taken into account. The MNE group identification iterates on the direct ownership information in ORBIS to account for missing information on the final owner of a firm. Two firms are assumed to be linked if one owns the other with a share of at least 50%. MNEs account for an important share of large firms and profits in many countries, particularly in smaller (more open) economies (Figure below).

Box 3.A1.2. Disclaimer on the data used in the empirical analysis *(continued)*

Distribution of firms in the sample, by firm type[9,10,11]

Panel A: As a share of total number of firms (only firms with more than 250 employees)

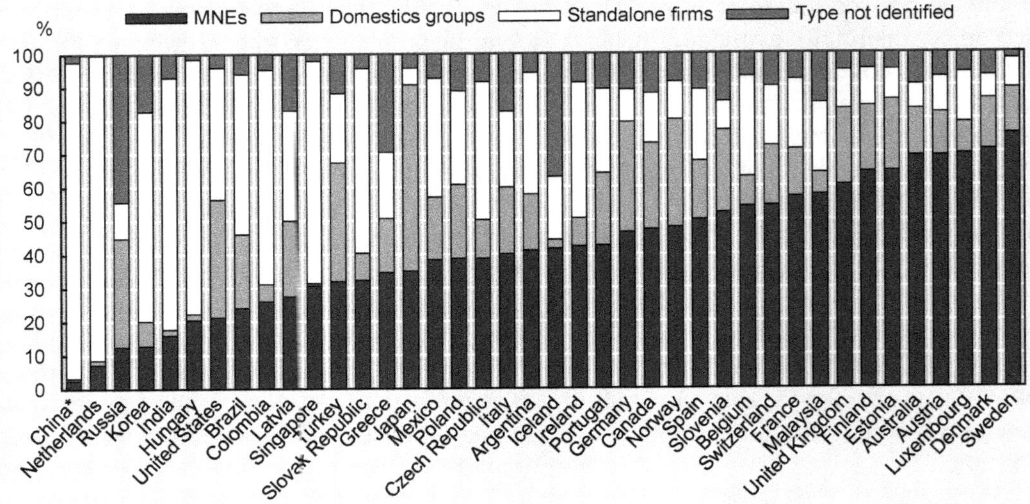

Panel B: As a share of reported pre-tax profits (only profitable firms)

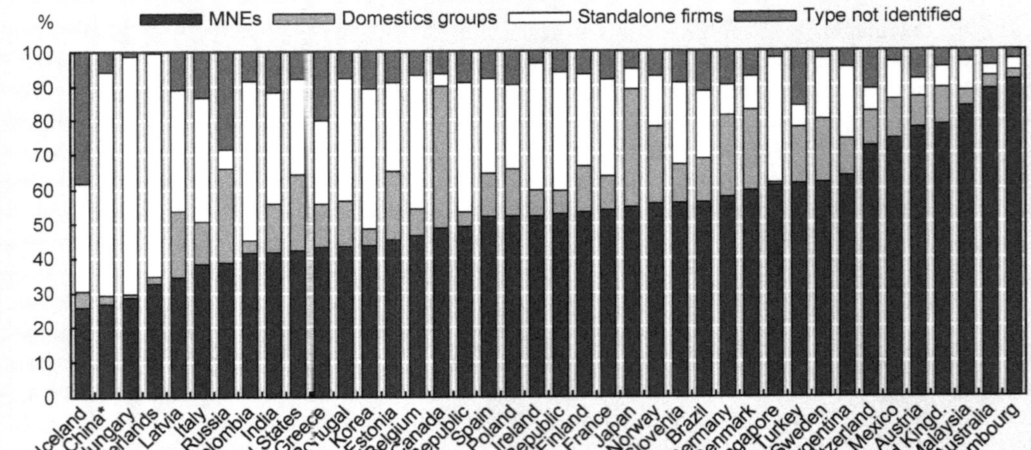

* People's Republic of China

Box 3.A1.2. Disclaimer on the data used in the empirical analysis *(continued)*

Quality of the sample and of the MNE group identification

The coverage of firms with available financial account data varies across countries. Compared with the actual population of firms (when data on the actual population is available), the coverage is above 50% in most European countries and less than 10% in most non-European countries. However, it is limited in some countries, including the United States, New Zealand and Chile (see Figure below). The distribution of observations across industries is somewhat higher in manufacturing than in services.

Representativeness of the final sample

Number of firms in the final ORBIS sample, as a share of the total in STAN business demography statistics, 2006[12]

Panel A: by country

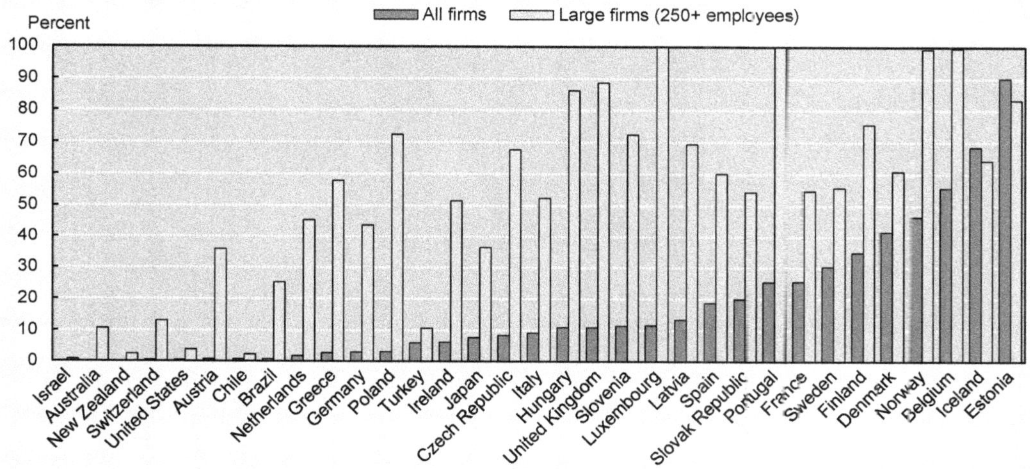

Note: The statistical data for Israel are supplied by and under the responsibility of the relevant Israeli authorities. The use of such data by the OECD is without prejudice to the status of the Golan Heights, East Jerusalem and Israeli settlements in the West Bank under the terms of international law.

Panel B: by industry

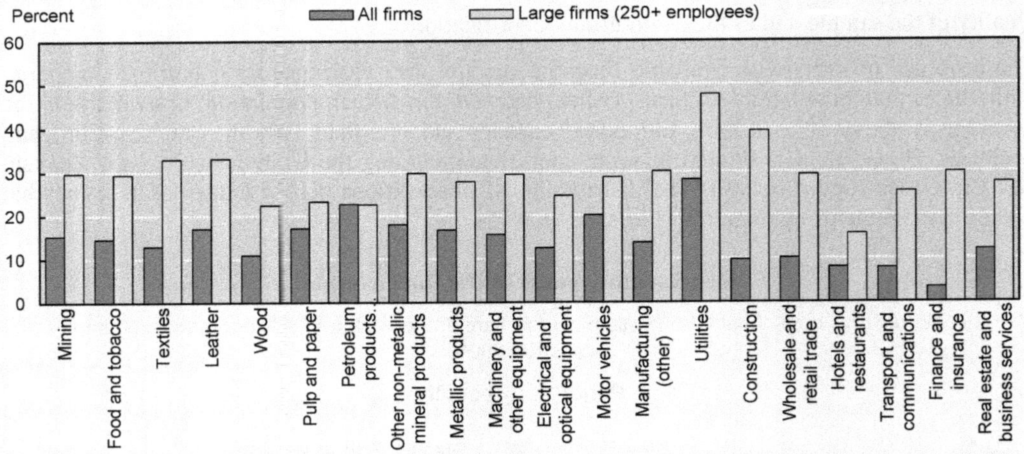

Source: OECD calculations based on the ORBIS database and OECD STAN business demography statistics.

For an average MNE group, more than 50% of the worldwide activity is covered, which is a higher share that in other recent studies (e.g. Huizinga and Laeven, 2008). An issue is the lack of financial data in certain no-corporate-tax countries. This is mitigated by the methodological approach, which only relies on links to these countries being identified, not on the availability of financial accounts in these countries. Still not all links are identified in ORBIS. It is difficult to assess the magnitude and importance of the missing links due to general lack of data on actual links. Nevertheless, an important number of links to no-corporate tax countries is identified (see Figure below). For example, among the top-500 United States firms (Fortune 500 list for 2013), Citizens for Tax Justice (CTJ, 2014) identify 362 firms having links to "tax havens". Of these 362 firms, 266 (i.e. 72%) are in the ORBIS sample. Among these 266 firms, at least one tax haven link is identified in ORBIS in 184 cases, i.e. 69% of the times (this represents just over half of top United States firms with tax haven links).

Given that financial reporting requirements are usually stricter for large firms, the coverage of the data is generally better for these firms. This would suggest that the coverage of MNE entities is better than average as they are generally large entities, although entities in large MNE groups can be small. It is possible that MNEs heavily involved in tax planning or using complex schemes (e.g. "stateless" entities for tax purposes) opt not to disclose their financial accounts to business registers if the repercussion of not complying with reporting is limited. This may result in under-sampling of such firms, which may bias the results when there are "non-random reasons for information to be missing (e.g. accounts in low-tax jurisdictions are less likely to be included in the dataset)" (Cobham and Loretz, 2014). This issue is addressed in the sensitivity analysis.

Finally, the current OECD-ORBIS database includes data up to 2010 and the analysis is based on the 2000-10 period. Since then, tax planning behaviours may have changed reflecting factors such as the growing importance of the digital economy and changes in anti-avoidance rules against tax planning and in global value chains. In addition, corporate tax rates have been cut in some countries.

Box 3.A1.2. Disclaimer on the data used in the empirical analysis *(continued)*

Identified links to no-corporate-tax countries of entities in the sample

Share of large MNE entities in the sample having links to countries not taxing corporate income[13,14]

Panel A: by country of headquarters

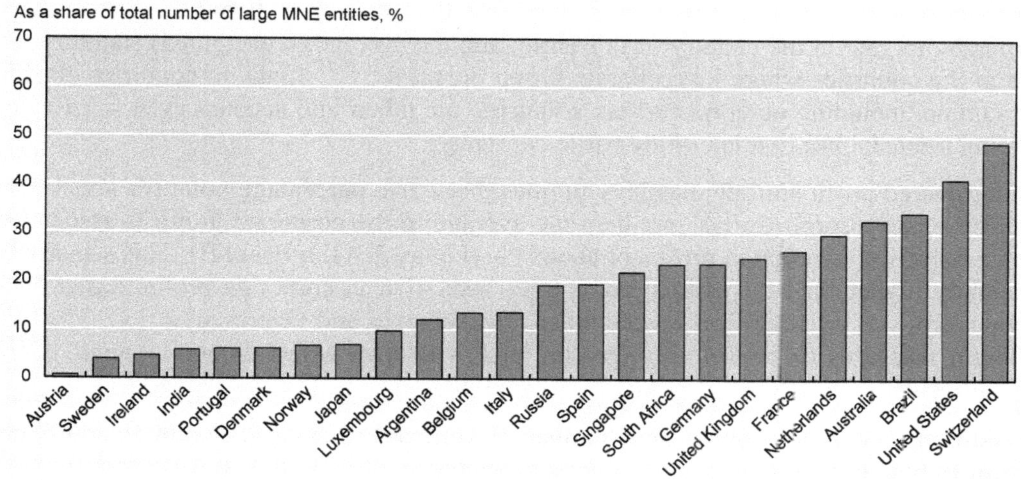

Panel B: by industry

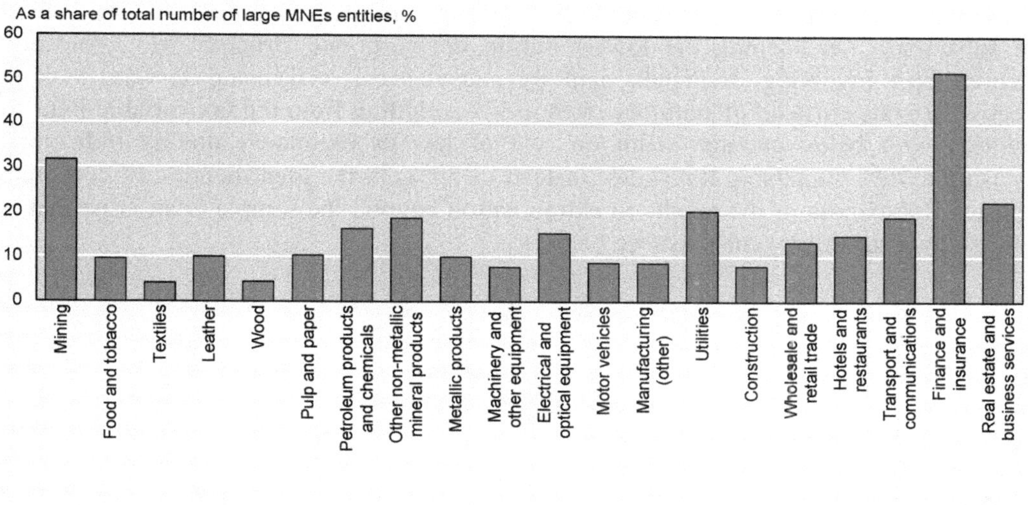

Profit shifting

The empirical strategy to identify profit shifting is to compare the profitability (measured as the ratio of pre-tax profit to total assets or employment) of MNE entities with similar characteristics (e.g. size, industry, etc.), but different opportunities to shift profits (see Box 3.A1.3 for details and Figure 3.A1.3, Panel A). These opportunities depend on the location of the other entities in the corporate group. Entities with links to lower-tax rate countries have opportunities to shift profits abroad, while entities with links to higher-tax rate countries may receive profits from abroad. In this study, the profit shifting opportunity of a MNE entity is measured by the difference between the statutory corporate tax rate in the country of this entity and the average (unweighted) statutory tax rate in the countries where its corporate group operates.[15,16,17] Links to countries outside the sample, including no-corporate-tax countries, are taken into account even in cases of missing financial information of the particular entity.

The estimated profit shifting elasticity implies that a one percentage point (or about 3%) higher statutory corporate tax rate than the average in the corporate group is associated with a reduction in reported profits of about 1% (Figure 3.A1.3, Panel B). This sensitivity is slightly higher than the estimate of a 0.8% reduction in corporate profits based on a meta-analysis of existing firm-level studies (Heckemeyer and Overesch, 2013). The two different measures of profitability (pre-tax profits to total assets or employment) yield similar results.

In addition, results are robust to a number of variants: (i) using different fixed-effects structures (e.g. country and country-interacted-with-time fixed-effects); (ii) restricting the sample to EU countries; (iii) restricting the sample to manufacturing firms; (iv) restricting the sample to sub-periods; (v) re-sampling observations to adjust for the relatively low representation of certain countries in the analysis; (vi) dropping all entities having at least one subsidiary, i.e. keeping the lowest tier in the corporate structure, (to avoid any potential bias involving dividends paid by subsidiaries); (vii) using forward-looking effective tax rates instead of statutory rates; (viii) excluding from the tax variable links to countries with below-average score on rule of law or regulatory quality indicators; (ix) using a 90% ownership threshold (instead of 50%) in the identification of corporate groups.[18] Robustness of the results to extrapolation beyond the sample is an issue that is addressed via sensitivity analysis (see below).

Figure 3.A1.3 Empirical approach on profit shifting: Illustrative example[19]

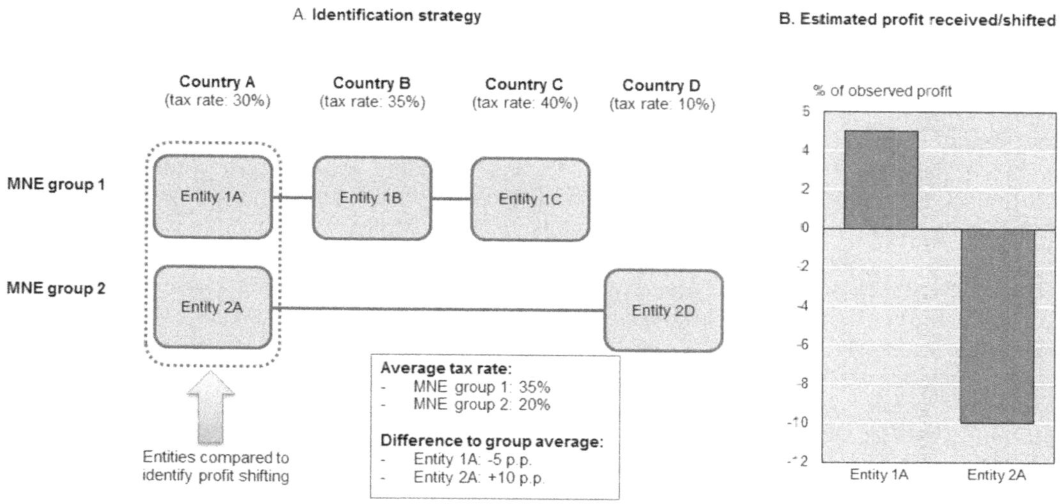

Box 3.A1.3. Empirical approach: Assessing tax planning based on firm-level data

The strategy to assess profit shifting is to compare the profitability of MNE entities with similar characteristics except for their links to countries with different tax rates. The hypothesis is that MNEs with links to lower-tax rate countries would report relatively low profits in entities located in higher-tax countries compared with similar firms that have no such links. In practice, the estimated equation is as follows:

$$Profitability_{f,g,c,i,t} = \alpha X_{f,g,c,i,t} + \beta\left(STAT_{c,t} - STAT\_group\_avg_{g,c,i,t}\right) + \delta_t + \delta_i,$$

where $Profitability_{f,g,c,i,t}$ is the profitability (the ratio of reported pre-tax profits to total assets or employment) of firm f (operating in MNE group g, country c and industry i) in year t. $X_{f,g,c,i,t}$ is a vector of determinants of true profitability, which includes both firm-specific characteristics (size, position in the group, presence of patents in the group) and macroeconomic variables (GDP growth, exchange rate, inflation, GDP per capita). $\left(STAT_{c,t} - STAT\_group\_avg_{g,c,i,t}\right)$ is the difference between the statutory tax rate in country c and year t and the unweighted average of the statutory tax rates in the countries where the multinational group g operates. Statutory rates are national averages (i.e. they do not reflect regional differences in rates) and do not take into account tax holidays. The tax sensitivity of profits is measured by the coefficient β, which is expected to be negative if profits are shifted to lower-tax rate countries. δ_t, δ_i are respectively time and industry fixed-effects to control for unobserved (non-tax) factors affecting profitability.*

Excluding country fixed-effects in the baseline estimation may bias the estimated tax sensitivity (upwards or downwards) since some unobserved country-specific factors may be captured by the tax sensitivity. However, such fixed-effects may also capture some profit shifting, which would result in underestimating profit shifting (Clausing, 2009; Buettner and Wamser, 2013). The results are qualitatively robust to including both country and country-interacted-with-time fixed-effects, although the tax sensitivity would be reduced by about 30%.

The strategy to assess (jointly) mismatches between tax systems and preferential tax treatment is to compare the effective tax rate (ETR) of a multinational entity in a given country to the ETR of a domestic (i.e. non-MNE) entity with similar characteristics. The ETR considered is the ratio of tax expenses over the profit reported in the financial statements of the firm, at an unconsolidated level (i.e. for each entity in the group). One caveat is that tax expenses reported in financial accounts are likely to differ from tax liabilities in tax data, for example due to differences in the inclusion of deferred tax expenses, other book/tax differences and differences in the tax residence of the affiliate.

The hypothesis is that if a multinational entity exploits mismatches to reduce its tax burden, it may report a high profit in its financial statements, but its taxable profit (and thus its tax burden) would be lower, for example because of the use of a hybrid instrument or entity. A hybrid instrument can result in an interest deduction in one country as it is treated as debt in this country and a non-taxable income in another country where it is treated as equity. As compared to a standard debt instrument, this would lead to a lower ETR (as measured with financial account data) in the receiving country. However, there would be no visible difference in financial accounts as compared to a standard equity instrument. The use of a hybrid entity will generally result in a lower ETR, as it can allow a MNE entity to report profits in a higher-tax rate country while paying the tax rate of a lower-rate (or no-tax) country. Another example is a dual resident entity which may claim more than one tax deduction for the same interest expense, thereby reducing its ETR. The effective tax rate of MNE entities can also be reduced by the exploitation of preferential tax treatment for certain activities or incomes (e.g. shifting patents to a patent-box country), to the extent that they benefit more than domestic firms, or because of negotiated tax rates. One caveat is that unobserved and inherent differences between MNE and domestic entities that are not related to tax planning (e.g. capital intensity) may also influence their relative ETRs.

Exploiting mismatches between tax systems may involve complex schemes with important fixed costs, suggesting that only large MNEs may engage in it. To account for this, the empirical approach is to compare the effective tax rate of multinational and domestic entities among different size classes. The estimated equation is as follows:

$$ETR_{f,c,i,t} = \beta_1 Large_{firm_{f,c,i,t}} + \beta_2 Small_{firm_{f,c,i,t}} \times MNE_{f,c,i}$$

$$+\beta_3 Large\_firm_{f,c,i,t} \times MNE_{f,c,i} + \beta_4 X_{f,c,i,t} + \delta_i + \delta_{c,t},$$

where $ETR_{f,c,i,t}$ is the effective tax rate of firm f (operating in country c and industry i) in year t, measured as tax expenses over reported profit. $Large\_firm_{f,c,i,t}$ and $Small\_firm_{f,c,i,t}$ are respectively dummies for large (over 250 employees, in line with the EU definition) and small entities. $MNE_{f,c,i}$ is a dummy equal to one when a company is part of a multinational group. $X_{f,c,i,t}$ is a vector of firm-specific controls (position in the group, presence of patents, profitability). The coefficients β_2 and β_3 measure the ETR differential between small (respectively large) MNEs and comparable domestic firms. The hypothesis is that these coefficients should be negative if MNEs exploit mismatches between tax systems and preferential tax treatment to reduce their tax burden. δ_i and $\delta_{c,t}$ are dummies for industry and for country-interacted-with-time, which capture the effect of countries having different (and time-varying) tax rates.

---

* Estimating profitability of individual affiliates is very difficult with available data, as reflected in only 1.5% of the variance across affiliates being actually explained. This is common among cross-sectional firm-level studies with many observations (see for example Beer and Loeprick, 2014). It reflects the intrinsic volatility of the profit rate, which is largely driven by (unobserved) firm-specific factors. If profitability is not captured by the non-tax variables, the estimated tax responsiveness could be affected.

Mismatches between tax systems and preferential tax treatment

Mismatches between tax systems have not received as much academic attention as profit shifting and little is known about their magnitude.[20] They are more difficult to identify than profit shifting, since a mismatch can exist in any pair of tax systems (and can be aggravated by the use of a third country in a tax planning strategy) regardless of their statutory tax rate. The hypothesis is that by exploiting mismatches between tax systems, for example in the form of hybrid entities or instruments, MNEs can reduce their effective tax rate (ETR) as measured with financial account data. The empirical strategy is to compare the effective tax rate (ETR) of a MNE entity on its reported profit to the ETR of an entity in a domestic group with similar characteristics (see Box 3.A1.3 for details). Differences in ETR between MNEs and domestic entities with similar characteristics may also capture negotiated lower tax rates for MNEs. In addition, they reflect preferential tax treatment of certain activities and incomes if MNEs have structured their activities to benefit more from this treatment than domestic firms (e.g. by shifting their patents to countries with preferential treatment of patent income).

One caveat is that tax expenses reported in financial accounts can differ from actual tax liabilities or cash taxes paid. Financial tax expenses include both current and deferred tax expenses, and can be affected by changes in countries' tax rates on deferred tax assets and liabilities. In contrast, tax accounting does not include the deferred tax expense.

The empirical analysis shows that the ETR of large (with more than 250 employees) MNE entities is on average 3.3 percentage points lower than that of comparable large domestic groups, even after controlling for a number of factors affecting firms' ETR (size, industry, position in the group, presence of patents, profitability, etc.). There is no such difference among smaller firms (less than 250 employees), which may reflect the existence of large fixed costs of setting up schemes to exploit mismatches between tax systems (e.g. complex structures or financial instruments, tax and legal advice). Possibilities to negotiate reduced tax rates and to exploit preferential tax treatment may also be greater among large firms. As the empirical results for profit shifting, the results are robust to a number of variants using the available sample of firms.

Trends in international tax planning

Changes in tax planning intensity can only be assessed over 2000-2010 with the available firm-level data. The empirical analysis suggests no clear trend over this period (Figure 3.A1.4). One possible explanation is that a potential increase in the tax planning intensity due to increasing globalisation and greater reliance on intangible assets has been offset by stricter anti-avoidance rules (see section 2.5).

Figure 3.A1.4 Trends in international tax planning, 2000-2010

Panel A: Profit shifting

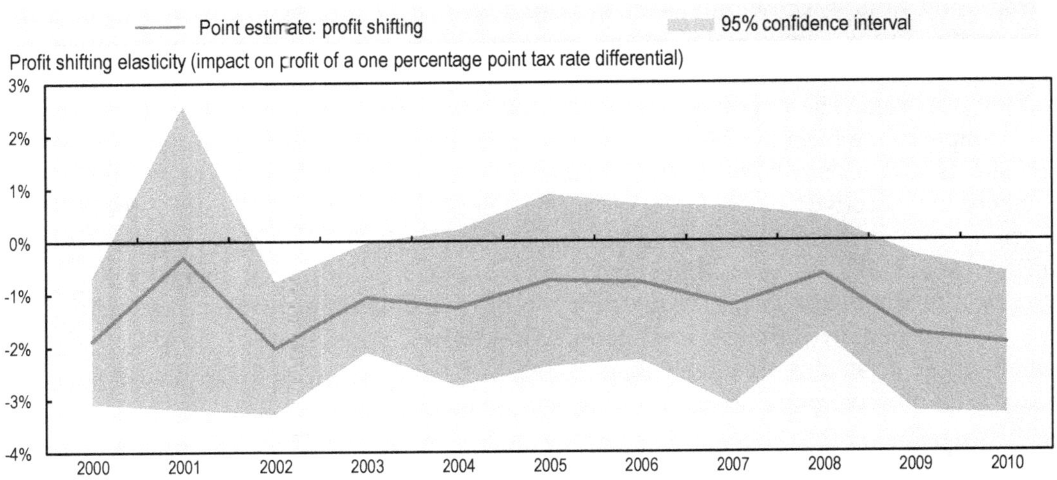

Panel B: Mismatches between tax systems including preferential tax treatment

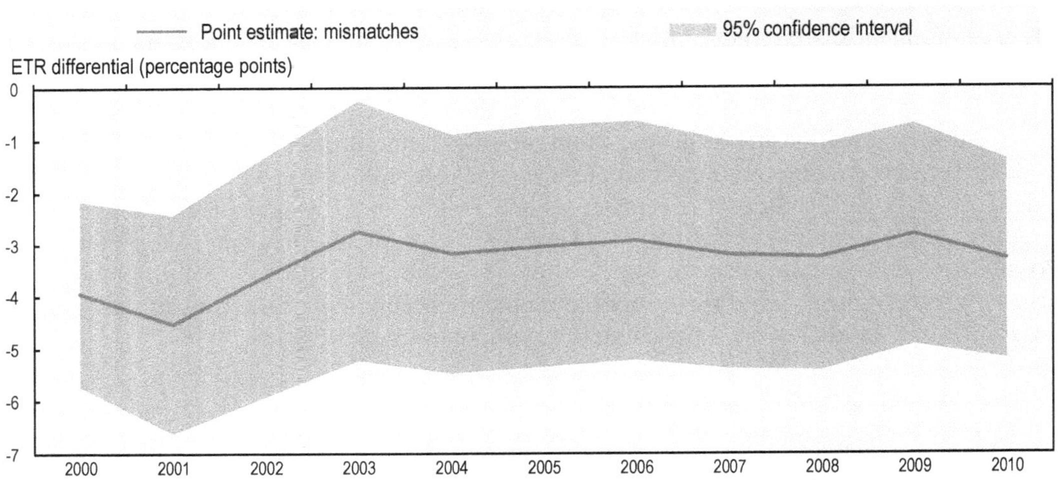

Note: Panel A shows that in 2000 a one percentage point higher statutory corporate tax rate than the average in the corporate group is associated with a reduction in reported profits of about 1.9%. Panel B shows that in 2000 the ETR of large MNE entities is on average close to 4 percentage points lower than that of comparable large domestic groups. The year estimates are obtained by interacting the tax planning sensitivities described in Box 3.A1.3 with a year dummy.

Identifying the main tax planning channels

The empirical approach in this study estimates the overall magnitude of tax planning as it is difficult to separate and quantify each channel such as transfer price manipulation and strategic location of external and internal debt. Nevertheless, it is possible with the available data to identify certain channels and certain types of MNEs engaging more intensively in tax planning.

Intangible assets are an important tax planning channel

MNEs can shift profits by locating intangible assets (e.g. patents, property rights, brands, know-how, etc.) and their associated revenues in lower-tax countries. This is facilitated by intangible assets (and the associated revenues) being easier to shift and more difficult to price and thus more susceptible to transfer price manipulation than other assets. Indeed, the share of patents that have been shifted, i.e. patents where the inventor is located in a different country than the MNE entity applying for the patent protection, varies significantly across countries (Figure 3.A1.5). Still, this can reflect factors other than taxes, such as outsourcing of R&D activities. More generally, patent data do not capture all types of intangible assets.

Figure 3.A1.5 Distribution of patents across countries

Panel A: Shifted and non-shifted patents as % of worldwide patents, 1998-2011[21]

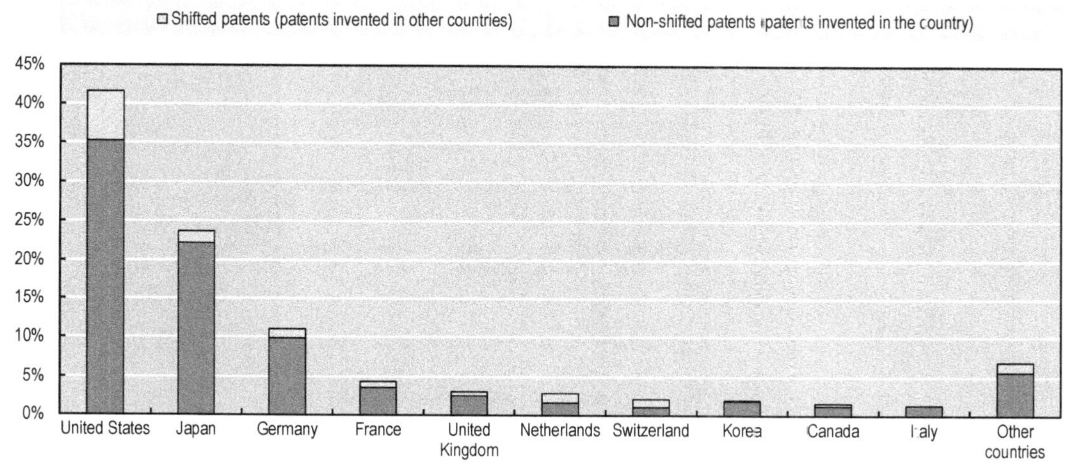

Panel B: Shifted patents as % of total patents in each country, 1998-2011[22]

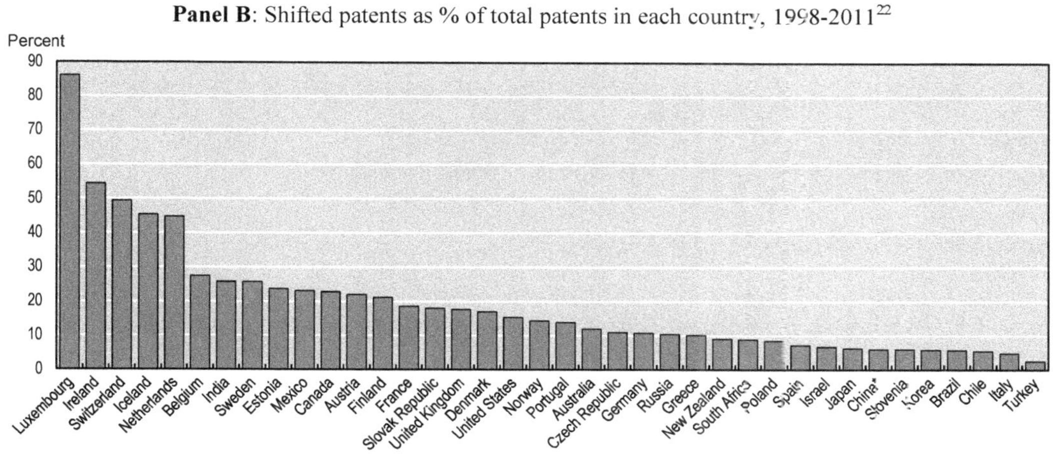

Note: The statistical data for Israel are supplied by and under the responsibility of the relevant Israeli authorities. The use of such data by the OECD is without prejudice to the status of the Golan Heights, East Jerusalem and Israeli settlements in the West Bank under the terms of international law.

* People's Republic of China.

Source: PATSTAT Database.

An increasing number of countries have preferential tax treatment of the income from intellectual activities (so-called "patent boxes" or "IP-boxes") (see Table 3.A1.1). In some countries, but not all, the preferential tax treatment is conditional on activity requirements and does not apply to acquired intellectual property unless it is further developed in the buying country (Evers et al. 2013; PWC, 2013).[23]

Table 3.A1.1 Tax treatment of intellectual property in selected OECD and G20 countries, 2014[24]

Country	Corporate tax rate	Patent box rate	Qualifying intellectual property	Acquired intellectual property	Year of introduction
Belgium	34	6.8	Patents, Supplementary Protection Certificates	Yes, if further developed	2007
China[1]	33	0-12.5	Patents, process innovation	na	2008
France	34.4	15.5	Patents, extended patent certificats, patentable inventions, manufacturing processes associated with patents, improvements of patents	Yes, under certain conditions	2001
Hungary	19	9.5	Patents, industrial designs, trademarks, copyrights, know-how, business secrets	Yes	2003
Luxembourg	29.2	5.84	Patents, designs, trademarks, brands, domain names copyrights on software	Yes	2008
Netherlands	25	5	Patents, Intellectual propert from R&D projects	Yes, if further developed	2007
Portugal	31.5	50% of gross income exempted	Patents, industrial designs or other protected intellectual property rights	Yes, if transfer complies with transfer pricing rules and country not considered a tax haven	2014
Spain[2]	30	60% of patent income exempted	Patents, secret formulas and procedures, plans, models	Yes, under certain conditions	2008
Switzerland (Niedwalden)	21.1	8.8	Patents, secret formulas and processes, trademarks, copyrights, software, know-how	Yes	2011
Turkey (Technology development zones)	20	20	Patents, licences, Intellectual propert from R&D projects	No	2001
United Kingdom	21	10	Patents, Supplementary Protection Certificates, certain other rights similar to patents	Yes, if further developed	2013

Notes:

1. People's Republic of China.

2. The corporate rate is reduced to 28% in 2015 and 25% in 2016 and onwards.

Source: Evers et al. (2013) and PWC (2013).

The empirical strategy to assess the tax sensitivity of the location of patents is to compare patent applications of MNE entities with similar characteristics except for their links to countries with different tax rates (Box 3.A1.4).[25] The hypothesis is that MNEs with links to countries with a lower effective tax rate on patent income (statutory rate or reduced rate for patents) would apply for fewer patents in entities located in higher-tax countries as compared to similar firms that have no such links. Similarly to the profit shifting analysis, taxes are measured by the difference between the corporate tax rate or the preferential tax rate on intellectual property income in the country of an entity and the average (unweighted) tax rate in the countries where the group operates. The analysis considers the impact of taxes on both shifted and non-shifted patents. Non-shifted patents are used as a proxy for R&D activities.

The empirical analysis suggests that preferential tax treatment attracts both patents invented in other countries and R&D activities. For instance, a 5 percentage point cut in the preferential tax rate on patent income is associated with an increase of 17% in the number of shifted patents, which represents a 2% increase in the total (shifted and non-shifted) number of patents. The same tax rate cut is also associated with an increase of 5% in the number of non-shifted patents, corresponding to a 4% increase in the total number of patents (Figure 3.A1.6). The relative importance of these two effects is likely to vary with the design of the preferential tax treatment, such as activity requirements.

Figure 3.A1.6 The effect of preferential tax treatment on the number of patent applications

Change in patent applications induced by a 5 percentage point cut in the preferential tax rate on patent income

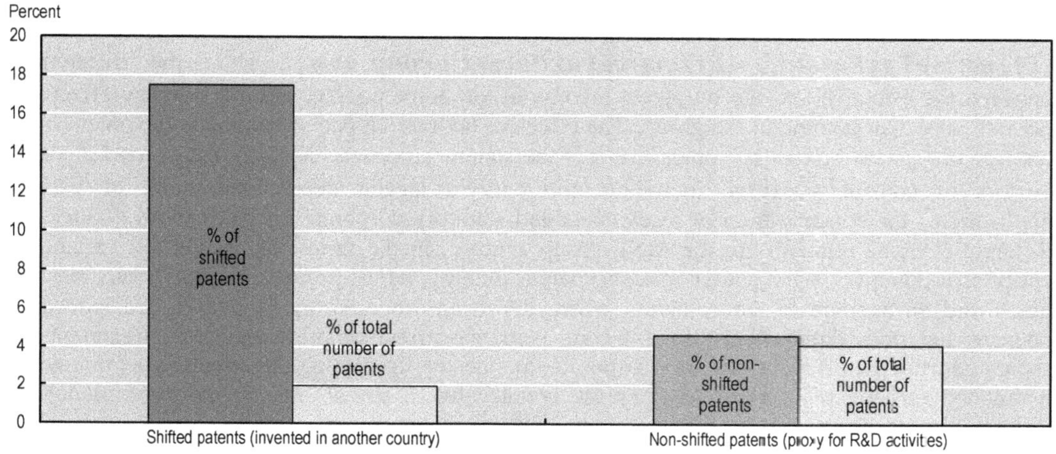

1. Shifted (non-shifted) patents are patents where the inventor is located in a different (the same) country than the MNE entity applying for the patent protection. A 5 percentage point cut in the preferential tax rate on patent income is associated with an increase of 17% in the number of shifted patents, which corresponds to 2% of all (shifted and non-shifted) patents. The effect is evaluated for an average country where the share of shifted patents is 11% (weighted average of available countries).

Box 3.A1.4. Empirical approach: Location of patents

The empirical approach to assess tax sensitivity of patent location is to compare the patent applications of MNE entities with similar characteristics except for their link to countries with different tax rates. The hypothesis is that MNEs with links to lower-tax countries would apply for relative fewer patents in entities located in higher-tax countries compared with other similar firms that have no such links. In practice, the estimated equation is as follows:

$$\begin{aligned} &\boldsymbol{Patents_{f,g,i,c,t}} \\ &= \boldsymbol{f\{(EffectiveTaxPatent_{c,t}} \\ &- \boldsymbol{EffectiveTaxPatent\_group\_avg_{g,i,c,t}), X_{f,g,i,c,t}, Y_{g,i,c,t}, Z_{c,t}, \delta_i, \delta_c, \delta_t, \varepsilon_{f,g,i,c,t}\}} \end{aligned}$$

where $\boldsymbol{Patents_{f,g,i,c,t}}$ is the number of patent applications to the three main patent offices in the world of firm $\boldsymbol{f}$ (belonging to group g operating in country $\boldsymbol{c}$ and industry $\boldsymbol{i}$) in year $\boldsymbol{t}$. $\boldsymbol{(EffectiveTaxPatent_{i,t} - EffectiveTaxPatent\_group\_avg_{g,i,c,t})}$ is the difference between the effective tax rate on patent income in the home country and the average effective tax rate on patent income in the group. The effective tax rate on patent income is the patent-box tax rate if a patent box exists; otherwise it is the statutory tax rate. $\boldsymbol{X_{f,g,i,c,t}, Y_{g,i,c,t}}$ **and** $\boldsymbol{Z_{c,t}}$ are vectors of control variables, including: the entity's lagged depreciated stock of patent applications, the concentration of researchers and statutory corporate tax rates (both defined in differential terms relatively to the MNE group average, in the same way as the tax variable), entity size dummies, headquarter dummy, parent dummy, MNE group size, R&D subsidies at home and on average in the countries where the group operates. $\boldsymbol{\delta_i}$ $\boldsymbol{\delta_c}$ and $\boldsymbol{\delta_t}$ are industry, country and time fixed-effects. In a second step, the effect of preferential tax treatment is separated from the effect of statutory corporate tax rates by interacting the effective tax rate with a dummy variable identifying whether the country has a patent box or not. The model is estimated successively for all, shifted and non-shifted patents.

The patent data is sourced from the OECD PATSTAT data matched with ORBIS data for firm characteristics. The sample consists of entities in 25 countries covering the years 2004-10. The equation is estimated using a negative binomial model, which is a non-linear model suited for high-variance count data, such as patent numbers.

Consistent with this, the profit shifting analysis confirms that profit shifting is significantly stronger – the tax sensitivity is about twice as large – among MNE groups with patents than for non-patenting MNE groups. Moreover, all else equal, patenting firms are found to have a lower ETR than non-patenting firms, which reflects the existence of preferential treatment for intellectual property and R&D tax credits in some countries. This difference is larger for MNEs than for domestic firms, suggesting that MNEs benefit more from these tax incentives by shifting patents and R&D investments to countries with preferential treatment for patent income and R&D investments.

MNEs manipulate the location of debt

One profit shifting strategy of MNEs is to locate external and internal debt in higher-tax rate countries, which allows MNEs to reduce their tax burden by deducting interest payments from taxable profits at a higher rate.[26] A number of studies have analysed the sensitivity of MNEs' capital structure to corporate taxation and find that firms' leverage depends on domestic and international taxation (e.g. Huizinga et al., 2008; Dischinger et al., 2010; Buettner and Wamser, 2013). Using German firm-level data, Møen et al. (2011) find evidence of both internal and external debt shifting and estimate that they are of about equal relevance.

An in-depth analysis of MNEs' allocation of external debt (i.e. third-party debt to credit institutions), relying on a similar approach as the profit shifting analysis, confirms that MNEs tend to locate external debt in higher-tax rate countries (see Box 3.A1.5). Specifically, the estimated debt-manipulation elasticity implies that a one percentage point higher statutory corporate tax rate of an entity than the average in the MNE group is associated with a 1.3% higher external debt for this entity. For the average entity, this would translate into a reduction in profit by about 0.2% (as compared to an overall reduction of 1% for profit shifting as a whole), accounting for 20% of overall estimated profit shifting. This is a lower-bound estimate, as the analysis only focuses on third-party debt and does not include the location of intra-group debt, which has been shown to be a significant tax planning channel (Buettner et al., 2012). In the financial account data used in this study, intra-group debt cannot be isolated.

Box 3.A1.5. Empirical approach: Manipulation of the location of external debt

The strategy to assess manipulation of the location of debt draws on Huizinga et al. (2008) and is similar to the profit shifting analysis. The idea is that the observed debt of an entity is the sum of a "true" and a manipulated debt. Manipulated debt would generally be positive in higher-tax rate countries and negative in lower-tax rate countries. The strategy is to compare the leverage of MNE entities with different opportunities to manipulate (i.e. shift or receive) debt, controlling for other characteristics influencing "true" debt. Manipulation opportunities are assessed based on the location of the other firms in the group and the statutory tax rate in these locations. A lower tax rate than the group average is assumed to be associated with shifting of debt to higher-tax rate countries, while a higher tax rate would be associated with receiving debt. Reflecting this strategy, the baseline equation is:

$$\frac{Debt}{Equity}_{f,g,c,i,t} = \alpha X_{f,g,c,i,t} + \beta\left(STAT_{c,t} - STAT\_group\_avg_{g,c,i,t}\right) + \delta_t + \delta_i$$

where $\frac{\boldsymbol{Debt}}{\boldsymbol{Equity}}_{\boldsymbol{f,g,c,i,t}}$ is the leverage (i.e. external debt-to-equity) ratio of MNE entity f, which is part of MNE group g and operates in country c and industry i, in year t. Debt refers to debt owed to financial institutions, as reported in an entity's financial accounts sourced from the ORBIS database. Importantly, it does not include intra-group debt, reflecting data limitations. $\left(\boldsymbol{STAT_{c,t} - STAT\_group\_avg_{g,c,i,t}}\right)$ is the difference between the statutory tax rate in country c and the unweighted average of the statutory tax rates in the countries where the multinational group of f operates. A positive $\boldsymbol{\beta}$ would indicate that debt is located in higher-tax countries. $\boldsymbol{X_{f,g,c,i,t}}$ is a vector of determinants of "true" debt including firm-specific controls such as size, position in the group (headquarters, other parent entity or non-parent entity) and the number of countries where its MNE group operates. Country or industry-specific controls are: GDP growth, value-added growth in the industry, development level (GDP per capita) and size of the credit sector (measured by private credit as a share of GDP and the share of employment in the finance industry). $\boldsymbol{\delta_t}$ and $\boldsymbol{\delta_i}$ are respectively time and industry fixed-effects.

Another way to assess the relative importance of profit shifting channels is to compare the tax sensitivity of pre-tax profit with the sensitivity of operating profit (i.e. profit before interest expenses and financial income). The tax sensitivity of pre-tax profit captures all profit shifting channels (transfer pricing, location of intangibles, location of debt, interest rate manipulation, etc.), while the tax sensitivity of operating profit does not include the location of debt and interest rate manipulation. For example, if the tax sensitivity of pre-tax profit were twice as large as the one of operating profit, debt manipulation would represent half of overall profit shifting. The empirical analysis does not find a statistically significant difference between the tax sensitivity of operating profit and that of total pre-tax profit. One caveat is that pre-tax profit includes financial income, i.e. interest income and dividends received. However, results are robust to dropping all entities with at least one identified subsidiary, which are the principal ones receiving dividends.

Summing up, the analysis suggests that transfer price manipulation, artificial allocation of legal ownership of intangible assets and manipulation of debt levels are important profit shifting channels. This is in line with recent literature findings (Heckemeyer and Overesch 2013; Buettner and Wamser, 2013).[27]

Treaty abuse is a way of implementing tax planning

MNE groups present in many countries have greater tax planning opportunities. Indeed, they have access to a broader range of (potentially mismatching) tax systems and pairs of bilateral tax treaties, creating scope for "treaty abuse". The empirical evidence suggests that both profit shifting and the exploitation of mismatches between tax systems are significantly more frequent among MNEs present in more than five countries. Their profit shifting propensity is more than twice as high as other MNEs and their propensity to exploit mismatches about 1.5 times higher

Overall effect of tax planning on the effective tax rate of MNEs

As a result of both profit shifting and mismatches between tax systems, the effective tax rate of large (more than 250 employees) MNE entities is on average 4-8½ percentage points lower than that of domestic group entities with similar characteristics along a number of dimensions (Table 3.A1.2). This differential is even higher among very large firms (more than 1 000 employees). The differential is also higher among patenting MNEs, which have a higher profit-shifting intensity than other MNEs and take greater advantage of tax incentives for R&D than domestic firms (by locating R&D and patents strategically). In contrast, the ETR differential is lower for smaller (non-patenting) MNE entities, as small MNEs appear to exploit profit shifting opportunities but not mismatches between tax systems.

Overall, the results suggest that there are two categories of tax planning MNEs. A first category is large MNE groups engaged in complex schemes often involving the exploitation of mismatches between tax systems, preferential tax treatment, abuse of bilateral tax treaties and profit shifting to low-or-no-tax countries. The empirical analysis suggests that tax planning can greatly reduce the effective corporate tax rates of these groups. The other category is smaller MNEs shifting profit via manipulation of the price of intra-group transactions and the location of debt, but not engaging in more complex tax schemes. This reduces their tax burden, but to a lesser extent than that of the first category.

Table 3.A1.2 Profit shifting and mismatches reduce the effective tax rate of MNEs[1]

Average differential in the effective tax rate between MNEs and domestic groups with similar characteristics
Percentage point

	Induced by:		
	Profit shifting	Mismatches between tax systems and preferential tax treatment	Total
Small MNE entity (<250 employees) as compared to a small non-MNE (domestic) entity	-2.0 [-1½ to -3½]	0.0	**-2.0 [-1½ to -3½]**
Large MNE entity (250+ employees) as compared to a large non-MNE (domestic) entity	-2.0 [-1½ to -3½]	-3.3 [-2½ to -5]	**-5.3 [-4 to -8½]**

1. The ranges around the average differential are computed using the sensitivity assumptions described in section 3.1.

Anti-avoidance rules can mitigate international tax planning

A variety of "anti-avoidance" rules exist in most countries to prevent tax planning strategies. Common ones include rules that hinder the manipulation of the price of transactions between related firms (transfer-pricing rules), rules that limit base erosion via interest deduction (e.g. thin-capitalisation and interest-to-earnings rules), specific rules applying to MNE income generated in foreign countries (controlled foreign company rules) and general and other specific anti-avoidance rules (GAAR and SAAR) (see Box 3.A1.6).

Withholding taxes on interest, royalties and dividends (i.e. taxes levied on these kinds of payments to non-resident entities) can influence cross-border tax planning opportunities even though they are not strictly speaking anti-avoidance rules. Withholding taxes influence firms' incentives to shift profit when they are levied at higher rates on payments made to residents of lower-tax rate countries. For instance, withholding taxes on interest income and royalties can discourage profit shifting via strategic allocation of debt and intangible assets, as they reduce the after-tax income of the firm in the receiving country.

Box 3.A1.6. Anti-avoidance rules

Some of the main anti-avoidance rules in domestic tax systems in OECD and G20 economies are (OECD, 2013):

- Transfer price rules require that cross-border transactions between related firms should be valued at market price (so-called "arm's length" principle). When no comparable transaction exists, different valuation methods can be used, for instance based on cost plus a fixed mark-up or using economic models to split the relevant profit among entities.
- Thin capitalisation rules and rules limiting interest deductibility disallow the deduction of certain interest expenses when the debt-to-equity or the interest-to-earnings ratio of the debtor is considered excessive. These rules apply either to total or related-party debt.
- Controlled foreign company (CFC) rules aim at eliminating the deferral of tax on certain income by using lower-tax foreign affiliates or the exemption on certain mobile foreign source income.
- General or other specific anti-avoidance rules prohibit "aggressive" tax avoidance, for instance, by denying tax benefits from a transaction that lacks economic substance.
- Anti-hybrid rules link the domestic tax treatment of instruments or entities with the tax treatment in the foreign country, thus eliminating the mismatch between tax systems. For instance, they may deny the deduction of interest if treated as non-taxable dividend in the recipient country.

A number of academic studies have classified countries according to the degree of strictness on specific anti-avoidance rules, such as transfer pricing regulations and rules against debt manipulation (e.g. Lohse et al., 2012; Lohse and Riedel, 2012; Blouin et al., 2014). However, there exists no classification of the overall strictness of the anti-avoidance stance.

Building upon these studies, a new, though limited, classification on the strictness of anti-avoidance and withholding taxes among OECD and G20 countries is developed in this study. Detailed tax rules vary significantly between countries and the classification aims at grouping countries along the key dimensions of anti-avoidance that are relatively easy to quantify and compare across countries, using simple and mechanical rules. The classification focuses on: (i) requirements regarding transfer pricing documentation; (ii) rules that limit interest deductions (i.e. thin capitalisation and interest-to-earnings rules); (iii) existence of a GAAR; and (iv) existence of a CFC rule. The classification also considers the level of withholding taxes on interests, dividends and royalties as they can influence MNEs' incentives to shift profit. Within the European Union, withholding taxes are set to zero by law.

On transfer pricing, interest deductibility and withholding taxes, the classification is based on a 0-1-2 scale, which captures the broad strictness of rules but may miss important country-specific details. On GAAR and CFC rules, a simpler 0-1 scale based on the existence of a rule is used, reflecting the difficulty to classify these country-specific rules in a harmonised way. The overall classification sums the 5 components. As a result, the classification runs from 0 to 8.

A caveat to this classification is that some aspects of anti-avoidance rules that are more difficult to compare across countries as well as country-specific details and enforcement practices (e.g. frequency of tax audits, penalties in case of non-compliance) are not captured. In addition, the classification does not distinguish between territorial and worldwide tax systems.

Information on some of the main anti-avoidance rules and withholding taxes among OECD and G20 countries is the basis for a new, though limited, composite anti-avoidance classification outlined in Box 3.A1.6 and presented in Figure 3.A1.7. This grouping builds upon earlier classification efforts in the literature (Lohse et al., 2012; Lohse and Riedel, 2012; Blouin et al., 2014). According to this grouping of countries, anti-avoidance rules appear to be comparatively strict in countries with relatively high corporate tax rates. This may reflect that, in countries with relatively high tax rates, firms have stronger incentives to avoid taxes, prompting governments to introduce stricter regulations.

A few existing studies have assessed the role of specific anti-avoidance rules for firms' behaviour, such as the impact of transfer pricing regulations on profit shifting (e.g. Lohse and Riedel, 2012) and the effect of thin capitalisation rules on firms' capital structure (e.g. Blouin et al., 2014). Generally, these studies find that individual anti-avoidance measures can reduce tax planning. However, there is no evidence of the overall impact of anti-avoidance rules and their implementation on tax planning.

Based on the slightly broader, but still limited, anti-avoidance classification presented in Figure 3.A1.7, the estimates in this study suggest that relatively stricter anti-avoidance rules are associated with lower profit shifting across OECD and G20 economies.[28] For instance, an increase in the strictness of anti-avoidance rules from moderate to relatively strict is associated with a reduction in profit shifting from that country by about one half. The empirical analysis also provides evidence that rules that limit base erosion via interest deductions are associated with reduced debt manipulation.

Figure 3.A1.7 Illustrative classification of anti-avoidance rules

Distribution of countries by degree of strictness of anti-avoidance rules and withholding taxes

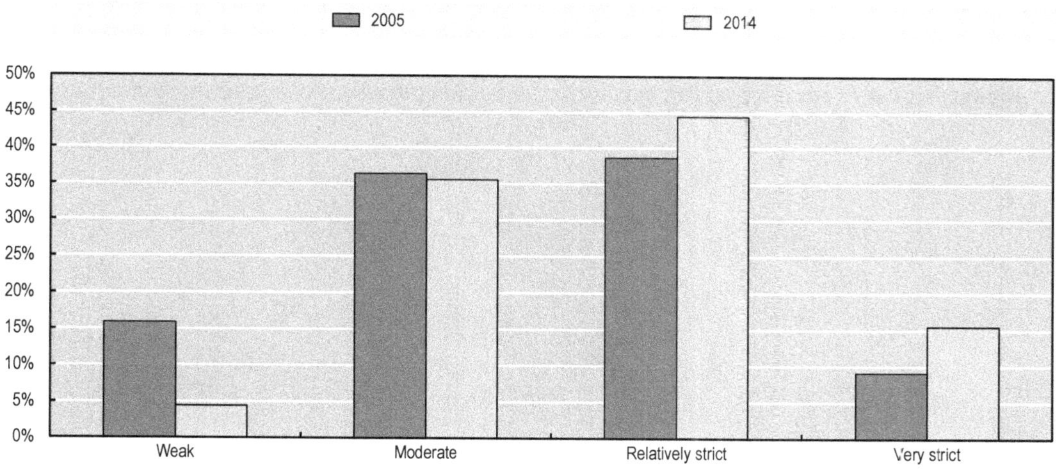

Note: 15% of countries in the sample (which includes all OECD and G20 countries) had "very strict" anti-avoidance rules in 2014. A "very strict" anti-avoidance rule corresponds to a score of 7-8 on the 0-8 indicator of anti-avoidance and withholding taxes described in Box 3.A1.6. A score of 8 is defined as the combination of strict documentation requirements on transfer pricing, a strict rule against debt manipulation, existence of a GAAR and a CFC rule as well as relatively high withholding taxes on interest, dividends and royalties. A "relatively strict" rule corresponds to a score of 5-6, a "moderate" to 3-4 and "weak" to 0-2. The indicator does not reflect the enforcement of existing rules.

Both tax planning and anti-avoidance entail compliance costs, reducing firms' profitability

Complex tax codes result in wasted resources for firms and tax administrations and can contribute to deter foreign investment. International tax planning also involves a collective waste of resources due to the costs associated with setting up complex tax schemes (e.g. tax and legal advice). One indication of resources spent on tax planning is the share of production of the "tax consultancy" industry in overall output (Figure 3.A1.8). Still, this indication is rough as this production category also includes non-tax-related activities, such as regular accounting and bookkeeping activities, the size of which varies across countries, depending among other things on industry structure.

One reason for the complexity of the tax system is that governments react to tax planning by some firms with anti-avoidance legislation that increases the administrative cost of all firms. For instance, Slemrod et al. (2007) suggests that tax complexity in the United Kingdom has increased mainly because of a significant volume of anti-avoidance legislation was added to the tax code. Consistent with this, the empirical analysis shows that anti-avoidance rules mitigate profit shifting, but are also associated with significantly lower average (pre-tax) profitability. The lower profitability may reflect resources spent on tax compliance. This adverse effect on average profitability is robust to controlling for the income level of a country, burdensome regulations in other areas and the statutory corporate tax rate. Compliance costs for firms as well as administration and enforcement costs for tax authorities are important to the assessment of the overall cost-benefit of anti-avoidance rules. Co-ordinating anti-avoidance rules across countries could reduce compliance costs for MNEs.

Figure 3.A1.8 Production of the accounting, bookkeeping, auditing and tax consultancy industry[29]

% of GDP, 2011

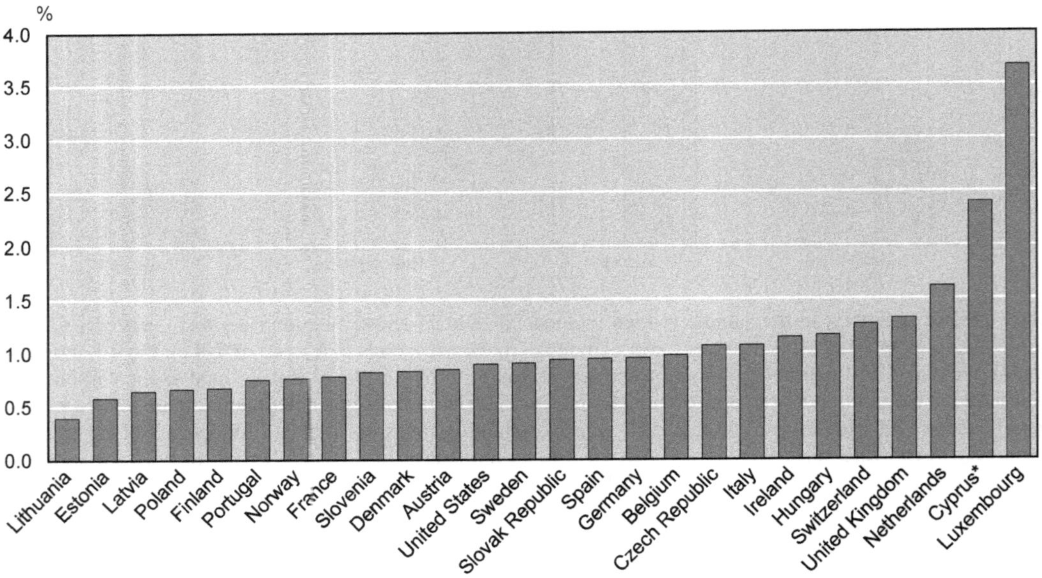

Note by Turkey: The information in this document with reference to "Cyprus" relates to the southern part of the Island. There is no single authority representing both Turkish and Greek Cypriot people on the Island. Turkey recognises the Turkish Republic of Northern Cyprus (TRNC). Until a lasting and equitable solution is found within the context of the United Nations, Turkey shall preserve its position concerning the "Cyprus issue".

Note by all the European Union Member States of the OECD and the European Union: The Republic of Cyprus is recognised by all members of the United Nations with the exception of Turkey. The information in this document relates to the area under the effective control of the Government of the Republic of Cyprus.

Source: Eurostat, BEA, OECD calculations.

Fiscal and economic implications of international tax planning

International tax planning affects both the size of the global corporate tax revenues and the distribution of tax bases and revenues across countries.[30] As the lost revenues would have been used to finance welfare or efficiency-enhancing public expenditures or to reduce other distortive taxes, such redistribution has real effects. Tax planning can also affect real activity in several other ways. As compared to a situation where tax planning would not be possible, tax planning MNEs have a lower tax burden, which may give them a competitive advantage over other firms. Also, the possibility to manipulate the location of internal and external debt reduces the effective cost of debt for MNEs, which can lead them to take on higher overall leverage. In addition, tax planning opportunities lessen the importance of corporate tax rates in shaping the allocation of MNEs' investment (both tangible and intangible) across countries.

Fiscal implications

Profit shifting redistributes corporate tax bases across countries and results in global tax revenue losses as shifted profits are taxed at a lower average rate than they would have been in the absence of profit shifting. While profit shifting entails gains or losses at the country level depending on the characteristics of tax systems, in the case of mismatches between tax systems (including preferential tax treatment) there are generally no gains in terms of tax revenues, but there can be ambiguity as to who has lost revenue. For example, both parties concerned by a scheme involving a hybrid security may (or may not) claim that they lost revenues. Another difficulty is to identify the most frequent schemes and countries involved in these mismatches.

The revenue effects are presented for hypothetical combinations of tax bases and tax rate differentials between tax rates faced by the average MNE entity in the home country and the tax rate faced by this hypothetical MNE on average in the other countries where it operates. They should be seen as illustrative and ranges reflecting the many uncertainties of the analysis are provided. The revenue estimates are based on the average tax planning propensity (both for profit shifting and mismatches) estimated over the full sample of countries, in combination with different hypothetical tax rate differentials and tax bases (i.e. the share of MNE profits in total corporate profits). It is important to note that the average propensity leaves aside certain country-specific differences in tax planning intensity, for example resulting from the strictness and enforcement of rules against tax planning.

Illustrative results for hypothetical cases

A number of assumptions are required to translate the estimated tax planning propensity into estimated effects on corporate tax revenues. One assumption is the share of MNEs in taxable profits, which in many countries is not readily available from tax statistics. Based on the sample of firm-level financial account data used in this study, this share ranges between 40% and 80% in most OECD and G20 countries. The revenue effects of tax planning are also based on the assumption that corporate tax revenues change in proportion with reported financial profits. This is an approximation because of potential differences between reported and taxable profits due to, inter alia, book/tax differences and tax credits. The effect of book/tax differences on the estimated revenue effects is ambiguous (Box 3.A1.7). By contrast, taking into account tax credits would increase the revenue effects where such tax credits are significant. Information on tax credits is limited and the available data suggest that they can vary substantially across countries and over time. The assumption in this hypothetical example is that tax credits represent 15% of CIT revenues before tax credits. Another key assumption is that firms outside the sample have similar structures and behave in a similar way as firms in the sample. Sensitivity analysis to this assumption is presented below.

Box 3.A1.7. The impact of book/tax differences and tax credits on tax revenue estimates

There exist few estimates of the difference between book and taxable profits. In the United States, the difference was volatile over 2006-10. Excluding the crisis-year 2008, the difference was relatively small on average over the period (Boynton et al., 2014; see Figure below). This pattern would suggest that differences in the timing of recognition of income and expenses are an important driver of book/tax differences (see Section 2.2 above on the sources of book/tax differences). In Germany, financial profits were 10% lower than taxable profits in 2009, with the difference being largest among firms engaged in corporate restructuring, but the corresponding information is not available for other years (Zinn and Spengel, 2012).

Book/tax differences in the United States[1]

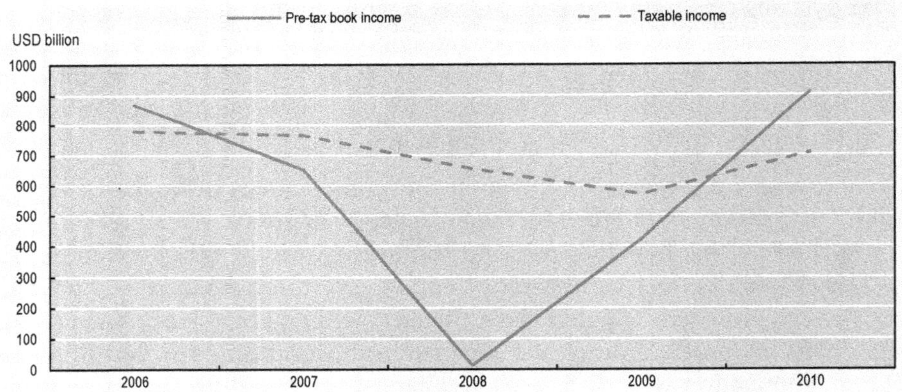

Source: Boynton et al. (2014). Data is for SEC 10-K corporations.

Book/tax differences can affect the estimation of the average tax planning propensity, which is based on financial account rather than tax data. Book/tax differences that are independent of tax planning (e.g. timing differences) likely create noise in the estimation, but are unlikely to bias the estimated tax sensitivity in any direction. In contrast, certain book/tax differences result from tax planning schemes (e.g. a dual residence scheme leading to the same interest expense being deducted in more than one country). These schemes would reduce taxable income relatively to book income (Lisowsky, 2010). Such schemes are not identified in the profit shifting analysis, but they are captured in the empirical analysis of mismatches between tax systems, which focuses on how reported profits are taxed.

Box 3.A1.7. The impact of book/tax differences and tax credits on tax revenue estimates *(continued)*

Book/tax differences can also affect tax revenue estimates for a given tax-sensitivity of reported profits. Indeed, these differences imply that corporate tax revenues may not change proportionately with profits reported in financial accounts. For example, if taxable profit is systematically lower (respectively higher) than book profit, shifting 5% of book profit would amount to shifting more (respectively less) than 5% of taxable profit and thus lead to a revenue loss greater (respectively smaller) than 5% of revenues.

Similarly, the existence of tax credits, if they are unaffected by profit shifting, can influence revenue estimates. Taking tax credits into account would increase estimated revenue effects (see Table below).

Illustrative example of the effect of book/tax differences and tax credits

	No tax planning	Tax planning	Share of tax planning
(1) Financial account profit	105.0	100.0	5.0%
(2) Taxable profit (assuming 10% lower tax than book profits)	94.5	89.5	5.6%
Tax rate	*30%*	*30%*	
(3) Tax before credits	28.4	26.9	5.6%
(4) Tax credits (assuming 15% of tax before credit)	4.0	4.0	
(5) Tax after credits	24.3	22.8	6.6%

Note: Profit shifting is assumed to reduce financial account (i.e. reported) profit by 5% (line 1). Assuming that taxable profits are 10% lower than financial profits, then profit shifting represents 5.6% of taxable profit (line 2). Assuming that tax credits represent 15% of tax before credits and are unaffected by profit shifting, revenue losses from profit shifting, revenue losses would represent 6.2% of tax revenues rather than 5% (line 5).

Based on these assumptions, illustrative tax revenue effects of tax planning in hypothetical cases are presented in Figure 3.A1.9. These estimates represent average effects for different combinations of statutory tax rate differentials and tax bases (i.e. shares of MNEs profits in total corporate profits). Clearly, actual tax revenue effects in a given country can deviate substantially from these hypothetical estimates. Indeed, the estimates rely on the observation that MNE entities that face higher-tax rate differentials tend to have more links to lower-tax rate countries and thus more profit-shifting opportunities than entities that face lower-tax rate differentials. However, profit shifting opportunities may differ from these averages, for instance because of differences in the strictness and enforcement of anti-avoidance rules. The extent of losses from mismatches between tax systems and preferential tax treatment can also differ from the cross-country average because of differences in tax rules as well as specific anti-avoidance rules (Figure 3.A1.10.). Thus, countries with higher statutory tax rates do not necessarily have higher revenue losses from multinational tax planning. In order to estimate the scale of profit shifting, it is necessary to consider real economic activity by companies in each country, such as FDI. Estimates are shown in Figures 3.A1.9 and 3.A1.11, but it should be noted that the scale of revenue loss cannot be explained only by corporation tax rate differentials. Especially when countries have effectively implemented substantive anti-avoidance tax rules, as shown in Figure 3.A1.10, the relationship between corporation tax rates and the scale of revenue loss by multinational tax planning could be significantly different from the results shown in Figures 3.A1.9 and 3.A1.11.

Figure 3.A1.9 Illustrative tax revenue effects of international tax planning in hypothetical cases

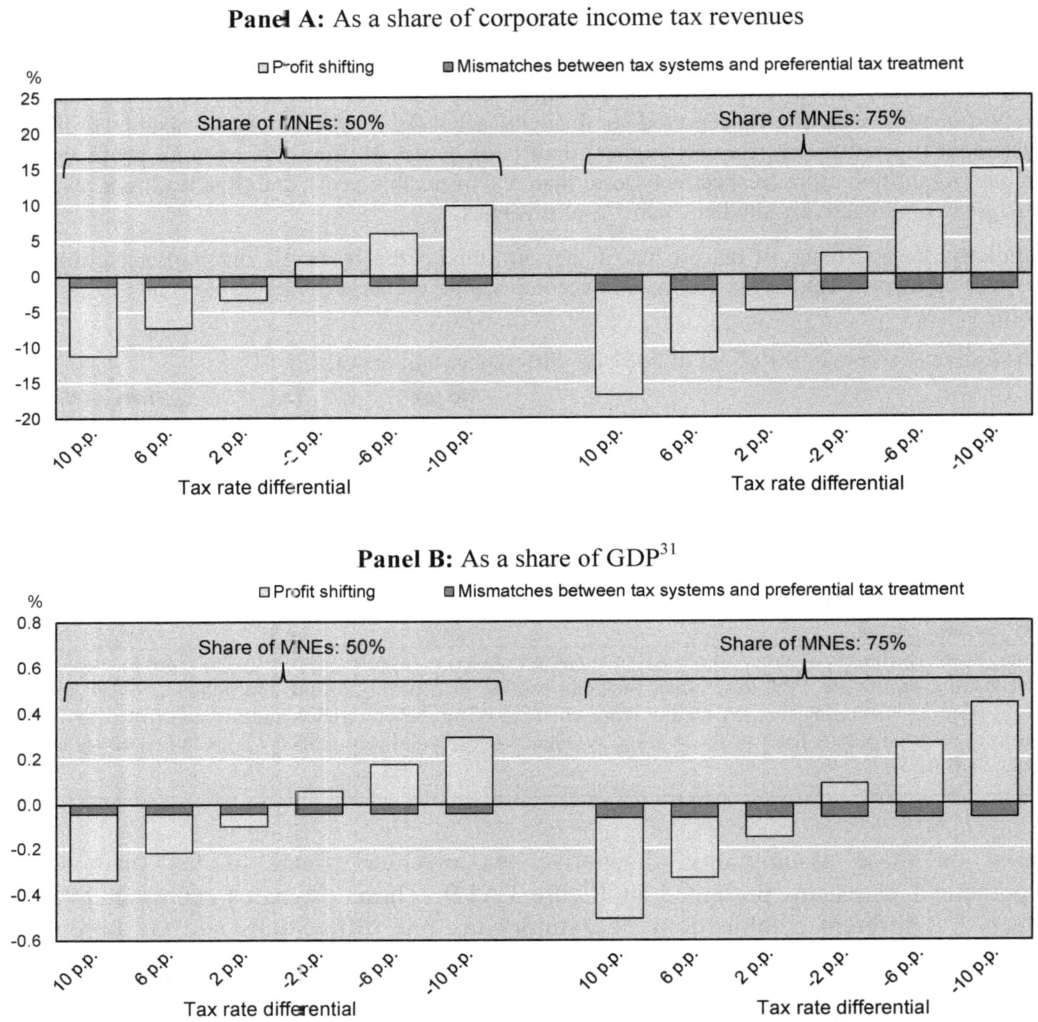

Note: For a country in which the average resident MNE would face a 10 percentage point higher tax rate than the average tax rate in the other countries where this MNE group operates and with a 50% share of MNEs in total corporate profits, the tax revenue loss from tax planning would represent on average about 11% of CIT revenues (or about 0.3% of GDP), most of which from profit shifting. These averages are presented as an illustration of the magnitude of tax planning. However, actual country-specific tax revenue effects can vary widely around these averages for many reasons, including cross-country differences in the strictness of anti-avoidance rules against tax planning and other country-specific tax rules.

Figure 3.A1.10 Illustrative tax revenue effects depending on the strictness of anti-avoidance rules

Example assuming a 6 percentage point tax rate differential between the resident rate and the average rate in the countries where the MNE groups operate

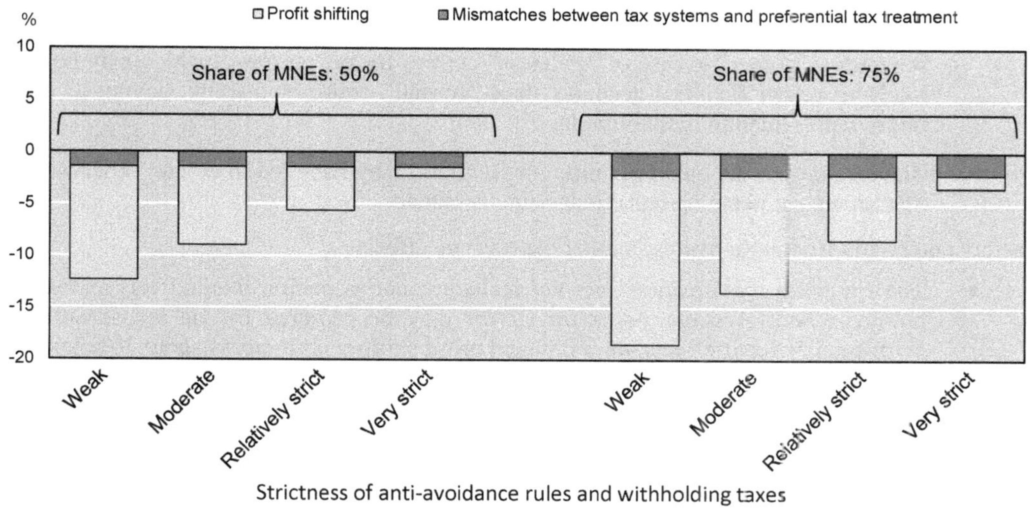

Note: For an average country with a 6 percentage point tax rate differential, a 50% share of MNEs in total corporate profits and weak anti-avoidance rules, the tax revenue loss from tax planning would represent on average about 12% of CIT revenues. The effect of anti-avoidance rules on the profit shifting intensity is estimated by refining the equation presented in Box 3.A1.3. The refinement consists of interacting the tax rate differential with the classification of anti-avoidance strictness. The resulting effect is positive, suggesting that profit shifting is reduced when anti-avoidance rules are relatively strict. The potential effect of anti-avoidance rules on mismatches between tax systems is not included since it could not be established empirically with the available data.

The revenue effects are surrounded by a number of uncertainties (Box 3.A1.8). Some factors may lead to an underestimation of revenue effects, such as the potential lack of financial or ownership information on certain entities involved in the most complex tax schemes. More generally, "unknown" tax planning schemes of MNEs may not be captured, although the empirical approach (based on the location of activity, profits and tax expenses) does not require knowing the details of schemes to estimate tax planning. On the other hand, certain assumptions may lead to an overestimation, such as not controlling for country fixed-effects in the estimation of the profit shifting sensitivity.

Box 3.A1.8. Main uncertainties surrounding the tax revenue estimates

Factors potentially leading to underestimating the revenue effects:

- Lack of financial or ownership information on some firms involved in complex tax schemes (e.g. specific case of "stateless" entities for tax purposes, which may be less likely to report financial accounts than "normal" entities), thereby leading to their under-representation in the sample.
- The cleaning of the data (e.g. dropping outliers) may have led to certain observations of extreme tax planning behaviour being excluded.

Factors potentially leading to overestimating the revenue effects:

- The empirical specification does not include country-specific fixed-effects and some not-controlled-for country-specific factors may be captured by the tax sensitivity. With country fixed-effects, the estimated profit shifting elasticity is about 30% lower.
- Inclusion of legislated tax incentives such as R&D tax credits or negotiated tax preferences, if MNEs exploit these incentives to a greater extent than similar domestic firms. These are not considered as BEPS behaviours.

Factors with ambiguous impact on the revenue effects:

- Corporate group structure is not exogenous to profitability. High-profitability MNE groups are more likely to set up affiliates in lower-tax countries, so as to shift profits there. Despite shifting part of their profits, these groups still report relatively high profits in higher-tax rate countries because of high "true" profitability. Based on the comparison with an average (less profitable) firm, the profits shifted by these groups may be underestimated. However, a symmetric effect exists in lower-tax rate countries, where these high-profitability groups may report relatively high profits not only because of profit shifting, but also because of higher "true" profitability. Thus, the overall effect on the tax sensitivity is ambiguous.
- Corporate tax revenues are assumed to change proportionately with financial reported profits. This may not always be the case because of differences between financial and taxable profits as well as tax credits (see Box 3.A1.7).
- Corporate tax rates have recently been cut in some countries. This may lead to smaller losses (or larger gains) in these countries. It also leads to larger losses (or smaller gains) in other countries which have not cut tax rates.

Reflecting these uncertainties, the revenue effects incorporate sensitivity to the following two sources of variation (Figure 3.A1.11): (i) taking a 95% confidence interval around the tax sensitivity estimate; and (ii) assuming that firms outside the sample have a 50% higher tax sensitivity than firms in the sample, where the sample coverage is assessed against the population of firms from the OECD Business Demography Statistics database (the weighted average of coverage is about 40%).[32]

Figure 3.A1.11 Revenue effects of tax planning: accounting for uncertainties

Panel A: Sensitivity to the estimated tax planning intensity[33]

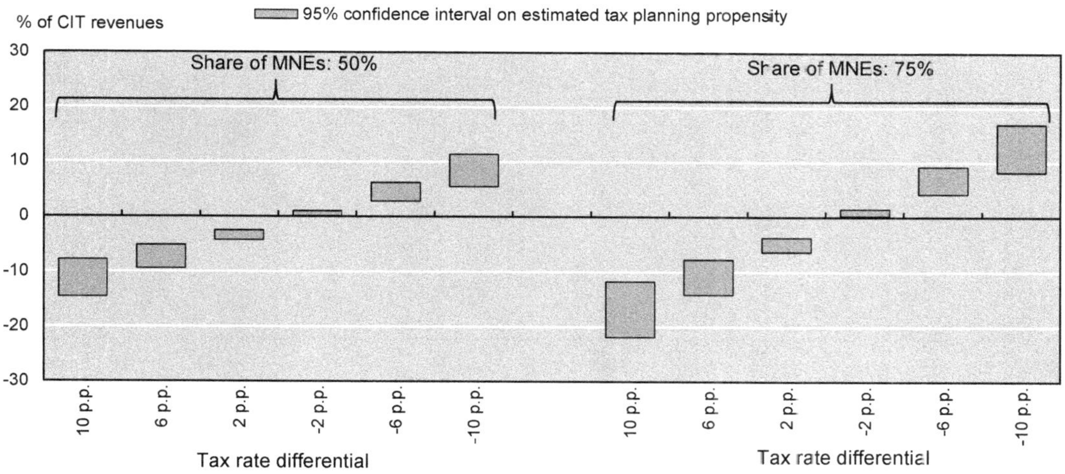

Panel B: Sensitivity to the tax planning intensity of firms outside the sample[34]

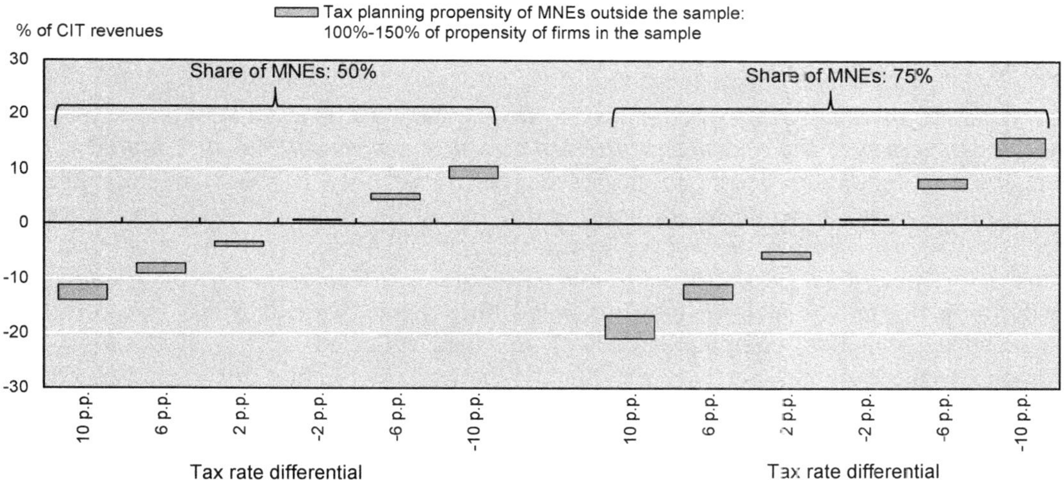

Panel C: Combined sensitivity

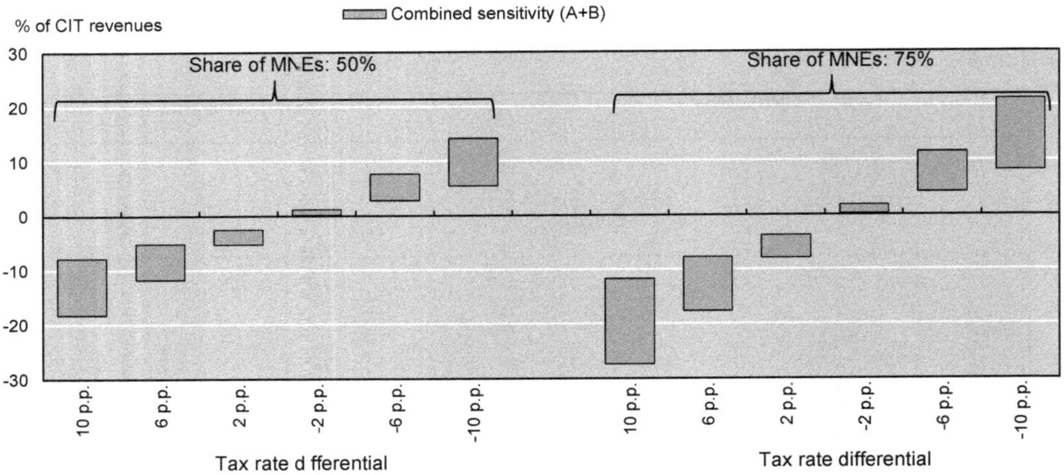

1. The revenue effect is based on the assumption that firms outside the sample have the same tax elasticity (i.e. profit shifting elasticity and average tax differential) as firms in the sample. The sensitivity analysis assumes a 50% higher tax elasticity of firms outside the sample relative to firms in the sample. The assumption is that 50% of firms are covered in the hypothetical country.

Global tax revenue loss

An estimate of the global revenue loss from tax planning is calculated based on the weighted average of the relevant parameters for the countries covered in this study. The weights are based on corporate tax revenues. Since only MNEs can shift profits internationally, tax revenue losses are proportional to the share of MNEs in corporate profits times the average extent of profit shifting by MNEs (i.e. the estimated tax sensitivity applied to the average tax rate differential). More precisely, the parameters underlying the global revenue loss are based on: (i) the share of MNEs in profits in financial account data complemented with tax data collected as part of the work on Action 11 (the weighted average is 59%); (ii) the average tax rate differential based on the actual links of MNE entities to other countries with different tax rates (the weighted average differential is 3.6 percentage points[35]); and (iii) tax credits as a share of pre-tax profits (the weighted average is 17%).[36]

Factoring in the uncertainties described above, the estimated total net revenue loss for the countries included in this study is in the interval of 4% to 10% of corporate tax revenues (Figure 3.A1.11). Globally, this corresponds to an accumulated revenue loss of about USD 0.9-2.1 trillion over the last ten years (2005-14) or about USD 100-240 billion in 2014.[37] Of these, about two-thirds are due to profit shifting and one-third to mismatches between tax systems and preferential tax treatment. A recent report by the IMF gives an estimate that falls in this range for the overall revenue loss, with an analysis based on macroeconomic data and comparing gross operating surplus with actual corporate income tax revenues (IMF, 2014). Based on FDI data, a preliminary report by UNCTAD estimates to around USD 100 billion the annual tax revenue loss from international tax planning through offshore investment for developing countries, a number of which are part of OECD or G20 (UNCTAD, 2015).

Competition implications

Tax planning can distort competition among firms and entail efficiency losses. Indeed, as shown above, the effective corporate tax rate of large tax planning MNEs can be sizeably lower than the rate of some other firms. This lower effective tax rate can give rise to an unintended competitive advantage of MNEs compared to other firms as it reduces the firms' tax costs (Overesch, 2009; OECD, 2013). This cost advantage can allow the MNE to gain market shares by reducing its price in line with its costs at least in the short term. In the longer term, once the MNE has gained a dominant market position, it may ultimately increase prices to raise profits. Alternatively, if the MNE is pursuing a strategy of competing on attributes other than the price (e.g. quality, service and branding), it may use the cost savings to further differentiate its products to achieve a larger market share and eventually a higher price and profit than its competitors (Porter, 1980). Finally, as tax planning reduces the cost of MNEs relative to other firms (entrants), MNEs can raise entry barriers by, for example, using the tax savings on spending on advertising and R&D (Sutton, 1991). Overall, the expected effect of tax planning is to increase the market share and after-tax profitability of tax planning MNEs at the expense of other firms.

Assessing the potential distortion to competition is difficult and little empirical evidence exists. This study uses a combination of firm and industry-level data to investigate if industries with a large share of MNEs with tax planning opportunities are more concentrated than other industries (see Box 3.A1.9). One way to assess the impact of tax planning on industry concentration is to compare it across countries having different anti-avoidance rules. The idea is that tax planning is more frequent when anti-avoidance is less strict, resulting in more concentrated industries than elsewhere. Controlling for other country and industry characteristics, this analysis suggests that industries with a strong presence of MNEs are less concentrated when anti-avoidance rules are stricter. Industry concentration is measured as the market share of the 10 largest entities divided by the market share of the 100 largest entities in an industry and country. For example, in an industry with a high share of MNEs among top-10 firms (the 75th percentile of the distribution), increasing anti-avoidance strictness by two notches (see Figure 3.A1.7) would reduce the combined market share of the ten largest firms in the industry by about 6 percentage points.

The study also investigates the implications of tax planning for price mark-ups of MNE groups using firm-level data (see Box 3.A1.9). Mark-ups are proxied by pre-tax operating profit divided by turnover, in line with Aghion et al. (2005). Along with the increased market concentration, estimates show that engaging in tax planning is associated with higher price mark-ups controlling for other factors affecting mark-ups such as size, productivity, leverage, presence of patents and exposure to foreign competition. For example, the mark-up of a MNE group is about 10% higher than that of a domestic firm, while the mark-up of a tax-planning MNE is up to 23% higher (Figure 3.A1.12, left panel). The effect is reduced in countries with stricter anti-avoidance rules against tax planning (Figure 3.A1.12, right panel). One caveat to these analyses is that the causality is unclear as more profitable firms may choose to set up affiliates in lower-tax countries (leading them to be identified as tax planners), suggesting that the results should be interpreted with caution.

Figure 3.A1.12 Mark-up rate and international tax planning

Mark-up rate premium over a non-multinational corporate group with similar characteristics1

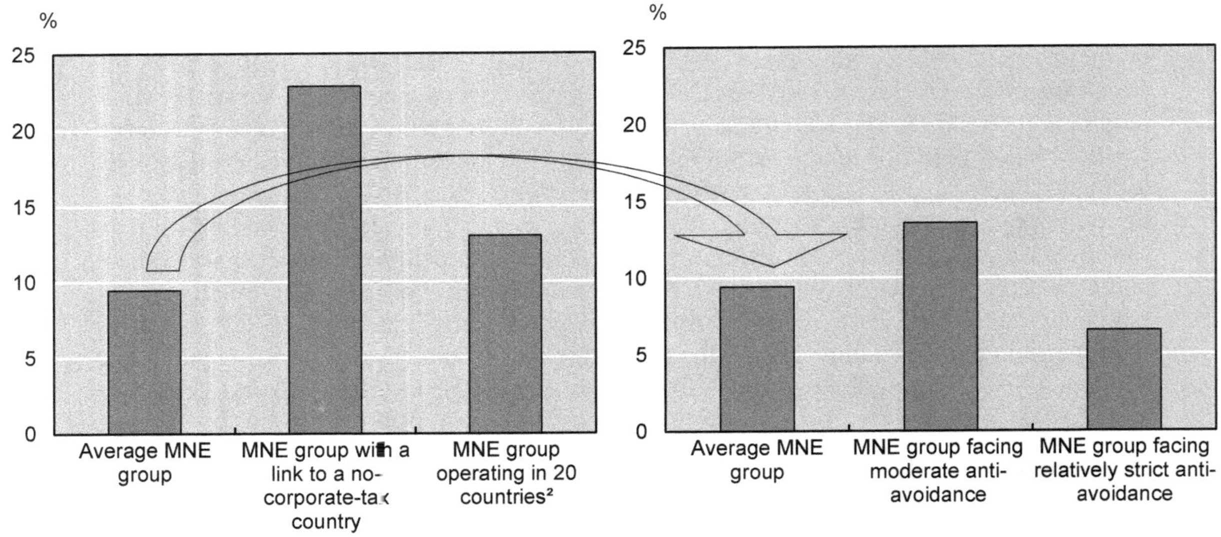

Notes:

1. The differences in mark-up between different types of firms are statistically significant at a 5% level.

2. The average MNE group operates in five countries. MNE groups operating in many countries have been shown to engage more intensively in international tax planning.

Distortions of competition lead to welfare losses as consumers face higher prices in some markets than otherwise. It can also, under certain circumstances, reduce innovation (Aghion et al., 2005; Gilbert, 2006). Reduced competitive pressures can also curb innovation incentives for MNEs themselves as it reduces the incentives to innovate to stay ahead of competitors (Aghion et al., 2005). Differences in the effective tax rate between MNEs and other firms may also contribute to a suboptimal allocation of capital in the economy as, by providing rates of return artificially altered by tax distortions, MNEs may crowd out investment by other (potentially more productive) MNEs and domestic firms.

Yet, MNEs are in general more productive and exposed to competition than other firms (e.g. Helpman et al., 2004; Bloom et al., 2012) and they can generate positive technological and productivity spillovers to other firms. If tax planning MNEs are more productive than the firms they crowd out, the overall effect on efficiency is unclear.

Box 3.A1.9. Empirical approach: Tax planning and competition

The empirical approach to investigate if tax planning affects competition explores two avenues: (i) assessing if industries with a strong presence of tax-planning MNEs are more concentrated; and (ii) assessing if MNE groups engaged in tax planning obtain different price mark-ups as compared to other firms with similar characteristics. The analysis draws on firm-level data from the ORBIS database to measure market concentration, mark-ups and the propensity of MNE groups to engage in international tax planning.

The estimated market concentration equation is:

$$Concentration_{i,c} = \gamma TaxPlanningIntensity_{i,c} + \delta_i + \delta_c$$

where $Concentration_{i,c}$ is the market concentration of industry *i* in country *c*, measured as the combined market share (based on turnover) of the 10 largest entities (based on unconsolidated accounts) in industry *i* and country *c*, divided by the combined market share of the 100 largest entities in the same industry and country. The analysis is based on 28 industries in 28 OECD and G20 countries. Tax planning intensity ($TaxPlanningIntensity_{i,c}$) is measured by the market share of MNE entities among top-10 firms in the industry multiplied by the strictness of anti-avoidance rules in country *c*. The idea is that tax planning is more intense in industries with a large share of MNEs, but less so in countries with relatively strict anti-avoidance rules. δ_i and δ_c are dummies for industry and country, which capture common characteristics of certain industries and countries.

The estimated mark-up equation is:

$$Markup_{g,i,c,t} = \alpha TaxPlanning_{g,i,c,t} + \beta X_{g,i,c,t} + \delta_i + \delta_t + \delta_c$$

where $\boldsymbol{Markup_{g,i,c,t}}$ is the mark-up rate of the MNE group g (consolidated accounts), which operates in industry i, in year t with headquarters in country c. The mark-up rate is proxied by the Lerner index or price-cost margin, measured as operating profit divided by turnover, in line with Aghion et al. (2005). The tax planning propensity ($\boldsymbol{TaxPlanning_{g,i,c,t}}$) is measured by four proxy variables: (i) a dummy variable for multinational (as opposed to domestic) groups; (ii) a dummy variable for MNE groups with links to no-corporate-tax countries; (iii) the number of countries where a MNE group operates; (iv) the average anti-avoidance strictness (as measured by the indicator defined in Box 3.A1.6) in the countries where the group operates. The control vector $\boldsymbol{X_{g,i,c,t}}$ is a set of group-specific variables potentially influencing the mark-up rate, including size, productivity, leverage, presence of patents (as a measure of innovative activities) and exposure to foreign competition (proxied by the average import penetration in markets where the group is active). $\boldsymbol{\delta_i}$, $\boldsymbol{\delta_t}$ and $\boldsymbol{\delta_c}$ are industry, year and country of headquarters fixed-effects.

All four measures of tax planning intensity have advantages and disadvantages. Comparing MNEs and domestic firms (option i) poses the issue of potential unobserved differences between them, although the extensive set of control variables included should minimise this issue. Comparing tax-planning MNEs (e.g. with links to no-tax countries, option ii) to other MNEs can pose reverse causality issues since ex ante more profitable MNEs have more incentives then other MNEs to set up affiliate in low-tax countries. The number of countries where a MNE operates (option iii) is also subject to reverse causality, since profitable firms are more likely to expand to other countries than other firms. Finally, MNE groups facing relatively strict anti-avoidance rules against tax planning (option iv) may have lower mark-up than other groups because of the compliance costs implied by these rules. Despite these limitations, the results are consistent across the various specifications, which supports the initial hypothesis that tax planning distorts competition.

Manipulation of the location of related and third-party debt: Implications for group leverage

In most OECD countries, the corporate tax system influences corporate financing decisions by favouring debt over equity, since interest payments on debt are generally deductible from taxable profits while dividends payments are not (de Mooij, 2012).[38] This can affect productivity if it distorts the allocation of investment towards firms that can raise debt easily over those that have to rely on equity finance, such as knowledge-based innovative firms investing in intangible assets (Arnold et al., 2011). This is an argument for advocating that corporate tax systems should aim at treating debt and equity-financed investment equally.[39]

International tax planning may compound this "debt bias" (e.g. de Mooij 2011).[40] The possibility to locate external and internal debt in entities in higher-tax rate countries lowers the marginal cost of debt at the MNE group level, which could lead MNE groups to increase their overall leverage.[41] Indeed, relying on group-level information on MNEs' overall external debt (consolidated debt at the corporate group level), the empirical analysis provides evidence that this overall leverage is sensitive to the possibility to locate external and internal debt in higher-tax rate countries – an area that has not yet been explored in the literature (see Box 3.A1.10). Group external leverage is found to be sensitive to the tax rates in the highest tax rate countries in the MNE group (e.g. the average of the two highest tax rates) and thus to the effective cost of debt in these countries. This suggests that MNE groups with the possibility to manipulate the location of debt have higher overall leverage as compared to other MNE groups.

Box 3.A1.10. Empirical approach: Tax planning and group external leverage

The idea is to assess the sensitivity of MNE groups' overall external leverage to changes in tax rates in the different countries where they operate. These changes can affect the location of group debt, but also its overall level by altering the effective cost of debt for the group. Overall group leverage is expected to be sensitive to the tax rate in the country of headquarters, where an important share of group debts is generally located, and in the higher-tax rate countries in the group, where MNE groups have been shown to shift debts.

The estimated equation is as follows:

$$\left(\frac{Debt}{Equity}\right)_{g,c,t} = \beta_1 STAT_{c,t} + \beta_2 STAT\_max_{g,c,t} + \alpha X_{c,t} + \delta_t + \delta_g,$$

where $\frac{Debt}{Equity_{g,c,t}}$ is the external (i.e. consolidated) debt-to-equity ratio of the MNE group g, with headquarters in country c, in year t. β_1 is the sensitivity of leverage to the statutory tax rate in the headquarters country ($STAT_{c,t}$) and β_2 the sensitivity to the average of the two highest tax rates among the countries where the group operates ($STAT\_max_{g,c,t}$). In alternative specifications, the average tax rate among all countries where the group operates and the average of the two lowest tax rates are also considered. $X_{c,t}$ is a set of firm-specific and macroeconomic control variables (e.g. profitability, GDP growth, interest rates). δ_t and δ_g are respectively time and group fixed-effects.

The source of data is consolidated financial accounts of MNE groups from the ORBIS database, over 2000-2010. The number of observations is about 15 000 group-year pairs, covering most OECD and G20 countries. Results are robust to: (i) replacing the average of the two highest tax rates in the group by the highest tax rate, or the average of the three highest; (ii) restricting the sample to EU countries; (iii) excluding financial firms.

For example, a MNE group with relatively high debt manipulation opportunities (e.g. the average of the two highest tax rates in the group is 40%, as compared to 35% for the average MNE) has 8% higher external leverage (Figure 3.A1.13, left panel). This finding is robust to a number of variants, such as adding control variables for macroeconomic developments or restricting the sample to only EU countries or non-financial firms. In addition, relatively strict thin capitalisation and interest-to-earnings rules against debt manipulation are found to lower the propensity of MNE groups to increase their external leverage through debt manipulation.

Figure 3.A1.13 MNE group external leverage and international tax planning

Leverage (external consolidated debt-to-equity) as compared to an average MNE group[1]

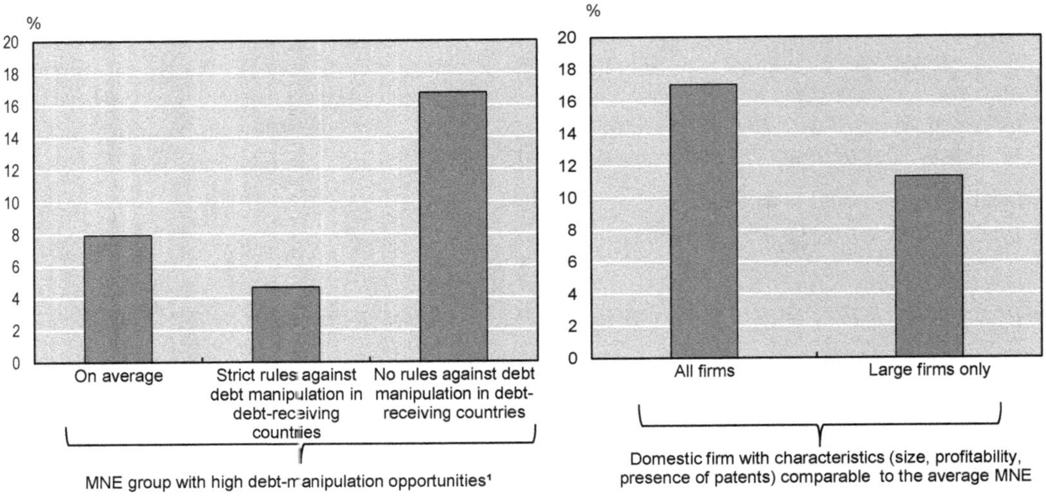

1. All differences are significant at a 5% level.
2. MNE groups with high debt-manipulation opportunities are groups facing a 5 percentage point higher statutory tax rate on average in the two highest-rate countries where they operate as compared to the average MNE group. For the average MNE group, this average is 35%, while for high debt-manipulation opportunities groups it is 40% (which corresponds to the 90th percentile of the distribution of this variable).

The empirical evidence suggests that strategic location of debt (internal and external) can increase the total debt of MNE groups. Yet, the external leverage of the average MNE group is found to be lower than that of the average domestic firm with comparable characteristics (Figure 3.A1.13, right panel), in line with most of the empirical literature (e.g. Burgman, 1996). This suggests that manipulation of the location of debt is not among the main determinants of MNE groups' external debt level, as it does not increase the average external leverage of MNEs above the average of domestic firms. Moreover, MNEs tend to have more diversified income streams as compared to domestic firms, making them less vulnerable to adverse income shocks (e.g. Baker and Riddick, 2013). Despite the additional external leverage induced by debt manipulation, the average MNE is therefore less likely than a domestic firm to have external debt levels that make it vulnerable to income shocks.

International tax differences, tax planning and the location of investments

Without differences in corporate tax rates and tax systems across countries, investment would be determined and located purely according to economic rates of return (assuming perfect mobility of capital and no other policy differences between countries). However, tax rates and systems differ and this creates distortions. Corporate income taxes affect firms' investment by reducing the after-tax return on investment. Indeed, recent OECD work found that corporate taxes reduce firms' investment, except for small and young firms (OECD, 2009; Arnold et al., 2011). Taxes can also affect firms' investment choices by favouring projects with a high after-tax rather than pre-tax return on capital (e.g. projects that can be more highly financed by debt). This may result in resources not being allocated to the most efficient projects or countries. In situations with tax distortions, tax planning may affect the impact of these distortions on investment and its location by reducing the effective cost of investing in high-tax countries.

International tax differences affect the location of foreign investment

Cross-country differences in corporate taxation influence the location of foreign investments and MNEs' foreign subsidiaries. Foreign investment, particularly investment in innovative activities, can generate knowledge spillovers with implications for human capital and productivity. Foreign investment can also increase competition from foreign firms in the domestic market, with positive productivity effects. There is a vast literature, including past OECD work, suggesting an adverse effect of host country corporate tax rate on foreign investment (Hajkova et al., 2006; OECD, 2007a; Feld and Heckemeyer, 2011). But corporate taxes are only one among many factors affecting firms' location choice (e.g. labour and product market regulation, size of the market, labour taxes, infrastructure, etc.). Its influence appears relatively small, for instance in comparison with labour taxes (Hajkova et al., 2006).

An example illustrates the effect of cross-country differences in corporate taxes for foreign investment, based on a tax sensitivity estimated on bilateral data on foreign direct investment (FDI) stocks (see Box 3.A1.11). More specifically, the sensitivity of FDI to corporate taxes is taken from past empirical OECD work, which controls for other determinants of FDI (e.g. income level, GDP, market size, distance between countries, product market regulation, employment protection legislation, labour taxes etc.). This estimate implies that a one percentage point increase in the corporate tax rate differential between two countries results in a 1.5% decrease in the gross bilateral FDI stock in the higher-tax rate country (Hajkova et al., 2006). Alternatively, an estimate based on a meta-analysis by Feld and Heckemeyer (2011) is used, with a tax sensitivity of 3 instead of 1.5. This higher sensitivity is because the meta-analysis does not control for the effect of policy determinants (other than corporate taxes) on FDI.

One caveat is that the available FDI statistics and the estimated tax sensitivity of FDI are distorted by international tax planning, for instance by large flows of interest income between countries. This is because the bilateral FDI statistics cannot separate investment income reflecting real activity from financial flows stemming from profit shifting.[42] Even so, the illustration gives an indication of the importance of taxes for foreign investment.

Based on these data and sensitivity, a tax-adjusted FDI stock is computed assuming that the statutory corporate tax rate at home is equal to the one in the host country for all pair of countries. For many pairs of countries this would involve a large tax change. In most countries, FDI positions explained by existing differences in corporate taxes account for less than 15% of inward FDI (based on the conservative OECD estimate of the sensitivity) (Figure 3.A1.14).[43]

Figure 3.A1.14 Share of inward FDI stock explained by tax rate differences between countries[1,2]

Average 2006-2011

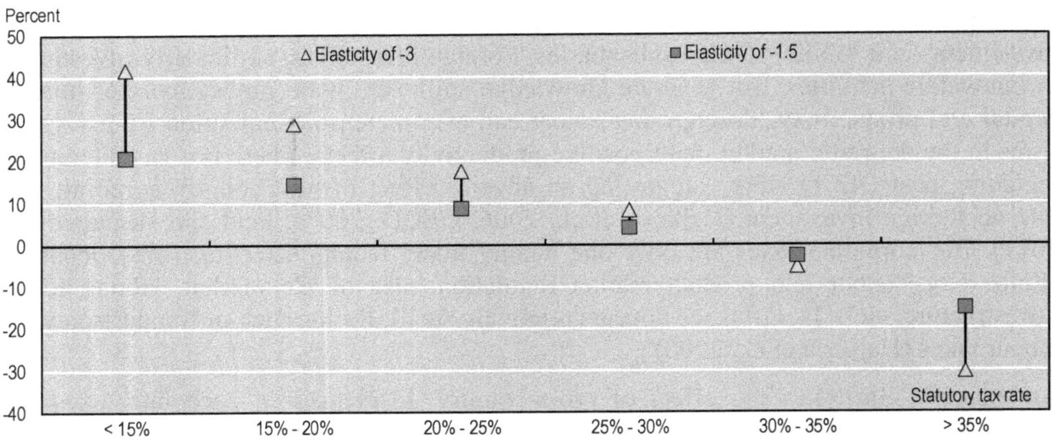

1. A positive figure indicates that the existing tax differences contribute positively to FDI. For example, without tax differences with other countries the FDI stock in a country with a tax rate below 15% would be about 20-40 percent lower (depending on the elasticity) than the actual stock.
2. The estimates are based on differences in statutory tax rates (the most widely available across countries). The estimates are similar when based on forward-looking effective tax rates instead of statutory tax rates.

In addition to differences in statutory corporate tax rates, preferential tax regimes (e.g. for intangible assets) and other characteristics of tax systems may influence the location of FDI. A potentially important factor is whether the home country of a MNE exempts foreign-source dividends from tax (i.e. territorial/source tax system) or subjects them to domestic tax while giving a credit for taxes paid in the host country (i.e. worldwide/residence taxation). Existing studies do not find a significant difference in the tax sensitivity of FDI under alternative tax systems (e.g. Hajkova et al., 2006). This may reflect tax deferrals and other tax planning strategies of MNEs as well as in practice that most countries do not have a "pure" territorial or worldwide system. A pure territorial system would tax all investments into a specific country in the same way regardless of home country, but would tax investment of the same MNE differently across countries. A pure worldwide system would do the opposite: it would tax investment of a MNE at home or abroad similarly, while treating investment of different MNEs into one country dissimilarly. Recently, there has been a trend towards territorial systems among OECD and G20 countries.

Box 3.A1.11. Cross-country differences in taxes and location of investment

The illustration relies on existing estimates of the sensitivity of FDI stocks to corporate taxation. Based on these tax sensitivities, a hypothetical bilateral FDI position in absence of differences between home and host statutory tax rates is computed for all pair of countries (estimates are similar when using forward-looking effective tax rates for a subsample of countries). The difference between actual and hypothetical inward FDI in a country reflects bilateral FDI positions, the assumed tax sensitivity and bilateral tax differences:

$$\Delta \boldsymbol{FDI}_{\boldsymbol{IN,host}} = \sum_{p} \boldsymbol{FDI}_{\boldsymbol{home \rightarrow host}} \times \boldsymbol{Tax\ sensitivity} \times (\boldsymbol{STAT}_{\boldsymbol{host}} - \boldsymbol{STAT}_{\boldsymbol{home}})$$

Bilateral gross FDI stocks are drawn from the OECD International Direct Investment database, covering 34 reporting countries and more than 200 partner countries over the period 2006-2011. In the statistics, foreign direct investment consists of capital shares and reserves, including retained profits, as well as net positions of loans, trade credits and securities.

The location of R&D activity and intangible assets are also influenced by taxation. As discussed, MNEs may locate income associated with patents and other intellectual property to countries with lower tax rate or preferential tax treatment on such income. However, MNEs do not locate the ownership of intellectual property only based on taxes. They often co-locate the ownership of intellectual property with the associated R&D activity (Griffith et al., 2014). Indeed, the empirical analysis suggests that R&D activities (proxied by patents where the inventor is located in the same country as the firm applying for the patent protection) are sensitive to tax rate differentials (see Box 3.A1.4).

Tax planning reduces the effect of tax rate differences on the location of investment by tax planning MNEs

Existing evidence, including recent OECD work, shows that a higher effective corporate tax rate in a country reduces firms' investment in that country (e.g. OECD, 2009; Djankov et al., 2010; Arnold et al., 2011). However, the possibility for MNEs with links to low-tax countries to reduce their effective tax rates by tax planning may make the location of their investment less sensitive to cross-country differences in tax rates. Thus, testing if (controlling for other factors affecting investment) the effects of high corporate tax rates on investment are weaker for such MNEs than for other similar firms without links to low-tax countries is an indirect way to verify the existence of tax planning.[44,45] International tax planning may reduce the effect of relatively high corporate taxation on tangible and intangible investment of tax planning MNEs, but at the cost of introducing distortions that are related to both the implied tax revenue losses and to the uneven playing field generated by differential effective taxation of different types of firms. Thus, across-the-board corporate rate reductions and base broadening would have more beneficial effects on the economy than "self-helped" reductions in effective tax rates by selected MNEs via tax planning behaviour.

Industry and firm-level evidence across a large set of OECD and G20 countries confirms that, while increases in corporate taxes tend to reduce firms' investment in a typical industry, the reduction in investment is lower in industries with a large share of tax planning MNEs (see Box 3.A1.12). For instance, a 5 percentage point increase in the effective (forward-looking) marginal corporate tax rate[46] would reduce investment on average across industries by about 5% in the long term (Figure 3.A1.15, Panel A). However, in industries with a high concentration of MNEs with profit shifting incentives, this effect would be nearly halved. This supports the hypothesis that tax-planning MNEs' investment is less sensitive to tax rates than other firms' investment. This is because tax-planning MNEs can achieve lower taxes through artificial arrangements without changing the location of the value-creating real economic activity. Moreover, stricter anti-avoidance rules against tax planning are found to raise the sensitivity of investment to tax rate changes (Figure 3.A1.15, Panel B).

Figure 3.A1.15 Tax planning reduces the effect of corporate taxes on tax planning MNEs' investment

Estimated long-term change in investment after a 5 percentage point increase in the corporate tax rate[47]

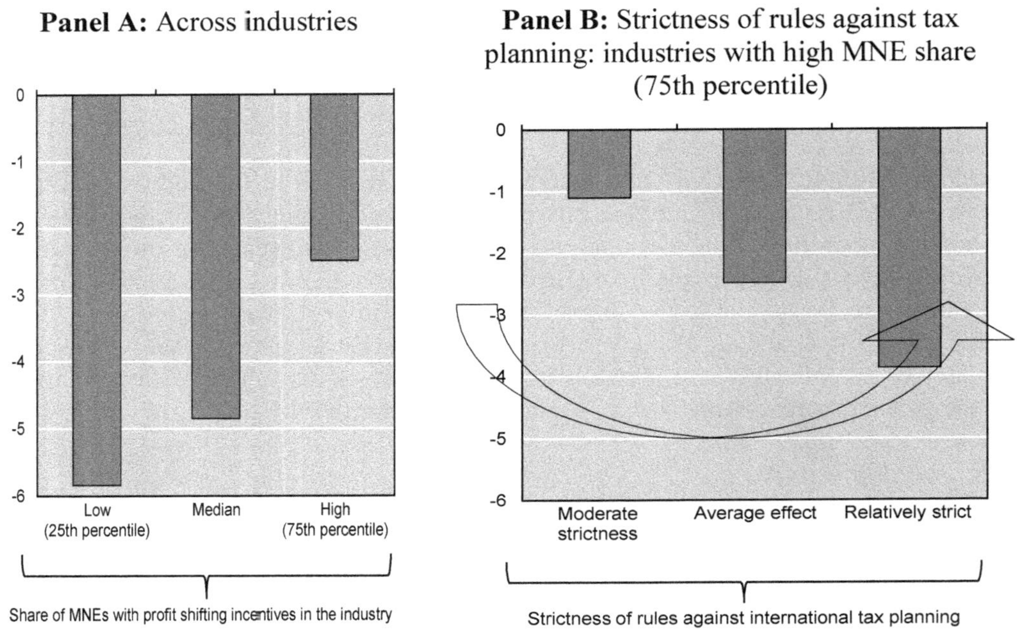

Box 3.A1.12. Empirical approach: Investment and tax planning

The effect of corporate taxes on investment is estimated with a similar strategy as in OECD (2009) (for details, see Schwellnus and Arnold, 2008; Vartia, 2008). The idea is to estimate an investment equation based on a neo-classical investment model (Hall and Jorgenson, 1967) to assess the impact of a tax rate change on firms having different tax planning incentives and opportunities. The analysis is conducted both at the industry and the firm-level. The industry level offers a better measure of investment, while the firm level offers a better measure of tax planning incentives. The two approaches give consistent results.

At the industry-level, the estimated equation is as follows:

$$Ivt\ rate_{c,i,t} = \alpha Ivt\ rate_{c,i,t-1} + \beta ETR_{c,t-1} + \gamma ETR_{c,t-1} \times Profit\_shifting\_MNEs_{c,i} + \theta VAgrowth_{c,i,t-1} + \delta_{c,i} + \delta_t$$

where $\boldsymbol{Ivt\ rate_{c,i,t}}$ is the investment rate (investment divided by lagged capital stock) in country c, industry i and year t, sourced from the World Input-Output Database (WIOD). $\boldsymbol{ETR_{c,t}}$ is the forward-looking effective marginal tax rate from the Oxford Centre for Business Taxation (results with the average effective rate are consistent but less statistically significant). $\boldsymbol{Profit\_shifting\_MNEs_{c,i}}$ is the number of MNE entities with profit shifting incentives among the 100 largest firms in country c and in industry i sourced from the firm-level database (ORBIS). An entity is considered as having profit shifting incentives if it faces a higher tax rate in its home country than the average (unweighted) in its corporate group, in line with the profit shifting analysis (Box 3.A1.3). The coefficient $\boldsymbol{\beta}$ reflects the tax sensitivity of the average firm, while $\boldsymbol{\gamma}$ reflects whether industries with a high concentration of profit-shifting MNEs are more sensitive than other industries. $\boldsymbol{VAgrowth_{c,i,t}}$ is the value-added growth of the industry – a high-growth industry is expected to have a higher investment rate. $\boldsymbol{\delta_{c,i}}$ and $\boldsymbol{\delta_t}$ are respectively fixed-effects for country-interacted-with-industry and time.

The sample consists of 30 industries in 29 countries over 1997-2009. The equation is estimated either with ordinary least squares or a generalised method of moments estimator that avoids the potential bias induced by the simultaneous use of the lagged dependent variable and fixed-effects. Results are consistent between the two estimation methods.

At the firm-level, the estimated equation is as follows:

$$\boldsymbol{Ivt\ rate_{f,c,i,t} = \beta ETR_{c,t-1} + \gamma ETR_{c,t-1} \times Profit\_shifting\_incentives_{f,c,i,t} + \theta VAgrowth_{c,i,t-1} + \delta_f + \delta_t}$$

where $\boldsymbol{Ivt\ rate_{f,c,i,t}}$ is the investment rate of firm f operating in country c, industry i and year t. The investment rate is measured as the change in fixed assets (at book value), net of depreciation (also at book value) and divided by lagged fixed assets, sourced from the ORBIS database. This measure is similar to Gal (2013). The effective tax rate and value-added growth variables are identical to the industry level analysis. $\boldsymbol{Profit\_shifting\_incentives_{f,c,i,t}}$ is the difference between the statutory tax rate in country i and year t and the average (unweighted) among the countries where the MNE group of f operates. $\boldsymbol{\delta_f}$ and $\boldsymbol{\delta_t}$ are firm and time fixed-effects. The sample consists of about 50 000 observations of MNE entity accounts in 18 OECD countries over ten years (2001-2010).

International tax competition

In an integrated global economy, countries may compete over mobile capital (tangible and intangible) by lowering effective and statutory corporate tax rates. One rationale for lowering tax rates is that it can attract foreign investment and increase domestic investments, with positive effects on growth. These investments can, in turn, create additional activity (e.g. employment opportunities, investment by intermediate suppliers, etc.), which further adds to growth and tax revenues.

One clear prediction from the tax competition literature is a reduction in tax rates, with a "race to the bottom" in the extreme case of a small open economy with perfect capital mobility (Devereux and Lorentz, 2012; Keen and Konrad, 2012). To the extent that the corporate tax is considered as more distortive than other taxes, a certain degree of tax competition may enhance economic efficiency. However, tax competition may also lower public spending and taxes below their efficient level and cause welfare losses, although this depends on what is considered the optimal level of public service provision (e.g. Wilson, 1999). Overall, in practice it is difficult to determine at what point tax competition produces negative effects for growth and welfare.

The empirical literature confirms that tax competition took place in past decades, as countries have responded to lower corporate tax rates elsewhere by reducing their own rates (Devereux and Sorensen, 2006; IMF, 2014). Furthermore, tax competition over corporate tax bases may have induced indirect spillovers on other tax bases. Pressures to reduce the corporate rate may have created pressures to reduce the top personal income tax rate because of the possibility to incorporate to reduce tax payments (OECD, 2009; Arnold et al., 2011; IMF, 2014). One marked change in taxation over the past decades is a reduction in top personal income tax rates and in progressivity in income taxes in OECD countries (OECD, 2009).

Tax planning provides incentives for tax competition as countries compete to attract profits generated by MNEs' activities elsewhere. This form of tax competition is not always transparent as it can occur through preferential regimes rather than on statutory rates. However, in the absence of tax planning, tax competition may not necessarily be less intensive. This is because the sensitivity of "real" investment to taxes may increase, as shown earlier. For instance, the estimates obtained with the methodology presented in Box 3.A1.12 suggest that the sensitivity of industry-level investment to the effective corporate tax rate would increase by about 30% if tax planning would be halved. In the absence of tax planning, higher-tax rate countries could become less attractive investment destinations for certain MNEs and may ultimately compete more fiercely to attract investment. At the same time, the additional tax revenues obtained in the short run by tackling tax planning could be used to reduce tax rates across the board or finance public spending, which could support private investment over the longer term.

Overall effect on efficiency and growth

International tax planning affects economic efficiency in several ways (Table 3.A1.3). Assessing the overall economic efficiency effect of tax planning is not easy as opposing factors are at play. One way to investigate this effect is to empirically examine if industries with a larger share of tax planning MNEs grow differently from other industries. Empirical analysis investigating if value-added growth differs across industries depending on the presence of tax planning MNEs, controlling for other factors affecting industry growth, yielded no clear evidence of a (positive or negative) impact of the presence of tax planning MNEs on industry growth.

Table 3.A1.3 Economic implications of international tax planning: summary of main findings

	Negative welfare effect	Positive welfare effect
Fiscal implications	Tax planning leads to tax revenue losses. The lost tax revenues could have been used to finance welfare or efficiency-enhancing public expenditures or to reduce other distortive taxes. Tax planning may also undermine the legitimacy of the tax system and reduce tax compliance among a wider set of taxpayers.	-
Competition between firms	Tax planning allows certain MNEs to increase their market power, resulting in more concentrated markets and higher price mark-ups. The reduced competitive pressure may hamper innovation and result in consumer welfare losses.	Welfare losses may be partially offset by the associated reallocation of resources to high-productivity MNEs.
Debt	The possibility to manipulate internal and external debt location reduces the effective cost of debt for MNEs and can lead them to take on higher overall external leverage.	-
Investment	Tax planning reduces effective tax rates at the cost of additional distortions (e.g. unlevel playing field between tax-planning MNEs and other firms) as compared with a situation in which corporate tax rates were cut across the board.	Tax planning reduces effective tax rates – and the associated drag on investment – for tax planning MNEs. Tax planning also reduces the effect of cross-country corporate tax differences on the location of investment by tax planning MNEs.
Tax competition	Tax planning provides incentives for tax competition as countries compete to attract profits generated by MNEs' activities elsewhere.	In the absence of tax planning, tax competition may not necessarily be less intensive, because the sensitivity of "real" investment to taxes may increase.

In any case, the welfare implications of tax planning go beyond economic efficiency. Tax planning redistributes corporate tax bases across countries, leading to revenue losses in higher-tax rate countries. These losses will either lead to lower government expenditures (which may reduce welfare) or may need to be offset by raising other distortive taxes on less mobile tax bases, which may entail a welfare loss. More broadly, tax planning may undermine the legitimacy of the tax system and reduce tax compliance among a wider set of taxpayers. This may hamper governments' ability to mobilise fiscal revenues due to lack of trust and perception of unfairness of the tax system. In turn, this can generate large compliance and administrative costs.

Discussion and concluding remarks

Corporate income taxes entail distortions and have been found to be more harmful for economic growth compared to other taxes at least at their observed level (OECD, 2007b; OECD, 2009; Arnold et al. 2011). Nevertheless, most countries levy corporate taxes. One reason is that the corporate tax plays a role as a "backstop" to the personal income tax. In the absence of a corporate tax, business income would not be taxed until it is realised as dividends or capital gains, which are often not subject to tax. By levying corporate income tax, governments reduce the opportunities for shareholders, especially non-resident, to shelter their income from taxation. In this area, new standards for automatic exchange of financial account information between countries (OECD, 2014d) may increase the possibility of taxing part of the corporate income at the personal level. Another argument for levying corporate income tax is that it could be designed to tax only economic rents (i.e. profits above a "normal" rate of return), in which case the economic distortions induced by the tax would be small (OECD, 2008).[48,49]

Globalisation creates additional challenges for corporate tax systems. Most corporate income tax systems were designed during a time when cross-border transactions, international trade and MNEs were less important than today. The issue is how to allocate the worldwide income of firms across the countries in which they are active. Provisions to deal with international trade and avoid double taxation or non-taxation of income have gradually been added to domestic tax systems. Nonetheless, as discussed, MNEs can often exploit the differences between tax systems to reduce their tax burden, with significant revenue losses for governments and globally.

This study provides robust evidence of such tax planning by MNEs. It highlights that international tax planning significantly reduces corporate tax revenues globally, though there is large uncertainty around the magnitude of the overall loss due to limitations in the currently available data. MNEs shift profit from higher to lower-tax rate countries. Large MNEs also exploit mismatches between tax systems and preferential tax treatment to reduce their tax burden. Transfer price manipulation, strategic allocation of intangible assets and manipulation of internal and external debt levels are found to be important profit shifting channels. Aside from its fiscal implications, tax planning is found to have effects on economic efficiency through various channels, including by affecting the sensitivity of the location of tax-planning MNEs tangible and intangible investments. Stricter anti-avoidance rules such as comprehensive documentation requirements on transfer pricing, rules against debt manipulation, GAARs and CFC rules as well as higher withholding taxes are associated with reduced tax planning, but also with higher compliance costs for firms. Co-ordinating anti-avoidance rules across countries could reduce these costs.

Bibliography

Aghion, P., N. Bloom, R. Blundell, R. Griffith and P. Howitt (2005), "Competition and Innovation: An Inverted-U Relationship", *The Quarterly Journal of Economics*, MIT Press, Vol. 120.

Atkinson, A. and J. Stiglitz (1976), "The Design of Tax Structure: Direct Versus Indirect Taxation", *Journal of Public Economics* 6.

Arnold, J., B. Brys, C. Heady, A. Johansson, C. Schwellnus and L. Vartia (2011), "Tax Policy for Economic Recovery and Growth", *Economic Journal,* Vol. 121.

Baker, H. and L. Ridick (2013), *International Finance: A Survey*, Oxford University Press.

Beer, S. and J. Loeprick (2014), "Profit shifting: drivers of transfer (mis)pricing and the potential of countermeasures", *International Tax and Public Finance,* No. 1.

Blomström, M. and A. Kokko (1998), "Multinational corporations and spillovers", *Journal of Economic Survey*, 12(3).

Bloom, N., R. Sadun and J. Van Reenen (2012), "Americans Do IT Better: US Multinationals and the Productivity Miracle", *American Economic Review,* 102.

Blouin, J., H. Huizinga, L. Laeven, and G. Nicodème (2014), "Thin Capitalization Rules and Multinational Firm Capital Structure", *IMF Working paper*, WP/14/12.

Boynton, C., P. De Filippes, E. Legel, and T. Reum (2014), "A First Look at 2010 Schedule M-3 Reporting and Schedule UTP", *Special Report, Tax Notes*, Internal Revenue Service.

Braconier, H., G. Nicoletti and B. Westmore (2014), "Policy Challenges for the Next 50 Years", *OECD Economics Department Policy Papers*, No 9, OECD Publishing.

Buettner, T., M. Overesch, U. Schreiber and G. Wamser (2012), "The impact of thin capitalisation rules on the capital structure of multinational firms", *Journal of Public Economics*, Vol. 96, Issues 11-12.

Buettner, T. and G. Wamser (2013), "Internal Debt and Multinational Profit Shifting: Empirical Evidence from Firm-Level Panel Data", *National Tax Journal*, 66 (1).

Burgman, T. (1996), "An Empirical Examination of Multinational Corporate Capital Structure", *Journal of International Business Studies*, No. 27.

Chamley, C. (1986), "Optimal Taxation of Capital Income in General Equilibrium with Infinite Lives", *Econometrica* 54(3).

Clausing, K. (2009), "Multinational firm tax avoidance and tax policy", *National Tax Journal*, Vol. 62, No 4.

Cobham, A. and S. Loretz (2014), "International distribution of the corporate tax base: Impact of different apportionment factors under unitary taxation", *Mimeo*, 2014.

CTJ (2014), "Offshore Shell Games", Citizens for Tax Justice.

Dahlby, B. (2011), "Global Value Chains, Foreign Direct Investment, and Taxation", mimeo, University of Alberta.

De Mooij, R. (2011), "The Tax Elasticity of Corporate Debt: A Synthesis of Size and Variations", *IMF Working Paper WP/11/95*, International Monetary Fund.

De Mooij, R. (2012), "Tax Biases to Debt Finance: Assessing the Problem, Finding Solutions", *Fiscal Studies, Institute for Fiscal Studies*, vol. 33(4).

Devereux, M. and P. Sorensen (2006), "The Corporate Income Tax: International Trends and Options for Fundamental Reform", European Commission, *Economic Papers* No. 264.

Devereux, M., B. Lockwood and M. Redoano (2008), "Do countries compete over corporate tax rates?" *Journal of Public Economics* 92(5-6).

Devereux, M. and S. Loretz, (2012), "What Do We Know about Corporate Tax Competition?", Oxford University Centre for Business Taxation, October, Working Paper 12/29.

Dharmapala, D. (2014), "What do we know about base erosion and profit shifting? A review of the empirical literature", *CESifo Working Paper*, No. 4612.

Dischinger, M., U. Glogowsky and M. Strobel (2010), "Leverage, Coporate Taxes and Debt Shifting of Multinationals: The Impact of Firm-specific Risk", *Mimeo,* University of Munich.

Djankov, S., T. Ganser, C. McLiesh, R. Ramalho and A. Shleifer (2010), "The Effect of Corporate Taxes on Investment and Entrepreneurship", *American Economic Journal: Macroeconomics,* Vol. 2 No. 3.

Evers, L., H. Miller, C. Spengel (2013), "Intellectual property box regimes: Effective tax rates and tax policy considerations", *ZEW Discussion Papers*, No. 13-070.

Feld, L. and J. Heckemeyer (2011), "FDI and Taxation: A Meta-Study", *Journal of Economic Surveys* (2011) Vol. 25, No. 2.

Fuest, C. and N. Riedel (2010), "Tax Evasion and Tax Avoidance in Developing Countries: The Role of International Profit Shifting", *Oxford University Centre for Business Taxation Working Papers,* 10/12.

Fuest, C. and N. Riedel (2012), "Tax Evasion and Tax Avoidance: The Role of International Profit Shifting", in *Draining Development?* editor P. Reuter, the World Bank.

Gal, P. (2013), "Measuring Total Factor Productivity at the Firm Level using OECD-ORBIS", *OECD Economics Department Working Papers*, No. 1049, OECD Publishing.

Gilbert, R. (2006), "Looking for Mr. Schumpeter: Where Are We in the Competition-Innovation Debate?", *Innovation Policy and the Economy*, Vol. 6 (eds. A. Jaffe, J. Lerner and S. Stern), National Bureau of Economic Research.

Golosov, M., A. Tsyvinski and I, Werning (2006), "New Dynamic Public Finance: A User's Guide", *NBER Macroeconomics Annual*.

Gravelle, J. (2015), *Tax Havens: International Tax Avoidance and Evasion*, Congressional Research Service, Washington D.C.

Gravelle, J. (2014), "International Corporate Tax Rate Comparison and Public Implications", Congressional Research Service, Washington D.C.

Griffith, R., H. Miller and M. O'Connell (2014), "Ownership of intellectual property and corporate taxation", *Journal of Public Economics* 112.

Grubert, H. (2003), "Intangible Income, Intercompany Transactions, Income Shifting, and the Choice of Location", *National Tax Journal* 56 No. 1.

Grubert, H. (2012), "Foreign Taxes and the Growing Share of U.S. Multinational Company Income Abroad: Profits, Not Sales, are Being Globalized", *Office of Tax Analysis*, Working Paper 103.

Hajkova, D., G. Nicoletti, L. Vartia and K. Yoo (2006), "Taxation and Business Environment as Drivers of Foreign Direct Investment in OECD Countries", *OECD Economic Studies* No. 43/2 2006.

Hall, R. and D. Jorgenson (1967), "Tax Policy and Investment Behavior", *American Economic Review*, Vol. 57.

Hanlon, M. (2003), "What can we infer about a firm's taxable income from its financial statements?" *National Tax Journal*, pages 831-863.

Heckemeyer, J. and M. Overesch (2013), "Multinationals' Profit Response to Tax Differentials: Effect Size and Shifting Channels", *ZEW Discussion Paper* No. 13-045.

Helpman, E., M. Melitz, and S. Yeaple (2004), "Export versus FDI with Heterogeneous Firms", *American Economic Review*, 94.

Huizinga, H. and L. Laeven (2008), "International profit shifting within multinationals: a multi-country perspective", *Journal of Public Economics*, No 92.

Huizinga, H., L. Laeven and G. Nicodeme (2008), "Capital structure and international debt shifting", *Journal of Financial Economics*, Vol. 88.

IMF (2014), "Spillovers in International Corporate Taxation", *IMF Policy Paper*, International Monetary Fund.

Joint Committee on Taxation (2014), "Technical Explanation, Estimated Revenue Effects, Distributional Analysis, and Macroeconomic Analysis of the Tax Reform Act of 2014", United States Government Printing Office, Washington.

Judd, K. (1985), "Redistributive Taxation in a Simple Perfect Foresight Model", *Journal of Public Economics*, 28(1).

Keen, M. and K. Konrad (2012), "International Tax Competition and Co-ordination", *Max Planck Institute for Tax Law and Public Finance Working Paper*, N°12/06.

Kydland, F. and E. Prescott (1977), "Rules Rather than Discretion: The Inconsistency of Optimal Plans," *Journal of Political Economy*, Vol. 85.

Lisowsky, P. (2010), "Seeking shelter: Empirically modeling tax shelters using financial statement information." *The Accounting Review*, Vol. 85, No. 5, pages 1693-1720.

Lohse, T. and N. Riedel (2012), "The impact of transfer pricing regulations on profit shifting within European multinationals", *FZID Discussion Papers*, No. 61.

Lohse, T., N. Riedel and C. Spengel (2012), "The Increasing Importance of Transfer Pricing Regulations – a Worldwide Overview", *Oxford University Centre for Business Taxation Working Paper*, No. 12.

Maffini, G. and S. Mokkas (2011), "Profit Shifting and Measured Productivity of Multinational Firms", *Oxford Bulletin of Economics and Statistics*, 73, 1.

Markle, K. and D. Shackelford (2011), "Cross-country comparisons of corporate income taxes", *NBER Working Paper*, No 16839.

Markusen, J., and A. Venables (1999), "Foreign direct investment as a catalyst for industrial development", *European Economic Review*, 43(2).

Modigliani, F. and M. Miller (1958), "The Cost of Capital, Corporation Finance and the Theory of Investment", *The American Economic Review*, Vol. 48, No. 3.

Møen, J., D. Schindler, G. Schjelderup and J. Tropina (2011), "International Debt Shifting: Do Multinationals Shift Internal or External Debt?", *CESifo Working Paper Series*, No. 3519.

OECD (2007a), Tax Effects on Foreign Direct Investment: Recent Evidence and Policy Analysis, *OECD Tax Policy Studies* No. 17, OECD Publishing, Paris, http://dx.doi.org/10.1787/9789264038387-en.

OECD (2007b), Fundamental Reform of Corporate Income Tax, OECD Tax Policy Studies No. 16, OECD Publishing, Paris, http://dx.doi.org/10.1787/9789264038127-en.

OECD (2008), "Reforming Corporate Income Tax", *Policy Briefs*, OECD Publishing.

OECD (2009), "Taxation and Economic Growth", *Economic Policy Reforms, Going for Growth*, Chapter 5, OECD Publishing, Paris, http://dx.doi.org/10.1787/growth-2009-en.

OECD (2013), *Action Plan on Base Erosion and Profit Shifting*, OECD Publishing, Paris, http://dx.doi.org/10.1787/9789264202719-en.

OECD (2014a), *Addressing the Tax Challenges of the Digital Economy*, OECD/G20 Base Erosion and Profit Shifting Project, OECD Publishing, Paris, http://dx.doi.org/10.1787/9789264218789-en.

OECD (2014b), *Neutralising the Effects of Hybrid Mismatch Arrangements*, OECD/G20 Base Erosion and Profit Shifting Project, OECD Publishing, Paris, http://dx.doi.org/10.1787/9789264218819-en.

OECD (2014c), *Countering Harmful Tax Practices more Effectively, Taking into account Transparency and Substance*, OECD/G20 Base Erosion and Profit Shifting Project, OECD Publishing, Paris, http://dx.doi.org/10.1787/9789264218970-en.

OECD (2014d), *Standard for Automatic Exchange of Financial Information in Tax Matters*, OECD Publishing, Paris, http://dx.doi.org/10.1787/9789264216525-en.

Overesch, M. (2009), "The Effects of Multinationals' Profit Shifting Activities on Real Investments", *National Tax Journal*, Vol. 62, No. 1.

Piketty, T. and E. Saez (2012), "A Theory of Optimal Capital Taxation", *NBER Working Paper*, No. 17989

Porter, M. (1980) "Competitive Strategy", Free Press, New York, 1980.

PWC (2013), Global Research and Development Incentives Group, November 2013.

Ragoussis, A. and E. Gonnard (2012), "The OECD-ORBIS Database: Treatment and benchmarking procedures", *Mimeo*.

Schwellnus, C. and J. Arnold (2008), "Do Corporate Taxes Reduce Productivity and Investment at the Firm Level?: Cross-Country Evidence from the Amadeus Dataset", *OECD Economics Department Working Papers*, No. 641, OECD Publishing.

Slemrod, J., J. Whiting and J. Shaw (2007), "Tax Implementation Issues in the United Kingdom", paper prepared for the IFS Conference on "Reforming the Tax System for the 21st Century: The Mirrlees Review", Cambridge, 12 April.

Sutton, J. (1991), "Sunk costs and market structure: Price competition, advertising, and the evolution of concentration", *MIT Press*, Cambridge, Mass.

UNCTAD (2015), "FDI, Tax and Development, The fiscal role of multinational enterprises: towards guidelines for Coherent International Tax and Investment Policies", *Working paper for review and feedback, 3/26/2015*.

Vartia, L. (2008), "How do Taxes Affect Investment and Productivity?: An Industry-Level Analysis of OECD Countries", *OECD Economics Department Working Papers*, No. 656, OECD Publishing.

Wilson, J. (1999), "Theories of Tax Competition", *National Tax Journal*, LII, No.2.

Zinn, B. and C. Spengel (2012), "Book/tax Conformity: Empirical Evidence from Germany", *ZEW Discussion Paper*, No. 12-051.

Notes

1. This annex was prepared by the OECD Economics Department in co-operation with the Centre for Tax Policy and Administration and has been approved by the OECD's Economic Policy Committee and the Committee on Fiscal Affairs.

2. More information about the ORBIS database is included in Box 3.A1.2.

3. The tax rate is the sum of the national and sub-national tax rate. For non-OECD countries, data are sourced from KPMG and refer to 2000 (Russian Federation refers to 2001 instead of 2000) and 2013.

4. The weighted average excludes Mexico due to missing data.

5. In the case of e-commerce or the sale of online services, there can be an ambiguity over where the profit of a firm is generated. For example, a firm may conduct substantial sales of goods and services in a market from a remote location and with minimal use of personnel (OECD, 2014a). As it is not possible to ring-fence the digital economy from the rest of the economy, no separate analysis was conducted of profit shifting associated with the digital economy. The assumption underlying the empirical analysis is that the location of assets (including purchased intangible assets reported in financial accounts) or employees represents a relevant proxy for the "true" activity of a firm.

6. MNEs may also shift certain activities (e.g. R&D activities) to benefit from preferential tax treatment on the related income. This is not considered as BEPS, but is included in the empirical analysis as it cannot be disentangled from BEPS channels with the available data. It was agreed in the BEPS Project that the preferential treatment of intellectual property should be coupled with "substantial activity" requirements to prevent harmful tax competition (OECD, 2014c).

7. In worldwide taxation systems, the location of headquarters determines the tax rate applying to worldwide profits. Thus, MNEs have an incentive to locate their headquarters in lower-tax countries (so-called tax inversion). However, the empirical analysis found no conclusive evidence that MNE headquarters are predominantly located in high or low-tax countries.

8. In some cases, reported and taxable profits differ because a firm exploits mismatches between tax systems to reduce its taxable profit (e.g. by deducting the same expense in more than one country) and thus its tax burden (Lisowsky, 2010). Such tax planning situations cannot be identified by analysing the location of profits using financial account data, but they are captured in the empirical analysis of mismatches between tax systems, which focuses on how reported profits are taxed.

9. "MNEs" are firms belonging to corporate groups present in at least two countries. "Domestic groups" are firms in corporate groups present in only one country. "Standalone firms" are firms belonging to no group (i.e. with no affiliate and no parent company). "Not identified" firms are assigned in different categories by the identification algorithm depending on the ownership threshold (i.e. 50% or 90%) chosen to link companies. All business forms (corporations, limited liability partnerships, etc.) are included in ORBIS data.

10. The share of domestic groups and MNEs appears implausibly low in the Netherlands, which probably reflects missing ownership links in the ORBIS database for this country. This may also be the case for other countries.

11. The data are based on the ORBIS sample used in the analysis and may not be representative of the underlying population, particularly for specific countries.

12. Only countries covered in the OECD STAN business demography statistics database are presented. Large firms are firms with more than 250 employees. When the number of employees is not available in ORBIS, turnover or total assets are used as alternative size measures (with respective thresholds of EUR 50 million and EUR 43 million, in line with the EU definition). Brazil and Iceland refers to manufacturing, Japan is 2012 in STAN as compared to 2009 in ORBIS (large firms is 50+ employees), Iceland 2005, Brazil 2008 and Switzerland 2009.

13. A MNE entity is considered as having a link to a given country if at least one entity in its corporate group is present in this country. A MNE entity is considered as large if it has more than 250 employees. The figures presented are computed based on all observations in the ORBIS sample used in this study over the period 2000-2010. Countries with less than 1200 observations of large MNE entities are not presented.

14. The data are based on the ORBIS sample used in the analysis and may not be representative of the underlying population, particularly for specific countries.

15. The statutory corporate tax is usually considered as the relevant tax rate on shifted profits (Gravelle, 2014). Lower effective tax rates (for example because of preferential tax treatment) are captured in the second part of the empirical analysis (mismatches between tax systems).

16. Using a weighted average is not straightforward. Weights based on activity levels may not reflect profit shifting possibilities as profits can be shifted to entities where the group has little activity. Weights based on profits or sales can pose endogeneity problems even in the case of lagging the relevant variable as there is a high correlation between past and current profits and sales.

17. In an alternative specification, the tax variable is split to assess separately profit shifting to no-tax countries and shifting between countries with positive (but different) tax rates. The result suggests that both types of profit shifting occur, with the profit shifting propensity (relative to tax rate differentials) being stronger between countries with positive tax rates.

18. A 50% threshold is commonly used in the tax literature for defining corporate groups (e.g. Huizinga and Laeven, 2008; Maffini and Mokkas, 2011). The rationale is that profit shifting would generally not take place between two companies that are not under the same control. By contrast, foreign direct investment statistics use a 10% ownership threshold.

19. The empirical approach is to compare in a regression analysis the profitability of MNE entities with different opportunities to shift profits, such as entities 1A and 2A. The entity 1A is expected to receive profits from other group members since it has a lower tax rate than them. In contrast, the entity 2A is expected to shift profits to other group members. The estimated tax sensitivity implies that a 1 percentage point statutory tax rate differential is associated with 1% higher (or lower) profit. This means that entity 1A is assumed to receive profits representing about 5% of its total profit, while entity 2A is assumed to shift about 10% of its profit. Details of the methodology are presented in Box 3.A1.3.

20. A few papers (e.g. Markle and Shackelford, 2011) include the effect of mismatches in their estimates, but without disentangling them from profit shifting.

21. Shifted (non-shifted) patents are patents where the inventor is located in a different (the same) country than the MNE entity applying for the patent protection. For example, the United States accounts for 42% of global patent applications, out of which 35% are invented in the country and 7% are invented in another country. Worldwide patent applications refer to the sum of patent applications (shifted and non-shifted) made by the 38 countries included in the analysis (see Panel B). Patent applications refer to applications to two major patent offices (i.e. the United States Patent and Trademark Office (USTPO) and the European Patent Office (EPO)) and patents filed under the Patent Co-Operation Treaty (PCT).

22. For example, in about 85% of patent applications in Luxembourg, the inventor is located outside Luxembourg.

23. It was agreed in the BEPS Project that the preferential treatment of intellectual property should be coupled with "substantial activity" requirements to prevent harmful tax competition (OECD, 2014c).

24. Existing intellectual property regimes in the OECD and G20 that do not meet the agreed standard for substantial activity should close to new entrants in June 2016 and stop operating in June 2021 (G20 communiqué, February 2015).

25. The patent protection may cover different countries than the one where the applying firm is located depending on the patent office where the patent is registered.

26. MNEs also have incentives to deviate from market interest rates on internal debt in order to shift profit. However, interest payments between related entities are generally regulated by the "arm's length" principle as other internal transactions.

27. Heckemeyer and Overesch (2013), based on a meta-analysis of 25 studies, estimate that debt manipulation accounts for about 30% of total profit shifting.

28. The indicator is compiled for 2005 and 2014. In the empirical analysis, the value for 2005 is used, which corresponds to the middle of the sample period.

29. The figure shows the percentage of GDP devoted to accounting, tax preparation, bookkeeping and payroll services, as a proxy for tax consultancy industry. It includes services unrelated to tax, but also excludes economic resources devoted to tax including tax legal services and corporations' in-house tax staffs.

30. The effect of international tax planning on other taxes and social contributions goes beyond the scope of this study. If international tax planning results from artificial financial flows and does not affect the location of "real" economic activity, the impact on other taxes and social contributions should be limited.

31. Figures as a share of GDP assume that CIT revenues represent 3% of GDP, which is close to the OECD average.

32. For Russian Federation, where no data is available in the OECD Business Demography Statistics database, a coverage rate of 70% is assumed. This corresponds to the average across European countries where comparison is possible. For non-European countries where no data is available in the OECD Business Demography Statistics database, a coverage rate of 5% is assumed.

33. The range is based on sensitivity around the point estimate of the tax planning sensitivity. The sensitivity analysis assumes a 95% confidence interval (i.e. about two standard errors on each side) around the point estimate of the profit shifting and mismatch estimates.

34. The revenue effect is based on the assumption that firms outside the sample have the same tax elasticity (i.e. profit shifting elasticity and average tax differential) as firms in the sample. The sensitivity analysis assumes a 50% higher tax elasticity of firms outside the sample relative to firms in the sample. The assumption is that 50% of firms are covered in the hypothetical country.

35. In the hypothetical example, the average tax rate differential corresponds to a statutory tax rate of 33%, which broadly corresponds to the weighted average of statutory tax rates over 2005-09 in OECD and G20 countries.

36. Data on tax credits is limited and the data used in this study were provided to the OECD as part of the work on Action 11 and most often refer to the year 2011. A caveat is that tax credits are volatile and that relying on data for only one year may not to be representative of the general size of tax credits.

37. The underlying assumption is that non-OECD and non-G20 countries lose on average 4-10% of corporate tax revenues, which is the same as the countries in the sample. On average in non-OECD non-G20 countries, corporate tax revenues as a share of GDP is about 50% higher than in countries in the sample (data on corporate tax revenues for these countries is sourced from available national sources and the IMF).

38. Other factors including the taxation of capital at the personal level can also affect financing decisions.

39. One option is to allow tax deductibility for the opportunity cost of equity finance (so-called allowance for corporate equity, ACE) as introduced in Belgium and Italy over the past decade. Another option is to remove interest deductibility altogether (so-called comprehensive business income tax, CBIT). These options are discussed extensively in the literature (e.g. OECD, 2007; de Mooij, 2012).

40. With complete markets and perfect information, there is no optimal debt-to-equity choice of firms (Modigliani and Miller, 1958). In reality, capital markets suffer from informational imperfections and non-neutral taxation. In a second-best world, changes in leverage due to taxation can either mitigate or exacerbate pre-existing distortions (de Mooij, 2011).

41. Manipulating the location of group debt may increase bankruptcy risks of the entities where debt is located if there is no perfect risk sharing within the group. However, MNE entities are generally thought to benefit from explicit or implicit guarantee from their parents (see Huizinga et al., 2008, footnote 9).

42. New international guidelines for compiling FDI statistics are currently being implemented. These guidelines recommend, among other things, to identify capital being channelled through special purpose entities, which are known to be used for tax planning. Once these data are available, the effect of tax differentials on FDI can be refined by excluding activities of special entities (see www.oecd.org/daf/inv/oecdimplementsnewinternationalstandardsforcompilingfdistatistics.htm).

43. In the case of location of investment, the relevant tax rate is the effective tax rate, as it takes into account the generosity of tax depreciation allowance of the investment and other tax provisions. The results presented in this study rely on statutory rates since effective tax rates are only available for a limited set of countries. However, the findings are robust to using effective rates for a smaller set of countries.

44. Few studies exist on the role of international tax planning for investment and most of the existing ones focus on one specific country, such as the United States or Germany (Grubert 2003; Overesch, 2009).

45. Using tax data for the United States, Grubert (2003) shows that R&D-intensive MNEs are more likely than other MNEs to invest in countries with either very high or very low tax rates. Investments in very-low-tax countries may serve in the setting up of tax-planning schemes. Investment in very-high-tax countries are attractive for tax-planning MNEs, since tax-planning allows them to avoid most of the high tax burden that non-tax-planning firms have to face in these countries.

46. Forward looking marginal tax rates are sourced from the Centre for the Oxford Centre for Business Taxation. They derive from modelling a hypothetical investment project taking into account all relevant tax provisions. By construction, they do not include the effect of international tax planning.

47. The corporate tax rate considered is the marginal forward-looking effective tax rate. All differences in the reaction of investment to tax rate changes are significant at a 5% level.

48. Dynamic inconsistency and lack of commitment in government policy may be another possible explanation for positive capital taxation as the policy maker has an incentive to tax capital once the investments is done to raise revenue (e.g. Kydland and Prescott, 1977; Piketty and Saez, 2012).

49. Another justification for capital income taxes is that they can provide insurance against future poor labour market outcomes (see Golosov et al., 2006). In a setting when there is uncertainty about individuals' future skills (productivity) and leisure is a normal good, more savings today, all else equal, will reduce work incentives later on. Thus, discouraging savings through capital income taxation increase the governments' ability to provide insurance against future labour market risks.

Annex 3.A2

A toolkit for estimating the country-specific fiscal effects of BEPS countermeasures

Introduction

When countries consider introducing BEPS countermeasures, estimates of the fiscal and economic effects may be needed. Tax policy analysts can provide government officials and other stakeholders with evidence-based analysis of the fiscal and economic effects of options to curtail BEPS behaviours.

The BEPS Action Plan states that "It is important to identify the types of data that taxpayers should provide to tax administrators, as well as the methodologies that can be used to analyse these data and to assess the likely economic implications of BEPS behaviours and actions taken to address BEPS". Action 11 also involves "ensuring that tools are available to monitor and evaluate the effectiveness and economic impact of the actions taken to address BEPS on an ongoing basis".[1]

This annex is intended to provide government tax administration and tax policy offices, as well as other stakeholders, with a toolkit of methodological approaches that could be used to estimate the fiscal effects of BEPS countermeasures. The fiscal effects estimates, which may incorporate taxpayer behaviour, are often an important starting point for analysis of other economic effects of legislative changes. While the toolkit discusses each of the BEPS Actions separately, the general estimation approach will be familiar to most government policy analysts responsible for analysing proposed tax legislation.

In a recent survey of the academic literature, Riedel (2014) notes: "The most convincing empirical evidence has been presented by academic studies that investigate specific profit shifting channels as their empirical tests are more direct and offer less room for results being driven by mechanisms unrelated to income shifting." This is an important insight in the discussion of the fiscal effects of BEPS countermeasures, and many of these empirical studies analysing specific profit shifting channels have been drawn upon in constructing the methodological approaches in this annex.

The toolkit presented in this annex focuses on practical approaches that tax policy analysts could use to estimate the fiscal effects of BEPS countermeasures for their country. Given that each country has different data and will begin from different starting points, several alternative approaches are often suggested. Some countries may introduce the full suite of BEPS countermeasures, while others may introduce selected BEPS countermeasures. For this reason, the proposed methodologies are distinguished by action. This is in line with the scope of Action 11 of the BEPS Action Plan.[2]

Government estimates of the fiscal effects of domestic tax law changes are not new, and some countries have already estimated the fiscal effects of certain BEPS-related tax policy measures. It is worth noting that individual country fiscal effects from unilateral measures do not take into account spillover effects in other countries. For example, implementing an interest limitation rule will reduce debt and interest deductions in the implementing country, but affected MNEs could shift debt and interest deductions to other countries with weaker rules. The effect on global BEPS and global revenue would be very different in respect of multilateral BEPS countermeasures compared to unilateral measures.

A number of governments view the closure of loopholes as base protection measures and, as a result, do not estimate the associated fiscal effects. This is also the case for many of the BEPS-related countermeasures, which may be treated as measures that protect forecasted budget revenue, not as incremental new revenue to the current-law revenue projections.[3] Thus, while a number of BEPS-related countermeasures have been enacted over the past ten years, they have sometimes been seen as measures to protect the tax base, and have not been officially scored as raising revenue relative to current tax projections.

Some countries have estimated the fiscal effects of BEPS-related countermeasures enacted or proposed. Table 3.A2.1 provides a summary of the fiscal estimates of BEPS-related countermeasures in selected countries as a percentage of their total corporate income tax (CIT) revenue. The revenue effects are approximate because the total CIT revenue does not always refer to the same year for which the revenue estimates were computed. Moreover, some revenue estimates refer to a period, but the number of years included is not always explicitly stated. Measures that were implemented in prior years may yield different fiscal estimates if estimated today or in future where general macroeconomic conditions may be different. For interest limitation rules in particular, because some of the fiscal estimates were introduced during a period of higher interest rates; introducing them in the current interest rate environment may result in a lower estimate. The fiscal estimates also depend on whether a country has implemented other policy measures simultaneously and how the estimates of these measures may have been integrated to avoid overlapping. Also, if these countries had existing countermeasures in place, then the fiscal estimate would only be for the incremental revenue effect of the new interest limitation rule, not the effect of the country's total interest limitation rule. The estimate would also be sensitive to the macroeconomic conditions at the time of introduction.

Table 3.A2.1. Government fiscal estimates of BEPS-related measures

Country	Measure	Year of enactment (unless stated otherwise)	Annual revenue effect as a percentage of total corporate income tax revenue
Denmark	Limited interest deductibility	2007	5.2%
France	Hybrid mismatch arrangements	2014	0.9%
Germany	Higher taxes on relocation abroad and more appropriate transfer pricing	2008	8.6%
Norway	Limited interest deductibility	2014	3.4%
Sweden	Interest deduction rules for internal debt	2013	8.5%
	Tax information exchange agreements	2010	0.6%
United Kingdom	Avoidance schemes using the transfer of corporate profits	2014	0.3%
	Hybrid mismatch arrangements	2017	0.2%
United States	Restrict deductions for excess interest of members of financial reporting groups and defer the deduction of interest expense related to deferred income	Proposal (2015) for enactment 2016	4.0%
	Tax currently excess returns associated with transfers of intangibles offshore	Proposal (2015) for enactment 2016	1.1%

Source: OECD Committee on Fiscal Affairs WP2 Country Survey

Analysing the fiscal effects of BEPS countermeasures provides a number of benefits. Fiscal estimates provide policymakers with at least a magnitude of the potential effects of policy actions, rather than relying on limited information relating to a select group of taxpayers or arrangements. Estimation and modelling requires analysts to make estimates and assumptions more explicit, even though key data may be incomplete. Understanding the limitations of the data can help improve available data over time. Fiscal estimation can provide important inputs to broader economic analysis of legislated changes by measuring the incentive effects, the level of the affected activities, and the potential taxpayer behavioural responses. For example, policy proposal or impact assessment documents produced by the ministry of finance and revenue authority in the United Kingdom, as well as policy costings provided in the United States, often include wide-ranging information and analysis in respect of tax policy proposals.[4] The information depends on the particular policy, but generally includes an overview of the current law and the proposed change under consideration; why government intervention is necessary; the policy objectives and intended effects; the alternate policy options and the basis for the recommended option; benefits and costs to government and other economic actors; additional factors, such as competition effects; and potential for behavioural responses.

General approach to undertaking a fiscal estimate

The following steps are important components of a revenue estimation exercise and could be used as a guide for estimating the fiscal effects of any new tax policy measure. This approach is likely to be particularly useful in the BEPS context as new countermeasures or improvements of existing countermeasures are proposed and enacted. It is important to recognise that all countries are different when it comes to the level of detail in respect of taxpayer data collected, and access to that data by tax policy analysts. For this reason, the most appropriate methodology will vary from country to country. Figure 3.A2.1 provides an overview of a potential approach that can be used in undertaking a fiscal estimate. This is followed by an explanation of each step.

Understanding the proposed change

Carefully evaluating and understanding the proposed legislative change is important. It is necessary to identify the key elements of the proposed change that are likely to have the greatest fiscal effect and can be captured with available data. It may be appropriate to place less reliance on policy design features that are more detailed and less likely to have a material effect on the fiscal estimate. Attempting to make a highly refined estimate with limited data and uncertainty about taxpayers' behaviours may not be worthwhile. While details matter, not all of them are important for incorporation in the economic analysis and identifying the key elements of the proposal is necessary for a reasonable estimate of the effect. Smaller issues could be referenced as potentially having an upward or downward bias on the revenue estimate.

The proposal needs to be compared to current law, regulations and practices as current practice will determine the counterfactual against which the countermeasure is measured. In many instances, BEPS countermeasures will be incremental to those measures already in place, such as thin capitalisation rules, transfer pricing rules and general anti-avoidance rules (GAAR). Some countries may already have legislation that is similar to or stronger than the proposed countermeasures, in which case the countermeasure, considered in isolation to other changes, may have no incremental effect on future revenues. It will also be important to determine the appropriate counterfactual and whether proposed countermeasures will be revenue protecting or revenue raising in nature.

Figure 3.A2.1. Potential approach to undertaking a fiscal estimate

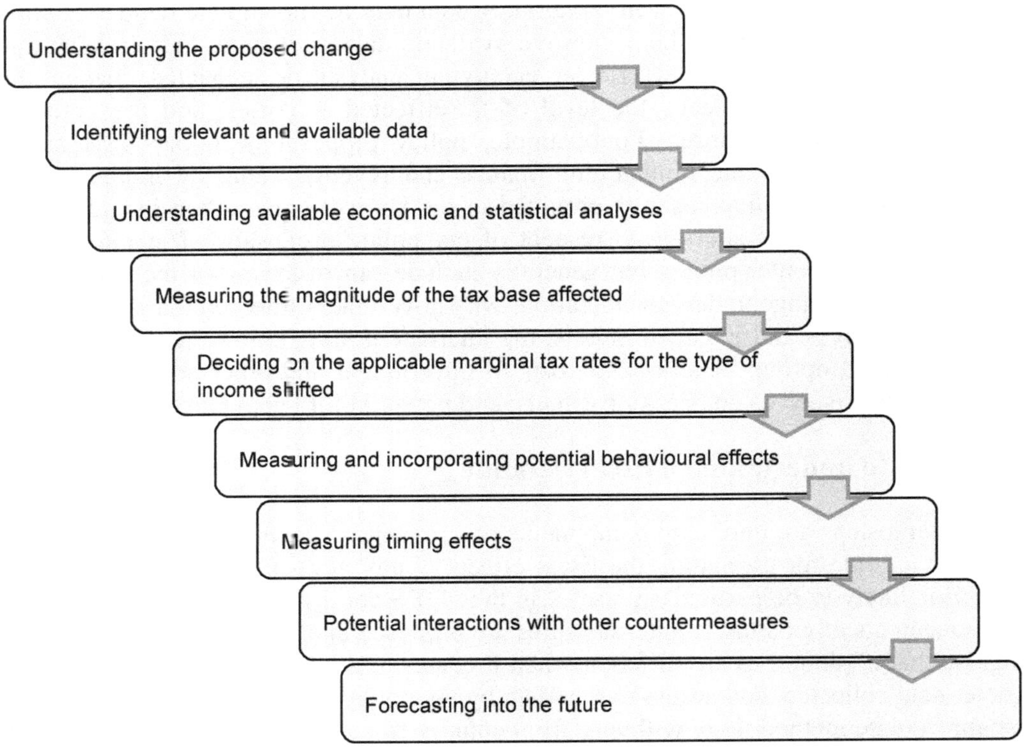

Identifying relevant and available data

Identifying the most relevant, currently available data is critical to the fiscal estimate. In some cases, such as individual income tax changes, tax analysts may have detailed tax return data which can be quickly used to simulate tax policy changes. In the business and corporate tax area, the data is typically much less available given the volatility of business income, the complexity of business structures, and the need to adjust for the carry-forward of tax losses, making the projection of corporate taxes more difficult than personal income taxes. The available data for international tax analysis of MNEs and BEPS is severely limited. However, it is common practice for government analysts of business tax policy changes to draw on databases from a variety of sources, not just from tax return information.

The availability of data will determine, to a large extent, the potential methodology that can be pursued. In the BEPS context, the best case scenario is having access to micro-level tax return information that highlights whether entities are affiliated with a MNE and distinguishes between related-party and unrelated-party transactions. Even tax return data may not have all of the information needed for the estimate and would need to be supplemented with other information.

Financial account micro-data may also be useful in the absence of tax return information. Extrapolation from the available financial account data to the universe of affected taxpayers will be necessary, especially given the missing data problems with available databases. Macroeconomic data may help calibrate financial account data and assist in an extrapolation. Caution must be exercised when interpreting the results from financial accounts due to the differences between tax expense reported for accounting purposes and the actual tax paid by a business. A good strategy would be to understand the potential sources of discrepancy and make suitable adjustments.

In the absence of a database of financial account micro-data, an alternative would be to analyse a statistical sample, or the financial statements of the top MNEs in the country. It is important to note that a statistical sample would be preferable to focusing on a concentrated group of MNEs. While focusing on the top MNEs may capture a significant proportion of the total economic activity affected, extrapolating beyond this group may result in an overestimate of the fiscal effect. Using a true statistical sample of taxpayers that would be affected by a policy measure would provide a better representation of the economy and thus a better sample from which to extrapolate. The number of groups chosen for the sample will depend on domestic factors and should have a good representation across sectors to adequately reflect sectorial contribution to GDP and whether certain sectors are more affected than others by the countermeasure(s) proposed.

If no micro-data is available, macro-data can be used. It is possible to find data on many of the transactions that are likely to be affected by BEPS, including imports/exports, sales, interest receipts and payments, and dividends and royalties. These are often available in national accounts and balance of payments (BOP) data. It is also possible that the data is available for bilateral exports/imports and/or FDI with other countries.

If no macro-data relevant to the countermeasure is available for the country, analogous data from similar economies could be sourced, as well as information from empirical studies. Some empirical studies have useful information on issues that relate directly to BEPS behaviours.

Understanding available economic and statistical analyses

When estimating the fiscal effects of a tax policy measure, there is often an array of literature and/or empirical studies available that have already investigated issues relating to the measure being enacted, and which can provide useful insights to tax policy analysts. In the BEPS-specific context, consulting existing studies that analyse certain tax-motivated behaviour, or which contain analyses on BEPS countermeasures in other countries, can add valuable insights to the estimation exercise. There are a number of empirical analyses of BEPS behaviours by MNEs, including in relation to transfer pricing, interest expense and treaty shopping. These analyses are important sources of information and can often assist analysts in refining a fiscal estimate. Some studies may show the behavioural responses to tax differentials or in relation to a specific measure that was implemented, while others provide useful information on relationships between variables that are integral to particular BEPS Actions (e.g. internal and external debt). Another example is an academic study that provides a better understanding of all treaty networks and those 'country routes' that are likely to be profitable from a tax planning perspective.

Measuring the magnitude of the tax base affected

Quantifying the magnitude of the tax base affected by a policy measure is a key element that often requires assumptions and judgement. It involves drawing on the relevant and available data and making necessary adjustments, after understanding the relationships between key variables. In the BEPS context, it is also critical to understand the various incentives to engage in BEPS behaviours as these will also affect the size of the affected tax base. Combining the knowledge from the prior steps effectively will enable an informed determination of the size of the tax base that is likely to be affected by the policy measure.

Deciding on the applicable marginal tax rate for the type of income shifted

Once the affected tax base has been calculated, it will be necessary to determine the applicable tax rate to apply to the estimated change in the tax base. This will depend on the type of income stream, whether the expansion in the tax base will be taxed at the margin, and the specific rules implemented. The simplest tax rate to use is the headline statutory tax rate, but in many cases (particularly in the BEPS context) this may not be the best choice given that many countries have special regimes that have substantially lower statutory CIT rates on certain income. For example, patent box regimes reduce the CIT rate on IP-related income and some countries have special arrangements with taxpayers that result in negligible tax liabilities. Effective tax rates may not be appropriate either; if an increase in the tax base should be taxed at the margin, an effective tax rate (ETR) would understate the fiscal effect in situations where investment allowances and tax credits reduce the ETR.

The starting point would be the applicable marginal tax rate (AMTR), which is the rate applied to an increase in taxable income as it would be taxed at the margin. Downward adjustments may be required for a variety of reasons. For example, businesses in an assessed loss position for tax purposes would not have their current tax liability affected by an incremental increase in taxable income. Having access to micro-data would not require an adjustment as the exact AMTR would be applied in the micro-simulation model. However, in recognition of the fact that a certain portion of firms would be in a tax loss position, a fiscal estimate relying on macro-data would require a downward adjustment in the statutory marginal tax rate. If no adjustment is made, it is likely to result in an overestimate of the fiscal effect.

Measuring and incorporating potential behavioural effects

It will be necessary to get a good understanding of the incentives for BEPS both prior to and subsequent to the enactment of proposed countermeasures. Incentives to engage in BEPS behaviours post-enactment are important for a dynamic estimate of the fiscal effects of the countermeasure(s) being analysed. It is also important to recognise that behavioural effects are not isolated to taxpayers. Behavioural effects can also occur as a result of domestic governments' reaction to other foreign governments' tax law changes and macroeconomic behavioural effects from these changes. However, for the purposes of this annex, only taxpayer behaviours are discussed.

Significant behavioural effects should be included to the extent data and available research allow. Since firms engage in profit maximising behaviour, tax policy analysts can assume that one of the routes firms use to achieve this objective is minimising their tax liability. Closing a loophole may result in MNEs finding alternate methods of eroding the tax base or shifting profits out of the country. This is important to recognise in a fiscal estimate as estimated increases in CIT revenue may not arise if MNEs find alternate methods to minimise their tax liability.

A simplifying assumption often used in tax policy analysis of smaller tax changes, as opposed to major tax reforms, is that the change will not have a significant macroeconomic effect. Since any business tax increase from reducing BEPS would result in lower taxes to other actors, increased government spending, or a reduction in the government's budget deficit, overall macroeconomic effects are unlikely to be significant given the offsetting effects. If significant macroeconomic effects are anticipated, the tax administration and tax policy offices would generally work with other government offices to estimate the overall budget effect.

Including behavioural responses for unilateral measures is different to doing so for multilateral action as discussed in the introduction. There are multiple empirical studies on taxpayer responses to tax rate differentials and specific tax policy changes that have been implemented, all of which can provide useful insights to analysts.

There are also factors outside of the legislated policy change that need to be factored into a fiscal estimate. In the lead up to introducing new legislation announced, many countries have processes in place that could include the release of a discussion document to seek public comments; parliamentary sessions; and engagement with taxpayers. The time taken for these processes can result in taxpayers changing their behaviour to avoid being affected by the new legislation. This is something that could be factored into behavioural responses.

The level of enforcement is also important. Weak enforcement could render a good policy measure ineffective if taxpayers can easily avoid paying the taxes due. For this reason, it may be appropriate to factor in a measure of expected effectiveness in terms of how successful the revenue authority will be at enforcing the countermeasure.

Measuring timing effects

Most governments estimate the fiscal effects of proposed legislation over several future years based on macroeconomic forecasts by other government offices. The effect of proposed changes depends on the timing of the implementation, phase-ins and any transition rules. Timing may also be affected by carry-forward rules, i.e. if deductions are disallowed in the current year, but become available in later years, such as with net operating loss carry-overs. Some proposals may have an effect on revenues before legislation is enacted or comes into effect if taxpayers react in advance of proposed legislation.

Potential interactions with other countermeasures

Recognising interactions between countermeasures is important to prevent double-counting from overlapping countermeasures or under-counting due to synergies between countermeasures. In large tax reform proposals, government analysts are routinely required to address the issue of overlap. They do this directly when considering the different provisions of a large tax reform, and also often use a revenue-estimating convention called "stacking". Stacking sets the order in which individual tax provisions of a tax package are estimated. For example, for a tax reform that includes both a tax rate change and a tax base change, the estimates of individual provisions will depend on the stacking order. If a tax rate reduction is stacked first, it will apply to the current-law tax base and thus result in a lower revenue estimate for the rate change than if a tax base increase is stacked first. The estimate of the tax effect of the larger tax base would also be smaller since it would apply to the lower tax rate. Alternatively, if the tax base increase is stacked first against the higher current-law tax rate, then its revenue effect would be larger, as would the tax rate reduction's tax effects, since the lower rate will be applied against the proposed larger tax base. In either case, the combined effect can be estimated accurately; stacking affects the size of the individual components, not the total, while reducing potential double-counting.

Stacking is important in estimating the fiscal effect of multiple policy measures to eliminate double counting. A few examples of potential overlaps in the BEPS context include: (1) if transfer pricing changes are stacked first, taxable income will be more appropriately taxed where the value is created based on the new transfer pricing rules, so taxable income that might be affected by Action 3 or Action 7 if implemented in isolation will have already been included in the Actions 8-10 transfer pricing fiscal estimates; (2) As both Action 4 and transfer pricing rules affect interest payments, caution will need to be exercised in terms of distinguishing between the correct pricing of interest (or payments equivalent to interest) and interest resulting from excessive leverage; and (3) while Action 2 would raise revenue by eliminating hybrid mismatch arrangements relative to current law in isolation, Action 4 and Action 6's fiscal effects could pick up most of the fiscal effects that Action 2 would otherwise have generated. Thus, stacking and potentially treating some countermeasures as integrity measures, which increase the effectiveness of other countermeasures, can significantly reduce the possibility of double-counting.

Synergies between multiple countermeasures are expected to have a more powerful effect on reducing BEPS behaviours than individual countermeasures in isolation. Thus, the sum of the parts may be less than the effect of the combined package. Countries could consider the likely effectiveness of the individual countermeasures as a specific parameter to be used in the estimate, as highlighted in the discussion of behavioural effects. The effectiveness parameter includes not only the coverage of the proposed legislation, but also the expected enforcement of the legislation. This parameter can be adjusted for certain countermeasures to incorporate potential synergistic effects, with possible sensitivity analysis around that adjustment.

Forecasting into the future

Fiscal estimates often require an extrapolation of the likely fiscal effects in the years following the year a new policy measure is implemented. Projecting into the future requires a reliance on GDP forecasts for the country and an estimation of how CIT revenues are likely to increase relative to GDP. This would involve analysing the responsiveness of CIT revenues relative to changes in GDP in prior years, as well as other factors that are likely to influence CIT revenues, such as the business cycle and whether there is a lag between when profits are reported and when tax revenues are reported.

Potential Methodologies by Action Item

Potential approaches to estimating the fiscal effects of individual Actions are set out below. The approaches pursued by countries will differ for many reasons, one of which is the availability of data. One country may have detailed tax return information that enables micro-simulations on a proposed countermeasure, while another country may have to rely more on macro-data. For this reason, two different routes are suggested for some of the Actions, depending on whether micro-data is available. There are areas of commonality though; for example, all countries will have to grapple with the question of likely behavioural responses and how to incorporate them into their estimates. Deciding on which approach is best and having learnt from best practices in other countries, government policy analysts can tailor the proposed methodologies to their domestic circumstances.

Since empirical studies have focused more on transfer pricing and the tax-motivated debt bias relative to other BEPS behaviours, the proposed methodologies for the individual Actions are arranged accordingly. The most comprehensive methodologies are provided for Actions 8-10 and 13 (transfer pricing) and Action 4 (interest limitation rules). Approaches to estimating the fiscal effects of the other Actions will also discuss the fiscal estimation issues involved in respect of those countermeasures and highlight potential available data. These Actions will contribute to addressing BEPS more effectively through increased disclosure, reducing harmful tax practices, improving dispute resolution, and speeding up the implementation of the treaty changes. In some cases, some of these Actions are designed as integrity measures complementing other Actions; such Actions will often enhance the effectiveness of other Actions such as transfer pricing rules and interest limitations.

Actions 8-10 and 13 (Transfer Pricing)

The overall objective of Actions 8-10 is the improved allocation of corporate taxable income to the countries where the economic activity generating the profits occurs. Specific objectives of the three Actions include developing rules that prevent BEPS caused by "moving intangibles among group members" (Action 8); "transferring risks among, or allocating excessive capital to, group members" (Action 9); and "engaging in transactions which would not, or would only very rarely, occur between third parties" (Action 10).

Understanding the proposed changes

The following changes or clarifications in the transfer pricing guidance will reduce the size of BEPS related to transfer mispricing and are particularly relevant to a fiscal estimate:

- Increased specificity in delineating the actual transactions in the context of a MNE group's economic activities and commercial and financial relations between the associated enterprises. This includes ensuring that both contractual arrangements and the actual conduct of the parties are taken into account in delineating the actual transaction for which it needs to be determined whether the conditions, including the price, are at arm's length;

- Providing for the possible non-recognition of transactions when they lack the commercial rationality of arrangements between unrelated parties;

- Strengthening the identification of risk in order to determine which associated enterprise assumes the risk for transfer pricing purposes. This includes ensuring that the assumption of risk by an entity is consistent with the exercising of control over the risk and with the financial capacity to assume the risk and is not only determined by the contractual assumption of risk;

- Providing for a more detailed evaluation of the activities related to the development, enhancement, maintenance, protection and exploitation of intangibles, and the allocation of profits generated by these intangibles in line with the importance of these functions;

- Provisions requiring that synergistic benefits deriving from membership of a MNE group are appropriately allocated through arm's length prices to members of the group contributing to the benefits;

- More detailed guidance on the pricing of transactions, including pricing of low value-adding services and commodities; and
- Introduction of measures to address the asymmetry of information between taxpayers and tax administrations, such as in the cases of hard-to-value intangibles and the timing of commodity transactions, thus preventing mispricing of transactions involving such intangibles and commodities.

In addition, Action 13 will enhance the relevance of transfer pricing documentation, and provide information about the MNE group's global allocation of revenues and activities. Mandatory Country-by-Country Reporting will provide more information to tax administrations to conduct risk assessments.

Data and methodology

Estimating the scale of transfer pricing-related BEPS and the effect of Actions 8-10 and 13 involves two distinct steps. First, an estimate is required of the net impact (increase or decrease) on CIT collections of BEPS relating to the mispricing of transactions. This estimate has two significant components: (1) the mispricing of transactions that are observed in a country's trade in goods and services data, and (2) BEPS-related transactions that are misallocated in the trade data for specific countries. An example of the second category would be missing royalty payments to a country that creates IP from in-country R&D expenditures, if BEPS attributes the value of the IP (and related income streams) to another country through transfer prices that are not in line with the location of activities that created the IP. Both aspects of the fiscal impact of BEPS should be included in the revenue estimates.

Second, an estimate of the overall impact of the proposed changes in transfer pricing rules and guidance presented in the Report on Actions 8-10 (*Aligning Transfer Pricing Outcomes with Value Creation,* OECD, 2015a) can be applied to the estimated scale of BEPS from mispricing to determine the expected changes in CIT revenues attributable to the implementation of the BEPS Actions. The purpose of the second step is to prepare a revenue estimate of the expected change in CIT revenues due to the adoption and implementation of the revised transfer pricing guidance. The extent of the changes adopted, as well as the timing of their implementation will vary from country to country.

The suggested methodology addresses: (a) mispricing of goods and services transactions between MNE entities, and (b) mispricing of interest payments among MNE entities.[5] The methodology described is based on country-specific, macroeconomic data on trade and interest flows to estimate the scale of BEPS and the fiscal effects of the guidance in the Report on Actions 8-10. Where other data, including firm-level micro-data or more disaggregated macro-data, is available for the country, analysts should take advantage of this. If information, such as that obtained from audits, is available, alternative methodologies may be appropriate.

a. Mispricing of goods and services

The estimation exercise begins with data on trade in goods and services, which includes the combined effects of mispricing of goods and services. In the presence of BEPS, it is expected that trade among MNE entities results in underreporting of profits in countries with marginal tax rates higher than the domestic country's marginal tax rate and over-reporting of profits in countries with lower marginal tax rates. This profit shifting occurs through the mispricing of transfer prices on MNE intra-firm trade flows of both exports and imports.

Detailed macroeconomic data on the total amount of annual exports and imports by country (for both goods and services, where available), as well as bilateral export and import flows with countries' trading partners, is available from the OECD *International Trade Account* data and IMF *Direction of Trade Statistics*.[6] To the extent that more detailed information from a national statistics office is available for individual countries, analysts should take advantage of such information.

The international trade data includes both goods and services for OECD and G20 countries, but data for service flows may be limited for other countries. Separate estimates of mispricing should be prepared for goods and for services when the data is available. International trade transactions in services include a number of components that may be affected by BEPS.

Revenue estimators need to understand what is included in the trade data. For example, recent changes to the international standards for reporting balance of payments statistics currently being implemented will expand available information on a country's trade in services related to intangible property. The new standards call for the capitalisation of R&D expenditures. This will provide a basis for reporting the value of transfers of the ownership of intangibles produced by R&D expenditures as a component of trade in R&D services. However, many intangible asset values are significantly greater than the capitalised value of their inputs, so potential shifted income may need to be adjusted from the reported trade value. This is in addition to the already included services data on the payments for the use of intellectual property.[7] In countries that have not yet adopted this change, the transfer of ownership rights in intangible property is unlikely to be included in the trade in services category.

Estimators must also consider potential transfer pricing adjustments to currently reported bilateral trade data. An example would be the potential reallocation of royalties paid by an operating affiliate in one country to a tax haven entity, which may not be fully reflected in royalties paid by the tax haven entity to the entity in the country actually conducting the R&D. In this triangular conduit trade example, actual trade data would not accurately reflect the expected income distribution.

Adjusting trade data to reflect MNE intra-firm transactions

Because BEPS mispricing occurs between MNE entities, it is necessary to reduce total trade flows to those that are potentially subject to mispricing among related companies. This requires estimating several key parameters:

- The percentage of international transactions accounted for by corporations subject to the CIT;[8]
- The percentage of the resulting trade flows accounted for by MNEs (i.e. the trade flows excluding exports/imports by domestic companies to/from unrelated parties); and
- The share of MNE trade transactions that represent transactions among related MNE entities.

There are several possible sources of information that could provide a basis for estimating these ratios. The first is tax return information of taxpayers identified as MNEs. The relative size of their taxable income or taxes paid, compared to other business taxpayers in the country, is a possible starting point. In addition, specific countries may conduct surveys of MNEs and other corporations that collect information on their activities, such as data on Activities of Multinational Enterprises (AMNE) that identifies intra-firm transactions.[9] Customs data and other national statistics could be used. If this type of information is not available for the country, reported ratios from other countries with similar economies and trade patterns could be used for the estimates.

Figure 3.A2.2 provides examples of the values for the key trade-related parameters for the limited number of countries that report this information.

The aggregate trade amounts can be multiplied by the above fractions to estimate the percentage of total trade accounted for by transactions between MNE entities.[10]

Figure 3.A2.2. Intra-firm transactions as a percent of selected trade statistics

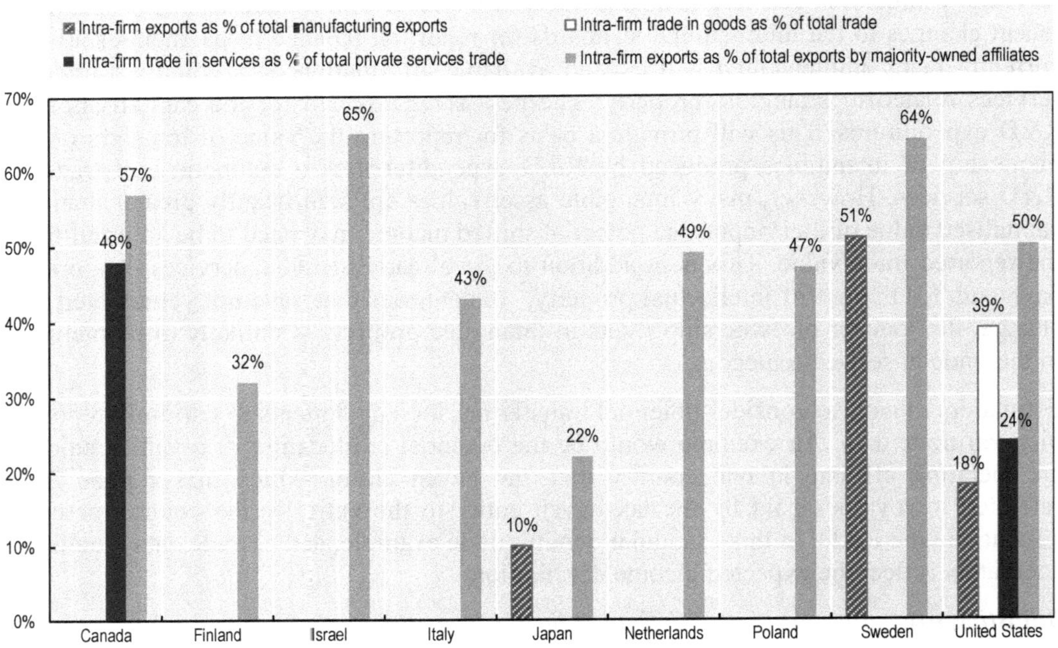

Source: Lanz and Miroudot (2011)

Notes:

1. The data is derived from AMNE and trade data for different years. In respect of intra-firm exports as a percentage of total exports by affiliates, data are for the year 2008 for Italy and the United States; 2007 for Israel, Japan, and Poland; 2006 for Finland; 2002 for Sweden and the Netherlands; 1994 for Canada. Data for Israel and Poland refer to the manufacturing sector only.

2. The statistical data for Israel are supplied by and under the responsibility of the relevant Israeli authorities. The use of such data by the OECD is without prejudice to the status of the Golan Heights, East Jerusalem and Israeli settlements in the West Bank under the terms of international law.

Adjusting for potential double counting

The resulting trade amounts determined in the prior step are the potential export and import flows that may be subject to BEPS-related transfer mispricing. However, there is one additional adjustment that could be made in determining the extent of BEPS mispricing. Increasingly, global value chains result in multiple cross-border transactions among MNE entities. As intermediate products and services move across borders through global supply chains, the value added in each country at each step in the production and distribution chain accumulates in the gross trade flows.[11] A portion of the trade flows represent MNE intra-firm sales. The question is how this "pyramiding" affects the accuracy of BEPS mispricing estimates based on the trade data.

While it is true that the intermediate goods and services lead to gross trade flows that overstate the value added contribution in each country in the supply chain, it does not necessarily follow that mispricing would only apply to the new value added by each country in the supply chain. Mispricing may still be based on the gross value of sales, not the smaller amount of in-country value added.

If a country determines that the use of gross trade data overstates the potential base for transfer mispricing, an adjustment could be made to reduce the trade figures to address this issue. For example, a country could reduce gross exports of goods by an estimated percentage of the export that is accounted for by imports of intermediate goods from other countries. A possible source for this percentage is the OECD *Trade in Value Added* database that includes an estimate of foreign value added as a percent of a country's exports.[12] This percentage ranges from 14% to 59% for OECD countries with a simple average of 30%. If a country is excluded from the OECD database, an estimate could be based on the figures for other countries with similar economies and trade patterns.

Trade-weighted marginal tax rate differentials

Profit shifting through transfer mispricing takes advantage of differences in marginal tax rates of related companies in different countries. Empirical studies have estimated the sensitivity of transfer prices to tax rate differentials independent of real economic factors. Applying the empirical results requires information on tax rate differentials.

The tax rate differentials are key variables used to estimate the degree of over or underreporting of profits due to BEPS. Since transfer pricing occurs at the margin (affecting the incremental income shifted), the appropriate tax rate is that applicable to the shifted (marginal) income, or the AMTR. The marginal tax rate is different to an average historical effective tax rate that could reflect non-marginal tax elements such as accelerated depreciation or tax credits. The marginal tax rate may be a country's top ("headline") statutory tax rate, but for certain types of income the marginal rate may be a special lower tax rate or an administratively-negotiated lower rate. For instance, a number of countries have special lower rates for income from certain intangible assets ("patent boxes") or other activities. These special lower rates can increase or decrease the tax rate differentials and thus result in greater incentives for transfer mispricing in the absence of safeguards to prevent this.[13] In most empirical studies, analysts have used headline statutory tax rates or average historical effective tax rates. More careful attention to AMTRs is needed in BEPS analyses of the expected revenue effects of countermeasures.

A trade-weighted value of AMTRs between a country and its trading partners can be estimated using pairwise trade flow data.[14] The tax rate differential for a country is equal to the home country AMTR minus the weighted average AMTR given each country's bilateral trade flows.[15] If data is available, the trade-weighted AMTRs should be calculated separately for exports and imports of goods and services.[16] This assumes that a dollar of shifted profits is taxed at the AMTRs.

It is possible that transfer mispricing could occur between related entities in two countries with the same headline statutory tax rate, either due to special tax rates or if one of the entities is in a net operating loss position. Transferring additional income from a profitable entity to a net operating loss entity would reduce current taxes as well as reduce the present value of taxes of the two related entities. The tax reduction could be a permanent reduction in tax equal to the statutory tax rate if the entity with the net operating loss would be unable to use those net operating losses in a future year due to carry-forward limitations.

For reference, the global weighted (by exports for the OECD and G20 countries) average tax rate differential, using 2014 statutory tax rates and 2012 trade flows, was 3.3 percentage points, implying a net shifting out of profits and thus decrease in corporate tax revenues.[17] Depending on the home country's AMTR relative to its trading partners, the AMTR differential could be negative, in which case the country could be benefitting from taxable income being shifted into the country with a coincident increase in corporate tax revenues. If the AMTR differential is positive, the country could be experiencing a shifting out of taxable income with a coincident decrease in corporate tax revenues. Countries with AMTRs in excess of the weighted average of their trading partners had a weighted average differential of 4.6 percentage points. The average tax rate differential for the group of countries with home country AMTRs less than their trading partners was -1.3 percentage points.

Transfer pricing responsiveness to tax rate differentials ("elasticities")

To translate the tax rate differentials into BEPS impacts, the differentials need to be multiplied by an estimate of the responsiveness (elasticity) of export and import prices to tax rate differentials. These "semi-elasticities" are estimates of the percentage change in trade prices in response to a one percentage point change in tax rate differentials, holding other factors constant.[18]

Table 3.A2.2 presents the elasticity estimates from specific empirical studies of the responsiveness of export and import prices for products to CIT rate differentials. The country and dataset used, time period covered, tax variable used, and estimated elasticity are shown for each study. There is a wide range of semi-elasticities (concentrated in the -0.65 to -1.6 range) varying by country, data availability and methodology. If feasible, countries should conduct their own empirical studies to determine a country-specific semi-elasticity. Alternatively, estimates from other countries with similar tax systems and economic structures could be used. Care should be taken to ensure the results are reasonable by, for example, seeing that the estimate of income shifted generally does not exceed any available estimates of profit margins.

A different elasticity may be applicable for goods and services. Some empirical studies have found that the responsiveness to tax rates is higher for entities with significant intangible assets, so mispricing of hard-to-value intangibles may be easier than mispricing physical goods.[19] Empirical analyses have also found larger mispricing among more highly differentiated physical goods.[20] The growth in importance of intellectual property within manufacturing and the production of products is making the distinction between goods and services in international trade increasingly unclear. For example, the price of exports of goods may reflect a price for the good itself plus an embedded, but not separately stated, charge for the use of intangible property, a service component. In this case, the transfer price of the good may include an element of BEPS related to the mispricing of the use of the intangible property that was produced in another country in earlier steps in the production chain.

Table 3.A2.2. Elasticity estimates of the responsiveness of intra-firm exports and imports to corporate income tax rate differentials

Study	Data	Time Period	Tax Variable	Elasticity
Bernard, Jensen and Schott (2006)	United States exporters arm's-length and intrafirm prices	1993-2000	STR	-0.65 to -1.6 semi-elasticities
Clausing (2003)	United States international trade transaction data	1997-1999	STR	-1.8 to -2.0 elasticities
Clausing (2006)	United States intrafirm trade balances by country	1982-2000	STR	-1.3 semi-elasticity
Overesch (2006)	German MNE balance sheet data for intrafirm sales	1996-2003	STR	-1.45 semi-elasticity
Davies, Martin, Parenti and Toubal (2014)	French exporter's arm's - length and intrafirm prices	1999	EATR	-0.24 elasticity
Vicard (2015)	French exporter's arm's- length and intrafirm prices	2000-2014	STR	-0.23 semi-elasticity
Cristea and Nguyen (2014)	Exports of Danish manufacturing firms	1999-2006	STR	-0.64 to -0.82 semi-elasticities

Notes: STR is statutory tax rate; EATR is the backward-looking average tax rate.

To calculate the percentage difference in the trade prices of exports and imports due to BEPS mispricing, the appropriately determined semi-elasticity value could be multiplied by the applicable differential tax rates in each country, before applying the resulting percentage to an estimated value of exports and imports with related parties in each country that are potentially subject to BEPS-related mispricing. The first part can be represented as:

Percentage difference in trade prices = (semi-elasticity) x ($AMTR_{home}$ – weighted average $AMTR_{trade\ partners}$)

For example, with a semi-elasticity of -1 and an AMTR differential of +5 percentage points, there could be a 5 percent reduction in trade prices.

With the simplifying assumption that there is no change in quantities traded as a result of the mispricing of exports and imports, the estimated percentage change in prices is equal to the percentage change in the value of trade. This calculation provides an estimate of the BEPS-related change in the value of imports and exports of goods and services due to the mispricing of observed transactions. In other words, it is an estimate of the change in value that would result if the BEPS incentive due to the tax rate differentials did not exist, assuming the estimated elasticities reflect only BEPS after accounting for real economic effects.

The final fiscal estimate assumption is that a one unit change in exports and imports translates into a one unit change in the CIT base. The resulting estimated change in a country's CIT tax base can then be multiplied by the AMTR to derive an initial estimate of the potential maximum annual CIT revenue impact of BEPS mispricing of reported goods and services. An adjustment would be required to recognise that a portion of firms may be in an assessed loss position for tax purposes.

Mispricing related to intellectual property

An important component of BEPS-related mispricing is the possible under-pricing (relative to arm's length prices) of the transfer of intangible assets from a higher to a lower-tax country. If under-pricing occurs, income (such as "buy-in" payments at the time of transfer or buy-in related royalty payments) for the entity in the higher-tax country will be understated as a result of the mispricing of the intangible transfer. In addition, the level of ongoing royalty payments to the affiliate for the use of intangibles may be mispriced.

The transfer pricing methodology for services would include an estimate of the mispricing of the related-party transfers of IP and royalty flows to the extent that these transactions are reported in a country's trade in services statistics. A significant trade in services category is "charges for the use of intellectual property." This includes charges (i.e. royalties and license fees) for the use of intangibles, including industrial processes, computer software, trademarks and other intellectual property.[21]

It is likely that this service category does not record all of the current-law payments for intangibles due to limitations in reporting coverage and in the classification of transactions. To the extent that transactions involving intangibles are underreported in the trade in services data, the estimating methodology will understate the amount of transactions potentially subject to BEPS.

Given the importance of intangible transactions in facilitating BEPS, the estimating methodology can be extended by analysing the trade in "charges for intellectual property" separately from other trade in services categories. If country-specific information is available on the extent of mispricing of the services from intangibles or the transfers of IP, based on taxpayer audits or empirical studies for example, this factor can be multiplied by the reported IP trade in services amount to derive a more accurate estimate of BEPS related to the intangibles. The more general elasticity approach would then be applied to the remaining trade in services categories.

It should be noted that the above methodology does not directly address the reallocation of revenue as a result of transfer pricing adjustments to the amount of observed royalties, or as a result of non-recognition of the transfer of intangibles for transfer pricing purposes under certain circumstances. The methodology, based on observed flows of services (including payments for intellectual property), would not pick up this revenue gain (or loss) due to the transfer pricing adjustments which reallocate the profits for tax purposes.

In this situation, revenue estimators should make a separate estimate of the impacts of the reallocation. Ex post audit experience may provide a basis for identifying the expected tax base change associated with this impact. The estimated change in the base would be multiplied by the AMTR to determine the revenue impact.

b. Mispricing of interest payments

BEPS can also result from overstating interest paid on intra-firm loans by entities in higher-tax countries and understating interest paid by entities in lower-tax countries. The trade flow data used to estimate the BEPS impacts of trade mispricing does not include interest payments and receipts.[22]

The IMF Co-ordinated Direct Investment Survey (CDIS) database provides data on BOP statistics for FDI payments and receipts of interest between related parties that could be used for estimating the revenue impact of interest payment mispricing. The data is for the interest component of the direct investment category of primary income international transactions. By definition, this data is limited to transactions among MNEs.[23]

The potential estimating methodology for the mispricing of interest payments follows that suggested for the mispricing of trade in goods and services:

- A weighted (by interest flows) average tax rate differential is calculated from the bilateral country information on interest payments and receipts of FDI interest;
- The tax rate differential is multiplied by an estimated semi-elasticity of the interest mispricing to tax rate differentials of other countries to estimate the degree of interest mispricing among MNE entities. The literature suggests that this semi-elasticity may be less than that for goods and services. If an elasticity estimate from the literature is used, the elasticity should be adjusted for any country-specific distinguishing factors such as relative transfer pricing rules or enforcement levels;
- The resulting change in interest payments and receipts is assumed to result in an equivalent change in interest expense/income and the CIT base; and
- The change in the CIT base is multiplied by the AMTR to determine the current-law revenue impact of BEPS profit shifting through the mispricing of interest.

It is important to note that there are other categories of possible mispricing induced by tax rate differentials, such as captive insurance payments and hedging transactions. Transfers to take advantage of unused net operating losses may not be induced by tax rate differentials, but also result in profit shifting. If there is country-specific information on the amount of these transfers, analysts should consider this information in estimating BEPS.

Although much international trade is undertaken by MNE corporations, increasingly non-corporate (or entity-level taxed) businesses are operating globally. Thus, transfer mispricing could also have adverse effects on other taxes, including personal income taxes, value-added taxes, and customs duties.

c. Combined fiscal estimate

Combining the fiscal estimates for the mispricing of goods, services and interest payments provides an aggregate estimate of the net revenue impact of BEPS under the current law (the "scale of BEPS"). This provides a starting point (or counterfactual) for estimating the expected fiscal impact of the revised transfer pricing guidance in the Report on Actions 8-10.

The first step in estimating the budget impacts of the combined guidance requires specifying the proposed or adopted administrative and legal changes that will better address transfer-pricing related BEPS. Each Action could have a different effect, or could be estimated jointly. The next step requires determining what percentage of current BEPS would be eliminated due to the revised transfer pricing guidance. In other words, what is the change in tax revenues that can be expected from the revised guidance? The following should be considered in estimating these fiscal impacts.

Adjusting for possible ranges of arm's length prices

Important institutional features of the transfer pricing compliance system may affect the size of expected collections from eliminating mispricing. For example, taxpayers provide a range of estimates for arm's length prices chosen to reflect comparable transactions among unrelated parties. Tax administrations generally accept transfer pricing estimates that fall within a range (e.g. inter-quartile) of the estimates. As a result, some of the estimated transfer mispricing may still fall within the acceptable transfer pricing range and not result in a change in taxable income. A second possibility is that audit resources are targeted on cases involving large expected outcomes. An adjustment factor could be applied to the estimate of collections from eliminating mispricing to account for such institutional features of the transfer pricing compliance system.

Additional adjustments

- The initial estimate of transactions at risk of mispricing could be reduced for certain types of trade considered to be less subject to mispricing;
- The extent to which existing anti-avoidance rules are already effective in the country should be factored into the fiscal impact estimates. An adjustment should be made to reflect the relative strength of the country's rules compared to the rules implicit in the elasticity estimate used and the revised guidance that is implemented; and
- The country-specific impacts of the revised guidance will also depend upon the timing of its implementation. This will affect the change in revenues calculated on an annual basis.

Possible sources of information to estimate the adjustments include:

- Input from income tax auditors and tax administrators on the potential impacts of the changes on both voluntary compliance and audit results;
- Revenue estimates prepared by estimators in other countries, including early adopters of the revised guidance;
- Results from empirical studies of profit shifting with different levels of transfer pricing rules and enforcement levels; and
- The first Country-by-Country Reports (CbCRs) will be filed for 2016 calendar year filers no later than 31 December 2017. Enhanced transfer pricing documentation, including CbCR information for MNEs with entities in the country, will thus be available for statistical analysis following the filing of these reports and will provide increased information for transfer pricing risk assessment. CbCR information will provide an additional resource for improving the marginal tax rate differential estimate with individual group data and for assessing this key percentage.

Similar to evaluating the scale of BEPS and the effects of other BEPS Actions, the fiscal effects of Actions 8, 9, 10 and 13 will not show up in a line on a future tax return. They will need to be estimated based on available evidence. The effects of the Actions will result in reduced mispricing as reported on the filed tax return, with a secondary effect of more effective enforcement against any remaining misreporting. Ex post evaluation of the estimated fiscal effects can involve conducting further empirical studies or examining future literature on estimated profit shifting and changes in transfer pricing assessments and settlements adjusted for levels of enforcement and other changes.

Potential interactions with other countermeasures

The fiscal effect estimate for the mispricing of interest interacts with the estimates of the fiscal effects of the countermeasures in the Report on Action 4 (*Limiting Base Erosion Involving Interest Deductions and Other Financial Payments,* OECD, 2015b). The transfer pricing revenue impacts in this section assume that the separate fiscal effects of countermeasures to reduce the strategic shifting of debt to high-tax countries are accounted for in the estimates of Action 4 countermeasures.

Action 4 (Interest Limitation Rules)

The objective of Action 4 is to reduce BEPS involving interest expense and other financial payments that are economically equivalent to interest expense. Action 4 calls for a best practice interest limitation rule for better aligning interest expense deductions with where the activities creating profits takes place.

Understanding the proposed best practice approach

In estimating the fiscal effect for individual countries of introducing the best practice interest limitation approach, it is important to encompass the key factors that are likely to drive a change in tax revenue. The main elements of the approach that are important for the fiscal estimate are:

- A fixed ratio rule: this limits an entity's net interest expense (NIE) to a fixed percentage of EBITDA[24]. The Report on Action 4 includes factors which a country should take into account in setting the benchmark ratio, within a corridor of 10% to 30%.
- A group ratio rule is encouraged in combination with a fixed ratio rule: this would allow an entity to deduct more interest expense in certain circumstances[25] but not more than the group's total external interest expense.
- Entities that will be subject to the rule: the fixed ratio rule should apply to taxable corporate and non-corporate entities (including permanent establishments) and, as a minimum, to entities that form part of a MNE group.[26] Where a group has more than one entity in a particular country, the country may apply the fixed ratio rule to the position of each entity separately, or to the overall position of all group entities in the same country. In addition, countries can determine whether to apply the rule to entities which are part of a domestic group and/ or stand-alone entities which are not part of a group.[27]
- Reducing the impact on certain entities: countries may apply a *de minimis* threshold to exclude entities with low NIE.
- Definition of NIE: for entities affected by the rule, NIE encompasses net interest payments to third parties, related entities and entities within the same group, regardless of whether the recipient is domestic or foreign. It also includes financial payments that are economically equivalent to interest, such as those which are linked to the financing of an entity that are determined by applying a fixed or variable percentage to an actual or notional principal over time The methodologies set out in the annex focus on NIE as captured in the National Accounts.[28]
- Definition of EBITDA: for the fixed ratio rule, the best practice approach recommends using an EBITDA based on tax numbers; and for the group ratio rule a country may provide for entity EBITDA to be calculated using either tax or accounting principles.

- Possible additional design features: allowing carry-forward of disallowed interest expense and/or unused interest capacity for use in future periods, or carry-back of disallowed interest expense into earlier periods.
- Specific rules to address issues raised by the banking and insurance sectors will be developed, with this work to be completed in 2016.

Since countries may opt for different fixed ratios and supplement the fixed ratio with additional design features of the best practice approach, some of which are outlined above, the design of the interest limitation rules introduced in each country will influence the estimation approach. In addition, countries differ in the level of detailed taxpayer data that government tax policy analysts have access to. The following section outlines a methodology (key steps, parameters, and assumptions) that may assist in estimation. The methodology is separated into two potential approaches – one using micro-data from tax returns or financial reports and the other using a macro-approach. The approaches can be used to estimate the change in fiscal cash collections on a year-by-year basis.

Data and methodology

Estimating the fiscal effect of interest limitation rules requires calculating the extent to which the CIT base will be broadened by limiting interest deductions, and applying the appropriate marginal tax rate to the increase in the base.[29] It is important to take into account the country's existing excessive interest deduction countermeasures to determine the incremental effect of the new rule. Also, it is important to recognise that taxpayers may change their behaviour in response to interest limitation rules, which would result in an adjustment to the static estimate. The magnitude of the behavioural response will depend on the design of the rule and the extent to which interest limitations are implemented on a multilateral basis, as well as non-tax determinants of capital structure, such as prevailing interest rates.

With regard to a counterfactual, some countries may have existing countermeasures to address excessive interest deductions in place, while others may not. For purposes of this analysis, the starting point assumes no existing interest limitation rules: asset-based rules (thin capitalisation rules) or interest limitation rules. If there are such rules, the amount of revenue currently collected from those rules should be determined if possible from tax returns, and then can be subtracted from the estimate relative to no interest limitation, to estimate the incremental effect of the new rules. Countries with existing countermeasures could opt to use current-law as the counterfactual in the estimation exercise.

Figure 3.A2.3 outlines the basic steps for estimating the fiscal effects of Action 4, depending on whether micro or macro-level data will be used. The steps for each approach are explained subsequently.

Figure 3.A2.3 Potential steps to follow once data availability has been determined

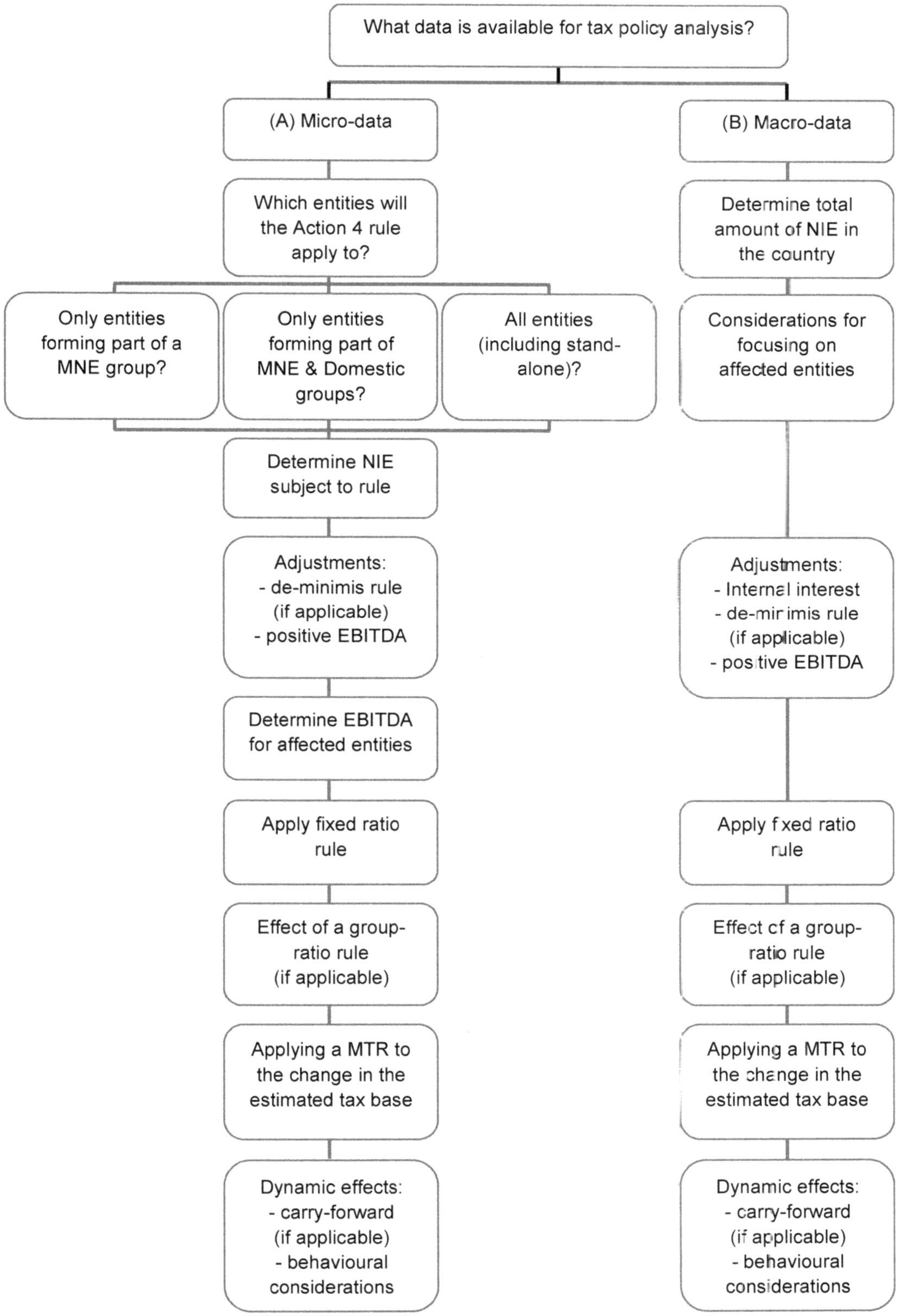

a. Micro-data approach

Ideally, government tax policy analysts in each country would have access to business tax returns to simulate the effects of the proposed interest limitation rule to obtain a static fiscal effect, taking into account the different provisions of the countermeasure and the AMTR of the additional income for different taxpayers. Individual company information with NIE, EBITDA, and taxable (or financial) income can be used to estimate the static fiscal effect for different fixed ratios, different *de minimis* rules, and different types of taxpayers affected. The effect of a group ratio rule, the effect of a carry-forward / carry-back rule, and behavioural effects would have to be separately estimated as adjustments to the static revenue effect.

If tax return information is not available, but individual company financial information is available, detailed simulations are possible, although adjustments for differences between financial account information and tax bases will need to be considered. Also, given potential lack of complete information from public financial accounts, macro-data for total interest receipts and payments recorded in the country could help extrapolate the micro-data to a total estimate.

Entities that will be subject to the rule

The first step is to determine which entities will be affected by the fixed ratio rule in the country. Given that the Action 4 best practice approach could have different impacts in addressing BEPS involving interest in the financial sector and other sectors, it will be necessary to focus only on entities in those sectors that are affected by the rule.[30] It will also be necessary to isolate the entities that the rule will apply to, e.g. only entities that form part of a MNE group, entities that form part of either a MNE or domestic group, or all entities including stand-alone entities. Based on the recommended approach, an entity belongs to a group if it is directly / indirectly controlled by a company, or the entity is a company which directly or indirectly controls one or more other entities. The ability to identify if the entity is part of a group will be important in determining which entities should be retained for micro-data analysis purposes. This may be problematic if, for example, taxpayer information does not provide the necessary information to distinguish whether or not an entity is directly controlled by a company. If the rule applies widely, including to standalone entities which are not part of a group, there would be no need to make this distinction. If relying on financial account micro-data, it is useful to note that control may be defined differently for financial reporting purposes, although where an entity is consolidated into a group's financial statements this will typically indicate that the entity is part of the group.

Determining NIE subject to the rule

Once the affected entities have been established, the amount of NIE paid by those entities will need to be determined to estimate the portion that would exceed the fixed ratio. The excess represents the estimated increase in the CIT base, prior to any adjustments. It is important to clarify what is included in NIE. Firstly NIE includes net interest payments by affected entities to (1) entities forming part of the same group, (2) related entities, and (3) third parties. It therefore pertains to both external and internal interest payments. Some countries have a group taxation regime that allows entities forming part of a group to file their tax returns jointly, as well as jointly compute tax calculations (e.g. setting off assessed losses between companies), while other countries require entity-level tax liability calculations and filing. This may be a consideration when calculating internal versus external interest. If information is collected on an unconsolidated basis, total NIE would reflect both internal and external NIE. If information is collected on a consolidated basis, internal interest payments would need to be estimated and added.

The Report on Action 4 recommends that countries also apply the rule to financial payments equivalent to interest payments to mitigate the likelihood of avoidance by taxpayers recharacterising interest payments into other forms similar to interest. For this reason, it will be necessary to determine whether micro-data is also available for capitalised interest on depreciable assets, the interest element of finance lease payments and imputed interest on convertible bonds, for example. A non-exhaustive list of examples is included in the Report on Action 4. Incorporating such interest payments into the micro-simulation exercise is likely to result in an upward adjustment to NIE.

Adjustments

Once affected entities and total NIE have been determined, certain adjustments may need to be incorporated. If the country legislates a *de minimis* threshold, all entities falling below the threshold that would benefit from the carve-out will need to be dropped from the population in the micro-simulation model. As part of the Action 4 best practice, it is recommended that such a threshold be based on the total NIE of all entities in the local group to avoid the possibility of fragmentation by establishing multiple entities, each of which falls below the threshold.

Determining the appropriate measure of EBITDA

At this point, there would be an estimate of total NIE paid by entities that would be affected by the rule. As NIE is the numerator in the fixed ratio rule, it will be necessary to establish EBITDA for each affected entity. The best practice approach recommends that the calculation of EBITDA be based on values that are determined under the tax rules of the country. An entity's EBITDA should be calculated by adding back to its taxable income, the tax values for: net interest expense and net payments equivalent to interest payments, as well as depreciation and amortisation.[31]

This will enable the calculation of a NIE/EBITDA ratio for each affected entity, i.e. the maximum amount that the entity would be allowed to deduct for tax purposes.

Applying the fixed ratio rule

The next step involves calculating the actual NIE that exceeds the fixed ratio (maximum level of NIE/EBITDA). The excess interest would be disallowed as a deduction from taxable income, resulting in an expansion in the corporate tax base. More than one fixed ratio could be simulated to estimate the effects of different ratios.

Effect of a group ratio rule

The Report on Action 4 sets out a framework for a group ratio rule. Further work on the design and operation of the rule will be conducted in 2016. If a group ratio rule is implemented in addition to the fixed ratio rule, this would be to the advantage of taxpayers and, to the extent that groups' ratios exceed the fixed ratio, would result in a reduction in total NIE affected. The Report on Action 4 notes that a country which introduces a group ratio rule may want to have a lower fixed ratio.[32]

Applying an AMTR to the estimated increase in the tax base to arrive at a static estimate

A micro-simulation model allows an appropriate tax rate to be calculated for each entity, which could be applied to the estimated increase in the CIT base. Since any increase in the corporate tax base will be taxed at the margin, the marginal tax rate is the most appropriate measure.[33] Using the top statutory tax rate may not be appropriate if there are lower tax rates on certain taxpayers and/or accumulated tax credits or offsetting losses that would lower the effective tax rate applied. It would be most appropriate to use the effective tax rate calculated from the micro-simulation and note that it may be a conservative estimate.

Incorporating behavioural effects

After estimating the static effects of the interest limitation rule, there are some considerations to take into account for a dynamic estimate, including the potential of carry-forward or carry-back rules and predictions on how taxpayers are likely to respond.

If, for example, the country is considering a carry-forward of disallowed interest, the initial year effect would be unchanged from the static fiscal effect, but future years' cash collections would be lower due to additional interest deductions claimed from the carry-forward. Similarly, if the country is considering a carry-forward of unused interest capacity, that would be equivalent to increasing the effective fixed ratio for those companies, thereby reducing future years' cash collections. In modelling the timing of cash collections when carry-forwards are allowed, the stock of unused interest or interest capacity should be estimated and then the projected usage of that capacity over time should be estimated. Information about the volatility of interest-to-EBITDA ratios over time by individual companies through panel time-series data would be optimal to incorporate into the modelling.

There are likely to be behavioural responses to the introduction of interest limitation rules. Companies could respond to the rules by:

- Substituting equity (new equity or retained earnings) for debt;
- Relocating internal debt among affiliates within the domestic or MNE group.

Apart from countries that have an allowance for corporate equity (ACE) system, substituting equity for debt would have a similar effect to the disallowance of interest. Countries with an ACE system would need to consider the design and whether there is potential for entities to receive a greater benefit from being able to deduct payments on equity as opposed to debt. If this is the case, the revenue effect could be close to zero. If entities switch to equity funding, it would be necessary to consider whether the decrease in lending could impact tax revenue on interest income if the counterparty lenders are tax resident in the country, as interest income would decrease with a decline in borrowing. This could be offset by an increase in dividend income, which could increase withholding tax (WHT) revenues.

Taxpayers could react by shifting internal debt to affiliates with lower NIE/EBITDA ratios, or to affiliates in jurisdictions where interest limitation rules are not binding. The degree of potential shifting is likely to be influenced by both tax and non-tax factors, including the design (and strictness) of the interest limitation rule; whether multilateral action is taken; the prevailing interest rate climate; and how flexible groups are given that they may have central financing functions and the transaction costs associated with shifting debt could be high.

Substituting equity for debt or shifting debt from the implementing country to another country would result in a revenue increase for the implementing country. Only if the shifting of debt is between entities within the same country, would the behavioural effect reduce the implementing country's revenue effect.

Since interest deduction limitations would result in an increase in the tax base, affected entities would experience an increase in their effective tax rate. Empirical studies showing behavioural responses to changes in tax rate differentials could provide some insights into the potential behavioural effects that may arise due to the enactment of countermeasures.

Ruf and Schindler (2012) summarise empirical evidence on the German interest limitation rules introduced in 2008. Buslei and Simmler (2012) and Dreßler and Scheuering (2012) find that firms respond by reducing debt-to-asset ratios.

b. Macro-data approach

If individual company tax return or financial information is not available for the analysis, then a macro-level approach can be attempted. The steps set out below offer a potential estimation strategy that countries could pursue.

Determining total NIE in the country

The first step involves estimating total NIE for firms that would be affected by the proposal. There may be different possibilities according to data sources available in the country:

- Aggregate tax data on interest receipts and payments (Revenue Authority).
- Aggregate financial account data on interest receipts and payments that may be broken down by sector (National Statistics Office).
- Aggregate financial account data on interest receipts and payments for the non-financial corporate sector (National Accounts).

If the Revenue Authority publishes aggregate information on interest payments and receipts, this is a good starting point. This information may be published for individuals/households and/or corporations, and may be broken down by sector. Drawing solely on data for entities subject to the CIT would result in an underestimate given that the best practice approach has a wider application, i.e. it includes non-corporate taxable entities, many of which may be subject to taxation at the individual/household level. There may be studies or other sources of data which could provide an idea of the portion of personal income taxpayers that are likely to be engaged in business activities. In addition, including all sectors could result in an overestimate, but this would also depend on whether sectors other than the financial sector are excluded. The financial sector generally receives more interest income than it pays and so may not result in an overestimate.

Some countries may have aggregate financial account data by sector available. This would provide aggregate NIE by sector, which is useful given that the Action 4 best practice could differ in its impact in addressing BEPS involving interest in the financial sector and other sectors. It will be important to determine which entities are included in the statistics in order to compare with the entities that will be affected by the rule. Depending on the design of the interest limitation rule, the affected entities in the data may be over or underrepresented.

If none of the abovementioned options is available, aggregate financial account data may be available for the non-financial corporate sector in the National Accounts – most likely produced by the central bank or National Statistics Office. The firms included in the non-financial corporate sector differ across countries and it will be necessary to check the approach taken in the country. Some countries, for example, include 'quasi-corporations' in this classification.[34] In the European Union (EU), only 7 out of 28 member countries (Cyprus[35], France, Hungary, Luxembourg, Romania, Slovak Republic and Spain) do not employ the concept of quasi-corporation in their national accounts and, among the remaining 21 member countries, only the Netherlands allocates all quasi-corporations to a single institutional sector (i.e. the household sector). Hence, 20 out 28 EU member countries have quasi-corporations in both their household and corporate sectors. Outside the EU, there are also differing approaches, for example the United States does not use the 'quasi-corporation' concept, while South Africa does.

The OECD publishes data on interest payments and receipts for most OECD member countries, as well as two non-OECD countries, one of which is a G20 country. Table 3.A2.3 provides the NIE figure for these countries in 2012.[36] The data provided for the majority of countries has been adjusted for financial services indirectly measured (FISIM), which estimates the difference between the higher interest rate that borrowers pay in return for the financial service and the reference rate.[37] Where information is available, it is indicated whether quasi-corporations are included in the non-financial sector.

The NIE figures in Table 3.A2.3 could be an over or under-estimate of affected NIE, depending on how the interest limitation rules are designed. This will depend on which entities are included in the National Accounts data compared to those affected by the rule. With respect to the former, there are two important considerations: whether quasi-corporations are included in the non-financial corporate sector, and whether interest payments and receipts are recorded on a legal entity or enterprise group basis. This will determine whether the aggregate NIE figure includes / excludes related party interest payments. If it is based on the legal entity, NIE would include intra-group interest payments and it will not be necessary to make an adjustment.

Table 3.A2.3. NIE by the non-financial corporate sector in billions of USD (2012)

Country	Entities included in non-financial corporate sector	USD bn
OECD		
Austria	Incl. quasi-corp	8
Belgium	Incl. quasi-corp	5
Chile*		5
Czech Republic	Incl. quasi-corp	4
Denmark*	Incl. quasi-corp	2
Estonia	Incl. quasi-corp	1
Finland	Incl. quasi-corp	7
France	Only corp	59
Germany	Incl. quasi-corp	19
Greece	Incl. quasi-corp	6
Hungary	corp	4
Ireland	Incl. quasi-corp	9
Italy	Incl. quasi-corp	47
Japan*		(9)
Korea*		30
Mexico*		44
Netherlands	Only corp	13
New Zealand		8
Portugal	Incl. quasi-corp	7
Slovak Republic*	Only corp	1
Slovenia	Incl. quasi-corp	1
Spain	Only corp	49
Sweden	Incl. quasi-corp	17
Switzerland		9
United Kingdom	Incl. quasi-corp	46
United States	Only corp	350
Non-OECD		
Colombia*		7
South Africa*	Incl. quasi-corp	4

* Countries where the figure adjusted for FISIM was not available

Source: OECD National Accounts Database

An additional consideration in estimating total NIE is whether the available data includes financial payments equivalent to interest. Interest expense may be capitalised into the cost of goods sold, embedded in purchases from other businesses, lease payments, payments under profit participating loans or under alternative financing arrangements, such as Islamic finance; or imputed on instruments such as convertible bonds and zero coupon bonds.[38] Focusing purely on interest expense would likely yield a conservative estimate. Depending on the definition of interest in the country, this could be mentioned as a likely source of downward bias or if information is available, an upward adjustment could be made to the change in the tax base.

Considerations for focusing on affected entities

Even though aggregate data does not allow distinction between stand-alone entities and those that belong to a domestic or MNE group, the design of the rule (i.e. which entities it would apply to) would influence the estimate of the fiscal effect.

There are a few scenarios which may require adjustments for affected entities. Examples of where an adjustment would be necessary include:

- The interest limitation rule could only apply to entities forming part of a MNE group, but aggregate NIE data includes all non-financial corporations. This would result in both an over and under-estimate of the change in tax base – an over-estimate in the sense that many corporations may not be part of a MNE group and an under-estimate in the sense that non-corporate entities may be part of a MNE group.
- The interest limitation rule would apply to entities forming part of a group (MNE and domestic) and stand-alone entities; however only aggregate NIE data from National Accounts is available which covers non-financial corporations, but excludes quasi-corporations. This would result in an under-estimate of the change in tax base.

While there may not be any micro-data to draw on, there are potential other sources that could be used to gauge the share of MNEs operating in the economy. For example, if the central bank or National Statistics Office produces data on net or gross operating surplus (NOS/GOS), it may be possible to find out the share of this that is attributable to MNEs and use this information to assist with applying a factor to aggregate NIE data (recognising that the share of NOS or GOS may not be directly linked to the share of NIE).

An additional strategy to find out more about MNE and domestic groups, as well as large stand-alone corporates, is analysing the financial statements of the top 25/50/100 groups/companies operating in the domestic jurisdiction as the largest groups are likely to have the biggest interest deductions, or alternatively a stratified statistical sample could be used. Deciding on an appropriate number of firms/groups will depend on the size of the economy and other domestic factors, such as whether there is an appropriate representation of sectors in the sample chosen. This could provide an indication of the total external NIE if considered on a consolidated basis, or total (internal and external) NIE if financial statements are published on an unconsolidated basis. This would provide a useful comparison to NIE published in National Accounts data.

Adjustments

If an adjustment is required to add internal interest, a parameter will be required that extrapolates from external NIE to total NIE. This would be necessary, for example, if relying on aggregate National Accounts data that collects information based on the enterprise group as opposed to legal entity as it would only include external NIE. Estimates of internal interest to total interest could be taken from empirical studies. Although not ideal, basing an adjustment for internal interest on the academic literature may be more accurate than implicitly assuming zero internal interest by MNE affiliates. The current literature, based on two datasets – the German Bundesbank MiDi dataset and the United States Bureau of Economic Analysis (BEA) dataset, finds the internal/external debt ratio averages around 0.4, while internal/total debt is approximately 0.3.[39] It should be noted that both Germany and the United States have higher than average statutory corporate tax rates, and thus may have higher internal debt ratios than countries with lower statutory corporate tax rates.

Implementing a *de minimis* rule to exclude entities from the rule requires a downward adjustment to the total NIE estimate. There may be information on small and medium-sized enterprises that is based on employees or turnover, which could be useful in making an adjustment.[40] Smaller firms may have higher interest ratios than larger firms, and academic studies find that domestic-only firms have higher interest ratios than similar sized MNE firms. However, if domestic-only firms are smaller than MNEs on average, the percentage of NIE above the *de minimis* threshold may be lower than the average for all firms.

Given that a fixed ratio rule would only affect entities in a tax-paying position, a downward adjustment could be made to reflect this. It is important to consider this in conjunction with the *de minimis* threshold as many of those in an assessed loss position may fall below the *de minimis* threshold. Even though micro-data may not be available, the Revenue Authority may produce aggregate statistics showing the portion of corporations in an assessed loss position. This could assist in deciding on a suitable factor for adjusting downwards, and could be more refined if the statistics are done by taxable income groups.

Applying the fixed ratio rule

This requires a determination of how much NIE would exceed the fixed ratio (NIE/EBITDA) and is challenging to do without access to any micro-data. Relying on financial statements of the top groups / corporations would be a good starting point, although this would be based on financial account, not tax, data. In addition, if relying on published consolidated information, this would exclude intra-group interest payments. Nevertheless, it may provide some assistance in making a reasonable assumption on the amount of NIE that would exceed the fixed ratio.

A further consideration is the likely heterogeneity of the NIE/EBITDA ratios within a MNE group. Micro-data for large non-financial MNEs shows that 45% of affiliates' gross interest expense (GIE) is in excess of their group's GIE/EBITDA ratio. Affiliates' GIE will include both internal and external interest as it is based on unconsolidated data, whereas group ratios only include external interest from consolidated data. Judgement will be required on whether to make an adjustment for this variation of fixed ratios within a group, which could be combined with an extrapolation to include internal interest.

Effect of a group ratio rule

For incorporating a group ratio rule, the approach will be the same as under the micro-approach above.

Applying an AMTR

Once the increase in the tax base (total NIE in excess of the NIE/EBITDA ratio) has been estimated, it will be necessary to apply an AMTR to the increase in the tax base. Given that the base broadening effect of interest limitation rules will result in more taxable income being taxed at the margin, the statutory tax rates may be a suitable starting point.[41]

Incorporating behavioural effects

The ability to carry forward either affected interest deductions or excess capacity results in a timing issue that will need to be factored into the annual estimates.

For behavioural considerations, the approach will be the same as under the micro-approach above.

Other countries' fiscal estimates of excess interest countermeasures

In addition to other countermeasures, Table 3.A2.1 provides the fiscal estimate of unilateral interest countermeasures in selected countries as a percentage of their total corporate tax revenue. Measures that were estimated or implemented in prior years would likely yield higher fiscal estimates compared with estimates produced today as these prior measures were introduced during a period of higher interest rates. The point in the business cycle at which the measure was estimated (and implemented) is also important as the revenue effects are shown as a percentage of CIT revenues, which are volatile across the cycle. The fiscal estimate also depends on whether a country implemented other policy measures simultaneously that may have influenced the fiscal estimate for interest countermeasures (e.g. depending on the order in which the estimates were stacked). Also, if these countries had existing interest limitations rules, then the fiscal estimate would be for only the incremental revenue effect of the new interest limitation, not the effect of the country's total interest limitation.

Potential interactions with other countermeasures

If implementing more than one BEPS countermeasure simultaneously, revenue estimates would need to take into account interactions of the various provisions. The Actions in respect of transfer pricing address the mispricing of interest, while Action 4 is focused on curbing interest deductions resulting from excessive leveraging. If both the transfer pricing guidance and interest limitation countermeasures are adopted, care will need to be taken to remove potential mispricing corrections from the Action 4 fiscal estimate.

Action 4 could also interact with the measures proposed under Action 2 (hybrid mismatch arrangements). Hybrid mismatch arrangement countermeasures may lead to the disallowance of certain interest expense deductions, which could reduce the interest-to-EBITDA ratio of firms affected by hybrid countermeasures. If data becomes available about reduced interest deductions from hybrid mismatch arrangements, or an estimate of that is made for another proposal, then it could be factored into the total NIE affected.

Action 1 (Address the Tax Challenges of the Digital Economy)

The Report on Action 1 (*Addressing the Tax Challenges of the Digital Economy*, OECD, 2015c) examines a number of tax policy issues specifically linked to the digital economy, its business models, and its key features. It notes that because the digital economy is increasingly becoming the economy itself, it would not be feasible to ring-fence the digital economy from the rest of the economy for tax purposes. Although the digital economy does not generate unique BEPS issues, some of its key features exacerbate BEPS risks. These risks are addressed in the BEPS Action Plan in the context of the work on Actions 3 (Strengthening CFC Rules), 7 (Preventing the Artificial Avoidance of PE Status), and 8-10 (Ensure that Transfer Pricing Outcomes are in Line with Value Creation).

Understanding the proposed change

The Task Force on the Digital Economy (TFDE) discussed and analysed several potential options to address these broader tax challenges raised by the digital economy issues. Specifically, they are considering three tax policy options for more effectively imposing taxes on activities related to foreign sellers without a PE in the country. The three tax policy options are:

- Modifications to the PE threshold and associated profit attribution rules for the CIT on the net income generated from remote sales of digital goods and services to in-country customers by a foreign producer without PE status under current law;
- The introduction of an excise tax on certain types of digital transactions; and
- The imposition of a WHT on the gross receipts from certain types of digital transactions.

Recommendations for enabling the collection of value-added tax (VAT) in business-to-consumer (B2C) digital transactions is included as part of the OECD *International VAT/GST Guidelines*, which will protect tax revenue.

Fiscal estimation issues

For estimating the direct tax fiscal effects of modifications to the permanent establishment threshold that affects remote sellers of digital goods and services, the approach will be the same as that described for the fiscal estimate of Action 7 below.

Estimating the fiscal effects of introducing an excise tax or the imposition of a WHT on certain types of digital transactions would follow the revenue estimating procedures outlined above in the section discussing the general approach to undertaking a fiscal estimate. Both taxes would be based on gross receipts of the identified transactions; therefore, the tax base should be similar under either proposal.

The first step in estimating the fiscal effects of adopting one of the alternative tax proposals would be to estimate the amount of existing sales for each type of eligible digital transactions that would be subject to the new excise or WHTs. Industry reports or country-specific estimates from public databases, such as the Eurostat e-commerce statistics, could be used to estimate the potential tax base, although the amount would need to be separated between the sales of remote sellers without a current PE from sales of remote sellers with a current PE.

It would be important to distinguish between sales to final customers (households) and intermediate sales to businesses in estimating the base. Potential behavioural responses should also be considered, such as reductions in the digital transactions in response to higher tax-inclusive prices along with substitution away from digital transactions from remote sellers without a current PE to alternative transactions (both digital and non-digital) from sellers with a PE. The resulting estimate of the change in the tax base would be multiplied by the applicable tax rates to determine the expected fiscal effects.

Finally, estimates of the fiscal effects of indirect tax changes through the collection of VAT in B2C transactions would be based on the expansion of the VAT tax base multiplied by the applicable VAT rates. Substitution of non-digital transactions for digital transactions would not affect the expected collections (except for scenarios where different VAT rates would apply).

Action 2 (Hybrid Mismatch Arrangements)

Understanding the proposed change

Hybrid mismatch arrangements are transactions which exploit cross-border differences in the treatment of instruments and entities to produce a mismatch in tax outcomes. A mismatch is either two deductions of the same payment (i.e. a double deduction (DD) outcome) or a deductible payment that is not included in the tax base by the recipient (i.e. a deduction/no inclusion (D/NI) outcome). Part I of the Report on Action 2 (*Neutralising the Effects of Hybrid Mismatch Arrangements*, OECD, 2015d) sets out recommendations for domestic rules intended to neutralise DD and D/NI outcomes for hybrid financial instruments (such as instruments which are considered debt in one country and equity in another) and hybrid entities (such as entities and arrangements that are considered fiscally transparent in one country and fiscally opaque in another). Part I of the Report on Action 2 further contains an imported mismatch rule that applies to both structured and intra-group arrangements and that can be applied to any payment that is directly or indirectly set-off against any type of hybrid deduction.

In the case of direct and indirect D/NI outcomes, part I of the Report sets out recommendations for rules to deny a deduction in the payer jurisdiction as a primary rule and, in the case of DD outcomes, the primary recommended rule is to deny a deduction in the parent jurisdiction. The hybrid mismatch rules also have secondary recommended rules that apply in the counterparty jurisdiction in the event that the primary rule is not applied.

Part II of the Report on Action 2 sets out recommended changes to the OECD Model Tax Convention aimed at ensuring that hybrid instruments and entities, as well as dual resident entities, are not used to obtain unduly the benefits of tax treaties and that tax treaties to not prevent the application of the changes to domestic law recommended in part I.

Potential data

An economic analysis of hybrid mismatch arrangements requires detailed company-level data. It requires not only information on transactions between related parties but also on their tax treatment in both the payer and recipient jurisdictions. Such data is rarely available through public sources, and only available to tax administrations making extra efforts to identify such arrangements, including requesting additional information from taxpayers. Estimates by government analysis would require information from tax administration audit teams about the number and scale of existing hybrid mismatch arrangements in the country.

Other countries' fiscal estimates

Several countries have introduced or proposed countermeasures intended to address DD and D/NI outcomes for which annual fiscal estimates have been made:

- France introduced in January 2014 measures limiting deductibility of interest if it is subject to a low tax rate at the level of the beneficiary. The estimated revenue effect is an increase in CIT revenue by 0.9%.
- The United Kingdom proposed in December 2014 measures in line with the Action 2 recommendations. The estimated revenue effect is an increase in CIT revenue by 0.2%.
- The United States proposed measures limiting deductibility of interest and royalties if there is no corresponding inclusion at the level of the recipient in the foreign jurisdiction. The estimated revenue effect is an increase in CIT revenue by 0.04%.[42]

These estimates assume a large behavioural response due to MNEs' ability to restructure their financial arrangements around unilateral countermeasures. For example, rules that deny a deduction for payments under a particular cross-border financing arrangement that give rise to a D/NI outcome may simply encourage taxpayer groups to enter into the same arrangement under the laws of another jurisdiction and then use a back-to-back loan structure to import the effect of the mismatch into domestic law, thus converting a direct D/NI outcome into an indirect D/NI outcome that is outside the scope of the country's rules.

The expected behavioural response to unilateral action by one country is the main reason for the low estimated revenue effects. The recommendations under Action 2 are intended to prevent taxpayers from obtaining any advantage under any jurisdiction in respect of these types of arrangements, making them more effective than unilateral and unco-ordinated action. If hybrid mismatch recommendations are implemented in many countries simultaneously with a rule to address indirect D/NI outcomes, there will be significantly less opportunity for companies to restructure their financial affairs to avoid the effect of the recommended rules. Thus, hybrid arrangements would be expected to increase corporate revenues by more than that generated from unilateral actions, provided multilateral co-ordinated implementation of Action 2 occurs. The revenue from implementation of the Action 2 recommendations is not expected to come from disallowed deductions or disallowed exemptions under the hybrid mismatch rules themselves, but rather from MNEs ceasing to structure themselves and their transactions in such a way as to exploit mismatches, and thus not claiming the deductions or benefitting from exempt income.

Potential interactions with other countermeasures

Rules recommended under Action 9 on transfer pricing of risk and capital and Action 4 on interest deductibility would decrease the benefit of many hybrid mismatch arrangements by limiting possibilities of achieving tax reduction via interest payments. In addition, the combination of hybrid mismatch arrangement rules with treaty abuse rules will reduce tax planning opportunities, and thus will have a greater effect together than the sum of the individual effects.

Action 3 (Controlled Foreign Corporation Rules)

The Report on Action 3 (*Designing Effective Controlled Foreign Company Rules*, OECD, 2015e) provides guidance based on best practices for the building blocks of effective CFC rules, while recognising that the policy objectives of these rules vary among jurisdictions. It identifies the challenges to existing CFC rules posed by mobile income, such as that from intellectual property, services and digital transactions, and allows jurisdictions to reflect on appropriate policies in this regard. The report emphasises that CFC rules have a continuing, important role in tackling BEPS, as a backstop to transfer pricing and other rules.

CFC rules are designed to protect a country's tax base by preventing shifting of mobile or passive income to a CFC. In the case of parents in territorial tax countries, CFC rules prevent the shifting of particular income to benefit from exempt foreign source income. In the case of parents in the countries that have a worldwide tax system with deferral, CFC rules prevent the shifting of particular income to benefit from deferral of such income.

Understanding the proposed change

The Report on Action 3 recommends that, in addition to corporate entities, CFC rules could also apply to partnerships, trusts and permanent establishments when those entities raise BEPS concerns, which could occur if they are either owned by CFCs or treated in the parent jurisdiction as taxable entities separate from their owners.

A tax rate exemption is recommended, pursuant to which CFC rules would not apply if the CFC's effective tax rate were higher than a set threshold.[43] The Report on Action 3 notes that resident shareholders should only be taxed on income earned by a foreign company if they appear to have had some input in how, when and where that income was earned. The Report on Action 3 recommends that CFC rules should at least apply both a legal and an economic control test so that satisfaction of either test results in control, and a CFC should be treated as controlled where residents directly or indirectly hold 50% or more of the voting rights, but the report allows the option for a lower control threshold if countries want to achieve broader policy goals or prevent circumvention of CFC rules.

Once an entity has been identified as a CFC, it is necessary to determine which income will be attributable to shareholders or controlling parties.[44] The Report on Action 3 describes multiple approaches to determining CFC income. CFC rules generally define attributable income in the context of income earned by CFCs raise BEPS concerns, which may include, among other things, income earned by CFCs that are holding companies, provide financial and banking services, engage in sales invoicing, as well as income from IP assets, digital goods and services, and captive insurance and re-insurance. The report describes three approaches: a categorical analysis, a substance analysis, and an excess profits analysis. Regardless of which approach is followed, the country will also need to decide whether the approach applies to entities or transactions. The Report on Action 3 notes that the transactional approach may be more consistent with both the goals of the BEPS Project and European Union law.

Depending on the definition of CFC income used in the country, the following types of income are often included in CFC rules:

- Dividends paid out of passive income that is not actively managed by the CFC.
- Interest and other financing income, unless the CFC had the required substance to earn the income and was not overcapitalised.
- Specific service income, unless the CFC had the required substance to earn the income, including:
  - Insurance income that was earned from a related party or where the parties to the insurance contract or the risks insured are located outside the CFC jurisdiction
  - Sales and services income
  - Royalties and other IP income

Once the level of CFC income has been determined, a tax rate is applied. CFC income is generally subject to the tax rate of the parent company in the parent jurisdiction. The Report on Action 3 also describes an option referred to as a "top-up tax", which would only subject CFC income to the difference between the tax paid in the CFC's jurisdiction and a threshold rate.

The fiscal analysis begins with the specific CFC rules adopted by a country. The Report on Action 3 sets out recommendations in the form of building blocks, but acknowledges that jurisdictions will have different policy objectives for their CFC rules. Therefore these recommendations are not minimum standards, but they are designed to ensure that jurisdictions that choose to implement them will have rules that effectively prevent taxpayers from shifting income into foreign subsidiaries.

Data and methodology

The analysis should identify the key elements outlined above to ensure that, where data permits, the appropriate income streams attributable to the appropriate entities are captured by the fiscal estimation exercise.

Estimating the amount of CFC income affected

If tax return information is available that identifies whether a domestic entity has a CFC, as well as the income earned by the CFC that should be attributable to the parent company, a micro-simulation exercise would be possible as all the CFC income could be identified and the appropriate tax rate calculated on an entity basis. For many countries, it may be the case that tax return information does not provide analysts with the necessary level of detail, such as disaggregated income sources defined as CFC income.

In such instances, a potential solution would be to identify income flows from passive assets held by entities in countries where the tax rate is lower than the tax rate threshold put in place for CFC rules. This would be similar to the strategy used by Ruf and Weichenrieder (2012; 2013) who analysed passive assets held by firms that were at least 90% owned by a German parent. The analysis was based on the MiDi dataset from the German Bundesbank, which provides balance sheet information on affiliates of German MNEs. Many countries may not have access to similar data which, in the absence of micro-data from tax returns, would require using macroeconomic data.

Relying on macroeconomic data could be done with some assumptions. It would be necessary to (1) identify those countries where CFCs' tax rates are likely to be below the threshold set for the tax rate exemption; (2) determine which types of income would be subject to the parent country's CFC rules and identify possible data; (3) assume the portion of these income streams that would be earned by CFCs controlled by domestic parent companies; and (4) assume the portion of the income that would be classified as CFC income. If information on income flows is not available, but balance sheet information is available, it may be possible to impute income from passive assets held using an assumed rate of return.

Table 3.A2.4 outlines potential data from five macro-economic sources that might be used to estimate CFC income.

Table 3.A2.4. Potential data sources for CFC income

Potential CFC income	Description	Potential Source
Dividends	Dividend income that should be classified as CFC income is likely to include dividend income from FDI equity holdings	Balance of payments data
Interest & other financing	Interest income that should be classified as CFC income is likely to include: • Lending to other affiliates (could be an overleveraged parent) • Bond holdings (portfolio investment) • Bank deposits (reflected in reinvested earnings)	Balance of payments data
Insurance income	Insurance income that should be classified as CFC income is likely to include insurance income from a related pary or where the parties to the insurance contract or the risks insured were located outside the CFC jurisdiction, unless the CFC had the required substance to earn the income.	Insurance income is captured in Trade in Services, which is recorded on a bilateral basis in the BOP, but is generally not broken down by disaggregated service items or affiliation.[45]
Sales and services income	Sales and services income that should be classified as CFC income is likely to occur as a result of the digital economy and/or when a CFC adds very little value but sells a good/service	Data on the value of purchases and sales via the internet (and/or networks other than the internet) of companies by country (EU, 2010-2014) http://ec.europa.eu/eurostat/web/information-society/data/database United States data on measuring the electronic economy: www.census.gov/econ/estats/ European Multi-Channel Online Trade Association: www.emota.eu/#!statistics/ccor
Income from IP, including royalties	Income from IP that should be classified as CFC income includes payments that reflect the returns on intellectual property. Ownership of acquired patent rights is another potential source for information given that payments for the use of IP are grouped with other service payments in the trade data.	These payments are captured in Trade and Services as described for insurance income and, for the majority of countries; it is not possible to separate the different service items.

Applying an appropriate tax rate

Once there is an estimate of CFC income, it will be necessary to apply an appropriate tax rate – either that of the parent country or a minimum tax – depending on the design of the CFC rules. The tax rate should be an AMTR since the additional CFC income would be incremental to the existing taxable income.[46]

Empirical literature

There are some empirical studies that examine the effect of CFC rules on MNE behaviour. The results generally show that the presence of CFC rules dissuade MNEs from using low-tax jurisdictions. Markle and Robinson (2012) investigate whether CFC rules, bilateral tax treaties and WHTs affect the tax behaviour of MNEs. Using ORBIS and COMPUSTAT data, the findings suggest that both the taxing of foreign profits (through a credit or worldwide system) and the presence of CFC rules reduce the likelihood of a MNE using a tax haven. In addition, the wider the scope of income that is subject to CFC rules, the lower the likelihood that a MNE uses "tax havens".

Ruf and Weichenrieder analysed the German CFC rules in two separate analyses. Both analyses are based on the German Bundesbank Micro-database Direct Investment (MiDi) data on German MNEs (outbound investment)[47]. The 2012 analysis investigates the effect of German CFC rules on the location of passive assets within German multinationals. The analysis investigates whether exceeding the tax rate threshold has an impact on the allocation of passive investment and finds that German CFC rules have a significant and predictable impact on multinational financing and are effective in limiting the shifting of passive assets. While passive investments make up a significant fraction of German outbound FDI, they found German CFC rules are effective in restricting investments in low-tax jurisdictions.

Their 2013 study investigates the effect of the change of Germany's CFC legislation in response to a decision by the European Court of Justice (ECJ), which ruled that German CFC legislation infringed on the freedom of establishment within the European Union, and thus could not be applied to CFCs in EU countries. The analysis found that after liberalising CFC legislation in response to the ruling, passive investments in low-tax European countries increased compared to low-tax non-European countries, signalling that the prior CFC rules limited shifting of passive investments of German MNEs to other EU countries.

Potential interactions with other countermeasures

There are interactions between CFC rules and transfer pricing rules. If, for example, CFC rules apply a sufficiently high rate of tax, certain transfer pricing outcomes may become irrelevant to the MNE as the benefit of engaging in transfer pricing manipulation would be removed. If proposed at the same time, a careful assessment of the likely interactions and overlap between the two countermeasures would be appropriate.

Action 5 (Harmful Tax Practices)

Current concerns on harmful tax practices are primarily about preferential regimes which can be used for artificial profit shifting, and a lack of transparency in connection with certain rulings. The Report on Action 5 (*Countering Harmful Tax Practices More Effectively, Taking into Account Transparency and Substance*, OECD, 2015f) sets out an agreed methodology to assess whether there is substantial activity in a preferential regime. In the context of IP regimes, consensus was reached on the "nexus approach". The nexus approach uses expenditure as a proxy for activity and allows a taxpayer to benefit from an IP regime only to the extent that the taxpayer incurred qualifying R&D expenditures that gave rise to IP income. The same principle can also be applied to other preferential regimes so that such regimes are found to require substantial activity where the taxpayer undertook the core income-generating activities.

In the area of transparency, a framework has been agreed for the compulsory spontaneous exchange of information on rulings that could give rise to BEPS concerns in the absence of such exchange. The results of the application of the existing factors applied by the Forum on Harmful Tax Practices (FHTP), and the elaborated substantial activity and transparency factors, to a number of preferential regimes are included in the Report on Action 5.

Understanding the proposed change

The work of the FHTP and the agreed approach on substantial activities will have positive impacts on CIT collections as the use of preferential tax rate regimes will be restricted to taxpayers with sufficient economic activities in the country. This will be expected to lead to an increase in taxes in the country with such a regime, as well as other countries.

In a country with a fiscal regime favouring geographically mobile income, Action 5 and the application of the elaborated substantial activity factor will reduce harmful tax practices and be expected to result in an increase in tax revenue, assuming no change in the base, due to the application of a higher general tax rate to the income that no longer qualifies for a preferential tax regime. Reduced harmful tax practices will help reduce BEPS and will be expected to lead to an increase in corporate tax bases and tax collections in other countries.

Empirical evidence

Several studies show that corporate tax rates are an important factor for patent location decisions and IP boxes have a strong effect on attracting patent registrations; it is recognised, however, that patent locations may not mirror the location of R&D activities. The studies use the number of patent applications as the dependent variable and the corporate tax rate as one of the explanatory variables. For example, Karkinsky and Riedel (2012), based on data from the European Patent Office (EPO) for a number of European countries over the 1978-2007 period, estimate a semi-elasticity of -3.8 to -3.5; that is, a 1 percentage point decrease in the rate of corporate tax translates into a 3.5 to 3.8% increase in patent applications in that country.

Griffith, Miller and O'Connell (2014), based on data from the EPO on patents located in 14 European countries, estimate semi-elasticities that range from -3.9 to -0.5. They also simulated the impact of the enactment of a new IP box on tax revenue and found that they result in losses in government revenues because they do not attract enough IP income to offset the revenue loss from the preferential tax rate application on current IP income.

While empirical studies show high responsiveness of MNEs to shifting mobile income, the responsiveness of shifting real economic activity is significantly smaller. DeMooij and Ederveen (2008) use a meta-analysis of other empirical studies to estimate an extensive FDI investment margin of -0.65, which is considerably smaller than the elasticities estimated for patent registrations. Similarly, a European Commission (2015) working paper reports relatively low estimates of the responsiveness of research and development expenditures.

A "nexus" requirement will reduce the amount of mobile income shifted as a result of preferential tax regimes, and will reduce BEPS associated with harmful tax practices.

Fiscal estimation issues

As a response to Action 5, countries will remove or amend certain preferential tax regimes. The effect on the country with an existing harmful tax practice can be estimated by the change in the tax base and the application of the higher general tax rate.

Revenue increases to other countries will more likely occur in the future as income shifting is reduced due to the reduction of harmful tax practices. One possible approach to estimating the fiscal effect would be to estimate the increase in the average AMTR, compared to what the average AMTR would have been with harmful tax practices, and use the methodology described in the transfer pricing Actions.[48]

The potential revenue gained from increased transparency due to the exchange of information will also be difficult to estimate, partly because the fiscal effects will depend upon the actions of other governments and the effect of reductions in harmful tax practices on relative marginal tax rates that create profit shifting incentives.

To the extent that additional information is received by a country as a result of the compulsory spontaneous exchange of information on rulings, tax administration auditors could provide insights on the potential revenue effects in the country.

Potential interactions with other BEPS Actions

There are potential overlaps with other BEPS Actions. Rules recommended under Action 8 on transfer pricing of intangibles would require any transactions which result in the shifting of income to take advantage of tax rate differentials are to be in accordance with the arm's length principle.

Action 6 (Prevent Treaty Abuse)

The Report on Action 6 (*Preventing the Granting of Treaty Benefits in Inappropriate Circumstances*, OECD, 2015g) includes a minimum standard on preventing treaty abuse including through treaty shopping and new rules that provide safeguards to prevent treaty abuse and offer a certain degree of flexibility regarding how to do so. The new treaty abuse rules address treaty shopping which involves strategies through which a person who is not a resident of a country attempts to obtain the benefits of a treaty concluded by that country e.g. WHT reductions, through an intermediary established in that state. More targeted rules have been designed to address other forms of treaty abuse.

Tax treaties are intended to reduce or eliminate double taxation of international income flows, including cross-border dividends, royalties and interest. In general, these income flows can be subject to several levels of taxation: CIT in the host country on profits realised in that country that are subsequently distributed as dividends, WHTs on international income flows, or CIT to be paid in the recipient country subject to double taxation relief, such as foreign tax credits or dividend participation exemptions.

Understanding the proposed change

The part of the Report on Action 6 that deals with treaty shopping provides that the OECD *Model Tax Convention* will include:

- A new preamble for tax treaties according to which tax treaties are not intended to create opportunities for tax evasion and avoidance, in particular through treaty shopping.
- A limitation-on-benefits (LOB) rule or a principal purposes test (PPT).

While the LOB rule addresses treaty-shopping situations based on the legal nature, ownership in, and general activities of, residents of a Contracting State, the PPT rule focusses on transactions, denying treaty benefits where one of the principal purposes for a transaction or arrangement was to obtain treaty benefits. Although the rules target treaty shopping differently, they would both allow treaty benefits to be granted to intermediaries in some cases, primarily where sufficient income-earning activities are exercised by these entities. There is agreement that, in these cases, the establishment of intermediaries is not motivated by treaty shopping considerations.

Data and methodology

Tax optimising MNEs make use of treaty networks to minimise their WHT payments by establishing intermediaries in conduit countries. While the simplest case involves only one intermediary, tax planning may involve the routing of international income flows via a chain of several conduit entities located in different countries. The effects of treaty shopping on country-level revenues, therefore, depend on the position of the country (within which the entity is located) in the treaty network. In principle, estimation requires not only information on statutory WHT rates, double taxation relief methods and existing tax treaties, but also on possible interactions across the treaty network.

Tax avoidance induces a diversion of international income flows, for instance through Special Purpose Entities (SPEs), which may not be captured by existing data sources. As a result, revenue effects may differ by country depending on its position in the treaty network and the routing of international investment flows.

An evaluation of the country's existing treaty network could be an initial step in the analysis of the fiscal effects of treaty shopping. Tax treaties are designed to reduce double taxation and stimulate reciprocal investment. The number of tax treaties and the amount of treaty-related tax reductions do not per se provide insights about the existence or the fiscal effect of treaty shopping. However, an indication about a country's exposure to treaty shopping may be obtained by identifying, first, potential conduit countries within its network and, second, total outbound payments to relevant entities. UNCTAD (2015) developed such an approach based on the bilateral corporate (inward) investment stock from the IMF CDIS. As a first step, conduit countries may be identified by a set of observable characteristics such as, for instance, low WHT rates, generous relief methods, preferential tax regimes and a large number of treaty links. Second, outbound payments to these countries can be retrieved from the CDIS. If bilateral SPE data is available, flows to SPEs in other countries may also be included. The sum of these outbound payments is an upper-bound estimate of the flows affected by treaty shopping.

The estimation of the fiscal effects of Action 6 countermeasures is dependent on available data sources. Countries where data on international income flows and WHT revenues are available will have a better empirical basis for their estimate. This approach is described in subsection (a). If this information is not available, estimation procedures will have to rely on other, often much less specific, data sources and results will therefore be less certain, as described in subsection (b).

a. Fiscal estimation based on country-specific data

Estimating the fiscal effects of Action 6 based on country-specific data requires information on the following key variables:

- Outflows of dividends, royalties and interest (by partner country);
- WHT bases if there are exemptions (by income type);
- WHT revenues (by income type); and
- Reduced treaty tax rates (by income type and country).

Although data on international flows of dividends, royalties and interest are publicly available from various sources, bilateral flows reported in these databases are typically incomplete due to confidentiality reasons.[49] The required information on income flows and WHTs may, in some countries, be available from the Central Bank or other public institutions.

Using this data, a fiscal estimate can be calculated by drawing upon of the following elements:

- Definition of the tax bases, accounting for exemptions and tax treaties;
- Weighted average WHT rate under current law;
- Outgoing dividend, royalty and interest payments affected by treaty shopping; and
- Weighted average WHT rate under the adoption of Action 6 countermeasures.

The first step in estimating the effects of treaty abuse countermeasures would be to derive an estimate of the tax base for each of the income types. It may be necessary to make a downward adjustment to the tax base to account for potential WHT exemptions, before applying an appropriate tax rate. If the tax base is not affected by tax treaties, the weighted average tax rate can be computed by weighting the bilateral tax rates (standard or reduced) by the income flow associated with the respective country-pairs. This is straightforward if outflows and tax rates are available by partner country. Otherwise, additional information, for instance, FDI stocks, can be used to determine the weights. If tax treaties affect the definition of the tax base, then a similar approach can be used. Exempted income flows which may become subject to taxation due to the countermeasures could be treated as zero-rated and included in the tax base.

To estimate the effect of the countermeasures an additional assumption about the expected increases in the average WHT rate need to be made. While this will entail estimation (i.e. with regard to the effectiveness of the countermeasures), available data on bilateral income flows may be used to provide empirical guidance. It has been suggested, for instance, that an initial evaluation of the treaty network may help identify potential conduit countries. Provided data on income flows to these countries is available, the magnitude of the affected outflows can be estimated. If bilateral income flows to conduit countries are not observed, other variables, such as e.g. FDI stocks, may be used as an approximation. Separate FDI data series on SPEs may also be drawn upon to obtain a more comprehensive picture of the relevant outflows (see UNCTAD, 2015, for a detailed description).

As treaty benefits will be denied for transactions motivated by treaty shopping under the Action 6 recommendations, the respective income flows will be reallocated for tax purposes. Outflows to conduit countries, for instance, may now be treated as if they were payments to the ultimate counterparty. The increase in the average WHT rate can be captured by an adjustment in the weights associated with each country pair. Since the final destination of the income flow in the counterfactual scenario remains unknown, a proportional increase in the weights of all non-conduit countries could be a reasonable starting point. Possible feedback based on audit experiences may also be used at this step.

Based on this approach, the affected outbound payments as well as the weighted average WHT rates under current law and Action 6 can be approximated. Since potential effects of the countermeasures on exempted income flows have been accounted for, the approximated tax base does not change in the Action 6 countermeasure fiscal estimate. The estimated revenue change equals the change in the weighted average WHT rate times the total outbound payments estimated to be affected by treaty shopping.

b. *Fiscal estimation based on publicly available data*

The approach presented in this section provides an example of how results from recent academic publications can be combined with publicly available data sources to derive an initial estimate. The following information is required:

- Outbound payments of dividends, royalties and interest from BOP statistics;
- Reduced treaty tax rates on royalties and interest; and
- Country-level tax revenue estimates from the network analysis by Van't Riet and Lejour (2014)[50]

BOP statistics include outgoing flows between related parties for dividends and interest (BOP, current account, primary income, direct investment income). However, royalty flows are not reported in the section on direct investment income but as a part of the goods and services section (BOP, current account, goods and services, charges for intellectual property). These flows include royalty flows between related and unrelated parties. While dividend and interest flows from portfolio investments are separated in the BOP data, further adjustments are necessary to isolate royalty flows between related and unrelated parties.

Publicly available data can be combined with results from a recent publication which provides information on country-level tax revenue effects with and without treaty shopping. Van't Riet and Lejour (2014) use a network approach to map the tax incentive structure faced by MNEs. The analysis includes 108 jurisdictions and builds on country level information on CIT, WHTs and double taxation relief methods. In addition, information on treaty benefits from existing bilateral tax treaties are used to calculate the tax minimising indirect payment route between all possible pairs of countries.

The analysis shows that the FDI-weighted world average tax rate on dividend flows, taking unilateral double tax relief and bilateral tax treaties into account, is around 11%.[51] Comparing taxation on indirect and direct routes shows that treaty shopping reduces the FDI-weighted world average by an upper bound of 44% (i.e. to 4.8%). While the world average effect may not be indicative for individual countries, the paper also includes a more detailed table providing revenue effects from WHT by country. Potential country-level WHT revenues with and without treaty shopping are reported as a percent of total outgoing dividend flows. Based on this information, a fiscal estimate of the maximum effect that could be obtained by eliminating treaty shopping can be derived by multiplying the results with corresponding outflows of FDI dividends. Information at the country level may be helpful to scale the upper bound estimate to a realistic estimate of the fiscal effects for the country.

Two sets of additional assumptions could be necessary for an analysis of the fiscal effects of Action 6 countermeasures. First, the results from the network analysis only include the effects from dividend payments between related parties. To account for the effects from royalty and interest payments, the revenue results from dividends could be applied to other income flows. This can be done by calculating the proportional reduction of statutory WHT rates on dividends that result from bilateral treaties and treaty shopping (i.e. indirect routing) respectively. Applying these proportions to statutory rates on royalties and interest may give a first approximation of the corresponding tax reductions on other outbound payments. In addition, the results may also be expanded to include income flows from portfolio investment. Although the treatment of portfolio dividends in tax treaties is typically different from the treatment of dividends between related parties, a similar approximation may be feasible, depending on the specific country context.

Common assumptions needed for both approaches

The fiscal estimates described in this section identify only an upper bound of the effects of treaty shopping. They assume that all MNEs use the tax-minimising route to channel international income flows. The estimates also do not correct for conduit arrangements that have non-tax related economic substance (e.g. in cases where regional holding companies are established in third countries to minimise transaction costs arising from language or time-zone differences).

Incorporating behavioural effects

MNEs may provide more substance to regional holding companies to satisfy LOB and PPT rules. In both cases, assumptions are needed to identify (a) the proportion to which conduit arrangements are supported by economic substance and (b) the effectiveness of the countermeasures. The first assumption should be based on further empirical evidence from the country-level, if possible. The second will depend on the countermeasures which are already in place, the capacity of the tax administration, and interactions with other countermeasures.

Both of the estimation procedures provide only a static estimate assuming that the amount and direction of outbound payments is unchanged. However, adoption of Action 6 countermeasures is likely to affect the composition of inbound and outbound income flows, thus leading to further effects on WHT revenues. For instance, if the multilateral adoption of Action 6 countermeasures leads to an increase in source country taxation, repatriation becomes less profitable and profits may therefore be reinvested in the source country or invested in other countries. The resulting dynamic effects on the composition of international income flows are not included in the proposed approaches. A more comprehensive analysis of this issue would need to be undertaken on a country-specific basis with available country-level data.

Potential interactions with other countermeasures

Action 6 interacts with Action 2 on hybrid mismatch arrangements as arrangements that are designed to exploit differences in tax treatment of instruments and entities are also often structured so as to take advantage of treaty benefits. Since zero-tax countries generally do not have treaties with other countries, Action 6 will provide a backstop to Action 2, further strengthening the elimination of BEPS through hybrid mismatch arrangements.

Action 7 (Permanent Establishment)

Tax treaties generally provide that the business profits of a foreign enterprise are taxable in a country only to the extent that the enterprise has a permanent establishment (PE) in that country to which the profits are attributable. The definition of PE included in tax treaties is therefore crucial in determining whether a non-resident enterprise must pay income tax in another country. The Report on Action 7 (*Preventing the Artificial Avoidance of Permanent Establishment Status*, OECD, 2015h) includes changes to the definition of PE in the OECD Model Tax Convention, which is widely used as the basis for negotiating tax treaties. These changes address business models which do not create tax nexus in the source state, including commissionaire arrangements instead of distributors or the artificial fragmentation of business activities.

Understanding the proposed change

The specific PE provisions being dealt with under Action 7 include the agency-PE rule and the specific exceptions. The recommendations will also address the issue of profit attribution once a PE is established, but these recommendations have not been finalised.

The specific Action 7 recommendations to reduce the artificial avoidance of PE status include:

- Changes to the agency-PE rule to ensure that where the activities that an intermediary exercises in a country are intended to result in the regular conclusion of contracts to be performed by a foreign enterprise, that enterprise will be considered to have a PE in the country unless the intermediary is performing these activities in the course of an independent business;
- Restricting all the exceptions to the PE rules to activities which are otherwise of a "preparatory or auxiliary character";
- A new anti-fragmentation rule; and
- Changes dealing with the splitting-up of contracts.

Data and methodology

Estimating the fiscal effects of Action 7 countermeasures will be difficult because the determination of a PE is fact-specific. It will be necessary to focus the analysis on MNEs with activities likely affected by a redefinition, such as commissionaire arrangements, to get a rough measure of the potential magnitude of the activity affected. One possible route would be to work together with relevant staff, including auditors, at the revenue authority, to understand the previous cases of PE audits and current investigations, as well as how the revised definition would affect the PE status of those and other companies. Once examples or a sample of potentially affected companies are identified, that sample can be extrapolated to the potential total economic activity affected by the Action 7 countermeasures in the country.

If it is possible to estimate the magnitude of the economic activities by the PEs being analysed, profits would need to be allocated between the PE and related parties. Further guidance with regard to this step of the estimation procedure can be obtained from the revised transfer pricing guidelines and the additional guidance on attribution of profits that will be developed in 2016.

Lowering PE thresholds implies that MNEs may now be subject to tax in locations where PE status was previously avoided. Economic activity previously subject to tax in another jurisdiction will now be subject to tax in the PE jurisdiction such that tax revenues could potentially decrease in one jurisdiction and increase in another.

Incorporating behavioural effects

As a consequence, MNEs may restructure their operations in line with the change in tax rate differentials. In some cases this may induce the MNE group to carry on the same activities through local subsidiaries or, in extreme cases, to discontinue some or all of its activities in a country. To the extent these reduced activities are then performed by local subcontractors or other firms with a PE in the country, there may be an increase in corporate tax collections. Measuring the shifted amount of additional economic activity and associated income as a result of the change in the definition of PE will be a difficult exercise. The amount of additional revenue in the PE jurisdiction will be the estimated increase in taxable income times the AMTR of that activity.

To monitor the fiscal effects of the BEPS countermeasure, audit results and new CIT information could be tracked after a country's adoption of Action 7's countermeasures. If the information is available for specific taxpayers, a net figure for revenue changes should be calculated, including tax increases for taxpayers where new measures give rise to PE status and the tax increases from economic activities of other in-country firms with a PE that would be increased when the artificial avoidance of PE status has been eliminated. Similar monitoring could be done for the jurisdiction where the income was previously reported.

Potential interactions with other countermeasures

Action 7 will have important linkages to Action 2 and 6, and the transfer pricing changes. Together with changes to tax treaties proposed in the Reports on Actions 2 and 6, the changes will lead to an increase in taxation in a number of cases where cross-border income would otherwise have been untaxed or would be taxed at very low rates as a result of the current provisions in tax treaties.

The BEPS countermeasures recommended by Action 7 are linked to the revised transfer pricing guidance of Actions 8-10. With the revised guidelines in effect, transactions between a company with newly established PE and related parties are to be priced at arm's length. Where some of the income from the operations of a newly established PE may have been shifted to a tax haven in the past, the income will now be assigned to where the economic activity generating that income is located.

Action 11 (Measuring and Monitoring BEPS)

The Report on Action 11 (*Measuring and Monitoring BEPS*, OECD, 2015i) includes an assessment of existing data sources relevant for BEPS analysis; indicators of BEPS; an initial economic analysis of BEPS and countermeasures (and the issues surrounding an economic analysis in the BEPS context); as well as recommendations for future data and tools necessary to better understand BEPS behaviours and monitor these behaviours and BEPS countermeasures over time. The issues raised and findings from the analysis of the scale and economic impact of BEPS and countermeasures will improve the understanding and visibility of these issues with policymakers and media. In addition, Action 11 highlights best practices in data collection and dissemination that could assist policymakers in more countries to have a better understanding of BEPS behaviours in their countries over time.

The measuring and monitoring of BEPS, such as that in the Report on Action 11, will provide increased transparency. Action 11 increases transparency with its macro analysis of the scale of BEPS and countermeasures, which complements the increased transparency of the individual company information of the other Actions. Action 11 will complement the increased transparency of Actions 5, 12 and 13.While not having a direct effect on corporate tax revenues, Action 11 will have an indirect effect through an improved understanding of the fiscal effects of BEPS behaviours by tax policy makers, tax administrations, taxpayers, the media and the public. The analysis of BEPS behaviours could highlight particular areas for increased tax enforcement, as well as raise the reputation costs of tax avoidance. With a better understanding of the BEPS behaviours and their potential fiscal and economic effects, Action 11 could contribute to prompting a more comprehensive implementation of BEPS countermeasures, which would result in tighter rules to counter BEPS. While not feasible to estimate a separate fiscal effect of Action 11, it may increase the willingness of policymakers to take action and improve the effectiveness of audit enforcement.

Action 12 (Disclosure of Aggressive Tax Planning Arrangements)

The Report on Action 12 (*Mandatory Disclosure Rules*, OECD, 2015j) includes recommendations for the design and implementation of mandatory disclosure regimes for potentially aggressive or abusive international tax planning strategies. The policy objectives include providing tax administrations with early information on tax planning strategies and deterring taxpayers from engaging in aggressive tax planning arrangements. The elements of Action 12 include:

- A modular design of mandatory disclosure rules;
- A focus on international tax schemes; and
- The design of enhanced models of information sharing among countries.

Fiscal estimation issues

Adoption of the Action 12 countermeasure will result in countries having the option to adopt new mandatory disclosure regimes or expanding existing regimes. The disclosure information will allow tax administrations to more effectively enforce existing domestic tax rules, as well as other BEPS countermeasures. As one transparency component of the BEPS project, Action 12's recommendations will increase the effectiveness of a country's enforcement efforts and will discourage taxpayers from taking aggressive tax positions in the first place.

Although implementation of new or expanded disclosure of aggressive tax planning arrangements would be expected to increase total corporate tax collections, it would be difficult ex ante to estimate the incremental improvement given the uncertainty of the behavioural effects of audit enforcement and taxpayer reactions. The empirical literature has focused more on the effects on financial reporting rather than actual taxes paid. Ex post, analysts could work with the audit teams to identify the increased effectiveness of audits and settlements on transactions identified through the increased disclosure.

Action 14 (Dispute Resolution Mechanisms)

The recommendations developed as a result of the work on Action 14 are intended to improve the effectiveness and efficiency of the mutual agreement procedure (MAP) in resolving treaty-related disputes; it is an important complement to the BEPS countermeasures, which could introduce elements of tax uncertainty, as well as the potential for unintended double taxation. The Report on Action 14 (*Making Dispute Resolution Mechanisms More Effective*, OECD, 2015k) specifically includes:

- Adoption of a minimum standard with respect to the resolution of treaty-related disputes, intended to ensure the full implementation of treaty obligations related to MAP, the implementation of administrative processes to promote the prevention and timely resolution of treaty-related disputes, and that taxpayers that meet the requirements of the MAP article can access the MAP; and

- A commitment by 20 countries (that accounted for 90% of outstanding MAP cases at the end of 2013) to provide for mandatory binding MAP arbitration in their bilateral tax treaties.

Fiscal estimation issues

If there is inconsistency in the implementation of the BEPS countermeasures there is the possibility that an unintended increase in double taxation could result in higher income tax collections than expected from the intended reduction in BEPS. This could be a potential component of the net revenue effect of other BEPS countermeasures.

Action 14 is designed to mitigate such unintended tax increases. The fiscal effect of an improved dispute resolution mechanism could be a decrease in the estimated net income tax revenues from other countermeasures. To the extent that improvements to the MAP and/or a MAP arbitration mechanism apply with respect to existing disputes, the disputes may be settled more quickly and a change in revenue could result from additional tax payments or refunds of previously collected amounts. A future change in tax collections from existing disputes might depend on whether countries require corporations to pay taxes on the disputed amounts.

It would be difficult to estimate the effect in advance of actual experience with improvements to the MAP and MAP arbitration. The results of a strengthened dispute resolution process, in terms of tax adjustments, could be tracked to provide an ex post estimate of the reduction in revenues due to the decrease in potential double taxation.

Action 15 (Multilateral Instrument)

The Report on Action 15 (*Developing a Multilateral Instrument to Modify Bilateral Tax Treaties*, OECD, 2015l) explores the feasibility of a multilateral instrument to modify tax treaties so as to implement the treaty-related BEPS measures and amend bilateral tax treaties. This is designed to significantly reduce the costs and time associated with bilateral treaty renegotiations for countries that choose to sign the instrument. A mandate has been developed for an ad-hoc group, open to the participation of all countries on an equal footing, to develop the multilateral instrument and open it for signature in 2016. So far, 88 countries are participating in the work on an equal footing.

Fiscal estimation issues

Where countries sign the multilateral instrument to modify their tax treaties, this could lead to an acceleration in the implementation of countermeasures and bring forward the fiscal effects. To the extent that the adoption of new countermeasures would require amendments to treaties which could require many years, the multilateral instrument may enable those amendments to take place quicker. If the multilateral instrument leads to the faster implementation of countermeasures then this will lead to a commensurate acceleration of the fiscal effects.

Summary

This annex provides potential approaches that could be used by government tax policy analysts to estimate the fiscal effects of BEPS countermeasures for their respective countries. A general approach is described before potential approaches are explained for the individual BEPS Actions. The proposed methodologies are set out according to the individual countermeasures of the BEPS Action Plan. Some methodologies are more comprehensive than others given the variation in data availability; the extent of insights from empirical studies; and depending on the design of the countermeasures. Countries will have different datasets and some may be more useful for particular BEPS countermeasures than others. It is recognised that estimating the fiscal effects of BEPS countermeasures may rely on applicable tax return data, financial account micro-data, macro-data (aggregated from tax return or financial accounts), a combination of micro and macro-data sources, or in some cases to data analogous to the country. Where possible, multiple approaches based on different sources of data are described.

As better data becomes available – both as a result of CbCR and countries recognising the need to draw on taxpayer micro-data to make more informed and evidence-based tax policy decisions – tax policy analysts will be in a better position to evaluate and monitor trends in BEPS behaviours and the effect of countermeasures.

An important consideration is the evaluation of ex post estimates relative to ex ante estimates. Separating the effects of unexpected macroeconomic changes from unexpected taxpayer behaviours from technical estimation issues can provide valuable learning to tax policy analysts as they assess the underlying causes in cases of large differences. Even small differences do not necessarily mean that all assumptions ex ante were correct. Evaluation of past estimates can improve understanding of key parameters, including behavioural changes.

Bibliography

Beer, Sebastian, and Jan Loeprick (2015), *Profit shifting: drivers of transfer (mis)pricing and the potential of countermeasures*, International Tax and Public Finance, Vol. 22(3), pp 426-451.

Bernard, Andrew B., J. Bradford Jensen and Pete K. Schott (2006), *Transfer pricing by U.S.-based multinational firms*, NBER Working Paper, No. 12493.

Blouin, Jennifer, Harry Huizinga, Luc Laeven, Gaetan Nicodeme (2014), *Thin Capitalization Rules and Multinational Firm Capital Structure*, IMF Working Papers, No. 14/12.

Buslei, Hermann, and Martin Simmler (2012), *The Impact of Introducing an Interest Barrier: Evidence from the German Corporation Tax Reform 2008*, DIW Discussion Paper, No. 1215.

Clausing, K. A. (2003), *Tax-motivated transfer pricing and US intrafirm trade*, Journal of Public Economics 87 (9-10), pp. 2207-2223.

Clausing, K. A. (2006), *International tax avoidance and U.S. international trade*, National Tax Journal, Vol. LVIV, No. 2.

Cristea, Anca D. and Daniel X. Nguyen (2014), *Transfer pricing by multinational firms: New evidence from foreign firm ownerships*, University of Copenhagen.

Davies, Ronald B., Julien Martin, Mathieu Parenti and Farid Toubal (2014), *Knocking on tax haven's door: Multinational firms and transfer pricing*, CEPII Working Paper, No. 2014-21.

DeMooij, Ruud A., and Sjef Ederveen (2008), *Corporate Tax Elasticities A Reader's Guide to Empirical Findings*, Oxford University Centre for Business Taxation, Working Paper, No. 08/22.

Dischinger, Matthias, and Nadine Riedel (2011), *Corporate taxes and the location of intangible assets within multinational firms*, Journal of Public Economics, Vol. 95(7-8), pp. 691-707.

Dreßler, Daniel and Uwe Scheuering (2012), *Empirical evaluation of interest barrier effects*, ZEW Discussion Papers, No. 12-046.

European Commission (2015), *Patent Boxes Design, Patents Location and Local R&D*, Taxation Working Paper No. 57.

Griffith, Rachel, Helen Miller and Martin O'Connell (2011), *Corporate Taxes and the Location of Intellectual Property*, CEPR Discussion Paper, No. DP8424.

Karkinsky, Tom, and Nadine Riedel (2012), *Corporate taxation and the choice of patent location within multinational firms*, Journal of International Economics, Vol. 88(1), pp. 176–185.

Lanz, R. and S. Miroudot (2011), *Intra-firm trade: Patterns, determinants and policy implications*, OECD Trade Policy Papers, No. 114, http://dx.doi.org/10.1787/5kg9p39lrwnn-en.

Markle, and L. Robinson (2012), *Tax Haven Use Across International Tax Regimes*, www.sbs.ox.ac.uk/sites/default/files/Business_Taxation/Events/conferences/symposia/2012/markle.

OECD, Activities of Multinational Enterprises (AMNE) database.

OECD (2008), Benchmark Definition of Foreign Direct Investment, 4th Edition.

OECD (2013), *Action Plan on Base Erosion and Profit Shifting*, OECD Publishing, Paris, http://dx.doi.org/10.1787/9789264202719-en

OECD (2015a), *Aligning Transfer Pricing Outcomes with Value Creation, Actions 8-10 - 2015 Final Reports*, OECD/G20 Base Erosion and Profit Shifting Project, OECD Publishing, Paris, http://dx.doi.org/10.1787/9789264241244-en.

OECD (2015b), *Limiting Base Erosion Involving Interest Deductions and Other Financial Payments, Action 4 - 2015 Final Report*, OECD/G20 Base Erosion and Profit Shifting Project, OECD Publishing, Paris, http://dx.doi.org/10.1787/9789264241176-en.

OECD (2015c), *Addressing the Tax Challenges of the Digital Economy, Action 1 - 2015 Final Report*, OECD/G20 Base Erosion and Profit Shifting Project, OECD Publishing, Paris, http://dx.doi.org/10.1787/9789264241046-en.

OECD (2015d), *Neutralising the Effects of Hybrid Mismatch Arrangements, Action 2 - 2015 Final Report*, OECD/G20 Base Erosion and Profit Shifting Project, OECD Publishing, Paris, http://dx.doi.org/10.1787/9789264241138-en.

OECD (2015e), *Designing Effective Controlled Foreign Company Rules, Action 3 - 2015 Final Report*, OECD/G20 Base Erosion and Profit Shifting Project, OECD Publishing, Paris, http://dx.doi.org/10.1787/9789264241152-en.

OECD (2015f), *Countering Harmful Tax Practices More Effectively, Taking into Account Transparency and Substance, Action 5 - 2015 Final Report*, OECD/G20 Base Erosion and Profit Shifting Project, OECD Publishing, Paris, http://dx.doi.org/10.1787/9789264241190-en.

OECD (2015g), *Preventing the Granting of Treaty Benefits in Inappropriate Circumstances, Action 6 - 2015 Final Report*, OECD/G20 Base Erosion and Profit Shifting Project, OECD Publishing, Paris, http://dx.doi.org/10.1787/9789264241695-en.

OECD (2015h), *Preventing the Artificial Avoidance of Permanent Establishment Status, Action 7 - 2015 Final Report*, OECD/G20 Base Erosion and Profit Shifting Project, OECD Publishing, Paris, http://dx.doi.org/10.1787/9789264241220-en.

OECD (2015i), *Measuring and Monitoring BEPS, Action 11 - 2015 Final Report*, OECD/G20 Base Erosion and Profit Shifting Project, OECD Publishing, Paris, http://dx.doi.org/10.1787/9789264241343-en.

OECD (2015j), *Mandatory Disclosure Rules, Action 12 - 2015 Final Report*, OECD/G20 Base Erosion and Profit Shifting Project, OECD Publishing, Paris, http://dx.doi.org/10.1787/9789264241442-en.

OECD (2015k), *Making Dispute Resolution Mechanisms More Effective, Action 14 - 2015 Final Report*, OECD/G20 Base Erosion and Profit Shifting Project, OECD Publishing, Paris, http://dx.doi.org/10.1787/9789264241633-en.

OECD (2015l), *Developing a Multilateral Instrument to Modify Bilateral Tax Treaties, Action 15 -2015 Final Report*, OECD/G20 Base Erosion and Profit Shifting Project, OECD Publishing, Paris, http://dx.doi.org/10.1787/9789264241688-en.

OECD, *Trade in value-added: Concepts, methodologies, and challenges (Joint OECD-WTO Note)*, www.oecd.org/sti/ind/49894138.pdf.

Overesch, Michael (2006). *Transfer pricing of intrafirm sales as a profit shifting channel: Evidence from German firm data*, ZEW Discussion Papers, No. 06-84.

Riedel, N., (2014), *Quantifying international tax avoidance: A review of the academic literature*, Paper prepared for the European Tax Policy Forum, mimeo.

Schindler, Dirk, and Martin Ruf, (2015), *Debt Shifting and Thin-Capitalization Rules - German Experiences and Alternative Approaches*, Nordic Tax Journal, Vol. 1, 17-33.

Ruf, M. and A. J. Weichenrieder (2012), *The taxation of passive foreign investment: lessons from German experience*, Canadian Journal of Economics, Vol. 45, No.4.

Ruf, M. and A. J. Weichenrieder (2013), *CFC legislation, passive assets and the impact of the ECJ's Cadbury-Schweppes decision*, CESifo Working Paper, No. 4461.

Schindler, Dirk, and Guttcrm Schjelderup (2013), *Transfer Pricing and Debt Shifting in Multinationals*, CESifo Working Paper Series, No. 4381.

Van 't Riet, M. and A. Lejour, (2014), *Ranking the stars: Network analysis of bilateral tax treaties*, CPB Discussion Paper, No. 290.

Vicard, Vincent (2015), *Profit shifting through transfer pricing: Evidence from French firm level trade data*, Banque de France Working Paper No. 555. DOI: http://dx.doi.org/10.2139/ssrn.2614864.

Merlo, Valeria, and Georg Wamser (2015), *Debt Shifting and Thin-capitalization Rules*, CESifo DICE Report, Vol. 12(4), pp. 27-31.

UNCTAD (2015), *FDI, tax and development*, UNCTAD Investment and Enterprise Division Working Paper.

Notes

1. Page 21 of the OECD (2013) *Action Plan on Base Erosion and Profit Shifting.*

2. Page 21 of the OECD (2013) *Action Plan on Base Erosion and Profit Shifting*: "*further work needs to be done… to monitor the impact of measures taken under the Action Plan to address BEPS. This should include outcome-based techniques, which look at measures of the allocation of income across jurisdictions relative to measures of value creating activities, as well as techniques that can be used to monitor the specific issues identified in the Action Plan.*"

3. Based on discussions by Delegates of the OECD's Committee on Fiscal Affairs Working Party No.2, and participating country Delegates.

4. See, for example, impact assessments on the HMRC website (available at www.hmrc.gov.uk/ria/#full) or Department of the Treasury (2015), (available at www.treasury.gov/resource-center/tax-policy/Documents/General-Explanations-FY2016.pdf).

5. The reduction in the CIT tax base due to the location of debt in entities in higher-tax countries is not included in the transfer pricing revenue impact estimating methodology. It should be included in the revenue impact analysis for Action 4 dealing with the allowance of interest deductions related to third-party and related-party loans.

6. The data includes detailed information on goods and services flows, by trade partner, and is available for the OECD and G20 countries. Information on trade in goods is available for additional countries from IMF data. Trade amounts would have to be imputed for the missing services trade data for selected countries.

7. For a detailed description of what is included in the trade in goods and services data, see IMF, Sixth Edition of the Balance of Payments and International Investment Position Manual (BPM6), available at www.imf.org/external/pubs/ft/bop/2007/bopman6.htm.

8. Note that the methodology is described in terms of CIT revenue impacts. The BEPS countermeasures would apply to all business income. To the extent that BEPS affects business profits reported on individual income tax returns and information is available, this additional revenue impact could be included in the BEPS impact calculations.

9. See OECD, *Activities of Multinational Enterprises (AMNE)* database.

10. The share of trade accounted for by transactions between MNE entities is available for a limited number of countries. See Lanz and Miroudot (2011), as well as data on MNE activities from specific countries, including the United States and Germany.

11. The trade amounts may include "round-trip" transactions among entities. For example, goods in process may be exported from an affiliate in country A to an affiliate in country B for further processing. The finished product may then be returned to the affiliate in country A as an import into country A. The full amounts of

both the export from country A and import into country A are included in the estimate of mispricing. National account statisticians are addressing this issue of double counting from the perspective of creating more accurate measures of trade flows that affect a domestic economy. See the OECD, *Trade in Value-Added: Concepts, Methodologies, and Challenges (Joint OECD-WTO Note)*.

12. See the OECD, *Trade in Value-Added: Concepts, Methodologies, and Challenges (Joint OECD-WTO Note)*.

13. One method of reducing this incentive is to require a greater level of in-country real activity (R&D, for example) to qualify for the special rates.

14. In calculating the trade-weighted AMTR, the AMTR for each of a country's trading partners identified in the bilateral trade data is multiplied by the share of a country's total worldwide exports or imports accounted for by the trading partner.

15. Alternatively, the calculations could be done at the level of trade flows between a country and each of the country's trading partners. In this case, it is not necessary to calculate a weighted average STR for among all trading partners.

16. The AMTRs would generally be the applicable tax rates for combined national and sub-national CIT rates.

17. These calculations use headline statutory tax rates except lower special tax rates that apply to royalty income in selected countries.

18. Although the value of the semi-elasticity is constant for all AMTR tax rate differential calculations, it does result in variations in the elasticity of response to these tax rate differentials. In other words, the larger the *percentage* change in tax rate differences, the higher the percentage change in export and import prices. Elasticities of trade pricing could be used for elasticities of net income to the extent that non-tax rate factors are fully specified and accurately measured in a regression equation. The percentage change in trade prices would affect net income due to tax rate differentials in the same way that net income is affected by tax rate differentials, over and above the estimated effect of non-tax factors. An extra dollar of revenue from trade mispricing results in an extra dollar of net income, similar to an extra dollar of net income from other profit shifting.

19. Sebastian Beer and Jan Loeprick, "Profit shifting: drivers of transfer mis(pricing) and the potential of countermeasures," International Tax Public Finance, published online 17 May 2014, find that profit shifting responsiveness is higher for subsidiaries with higher ratios of intangible to total assets. Matthias Dischinger and Nadine Riedel, "Corporate taxes and the location of intangible assets within multinational firms," *Journal of Public Economics* 95 (2011) also find that an affiliate's pre-tax income response is more sensitive to tax rate differentials for groups with high ratios of intangibles to sales. See also the results discussed in Annex 1.

20. See for example, Andrew B. Bernard, J. Bradford Jensen, Peter K. Scott, "Transfer Pricing by U.S.-Based Multinational Firms," National Bureau of Economic Research, Working Paper 12493, August 2006.

21. While royalty payments for the use of intellectual property are included in the charges for the use of intellectual property category, the value of sales of the outcome of R&D are reported in the other business services category. These transactions, including the sale of intangible property among MNE entities, are included in the trade in services flows that are the beginning point for the transfer pricing revenue analysis.

22. The financial services in the service trade data include brokerage, underwriting, credit card and management and advisory services. Interest payments and receipts are included in the primary income accounts.

23. The data is captured for those entities where there is at least a 10% ownership link.

24. As per paragraph 82 of the Report on Action 4, it is recommended that a fixed ratio rule should measure earnings using EBITDA. However, a country may apply a fixed ratio rule which measures earnings using EBIT, so long as the other elements of the rule are consistent with the best practice in this report. Since EBITDA is the recommended approach, the approach outlined for the fiscal estimate will refer to EBITDA. If the country opts for EBIT in the design of interest limitation rules, the fiscal estimate should be based on EBIT.

25. As per paragraph 24 of the Report on Action 4, countries are encouraged to combine a robust and effective fixed ratio rule with a group ratio rule which allows an entity to deduct more interest expense in certain circumstances. A group ratio rule may be introduced as a separate provision from the fixed ratio rule, or as an integral part of an overall rule including both fixed ratio and group ratio tests.

26. An entity is part of a group if it is directly/indirectly controlled by a company, or the entity is a company which directly or indirectly controls one or more other entities. A group is considered to be multinational if it operates in more than one jurisdiction, including through a permanent establishment.

27. Countries which are European Union (EU) Member States would need to take into account EU law considerations in designing their domestic rules, to ensure they are compliant with EU law. The Report on Action 4 includes an annex detailing the necessary considerations.

28. The Action 4 best practice approach refers to a non-exhaustive list of examples. Details matter and each country would need to determine whether the definition of interest used for an interest limitation rule as per the best practice approach is appropriately captured in the fiscal effect calculations. If it is impossible to incorporate all payments equivalent to interest, it could be noted that the fiscal effect may be understated.

29. The interest limitation would apply to all business, irrespective of legal form. The description will refer to CIT, but would be equally applicable to personal income tax base changes of non-corporate businesses and their owners.

30. Further work will be conducted, to be completed in 2016, to identify targeted rules to deal with the base erosion and profit shifting risks posed by banks and insurance companies.

31. Please see the Report on Action 4 for a discussion on why tax exempt income, such as exempt dividend income or foreign earnings that are tax exempt, should not form part of the entity's EBITDA figure. The rationale behind excluding exempt dividend income is to address concerns related to the outbound investment scenario as described in Action Item 4.

32. See paragraph 115 of the Report on Action 4.

33. See the discussion on applicable marginal tax rates in the transfer pricing section (Actions 8-10 & 13).

34. Quasi-corporations are unincorporated corporations that keep a complete set of accounts so they can be separated. If the unincorporated enterprise does not keep a complete set of accounts then it is classified within the household sector.

35. Note by Turkey: The information in this document with reference to « Cyprus » relates to the southern part of the Island. There is no single authority representing both Turkish and Greek Cypriot people on the Island. Turkey recognizes the Turkish Republic of Northern Cyprus. Until a lasting and equitable solution is found within the context of United Nations, Turkey shall preserve its position concerning the "Cyprus issue".

Note by all the European Union Member States of the OECD and the European Union: The Republic of Cyprus is recognized by all members of the United Nations with the exception of Turkey. The information in this document relates to the area under the effective control of the Government of the Republic of Cyprus.

36. NIE is calculated by subtracting interest receipts from interest payments and multiplying by an average exchange rate for 2012 where applicable.

37. Banks generate service income by lending at a higher rate of interest than they borrow. This is considered a service for bringing the lenders and borrowers together. Since depositors receive a lower rate of interest than the 'reference rate', the interest received is increased by the amount of the difference between the reference rate and the rate that depositors actually receive. Depositors immediately use this increase in income to purchase the service. Conversely, borrowers pay a higher rate of interest (than the reference rate), some of which reflects payments for a service. The National Accounts subtract the difference between the higher rate that borrowers pay and the reference rate. Again this difference is immediately used by borrowers to purchase this service.

38. See list provided in description of key issues for Action 4.

39. Schindler et al. (2013), Blouin et al. (2014) and Wamser et al (2015).

40. The Business and Industry Advisory Committee to the OECD presented numbers in the Action 4 Focus Group meetings showing the distribution of large public firms by different external interest ratios.

41. Please see the discussion on applicable marginal tax rates in the transfer pricing section (Actions 8-10 & 13)

42. This estimate is stacked after many other proposals such that some of the revenue effects are reflected in other estimates.

43. Action 3 notes that this method generally recognises that even in a situation where the statutory tax rate is not considered a low tax rate, low taxation may occur as a result of (1) reducing the tax base or (2) lowering the tax burden by subsequent rebates of taxes paid or through non-enforcement of taxes.

44. Determining attributable income would be unnecessary for countries that opt for a full-inclusion system, i.e. once an entity is classified as a CFC, all income is treated as CFC income, which is relevant in the context of worldwide tax systems.

45. There are exceptions: United States intra-firm imports and exports are collected for disaggregated service items, and both Canada and the United States break down services trade by affiliation (Lanz & Miroudot, 2011).

46. See discussion on the applicable marginal tax rate (AMTR) in the section on transfer pricing (Actions 8-10 & 13).

47. In the case of the 2012 study, the data was supplemented with information on national characteristics from the World Bank Development Indicators and with tax rate information from PWC, the Bureau of Tax Policy Research at the University of Michigan, KPMG, and other sources.

48. Please see the discussion on applicable marginal tax rates in the transfer pricing section (Actions 8-10 & 13).

49. The sources include the IMF Balance of Payments Statistics and the OECD International Direct Investment Database. In compiling and presenting FDI statistics, compilers in many countries may encounter the possibility of confidential data occurring in the results to be disseminated. FDI information can be regarded as being confidential in a primary sense for a number of reasons: (i) if a compiler declares it to be confidential, (ii) if there is only one or at most two entities giving rise to the information, or (iii) if the contribution of a particular enterprise (or even two enterprises) dominate(s) the contributions of all other entities (OECD, 2008).

50. The applicable information can be found in Table B6 of the paper.

51. Note that this result refers to the combined remaining tax rate, potentially including CIT in the recipient country, depending on the relief method.

Chapter 4

Towards better data and tools for monitoring BEPS in the future

Key points:

- The limitations of currently available data and the complexity of BEPS mean that improved data and tools are necessary if the global community is to obtain a clearer picture of the scale and impact of BEPS and properly monitor the effectiveness of the measures implemented under the BEPS project.
- Given the large, and soon to be expanded, volume of data in the hands of tax administrations, this report's recommendations focus on the need for governments to work more closely together to make better use of data that is already (or has been agreed, as part of the BEPS project, to be) collected. In particular, statistical analyses based upon data collected under the Action 13 Country-by-Country Reports have the potential to significantly enhance the economic analysis of BEPS.
- This report makes the following recommendations:
  - The OECD should work with all OECD members and BEPS Associates (including all G20 countries) and any country willing to participate to publish, on a regular basis, a new Corporate Tax Statistics publication, which would compile a range of data and statistical analyses relevant to the economic analysis of BEPS in an internationally consistent format. Among other information, this publication would include aggregated and anonymised statistical analyses prepared by governments based on the data collected under the Action 13 Country-by-Country Reports.
  - The OECD should work with all OECD members, BEPS Associates and any willing participating governments to produce periodic reports on the estimated revenue impacts of proposed and enacted BEPS countermeasures.
  - The OECD should continue to produce and refine analytical tools and BEPS Indicators to monitor the scale and economic impact of BEPS and to evaluate the effectiveness and economic impact of BEPS countermeasures.
  - Governments should improve the public reporting of business tax revenue statistics, particularly for MNEs.
  - Governments should continue to make improvements in non-tax data relevant to BEPS with wider country coverage, such as for FDI associated with resident SPEs, trade in services and intangible investments.
  - Governments should consider current best practices and explore new approaches to collaborating on BEPS research with academics and other researchers. Governments should encourage more research on MNE activity within tax administrations, tax policy offices, national statistical offices (NSO), and by academic researchers, to improve the understanding of BEPS, and to better separate BEPS from real economic effects and non-BEPS tax preferences.

- Monitoring BEPS in the future will require that governments make better use of the data that is already (or has been agreed, as part of the BEPS project, to be) collected. Additional and more in-depth analysis of BEPS and the publication of statistical results and aggregate tabulations of MNE taxes and activities by individual countries will also be important to evaluating the effectiveness of BEPS countermeasures.

4.1 Introduction

268. The limitations of currently available data and current estimation methodologies mean that improved data and tools will be necessary if the global community is to obtain a clearer picture of the scale and impact of BEPS and properly monitor the effectiveness of the measures implemented under the BEPS project.

269. Chapter 1 included an assessment of currently available data, which concluded that the significant limitations of existing data sources mean that, at present, attempts to construct indicators or undertake economic analyses of the scale and impact of BEPS are severely constrained and thus must be heavily qualified. More comprehensive and more detailed data regarding MNEs is needed to provide a more accurate assessment of the scale and impact of BEPS.

270. Chapters 2 and 3 noted the difficulties in constructing BEPS indicators as well as undertaking economic analysis with the currently available data. At present, in addition to the data limitations, there is also a lack of detailed information on countries' tax rules and aggregate tax bases, which are all needed for improved cross-country economic analyses of BEPS and the effects of BEPS countermeasures. Economic analyses must separate BEPS behaviours from both the effects of real economic factors as well as the effects of non-BEPS tax preferences such as R&D tax incentives and other legislated special rates, deductions and exemptions.

271. Governments, and in particular tax administrations, already collect an array of information regarding the tax affairs of MNEs and their affiliates. The scope and value of this information will be increased as a result of the work undertaken as part of Action 5 (spontaneous exchange of rulings), Action 13 (transfer pricing documentation), and where implemented, Action 12 (disclosure of aggressive tax planning arrangements). While the need to improve the economic and fiscal analysis of BEPS requires greater access to this data, any recommendations around the availability of data in the future must take into account the need to protect the confidentiality of taxpayer information and minimise the administrative burden for governments and taxpayers.

272. Given the large, and soon to be expanded, volume of data in the hands of tax administrations, this report's recommendations focus on the need for governments to make better use of data that is already (or has been agreed, as part of the BEPS project, to be) collected and share best practices. Tax administrations can maximise the benefits of available information by increasing access to this data for research purposes under strict confidentiality rules. In addition, as statisticians continue to improve National Accounts with the measurement of foreign direct investment (FDI) through special purpose entities (SPEs) and other conduits, more disaggregation of bilateral trade in services data including payments for intellectual property and management services, and the measurement of intangible investments, these changes will provide further assistance to future economic analysis of BEPS.

273. The tools to be used to analyse and publish data in the future should be developed in a consistent and co-ordinated way so that when better data becomes available in the future it can be analysed and published in its most meaningful form. Increased analysis and publication of statistical results, particularly in the form of aggregate tabulations of taxes and activities of MNEs by individual countries will be important in better understanding BEPS.

274. Analyses of BEPS countermeasures may be useful for individual countries as they consider enactment and implementation, as well as monitoring the effects of countermeasures on BEPS going forward. Countries will differ in terms of the specific BEPS countermeasures adopted (some already have implemented certain BEPS countermeasures) and in the timing of their implementation. Improvements in the data and tools for analysis of BEPS and BEPS countermeasures are critical for policymakers, and those improvements will need to be undertaken by individual countries as well as international organisations.

4.2 Background

275. The future path of BEPS measurement is clearly dependent on increasing the quality and relevance of data available to improve indicators and economic analyses of BEPS, as shown in Figure 4.1. In the current state of BEPS analysis, analysts are generally exploiting the available data, although some of the data already being collected are not currently being compiled for analysis and access is often limited. While there are some new and innovative types of analysis of BEPS being undertaken, all analyses are constrained by significant data limitations. The academic community has demonstrated its creativity in examining new dimensions of BEPS to explore with currently available data, but there are diminishing returns to working with the current data, particularly non-tax return data.

276. The objective is that, in the future, better data will allow new and more refined indicators as well as refined economic analysis of BEPS and the effectiveness of BEPS countermeasures. Better data has a number of different dimensions.

- More relevant BEPS information (i.e. total MNE tax payments by country, tax residence of the entity rather than simply country of incorporation, related party transactions and structures).
- More coverage of companies, countries, and MNE relationships.
  - More complete set of companies (e.g. fewer missing entities and groups and better coverage across all countries).
  - More complete information from currently available company tax and non-tax records (e.g. fewer missing financial variables).[1]
  - Clear identification of MNE companies on tax return forms, both domestic companies of foreign MNE parents and domestic parents of foreign affiliates. Improved linkages between related entities and the overall MNE group information.
  - Expanded linkages between tax and other financial information.
- Increased access to available data for government analysts and academic researchers under strict confidentiality and access requirements.
- Increased data consistency across countries.

- More timely information with shorter time lags.

277. Initiatives could be taken in the areas described above that would improve the available data, increase the signal-to-noise ratio in future BEPS analyses, and help separate BEPS from other factors.

Figure 4.1. Future path of BEPS measurement

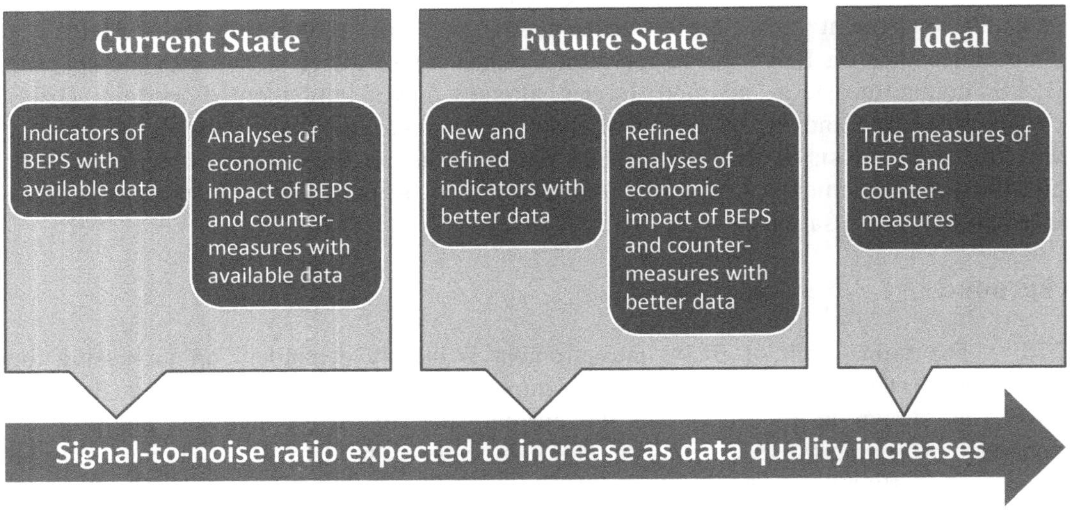

278. Existing arrangements, in relation to the collection, analysis, publication and provision of access to tax data, differ across countries. When considering existing data, three key issues must be considered: availability, coverage, and international consistency. Each of these is discussed in the next section.

4.2.1 Availability and access to data for BEPS analysis

279. The first key issue is the "availability" of current data. Governments, and in particular, tax administrations, already collect a vast array of information regarding the tax affairs of MNEs and their affiliates. Tax data is collected for the principal function of tax administration and government tax policy consideration and advice. Government analysts within tax administrations, and often within other government tax policy offices[2], generally have the ability to research and analyse the individual tax return data collected to help develop and evaluate government tax policy and inform advice.

280. In some countries, a significant portion of the tax return information is compiled into databases and is available for tax policy analysis. Often, aggregated tax data will be provided by individual countries to international and regional organisations so that the data can be compiled in a consistent manner for cross-country comparison and analysis, such as the OECD's annual *Revenue Statistics* publication. The data is aggregated so as to ensure that the confidentiality of taxpayer information is preserved.

281. Access to more detailed tax return data can in some countries be granted to researchers and academics. In some cases, qualified researchers may be engaged directly by government under strict confidentiality rules to assist the government in its analysis of the tax data for tax administration and tax policy purposes. In some countries, tax policy analysts can request access to tax return data, under strict confidentiality rules and other

conditions of access, to conduct their own research or special studies of tax return information for the purposes of tax policy or economic analysis.

282. Box 4.1 outlines some examples of best practices concerning data availability for the purpose of tax analysis of corporate tax and MNEs. As can be seen from the examples of best practices, an important factor in the availability of current data is whether data that has been provided to tax administrations is compiled into an electronic database that is easily accessible by government tax analysts. Increased electronic filing of corporate income tax returns will make the compilation of more data less resource intensive for tax administrations.

283. While electronic filing systems are helpful, where information is not collected in a standardised format, compilation will involve searching for the specific data item (often with different terminology across different datasets) and then sorting into standardised categories. Unless there is a tax form which taxpayers are required to complete, it is likely that the information will not be compiled for tax policy analysis without requiring significant extra resources and effort.[3] Additional information requested on tax returns that may not be required for the calculation of tax liability, such as information on balance sheets or specific income and expense items may not be completed by taxpayers with the same degree of care and diligence.

Box 4.1. Some best practices in data availability for tax analysis of corporate tax and MNEs

Published aggregated tables of MNE tax data: The United States Internal Revenue Service publishes special tabulations every other year of information from foreign affiliates of United States MNEs (information Form 5471 including Schedule M) and from domestic affiliates of foreign MNEs (Form 5472). The tables present aggregated totals of the components of taxable income and deductions by country and industry, including in the case of Form 5472 detailed aggregated transactions with related parties.

Information on cross-border related party transactions: The Australian Taxation Office requires certain taxpayers to complete an annual international dealings schedule, which contains a specific section on international related party transactions.[4] The specific section is required to be completed where the total amount of their international related party transactions exceeds AUD 2 million. In addition, for the countries with the three largest related party transaction totals, the taxpayer is asked to specify the country and detail the activity type and the aggregate transaction amount (expenses/losses plus revenue/gains). The schedule also requires notification of restructures, dealings in intangibles, derivatives transactions and information on the number of CFCs in each country and an explanation of thin capitalisation arrangements on the Australian side.

Access to qualified academic researchers under strict confidentiality rules: 15 OECD countries[5] currently have special programs that provide qualified academics with access to corporate tax return data for analysis under strict confidentiality rules. These programs enable sophisticated empirical analysis of tax return data, complementing analysis of non-tax return data, while maximising the benefit of existing data. See case study box of these programs.

Quantifying corporate tax preferences: A number of countries regularly publish the fiscal cost of special tax rates, deductions, exemptions and credits in their corporate income tax. Although there can be conceptual and measurement issues with some preferences, most corporate tax preferences are readily measurable such as corporate tax credits, special low tax rates, and deductions in excess of 100% of expenditures.

Box 4.1. Some best practices in data availability for tax analysis of corporate tax and MNEs *(continued)*

Analysis of MNE investments: The German Bundesbank, the Japan External Trade Organisation, and the United States Bureau of Economic Analysis conduct special surveys of the multinational affiliates' operations. While not tax focused, the information from these surveys has provided academic researchers operating under strict confidentiality rules with an important source of data about MNE behaviours. Concerns about MNE response rates have limited any matching of these investment surveys with tax return information.

Aggregate audit analyses: Several countries report on their corporate audit and enforcement activities, including amounts assessed and assessments collected. These analyses have not separated MNEs from other corporations, and generally do not separately report by type of assessment, such as specific BEPS behaviours. Several commentators on the Action 11 Public Discussion Document suggested aggregated data from audits and examinations would aid in the analysis of BEPS.

International and regional tax statistics: Consistent, comparable, and quality-checked tax statistics are extremely important for policymakers and other tax stakeholders. The OECD Revenue Statistics and Tax Policy Database provide detailed information on a comparable basis for OECD countries and an increasing number of non-OECD countries in its regional publications.

Matching available databases: Separating BEPS behaviours from real economic effects will require data on real economic variables. Several tax administrations, policy offices and other researchers supplement corporate tax return information with other databases to maximise the available information. The Australia Taxation Office compares and contrasts corporate tax return data with the databases of external agencies and organisations in order to ensure compliance with tax obligations.[6]

Better utilisation of technology in collection and compilation of taxpayer data: Access to and compilation of taxpayer data could be eased by the use of a digital system to collect and store it. Brazil has unified tax and book-keeping information through a digital system; the Sistema Público de Escrituração Digital, at the federal, state and municipal levels. In addition, Japan's Kokuzei Sogo Kanri system links all regional tax information for analysis.

Focus on data quality: Data quality can be enhanced by dedicated personnel focused on improving the accuracy and completeness of data obtained from tax forms. The Department of Finance, the Canada Revenue Agency and Statistics Canada have established a joint committee for data quality, supported by working groups with subject matter specialists in areas including: corporation and individual reporting, partnership and trust reporting, international reporting, and sales tax reporting. The working groups meet regularly to address issues that arise, discuss information technology system and/or form changes that are necessary to reflect legislative amendments, and develop ways to improve data quality.

Statistical sampling: Even with electronic records, statistical sampling can be a useful tool to examine tax return data too voluminous to approach with other techniques, such as quality assurance and imputations. Statistics compiled by the United States Internal Revenue Service (IRS) Statistics of Income (SOI) Division are generally based on statistical sampling. Returns are assigned to sampling classes (or strata) based on criteria including the form type filed, various income factors or other measures of economic size, and industry. Statistical samples are then selected from each stratum and can be extrapolated to population totals.

4.2.2 Coverage of data for BEPS analysis

284. The assessment of existing data in Chapter 1 outlined a number of current coverage issues that need to be addressed to better analyse BEPS. Some of the issues will be addressed by the additional information required under Actions 5, 13 and, where implemented, Action 12 of the BEPS project. These will potentially lead to significant improvements in the scope of tax data available to governments, including details of the entire MNE group and all of its entities by country of tax jurisdiction. These future data collected from the Action Plan are described later in this chapter.

285. Coverage of data also includes information that national tax administrations have, but is not presently compiled and analysed. For example, an important missing element is the corporate and other tax payments of MNEs in countries. Many countries do not currently analyse their corporate income tax return information on this important dimension. Other taxes paid by MNEs (i.e. withholding taxes, non-refundable VAT on business inputs, property taxes) can affect location decisions, so are important for separating BEPS corporate income tax effects from other non-BEPS policy factors.

286. Information on non-BEPS corporate tax policies that reduce taxes of MNEs, and also domestic companies, are needed to separate the effects of BEPS from other factors. Many countries have tax expenditure analyses which quantify the tax lost from special preferences, concessions and tax credits. Although there are conceptual and measurement issues with tax expenditures, estimates of corporate tax credits, special tax rates, and deductions in excess of 100% of expenditures are generally not affected by these issues, and would be more amenable to international comparisons. More information on business tax preferences by MNEs and domestic-only businesses would aid BEPS analysis in the future.

4.2.3 Internationally consistent analyses of BEPS

287. As important as it is for individual countries to undertake their own analyses and publish their own country-specific statistics, it is also important to improve BEPS analysis at the global level. Better BEPS economic analysis at the global level requires data with more comprehensive country and industry coverage by type of taxpayer.

288. The benefits of those individual country analyses can be maximised if national statistics are available and compiled in a consistent and reliable manner to facilitate cross-country analyses. BEPS is a global issue, and if it is reduced in one jurisdiction but then shifted to another jurisdiction through tax planning, then total BEPS has not been reduced. It will be important to monitor BEPS statistics on an international basis, with as many countries volunteering to share data as possible and, preferably in an internationally consistent format.

289. International statistics on FDI, trade and many other economic measures are compiled, analysed and published by a number of international organisations as well as by some academic organisations. The *OECD Tax Database* and *OECD Revenue Statistics* currently provide tax rate information for OECD countries and detailed revenue statistics for over 50 countries on a consistent, standardised, and quality-assured basis. More comprehensive cross-country tax data, particularly on business taxes and BEPS-related metrics, would be important for improving international analyses of BEPS.

Box 4.2. Case studies of tax administrations' collaborations with qualified researchers

Fourteen OECD countries, and a number of non-OECD countries, have special programs to allow access to tax return information under strict confidentiality rules to qualified researchers. Three of the programs are described below.

Canada: Statistics Canada houses the Canadian Centre for Data Development and Economic Research, which maintains business-related micro datasets, including income tax returns filed by all corporations. In order to respect taxpayer confidentiality, researchers do not have access to the names of tax filers or direct access to the data. Researchers are only able to access the data from Statistics Canada's offices in Ottawa. Data analysis programs must be developed using a synthetic dataset in which firm entries are interchanged to prevent researchers from identifying specific firms.

United Kingdom: The United Kingdom's revenue authority, Her Majesty's Revenue and Customs (HMRC), currently allows access to tax return information under certain conditions. The HMRC Datalab is a secure environment where legally authorised researchers can access, free of charge, confidential taxpayer and de-identified data to undertake research that serves one of the HMRC's functions and benefits the wider research community. There is ongoing collaboration with other United Kingdom Research Data Centres and international connections have been made as part of the Data without Boundaries project. Projects on corporation tax have outnumbered those on other forms of taxation, and research has provided lessons on which to draw for future policy analysis. There are some challenges that the HMRC is working on resolving, including legislative restrictions to data access; a continually evolving landscape that requires adaptation; public perceptions on data sharing; balancing resources; and different working cultures and expectations. As of May 2015, 47 projects had been approved, 60 researchers trained, and more than 30 publications have been published by Datalab researchers.

United States: The United States IRS SOI Division endeavours to increase the use of its tax micro data by researchers outside the Federal government with its Joint Statistical Research Program. Researchers who apply and are selected partner with SOI staff on projects that advance the understanding of how existing taxes affect people, businesses, and the economy, and provide new understanding of taxpayer behaviour that can aid in the administration of the United States tax system. Such research can lead to the development of new datasets useful for future tax administration research, as well as new tabulations that can be released to the public. Research papers are made available to the public as working papers and may also be submitted for publication in economic or statistical journals. SOI staff participate in all phases of selected projects, including research, analysis, and presentation of findings.

4.3 Classification of analytical tools to turn data into insights

290. Data alone will not increase the understanding of BEPS. Analytical tools must be used to provide insights from those data. Analytical tools range from descriptive statistics (e.g. ratios of FDI to GDP, effective tax rates) to aggregate tabulations (e.g. ETRs by industry or country), to indicators (e.g. effective marginal or average tax rates, indicators included in Chapter 2), to multivariate statistical analyses (e.g. measuring relationships while holding other factors constant), to economic modelling (e.g. revenue effects of proposed measures and effectiveness evaluations). Enhanced data would enable all of the tools to increase the understanding of BEPS and the effects of BEPS countermeasures.

- Descriptive statistics can provide significant insights, particularly if they are put in context, such as FDI relative to a measure of the country's overall economic activity. Better data can expand the number of descriptive statistics and refine existing statistics. Future improvements in FDI special purpose entity data would make it feasible to construct one of the potential future indicators in Chapter 2. Better data can be used to calibrate MNE ETRs in each country, such as the extent to which MNEs are reporting income in zero-corporate tax countries.

- Aggregated tabulations are an important resource for analysing and understanding BEPS by external stakeholders given confidentiality considerations. Aggregate tabulations can overcome many confidentiality issues, by providing confidentiality and anonymity, while showing detailed information about groups of similar corporations. The United States IRS publishes detailed tabulations from tax forms filed by foreign affiliates of United States parents and United States affiliates of foreign parents, by country and industry.[7] More sophisticated statistical analysis can be undertaken based on aggregated tabulations, although more limited than statistical analysis with individual taxpayer data. Aggregated tabulations showing the percent of foreign source income from selected no-tax countries is often cited in policy debates.[8] Aggregate tabulations could also improve the understanding of differences between tax and financial records.

- Indicators will also be improved with better data, as discussed in Chapter 2. In addition, better data can assist in improving effective tax rate measures. Effective marginal and average tax rates of hypothetical companies can illustrate the effects of different countermeasures. One of the difficulties of effective tax rates in the international tax area is calibrating the measures to different groups, rather than to just a few hypothetical firms. Isolating the impacts of the tax policy settings of a particular country presents another difficulty. Better data can help calibrate effective tax rate metrics for policy analysis of BEPS countermeasures.

- Multivariate statistical analysis is a powerful analytic tool, but generally requires individual taxpayer data, which for tax return analysis raises confidentiality issues, or many years and/or countries for macroeconomic data. Statistical analysis of individual taxpayer data allows the effect of individual factors, such as taxes, to be analysed holding other factors (e.g. economic determinants of profit) constant. Although statistical analysis of individual tax returns may not be possible beyond tax administrations without expanded access that ensures taxpayer confidentiality, the results of statistical analyses could be released publicly while addressing confidentiality concerns. This occurs regularly with both tax and non-tax corporate data in several countries, both by government researchers and in some countries under special programs for qualified academic researchers.

- Economic modelling often uses the other analytical tools to evaluate the fiscal and economic impacts of tax policy changes. Annex 3.A1 uses multivariate statistical analysis to analyse a number of economic effects of BEPS. Annex 3.A2 provides a toolkit for deriving an estimate of the fiscal effects of the individual BEPS Action Plan countermeasures for individual countries. Economic modelling could be used to evaluate the effectiveness and economic impact of actions to address BEPS.

291. Advances in the use of analytical and monitoring tools are being made by researchers alongside improvements in the available data. Academic researchers have extended empirical analyses through "meta-analyses" of multiple empirical studies of the same phenomena and by analysing BEPS through tax rate differentials between affiliates or between parent entities. Continued improvement in analytical techniques and approaches, such as analysing MNE entities' share of profitability and economic activity of the entire MNE group are promising approaches.

4.4 A classification of the types of data

292. A classification of the types of data can help form the basis of recommendations regarding new tools and data under Action 11. The BEPS Action Plan makes it clear that any recommendations should have regard to the need to protect the confidentiality of taxpayers and minimise the administrative costs to governments and taxpayers.

293. It is also worth noting that some of the potential recommendations that could be made regarding data and monitoring tools for the future may involve matters within the domain of tax policy and tax administration, and some will relate more generally to the work and responsibilities of national statistical offices and other non-tax government agencies and institutions. These are all important distinctions that should be borne in mind when considering the range of potential recommendations regarding new tools and data for BEPS analysis.

294. Figure 4.2 shows a schematic of data important for analysis of BEPS and BEPS countermeasures. Data can be divided into categories, starting with tax and non-tax data. Data can then be divided into data already (or soon to be) collected and data not collected. Currently collected data is likely to be available sooner than data that is scheduled to be collected under new arrangements proposed under other Actions of the BEPS project. Changes in processing currently collected data, however, could take several years to implement and complete.

Figure 4.2. Data important for analysis of BEPS and countermeasures

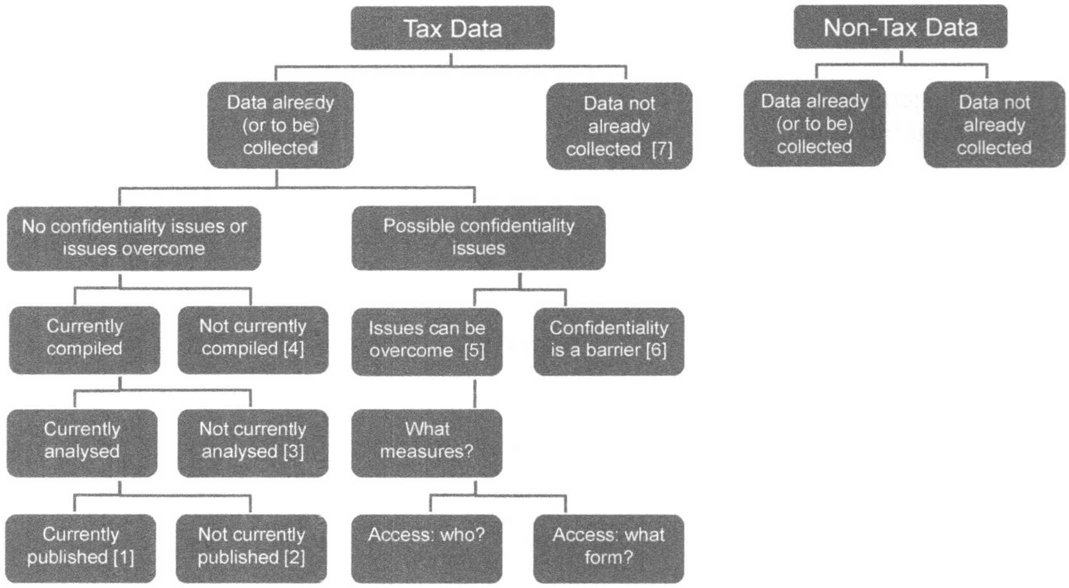

295. Data already being collected can be divided between data that does not involve any confidentiality issues (or where those issues have already been overcome) and data that has potential confidentiality issues. If there are possible confidentiality issues, then those data can be divided into those where confidentiality issues might be overcome and those where confidentiality issues will continue to be a barrier to access. Where there are current confidentiality issues that might be overcome, consideration must be given to determining what types of measures (e.g. legislative, administrative, etc.) are necessary to address those confidentiality concerns, and then who might gain access (e.g. other government analysts, academic researchers) and in what form would that access be granted. In response to a questionnaire circulated by WP2 of the Committee on Fiscal Affairs in June 2015, 17 of the 38 country respondents indicated that their tax administrations provide access to information on payments between related parties from tax return data to other government tax policy analysts.[9] In 16 of the 38 respondent countries, tax administrations allow access to corporate tax data to qualified academic researchers and national statistical offices under strict confidentiality rules.

296. If data is collected and does not have confidentiality issues, there are still issues of whether the data is compiled such that it can be analysed without excessive resource costs. New electronic search technologies can now help pull information from open-ended text, but these processes still remain labour intensive. Resource constraints may prevent even compiled data from being analysed. Tax administrations may have many other priorities that take precedence before tax policy analysis is undertaken. Finally, when data is analysed, it may not be published for a wider audience, again due to resource constraints or other limitations. A number of tax administrations compile, analyse and publish aggregated tables of corporate tax data without confidentiality issues.

297. Figure 4.2 specifically identifies seven categories of tax data, where future actions may be considered to improve the available data and analysis of BEPS. A number of potential future actions are identified below for each of the seven data groups, ranging from consideration of additional metrics and analyses for tax data already collected, analysed and published to focusing efforts on other groups of data when tax or non-tax data has confidentiality issues.

1) Tax data already collected without confidentiality issues, currently compiled, analysed and published
   - Consider additional metrics and analyses (e.g. specific analyses of MNEs, expanded access to researchers under confidentiality arrangements)
   - Consider standardised formats for international comparability

2) Tax data already collected without confidentiality issues, currently compiled and analysed, but not published
   - Consider additional metrics and analyses (e.g. specific analyses of MNEs, expanded access to research under confidentiality arrangements, merging databases)
   - Consider publishing analyses, and in standardised formats for international comparability

3) Tax data already collected without confidentiality issues, already compiled but not analysed
   - Consider additional analyses of the compiled data, and publication (e.g. specific analyses of MNEs, expanded access to research under confidentiality arrangements, merging databases)

4) Tax data already collected without confidentiality issues, not currently compiled
   - Consider which data is most useful for analysis (e.g. their benefits) and the cost of compilation (e.g. specific analyses of MNEs, merging databases)
   - Consider processes to reduce compilation costs (e.g. statistical sampling)
   - Consider how data may be compiled in standardised formats for international comparability

5) Tax data already collected, but possible confidentiality issues which may be overcome
   - Consider what measures need to be taken to overcome confidentiality barriers
   - Consider who could have access (e.g. government tax policy analysts)
   - Consider what form the access could take (e.g. aggregated anonymised tabulations)

6) Tax data already collected, but confidentiality is a barrier
   - Consider available alternatives to maximise benefit of data within confidentiality limits (e.g. aggregated anonymised tabulations, access to qualified researchers under strict confidentiality rules)

7) Tax data not already (or not agreed to be) collected
   - Focus on maximising the analysis and publication of tax data already collected

298. Monitoring BEPS in the future will require taking better advantage of currently available (and soon to be provided) data in the hands of tax administrations. Increased analysis and publication of statistical results and aggregated tabulations of MNE taxes and activities by individual countries will be important to evaluating the effectiveness and economic impact of BEPS countermeasures and ensuring that BEPS is properly monitored in the future.

4.5 Data collected in response to the Action Plan in the future

299. The scope and value of information collected by governments will be enhanced as a result of the work undertaken as part of Action 5 (spontaneous exchange of rulings), Action 13 (transfer pricing documentation) and, where implemented, Action 12 (disclosure of aggressive tax planning arrangements) of the BEPS Action Plan. In particular, the additional information from Action 13 will provide governments with more information on MNE groups' allocations of their global economic activities and the amounts of taxes they pay in each country.

300. The Action 13 Country-by-Country Reports (CbCR) will be important for improving high-level transfer pricing risk assessments. The Report on Action 13 (*Transfer Pricing Documentation and Country-by-Country Reporting,* OECD, 2015)

states that CbCR "may also be used by tax administrations in evaluating other BEPS related risks and where appropriate for economic and statistical analysis."[10] While the use of CbCR data is restricted to governments, statistical analyses based on the data included in the CbCR have the potential to greatly improve future BEPS analyses. The conventional statistical and economic analyses examining profit rates of individual affiliates based on economic factors as well as tax rate differentials could be improved. Unlike analyses of financial statement data, the statistical analyses based on CbCR data will be able to use actual income taxes paid to the tax jurisdiction of the entities, and will include all entities of the MNE group.[11] The CbCR will be required of MNE groups with annual consolidated group revenue in the preceding year of EUR 750 million or more, which is estimated to exclude 85-90% of MNE groups while still covering MNE groups responsible for approximately 90% of global corporate revenues.

301. One of the benefits of CbCR is that there is a standard reporting template for filing which will maintain consistent reporting rules across countries as a means of limiting taxpayer compliance costs. The standard reporting template and its conversion to electronic files will also enable less costly compilation of the included data by tax administrations. MNEs will also file a master file, which provides an overview of the MNE group business and its overall transfer pricing policies, and a local file, which provides more detailed information relating to specific intercompany transactions. The local file will include important information about transactions between related parties, such as interest and royalties.[12] This information would be helpful to analyse BEPS, but will not be provided in a standard template. Tax administrations will have access to the data, but it will require more resources to extract and compile the information.

302. The first CbCR will be filed for 2016 calendar year filers no later than 31 December 2017. Thus, some CbCR data will be available for statistical analysis as early as the end of 2017. However, more complete data for 2016 will not be available until later. Tax administrations and government tax policy analysts will want to be ready to quickly analyse the data when it becomes available.[13]

303. Statistical analysis in the form of aggregated and anonymised tabulations based on CbCR data would provide governments with a complete view of the largest MNEs' global activities for the first time. These statistical analyses would not disclose individual taxpayer specific information, and any publication would depend on the country's confidentiality rules. In addition, governments should consider other immediate compilation, analysis, publication and access improvements in other MNE corporate data for analysing BEPS and BEPS countermeasures in the meantime. Increased benefits could be obtained from the publication of such data in aggregated and anonymised form, especially if such analyses are tabulated using a format that is consistent across countries. To achieve such consistency, greater co-ordination between governments would be required.

304. Given confidentiality considerations, tax administrations and some government offices are the only ones with access to tax return information of MNEs operating in their countries.[14] When the first CbCR become available to governments in 2017, access to the reports will be limited to those government offices. During the public consultations on the Action 11 discussion draft, a number of commenters suggested that a formal repository or global database of MNE CbCR should be created. Given concerns around confidentiality, there are no plans for such an approach,[15] however, there would clearly be considerable benefit for BEPS analysis in developing an internationally co-ordinated approach to

compiling the results of statistical analyses that are aggregated, anonymised, and based upon global CbCR data.

4.6 Recommendations

305. It is clear from the assessment of current data that analyses of BEPS with non-tax return information provide an incomplete picture. Using publicly available non-tax return data has shown the presence and significance of BEPS, but has not provided clear measures of the scale and scope of BEPS. Non-tax return information does not have complete coverage, and those companies that are missing or not reporting financial information may be undertaking significant BEPS. Non-tax return information does not allow the separation of BEPS impacts from the impacts of non-BEPS tax preferences. For example, ETRs could be reduced by enacted tax incentives and special tax rates, as well as BEPS behaviours.

306. Thus, better analysis of BEPS in the future will require more analysis of tax return data by individual countries' tax administrations and/or their tax policy offices. Given the large, and soon to be expanded, volume of data in the hands of tax administrations, this report's recommendations focus on the need for governments to work more closely together to make better use of data that is already (or has been agreed, as part of the BEPS project, to be) collected. Consistent with this approach, this report makes the following recommendations:[16]

Recommendation 1

The OECD should work with all OECD members, BEPS Associates and any country willing to participate to publish, on a regular basis, a new Corporate Tax Statistics publication, which would compile a range of data and statistical analyses relevant to the economic analysis of BEPS in an internationally consistent format. Among other information, this publication would include aggregated and anonymised statistical analyses prepared by governments based on the data collected under the Action 13 Country-by-Country Reports.

307. The OECD, through WP2 of the Committee on Fiscal Affairs, should work with OECD members, BEPS Associates and any willing participating countries to develop appropriate data classification guidelines and a standardised reporting template and process, which will allow for the compilation and publication on a regular basis of internationally consistent and comparable corporate tax statistics, which could include the following:

- Total corporate/business tax revenues collected by governments
- MNE share of corporate/business tax collected
- Breakdown of business taxes by industry/sector
- Summaries of countries' statistical aggregated analyses based on data obtained from CbCR
- Key income and expense items of the corporate tax base

- Identification and quantification of tax credits, special low tax rates, and other tax preferences
- Corporate withholding taxes

308. These statistics would be provided in an aggregated and anonymised form to ensure that taxpayer confidentiality is strictly preserved.

309. Current cross-country analyses of corporate tax systems often use a crude measure of the corporate tax base, by dividing corporate tax collections by the headline statutory tax rate. This significantly understates the corporate taxable income by ignoring corporate tax credits and special low tax rates, and could be improved with additional information on corporate tax preferences.

Recommendation 2

The OECD should work with all OECD members, BEPS Associates and any willing participating governments to produce periodic reports on the estimated revenue impacts of proposed and enacted BEPS countermeasures.

310. The OECD, through WP2 of the Committee on Fiscal Affairs, should work with participating governments to develop a standardised reporting template and process, which will support the publication of periodic reports on the estimated revenue impacts of proposed and enacted countermeasures.

311. These reports could monitor the expected revenue impacts of proposed reforms and the estimated revenue impact of enacted reforms. Improved metrics of existing and future BEPS countermeasures could be developed for cross-country research by analysts.

Recommendation 3

The OECD should continue to produce and refine analytical tools and BEPS Indicators to monitor the scale and economic impact of BEPS and to evaluate the effectiveness and economic impact of BEPS countermeasures.

312. Chapter 2 presents a "dashboard" of BEPS Indicators. While these indicators are not intended to precisely measure the scale of BEPS, they do provide clear indications of the existence of BEPS and with improved data and further refinement over time may prove useful in monitoring trends and changes in BEPS.

313. As further data becomes available, not only will this lead to refinements in the indicators presented, but may also allow for new and enhanced indicators to be constructed, including those indicators identified in Chapter 2 as possible future indicators.

314. Annex 3.A2 presents a toolkit for analysing the fiscal effects of BEPS countermeasures for governments to use in their consideration of estimating future revenue effects. The toolkit could be expanded to include the availability of statistical analyses based on data collected under Action 13's Country-by-Country Reports. The

toolkit could also be refined with the shared experience of government estimators and analysts who have estimated the effects of countermeasures in different countries.

Recommendation 4

Governments should improve the public reporting of business tax statistics, particularly for MNEs.

315. Many countries currently do not separately identify MNEs for statistical reporting of business tax statistics. The Action 13 Country-by-Country Reports will identify large MNEs present in a country. Separate business tax statistics for in-bound MNEs (domestic affiliates of foreign parents), out-bound MNEs (domestic parents with foreign affiliates) as well as domestic-only businesses may be able to be compiled. Special tabulations from the local files of the Country-by-Country Reports may provide more detail about MNEs' tax situation beyond the information in the standardised reports.

316. In the case of a large number of countries, including many low-income and developing countries, there is a need for the improved compilation and publication of basic, and expanded, revenue statistics. Increased information about incentives provided to MNEs may also provide a starting point for an evaluation of their effectiveness.

317. Research on BEPS has been hampered by the lack of basic, quality revenue statistical data. This is a fact for all countries, but is especially the case for developing countries, where studies by academic researchers have highlighted the importance of being able to access more information on BEPS in developing countries. Increased technical assistance and support from developed countries should be provided. The OECD Revenue Statistics and Regional Revenue Statistical publications provide a possible template for the collection of data for countries that do not currently publish regular, comparable and internationally consistent revenue statistics.

Recommendation 5

Governments should continue to make improvements in non-tax data relevant to BEPS, such as by broadening country coverage and improving data on FDI associated with resident SPEs, trade in services and intangible investments.

318. While CbCR has the potential to greatly enhance micro-level tax data of MNEs, continued improvement in non-tax macroeconomic data and micro-level data will assist future analysis of BEPS. Recent analyses of trade data, investment and FDI data have provided important insights to the analysis of BEPS. Wider coverage of countries included in these international statistics would be beneficial.

319. The *Benchmark Definition of Foreign Direct Investment, 4th* edition (BMD4) recommends that countries include transactions with Special Purpose Entities (SPEs) in their FDI statistics to ensure comparability with other countries. It also provides guidance on compiling FDI statistics that exclude transactions with SPEs, but does not recommend specific identification of SPEs and other conduits. These statistics enable policymakers to assess the impact of FDI into their economies because the statistics will better reflect FDI

into businesses with a real presence in the economy. These statistics also better measure outward investment from countries by removing funds that pass through their economy but originate elsewhere. Additional countries reporting SPEs would enable improved analyses.

320. Improvements in the measurement of intangibles investments, including the capitalisation of investments in research and development, will enable researchers to better identify the contributors to profitability and the scale of their contribution. Detailed analyses of trade statistics and investment surveys have been used by researchers to analyse BEPS, but have been limited to only a few countries.

Recommendation 6

Governments should consider current best practices and explore new approaches to collaborating on BEPS research with academics and other researchers. Governments should encourage more research on MNE activity within tax administrations, tax policy offices, national statistical offices, and by academic researchers, to improve the understanding of BEPS, and to better separate BEPS from real economic effects and non-BEPS tax preferences.

321. Research by academics, national statistical offices[17] and other tax policy analysts is important to advancing the progress of the economic analysis of MNEs, BEPS and any BEPS countermeasures. There are numerous examples of best practices, many of which have been set out earlier in this chapter, where governments have made tax return data available to researchers under strict confidentiality and access requirements. Governments should look to existing best practices and consider options for improving collaboration with academics and researchers in the future.

322. In many countries, the collection of business statistics data used in compiling national accounts makes no distinction between whether the firms are foreign affiliates or domestically owned. Where available, the data shows significant differences across these categories of firms.

323. Since separating real economic effects from BEPS is important, non-tax research is needed on a number of issues, including:

- What contributes to value added by businesses and particularly MNEs
- The measurement and contributions to value of intangible assets
- Understanding sources of differences between MNEs and domestic-only companies
- Non-tax determinants of MNE location decisions

4.7 Conclusion

324. The recommendations made in this report, combined with new statistical analyses possible based on data from Actions 5, 13, and, where implemented, Action 12 will enable policymakers in the future to have stronger economic analyses of BEPS and the effects of BEPS countermeasures.

325. More information about BEPS will be needed to monitor the effects of the BEPS program in the future, since BEPS is a global problem and individual country tax administrations have the best data. Better data and tools for analysing BEPS are critical to

separating the effects of BEPS from real economic activity and non-BEPS tax preferences.

326. Better data and improved analyses should be a priority to ensure that all stakeholders have a better understanding of the fiscal and economic effects of BEPS, and the impact of BEPS countermeasures and their effectiveness over time. Improved data and analysis will assist policy makers by underpinning future decisions with an even stronger evidence base and will, over time; help build greater trust and confidence among all taxpayers in the effectiveness of the international tax rules.

Bibliography

Keightley, M. P. and J. M. Stupak (2015), *Corporate Tax Base Erosion and Profit Shifting (BEPS): An Examination of the Data*, United States Congressional Research Report.

Mahoney, L. and R. Miller (2013), *Controlled Foreign Corporations*, United States Internal Revenue Service Statistics of Income SOI Bulletin, Winter 2013.

McDonald, M. (2008), *Income shifting from transfer pricing: Further evidence from tax return data*, United States Department of the Treasury, Office of Tax Analysis, OTA Technical Working Paper 2.

OECD (2015), *Transfer Pricing Documentation and Country-by-Country Reporting, Action 13 - 2015 Final Report*, OECD/G20 Base Erosion and Profit Shifting Project, OECD Publishing, Paris, http://dx.doi.org/10.1787/9789264241480-en.

Sullivan, M. A. (2010), *Transfer Pricing Issues in a Global Economy*, Testimony before the UNITED STATES House of Representatives Ways and Means Committee, July 22, 2010.

Notes

1. Many financial statement databases include observations for companies but without accompanying financial information. Several government tax policy analysts have noted that tax return information that is not specifically required for the tax liability calculation are not as complete as the tax return lines for the tax liability calculation, such as balance sheet data on assets and liabilities or data on information returns.

2. Based on June 2015 survey responses of 30 OECD countries, just over half of the countries' tax policy offices have access to individual company tax return information.

3. Statistical sampling is used by some tax administrations to reduce the cost of compiling information while maintaining a representative sample. In some cases, analysis of the top 100 or 500 companies can provide significant insights, since they often account for a large percentage of the total tax under consideration.

4. www.ato.gov.au/uploadedFiles/Content/MEI/downloads/International-dealings-schedule-2015.pdf.

5. The OECD countries that grant access to tax return data, under strict confidentiality conditions, to qualified (non-government) researchers include: Belgium, Canada, Finland, France, Germany, Ireland, Italy, Korea, Netherlands, New Zealand, Sweden, Switzerland, the United Kingdom and the United States. South Africa also grants access to these data to researchers.

6. Another example can be found in McDonald (2008), "Income Shifting from Transfer Pricing: Further Evidence from Tax Return Data," where Compustat data was merged with tax return records in order to add financial information for United States parents of CFCs.

7. Lee Mahoney and Randy Miller, "Controlled Foreign Corporations," United States Internal Revenue Service Statistics of Income SOI Bulletin, Winter 2013.

8. Martin A. Sullivan, "Transfer Pricing Issues in a Global Economy," testimony before the United States House of Representatives Ways and Means Committee, July 22, 2010. Mark P. Keightley and Jeffrey M. Stupak, "Corporate Tax Base Erosion and Profit Shifting (BEPS): An Examination of the Data," United States Congressional Research Report, April 30, 2015.

9. Questionnaire conducted by Working Party No.2 of the Committee on Fiscal Affairs in June 2015. The 29 OECD country respondents were: Australia, Austria, Belgium, Canada, Chile, Czech Republic, Denmark, Finland, France, Germany, Hungary, Iceland, Ireland, Italy, Japan, Korea, Luxembourg, Mexico, Netherlands, New Zealand, Portugal, Slovak Republic, Slovenia, Spain, Sweden, Switzerland, Turkey, United Kingdom and United States. The other country respondents were: Argentina, Brazil, Bulgaria, Colombia, India, Latvia, the Philippines, Singapore and South Africa.

10. Paragraph 25 of the Action 13 2015 Deliverable: Guidance on Transfer Pricing Documentation and Country-by-Country Reporting.

11. Country-by-Country Reporting will include for each jurisdiction:

- Total revenue, plus unrelated party revenue and third-party revenue
- Profit/loss before income tax
- Income tax paid on a cash basis
- Income tax accrued for the current year
- Stated capital
- Accumulated earnings
- Number of employees
- Tangible assets other than cash and cash equivalents
- Listing of constituent entities resident in the tax jurisdiction, the tax jurisdiction or incorporation if different than the jurisdiction of residence, and main business activity by category

"It is mandated that countries participating in the BEPS project will carefully review the implementation of these new standards and will reassess no later than the end of 2020 whether modifications to the content of these reports should be made to require reporting of additional or different data." Ibid, p.5.

12. Other related party transactions that have been analysed for BEPS issues, include dividends, cost sharing, property right, sales of stock in trade, and serve transactions.

13 When calculating effective tax rates (e.g. income tax paid as a percent of profit), it will be important to separate firms with positive profits from firms with losses, otherwise the aggregated effective tax rates will be overstated.

14. 45% of OECD countries reported special programs to enable qualified academic researchers access to corporate tax data under strict confidentiality rules.

15. Implementation of CbCR has a specific framework of only government-to-government exchanges.

16. It is noted that countries, especially those with a more decentralised tax system, will need sufficient time to analyse and/or implement the recommendations set out in this chapter.

17. National statistical offices are making advances in the development and collection of economic data that will assist researchers in measuring and monitoring BEPS. As reported in the summary of a recent conference on national accounts organized by the Conference of European Statisticians, national statistical offices are developing additional data sources to measure economic activities of MNEs and global value chains. Examples of new developments include integrating data from multiple sources, both macro and micro, disaggregating FDI statistics, and extending trade statistics, such as trade in value added, to more accurately measure the influence of international trade on domestic economies.

ORGANISATION FOR ECONOMIC CO-OPERATION AND DEVELOPMENT

The OECD is a unique forum where governments work together to address the economic, social and environmental challenges of globalisation. The OECD is also at the forefront of efforts to understand and to help governments respond to new developments and concerns, such as corporate governance, the information economy and the challenges of an ageing population. The Organisation provides a setting where governments can compare policy experiences, seek answers to common problems, identify good practice and work to co-ordinate domestic and international policies.

The OECD member countries are: Australia, Austria, Belgium, Canada, Chile, the Czech Republic, Denmark, Estonia, Finland, France, Germany, Greece, Hungary, Iceland, Ireland, Israel, Italy, Japan, Korea, Luxembourg, Mexico, the Netherlands, New Zealand, Norway, Poland, Portugal, the Slovak Republic, Slovenia, Spain, Sweden, Switzerland, Turkey, the United Kingdom and the United States. The European Union takes part in the work of the OECD.

OECD Publishing disseminates widely the results of the Organisation's statistics gathering and research on economic, social and environmental issues, as well as the conventions, guidelines and standards agreed by its members.

OECD PUBLISHING, 2, rue André-Pascal, 75775 PARIS CEDEX 16
(23 2015 36 1 P) ISBN 978-92-64-24133-6 – 2015

www.ingramcontent.com/pod-product-compliance
Lightning Source LLC
Chambersburg PA
CBHW061204240926
51846CB00006B/1114